AFRICAN STUDIES
HISTORY, POLITICS, ECONOMICS, AND CULTURE

Edited by
Molefi Asante
Temple University

A ROUTLEDGE SERIES

African Studies
History, Politics, Economics, and Culture
Molefi Asante, *General Editor*

TRANS-ATLANTIC MIGRATION
The Paradoxes of Exile

Edited by
Toyin Falola and
Niyi Afolabi

Routledge
New York & London

Routledge
Taylor & Francis Group
711 Third Avenue,
New York, NY 10017

Routledge
Taylor & Francis Group
2 Park Square
Milton Park, Abingdon
Oxon OX14 4RN

Routledge is an imprint of Taylor & Francis Group, an Informa business

First issued in paperback 2012

© 2008 by Taylor & Francis Group, LLC

Library of Congress Cataloging-in-Publication Data

Trans-Atlantic migration : the paradoxes of exile / edited by Toyin Falola and Niyi Afolabi.
    p. cm. -- (African studies)
    "Drawn from an international conference on movements, migrations, and displacements, and held at the University of Texas-Austin in March 2006."
    Includes bibliographical references and index.
    ISBN 978-0-415-96091-5
    1. Africans--Foreign countries--Congresses. 2. Africans--Migrations--Congresses. 3. Migration, Internal--Africa--Congresses. 4. Immigrants--Africa--Congresses. 5. African diaspora--Congresses. 6. Africa--Emigration and immigration--Congresses. I. Falola, Toyin. II. Afolabi, Niyi.

DT16.5.T73 2007
304.8096--dc22   2007015348

Visit the Taylor & Francis Web site at
http://www.taylorandfrancis.com

and the Routledge Web site at
http://www.routledge.com

ISBN-13: 978-0-415-96091-5 (hbk)
ISBN-13: 978-0-415-54249-4 (pbk)

To Omi Osun (Joni Jones) for her Yoruba Spirituality

&

To the memory of millions—nameless and forgotten—who perished in the trans-Atlantic journeys

Contents

List of Tables

List of Figures

Preface

Trans-Atlantic Migration: The Paradoxes of Exile argues that new cadres of African immigrants are finding themselves in the New World—mostly well educated, high-income earning professionals, and belonging to the category termed "African brain drain," they constitute the antinomy of those Africans who were forcibly removed from Africa during slavery. Yet, along with this sense of freedom and voluntary migration comes a paradox—that of living in two worlds and negotiating the pleasures and agonies that come with living in exile. For the new African immigrant, the primary factor motivating migration is the desire for a better life—whether fleeing political persecution, economic crisis, refugee crisis, or a combination thereof. The overall consequences include displacement, alienation, and the not so enchanting realities of exile. In its encompassing structure and multivalent perspectives, *Trans-Atlantic Migration: The Paradoxes of Exile* sets in motion the shifting theoretical and pragmatic verity that the new African diaspora and transatlantic migrations are paths laden with paradoxes that only time, negotiations, compromises, and a sense of identities can ultimately resolve.

While a few studies have attempted to expose the emerging trans-migrational trends in the 80s and 90s such as Toyin Falola's focus on African intellectuals in a changing world order as in *Nationalism and African Intellectuals* (2001) and Lawrence Okafor's *Recent African Immigrants to the USA* (2003) among others, no other study comes close to the scholarly intentions of *Trans-Atlantic Migration: The Paradoxes of Exile*, in its intellectual scope, cogency, and interdisciplinary orientation. Based on a major international conference held at the University of Texas-Austin (March 24–26, 2006) on the problematic of "Movements, Migrations, and Displacements," this volume brings together thirteen cogent essays on the new wave of migration patterns and the role of Africans in the reconfiguration of the global economy and transnational, cultural, and environmental discourse.

Broadly framed as a dialogue between the implied antithesis of the diaspora of slavery, the diaspora of colonialism, and the voluntary diaspora to the United States, Canada, and Latin America, the main arguments of *Trans-Atlantic Migration: The Paradoxes of Exile* may be summed up as follows: (i)That the exigency of migration has significant unintended consequences. (ii) That any displacement from a "comfort zone" triggers survival mechanism. (iii) That there is a correlation between economic gain and brain drain. (iv) That voluntary migration implies hopes, dreams, and a sense of peace among African immigrants. (v) That there is a subtle relationship between the dynamics of Atlantic slavery and the unintended consequences faced by African immigrants in terms of reverse patterns of postmodern migrations from Africa. (vi) That migrant African professionals in the USA see their "displacements" more as an opportunity for professional development than loss of patriotism. (vii) That the implications for US African policy can lead to an improved partnership between USA and Africa through productive dialogue between local and international development agencies. (viii) That the processes of adaptation and integration for African immigrants must be studied and analyzed from an interdisciplinary perspective to highlight the journey to citizenship not necessarily as the attainment of the "American dream" alone but the possibility to simultaneously contribute to Africa that was voluntarily left due to economic exigencies. (ix) That such a study must involve the entire African communities located in major American cities (New York, Chicago, Washington, Atlanta, Houston, Dallas, Los Angeles, etc) and those along the southern pull of New Orleans, Alabama, Mississippi, etc. (x) That the refugee situation as well as the economic crises in Africa have a direct bearing on African immigration to the USA, hence, must also be factored into the discussion of how the first generation of "new African Americans" (new minorities) will be received or is being received such as the election of Barak Obama (Kenya) to the US Senate in 2004 and the viable possibility of his presidential ambition in 2008.

We want to thank all the contributors who, despite security and financial concerns, traveled long distances to be with us in Texas. Presenters and participants engaged in lively discussion throughout the three-day period. Such an undertaking does not come without copious debts. We are grateful to a host of graduate students (Roy Doron, Tyler Fleming, Matthew Heaton, Ann Genova, Adam Paddock, and Saheed Aderinto); the technical personnel (Sam Saverance); and many staff at the University of Texas (Gail Davis, Laura Flack and Martha Gail Moore). The organizations and departments that supported us financially include the Departments of History, Government, and English, the Center for African and African American Studies, the Office of the Vice President, College of Liberal Arts, Office of the Dean of Students, the Texas Cowboys Fund, The Louann and Larry Temple Fund, The Frances Higgenbotham Nalle Fund, and Dedman College, Southern Methodist University, Dallas. We are also grateful to Dr. Vik Bahl of Green River Community College in Auburn, Ms. Ronke Obadina of Austin, and Dr. Segun Fayemi of New York for their commitment to the conference.

Toyin Falola, University of Texas at Austin

Niyi Afolabi, University of Massachusetts at Amherst

Chapter One
Introduction: Prospero's Ripples, Caliban's Burden

Toyin Falola and Niyi Afolabi

OVERVIEW

This book integrates the discussion of the "new" trans-Atlantic migration with the issues of exile in their varied manifestations. Conceptually, it takes the position that "uprooted migrants" are part of a new diaspora that the era of globalization, shifting cultural identities, and labor dynamics are complicating beyond the legacy of slavery and abolition. Drawn from an international conference on "Movements, Migrations, and Displacements," and held at the University of Texas-Austin in March 2006, this volume brings together prominent and emerging scholars who share their expertise on the subject from multivalent perspectives.

Divided into three main parts, namely "Paradoxes of (Im)Migration and Exile," "Migration, Labor Conflicts, and Development," and "Migration and Survival Politics," these thematic clusters sum up issues that are both intellectually provocative and stimulating. Let us cite extensively from the welcome address of the convener, Professor Toyin Falola, whose laconic vision of the conference has generated an edited volume of a compelling breadth—a timely venture that sets out to explore major topical issues confronting Africa and the World especially regarding issues of African migration:

> Africans have always been on the move, ever since the time they created civilization and scattered it around the continent and elsewhere. . . . We are ready to listen to fresh ideas on new cultural, historical, sociological, methodological, and theoretical questions that will address relevant, recurring and urgent issues or raise neglected topics. . . . The richness is reflected in the wide variety of issues that are represented . . . migration and shifting identity; hybridity and transculturation, the

impact of Western and Asian settlers in Africa, trans-national struggles and ideas, and the African diaspora in other continents. Other major issues include those with regard to refugees, the representations of migrations in literature, films, and media, exile and homecoming narratives, sociological issues such as crime, juvenile delinquency, unemployment, family structures, gender and generational disparities, and memoirs of migrancy.[1]

In this cogent statement lies the main thrusts of new diaspora waves including the reverse diaspora—an area that is currently broached and worthy of more in-depth study.

PART I: PARADOXES OF (IM)MIGRATION AND EXILE

This section focuses on the contradictions of migration and the agonies of exile. The three chapters bring together perspectives on immigrant incorporation, democratic struggles by Nigerian exiles in the face of a Nigerian military dictator, and the stereotypical portrayals of African immigrants in mostly Hollywood movies. Despite their varying strategies to stimulate the critical perspective of the reader, these chapters actually deal with emotional issues of displacement, nostalgia, discrimination, and efforts to bring about some psychological balance to their alienating existence. While there are many paradoxes faced by African immigrants, some are quite compelling that they are usually unspoken. When African immigrants their homelands except if under the conditions of refugee crisis, the usual thinking that their displacement is temporary and the wish to return lingers on until five years become ten, then twenty, and then permanent exile. In the final analysis, African immigrants in dealing with sometime hostile circumstances, face the reality that they may never return home, or at least not in the immediate. And this is where immigration becomes a liability—the reality or the possibility that the immigrant may die in exile. Historically, exile or banishment from one's country is a form of punishment for a capital offense. A situation where thousands of Africans are embracing exile as opposed to their former "homelands" is truly paradoxical, causing for urgent assessment of what went wrong in Africa especially in the last twenty years when immigration to the United States has tripled.

While Chapter one primarily serves as an introduction to the volume, in chapter two, "Paradoxes of Immigrant Incorporation: High Achievement and Perceptions of Discrimination by Nigerians in Dallas / Fort Worth, Texas (USA)," Dennis D. Cordell analyzes the paradoxes of immigrant incorporation among Nigerians in the Dallas-Forth Worth-Texas area

(DFW). Using the variables of education, household income, and perception of discrimination, this chapter concludes that despite the high level of accomplishments and achievements before and after integration into the American society, Nigerian immigrants still feel alienated and not fully assimilated. This chapter is a comparative analysis of the extent of integration of Nigerian immigrants in Dallas-Fort Worth, Texas. According to Cordell, the study draws from qualitative and quantitative data collected from a convenience sample of 100 households in the Nigerian community, supplemented by census data and field reports—all collected in the course of a recent National Science Foundation research fellowship.

The Nigerian community in DFW, like the Nigerian immigrant community nationally, is characterized by very high levels of educational achievement and quite high economic status. At the same time, Nigerian immigrants perceive that racial and ethnic discrimination and their accents are major obstacles to integration into American society. In discussing the challenges faced by the Nigerian community in DFW, Cordell describes their educational and economic achievement while interpreting their perceptions of discrimination and other obstacles posed by the differently accented English of many in the community. As Cordell argues, the chapter challenges the popular assumption that "successful" immigrant incorporation is only a question of achieving high levels of income and education. The chapter concludes, with comparisons between the Nigerian community in DFW and African immigrant communities elsewhere in the country, that Nigerian immigrant community in DFW has achieved the same if not higher level of accomplishments as other immigrants from the African diaspora.

While the accomplishments of Nigerians abroad are praised in the previous chapter, these same achievements are turning into a threat in the face of dictatorship in Nigeria. Under Sani Abacha, many intellectuals and successful entrepreneurs had to flee Nigeria for fear of political persecution, imprisonment, and death. In chapter three, "Nigerian Exiles, Democratic Struggles, and the Notion of Sacrifice," Anthony Agbali compellingly studies the overlap between political and economic history as it relates to the problematic of exile within the context of Nigerian exiles during Abacha dictatorial years. While the study focuses primarily on the Abacha dictatorial regime and its impact on the wave of exiles from Nigeria towards Euro-America, the author painstakingly historicizes the patterns of exile from Nigeria specifically for example during and right after the Civil War and even before. The author advances in theory and practice, the notion of hiatus (interruption and reconnection)—combining primary and secondary archival research to make compelling comments on the connection between Abacha dictatorship, exile, and the struggle for democracy in Nigeria.

In chapter four, "Immigrants' Pilgrimage and Imaginations: The Cinematic Portrayals of African Immigrants in Movies," Raphael Obotama provides a reflexive, comparative, and analytical piece on the stereotypical portrayal of African immigrants both on the continent of Africa and in the New World. The film selection is judicious and insightful, focusing on how stereotypes are challenged and reinforced. The four movies provide a comparative prism from which to ponder the manipulation of popular culture by the media to disseminate negative images that have their origins in colonial images of Africa. The chapter succeeds in calling into question these negative images while also countering the stereotypical images with positive ones such as seeing the contribution of African immigrants as a form of cultural enrichment for the new society in which they find themselves. As a comparative study, the chapter focuses essentially on the portraits of African immigrants in such movies as *Coming to America, Coming to South Africa, The Dirty Pretty Thing* and *Secret Laughter.* Since the cinematic imagination also constructs social epistemological notions based upon real or imagined ontological frameworks, Obotama argues that these portrayals betray the challenging processes of African immigration experience and the modalities of adaptation and integration in new spaces.

PART II: MIGRATION, LABOR CONFLICTS, AND DEVELOPMENT

The pressures to immigrate are structurally and strategically conditioned by the prevailing socio-economic and political situation of the emigrating countries. This section deals with the interconnected nature of migration, economic motivations, and development. Given the complexity of the African migration reality, there may not be a unilateral explanation for labor migration from Africa. Martin and Taylor (2001) have identified three assumptions that sum up their thesis that "economic and job growth reduce emigration pressures."[2] First, it is assumed that immigration into the industrial democracies will continue through front, side, and back doors, and migration policies can affect the number, characteristics and expulsion/integration prospects of immigrants. Second, it is assumed that this inevitable migration should be managed, and primarily in the interest of the immigration country. Third, it is assumed that economic policies can play important direct and indirect roles in managing migration (95–96).

In the African context, migration can only be managed by both the developed and developing countries but due to a series of recent complex realities in Africa, especially since the 1980s, the upper hand of immigration management seems to be in the West. It is remarkable for example that right after African independence in the 1960s, Africans migrating to the West either for higher education or for economic reasons, were not and could not have be considered "economic refugees" as many Africans are called today for the simple reason that African economies were booming and were at their peak since Europe left Africans (without economically leaving) to manage their own destinies. Migration then was for development while migration today is primarily for economic and political survival.

Focusing on a number of case studies, such as Nigeria, Ghana, French Sudan, and South Africa, the four chapters in this section grapple with issues of brain drain, brain gain, and brain circulation; the significance of land, history, and labor among migrant farmers; gender biases in African historiography; and the hardships of African migrants within Africa. In chapter five, "The Uprooted Emigrant': The Impact of Brain Drain, Brain Gain and Brain Circulation on Africa's Development," Godwin S. M. Okeke adds an unusual "positive" spin to the debate on brain-drain versus brain gain, with a compromise approach appropriately termed "brain circulation." Yet, this notion of "circulation" is not without its problems. Circulation for whom and in whose interest? If the gain is viewed from the perspective of those African professionals who return home to ameliorate and contribute to the respective societies they once left, the percentage of those "returnees" is quite negligible as compared to those who stay on. And this is the crux of the dilemma. The chapter is quite persuasive in the attempt to transform the conflicting brain gain/brain drain debate into a win-win paradigm by suggesting other options—namely the "diaspora option," "virtual linkages" etc. One can only hope that Okeke's positive conclusion materializes in not too long a future—in terms of the "brain circulation" thesis geared towards bringing about a more "stable world order."

While "brain circulation" constitutes the alternative paradigm for conflict resolution in international migration as proposed by Okeke, an unusual competition, appropriately termed "walking for land" is set in motion in chapter fourteen to resolve land conflict between two ethnic groups in Ghana. In chapter six, "Walking for Land, Drinking Palm Wine: Migrant Farmers and the Historicity of Land Conflict in Brong Ahafo, Ghana," Isidore Lobnibe analyzes a humorous and compelling case-study of the "colonial" approach to land/border dispute in Ghana and its impact on the local disputants. The chapter narrates a competition between the disputing parties in terms of the challenge of walking from each party's abode to the other is fascinating. Yet, the role of palm wine in the competition and its implied meaning as a stimulant gives a stereotypical image of Africans as "lazy drunks" who can easily be manipulated passively such as in the case of colonialism. While the author succeeds in the argument that versions of history constitute a strategy for landless migrants to make a case for their ownership of a disputed land, he also emphasizes that the victory of the Dormaa over the Wenchi is only one version of history. In sum, the chapter makes a compelling case for the role of oral histories in the discourse of land ownership and inter-migrant relations.

Our discussion of African migrations will be incomplete without addressing issues of gender in migration. In chapter seven, "Migrants in French Sudan: Gender Biases in the Historiography," Marie Rodet challenges gender biases in African historiography and African migrations scholarship by invoking the fact that colonial attitudes towards women were based on seeing women as "accompanying spouses," "passive migrants," and "domestic workers" etc, as opposed to "labor migrants" that captures the category in which men were classified. In addition to a critique of insufficient studies on African female migrations, Rodet argues that African historiography on female migrations is gender biased and must be redressed. This study contributes to such balanced and gender-conscious research in African studies. The case-studies of the *Cercles* are particularly informative and provocative about gender roles, biases, and relations in migration.

African migration studies as an emerging sub-field in African studies has focused primarily on the patterns of migration from Africa to the West and less on intra-African migration. This research attitude may be attributable to other competing issues of refugees and internally displaced persons in Africa. Indeed, it is rewarding to compare the experiences of African migrants in other African countries to the experiences of African migrants in the African diaspora. Apparently, the same issues of adjustment conflicts between migrants and locals especially when it comes to employment cannot be overemphasized. In chapter eight, "The Impact of the Relationship between Migrants and Traditional Authorities on South African Mining Communities" Charity Chenga and Freek J. Cronjé analyze a fascinating case study of how the attitudes of traditional authorities towards migrants impact the adjustment/settlement of these workers. While migrants are generally willing to work hard in the mines since they are coming from African countries with worsening economic conditions, traditional authorities see as them as "threats" to their own economic survival and often accuse them of spreading sexually transmitted diseases as well as other social problems in terms of how these migrants affect their children negatively. In their turn, these labor migrants see the traditional authorities as lazy and socially dependent. Chenga and Cronjé conclude that both parties must see each other as global partners—traditional authorities in particular must see migrants as contributors to global values to which traditional values can equally benefit.

PART III: MIGRATION AND SURVIVAL POLITICS

Ultimately, African migration is a form of politics, not necessarily of the "belly" alone, but of survival. This section is perhaps the most encompassing in that it incorporates many aspects of migration and survival politics. The four chapters engage issues as far-flung as Pan-Africanism[3] and Nkrumah, cultural adaptation of African migrants in South Africa, and Asian Diaspora in Africa. In chapter nine, "Cultural and Ethnic Accommodation of New-Comers in South Africa," Gxowa-Dlayedwa Zodwa probes into the political nature of cultural and ethnic conflicts between South Africans and non South Africans. The three chapters closing the volume vary in their thematic concerns which range from the migration of ideas such as Pan-Africanism to the dynamic settlement of Asians in Africa. In chapter ten, "Pan-Africanism: The Impact of the Nkrumah Years 1945–1966," Obinna Onwumere provides a biographical analysis of Nkrumah's London years and their significance for the development of Nkruma's ideals with regards to freedom and human dignity. Chapter eleven, "African Political Instability and the Search for an Inclusive Society," Chika B. Onwuekwe theorizes on the fact that migration trends in Africa are the consequences of political disease and economic mismanagement. In a bold indictment of the political institutions and "rulers" (as opposed to leaders) that / who have betrayed Africa. The chapter opines that until Africa gets its leadership in order, human capital will continue to be lost, regrettably. Chapter twelve, "A Critical Analysis of the Social and Economic Impact of Asian Diaspora in Kenya" Francis Ogino, Felix Kiruthu, and Winston Jumba Akala, critically expose the historical background of Asian diaspora in Kenya, the economic contributions as well as some of Asians' "amoral" cultural practices. The chapter is particularly significant in its incisive study of how migration could be a double-edged phenomenon—that is, the idea of Asians, while somewhat culturally alienated in Kenya, are politically influential given their economic contributions to the society.

NOTES

1. Toyin Falola, "Welcome," Conference Program, *Movements, Migrations, and Displacements in Africa,* Africa Conference 2006, The University of Texas at Austin, March 25–27, 2006), 1.
2. Philip L. Martin and J. Edward Taylor, "Managing Migration: The Role of Economic Policies," *Global Migrants, Global Refugees: Problems and Solutions,* Aristide R. Zolberg and Peter M. Benda eds., New York: Berghahm Books, 2001, 95.

3. The Pan-African idea must not be seen as being "out of place" in the context of migration. Indeed, the notion of migration is not limited to people but also of ideas. In this context, Nkrumah's role is significant as the father of Pan-Africanism, one who championed the recuperation of African unity worldwide and an attempt at formulating a global African identity.

REFERENCES

Achanfuo-Yeboah, David. "Grounding a Theory of African Migration in Recent Data on Ghana." *International Sociology* 8 no. 2 (1993); 215–226.

Adepoju, Aderanti. "Linkages between Internal and International Migration: The African Situation." *International Social Science Journal* 23 (1984); 145–155.

———. "Issues and Recent Trends in International Migration in Sub-Saharan Africa." *International Social Science Journal* 52 no. 3 (2000); 383–389.

Akpraku, Kofi K. *African Émigrés in the United States: A Missing Link in Africa's Social and Economic Development*. New York: Praeger, 1991.

Allen, Tim and Hubert Morsink, eds. *When Refugees Go Home: African Experiences*. Trenton, NJ: Africa World Press, 1994.

Allen, Tim, ed. *In Search of a Cool Ground: War, Flight & Homecoming in Northeast Africa*. Trenton, NJ: Africa World Press, 1996.

Arthur, John A. *Invisible Sojourners: African Immigrant Diaspora in the United States*. Westport: Praeger, 2000.

Bailey, Samuel L and Eduardo José Míguez, eds. *Mass Migration to Modern Latin America*. Wilmington, DE: Scholarly Resources, 2003.

Bloch, Alice. "Emigration from Zimbabwe: Migrant Perspectives." *Social Policy and Administration* 40 no. 1 (2006); 67–87.

Brettell, Caroline and James Hollifield, eds. *Migration Theory: Talking Across Disciplines* (New York: Routledge, 2000.

Castles, Stephen and Mark J. Miller. *The Age of Migration: International Population Movements in the Modern World*. New York: Guilford Press, 1993.

Clark, Kamari Maxine. *Mapping Yoruba Networks: Power and Agency in the Making of Transnational Communities*. Durham: Duke University Press, 2004.

Cohen, Lucy M. *Culture, Disease, and Stress among Latino Immigrants*. Washington: Smithsonian Institute, 1979.

Crush, Jonathan and Clarence Tshitereke. "Contesting Migrancy: The Foreign Labor Debate in Post-1994 South Africa." *Africa Today* 48 no. 3 (2001); 49–70.

Daniel, Yvonne. *Dancing Wisdom: Embodied Knowledge in Haitian Vodou, Cuban Yoruba, and Bahian Candomblé*. Urbana: University of Illinois Press, 2005.

El-Khawas, Mohamed A. "Brain Drain: Putting Africa between a Rock and a Hard Place." *Mediterranean Quarterly* 15 no. 4 (2004); 37–56.

Fabre, Geneviève and Klaus Benesch. *African Diasporas in the New and Old Worlds: Consciousness and Imagination*. Amsterdam/New York: Rodopi, 2004.

Falola, Toyin. "Nigeria in the Global Context of Refugees: Historical and Comparative Perspectives." Paul Lovejoy and Pat Williams, eds. *Displacement and The Politics of Violence in Nigeria*. Leiden and New York: Brill, 1997; 5–21.

———. "Intellectuals and Africa in a Changing World Order." *Nationalism and African Intellectuals*. New York: University of Rochester Press, 2001; 262–293.

Falola, Toyin and Matt D. Childs, eds. *Yoruba Diaspora in the Atlantic World.* Bloomington, IN: Indiana University Press, 2005.

Gordon, April. "The New Diaspora: African Immigration to the United States." *Journal of Third World Studies* 15 (1998); 79–110.

Hagopian, A. et al., eds. "The Flight of Physicians from West Africa: Views of African Physicians and Implications for Policy." *Social Science and Medicine* 61.8 (2005); 1750–1760.

Hammar, Thomas et al., eds. *International Migration, Immobility and Development: Multidisciplinary Perspectives.* New York: Berg, 1997.

Hear, Nicholas Van. *New Diasporas: The Mass Exodus, Dispersal and Regrouping of Migrant Communities.* Seattle: University of Washington Press, 1998.

Henderson, George and Martha Primeaux. *Transcultural Health Care.* Menlo Park, CA: Addison-Wesley, 1981.

Kibreab, Gaim. *African Refugees: Reflections on the African Refugee Problem.* Trenton, NJ: Africa World Press, 1985.

Kiluva-Ndunda, Mutindi Mumbua. "The Impact of Development on Women's Health and the Environment." *African Women & Globalization: Dawn of the 21ˢᵗ Century.* Jepkorir Rose Chepyator-Thompson, ed. Trenton, NJ: Africa World Press, 2005; 215–224.

Kiple, Kenneth F. *Another Dimension to the Black Diaspora.* Cambridge: Cambridge University Press, 1981.

Kramer, Elizabeth J. et al. eds. *Immigrant Women's Health: Problems and Solutions.* San Francisco: Jossey-Bass, 1999.

Lanza, Robert. *The Health and Survival of the Human Species in the 21st Century.* Santa Fe, NM: Health Press, 1996.

Lesser, Jeffrey, ed. *Welcoming the Undesirables: Brazil and the Jewish Question.* Berkeley: University of California Press, 1994.

Lesser, Jeffrey, ed. *Negotiating National Identity: Immigrants, Minorities, and the Struggle for Ethnicity in Brazil.* Durham: Duke University Press, 1999.

Lindsay, Beverly, ed. *African Migration and National Development.* University Park: Pennsylvania State University Press, 1985.

Macklin, Audrey. "Our Sisters from Stable Countries": War, Globalization, and Accountability." *Social Politics: International Studies in Gender, State and Society* 10 no. 2 (2003); 256–283.

Makoni, Sinfree, et al. eds. *Black Linguistics: Language, Society, and Politics in Africa and the Americas.* Foreward by Ngugi wa Thiong'o. London/New York: Routledge, 2003.

Martin, Philip L. and J. Edward Taylor. "Managing Migration: The Role of Economic Policies." *Global Migrants, Global Refugees: Problems and Solutions.* Aristide R. Zolberg and Peter M. Benda eds. New York: Berghahm Books, 2001; 95–120.

Meissner, Doris et al., eds. *International Migration: Challenges in a New Era.* New York: The Trilateral Commission, 1993.

Mobasher, Mohsen M and Mahmoud Sadri. *Migration, Globalization, and Ethnic Relations: An Inetrdisciplinary Approach.* Upper Saddle River, NJ: Pearson Prentice Hall, 2004.

Muller, Gilbert H. *New Strangers in Paradise*. Lexington KY: University Press of Kentucky, 1999.

Nelson, Lise and Joni Seager eds. *A Companion to Feminist Geography*. Malden, MA: Blackwell Publishers, 2005.

Okafor, Lawrence A. *Recent African Immigrants to the USA: Their Concerns and How Everyone Can Succeed in the USA*. New York: Rosedog Press, 2003.

Olaniyan, Tejumola. "African Writers, Exile, and the Politics of a Global Diaspora." *West Africa Review* 4 no. 1 (2003); 1–4.

Patterson, Andrew and Glenda Kruss. "Educational Migration and Its Effect on Access to Schooling in South Africa." *South African Journal of Education* 18 no. 3 (1998); 149–156.

Pond, B. and B. McPake. "The Health Migration Crisis: The Role of Four Organizations for Economic Cooperation and Development Countries." *Lancet* 367 (2006); 1448–1455.

Ranger, Terence. "Studying Repatriation as Part of African Social History." *When Refugees Go Home*. Tim Allen and Hubert Morsink, eds. Trenton, NJ: Africa World Press/United Nations Research Institute, 1994, 279–294.

Reimers, David M. *Other Immigrants: The Global Origins of the American People*. New York: New York University Press, 2005.

Scott, Frankilin D. Ed. *World Migration in Modern Times*. New Jersey: Prentice Hall, 1968.

Sheldon, Kathleen, ed. *Courtyards, Markets, City Streets: Urban Women in Africa*. Boulder, CO: Westview Press, 1996.

Schulman, Steven, ed. *The Impact of Immigration on African Americans*. New Brunswick: Transaction, 2005.

Simelane, H.S. "The State, Chiefs and the Control of Female Migration in Colonial Swaziland, c. 1930–1950s." *Journal of African History* 45 no. 1 (2004); 103–124.

Stilwell, B. et al. "Migration of Health-Care Workers from Developing Countries: Strategic Approaches to its Management." *Bulletin of the World Health Organization* 82.8 (2004): 595–600.

Sutlive, Vinson H. and Tomoko Hamada. *Physicians and Health Care in the Third World* (#55). Williamsburg: VA: Studies In Third World Societies/College of William & Mary, 1994.

United Nations. *Health and Mortality: Issues of Global Concern*. New York: United Nations, 1999.

Weiner, Myron. *The Global Migration Crisis: Challenge to States and to Human Rights*. New York: Harper Collins, 1995.

White, Evelyn C. *Black Women's Health Book: Speaking for Ourselves*. Seattle, WA: The Seal Press, 1990.

Zegeye, Abebe. *Forced Labour and Migration: Patterns of Movement within Africa*. London/NewYork: Zed Books, 1989.

Zeleza, Paul Tiyambe. "The African Academic Diaspora in the United States and Africa: The Challenges of Productive Engagement." *Comparative Studies of South Asia, Africa and the Middle East* 24 no. 1 (2004); 261–275.

———. "The Politics and Poetics of Exile: Edward Said in Africa." *Research in African Literatures* 36 no. 3 (2005); 1–22.

Part I

Paradoxes of (Im)migration and Exile

Chapter Two

Paradoxes of Immigrant Incorporation: High Achievement and Perceptions of Discrimination by Nigerians in Dallas/ Fort Worth, Texas (USA)

Dennis D. Cordell

INTRODUCTION

The Nigerian community in Dallas/Fort Worth, Texas (DFW), like the Nigerian immigrant community nationally, is characterized by very high levels of educational achievement, and quite high economic status. At the same time, Nigerian immigrants perceive that racial and ethnic discrimination and their accents are major obstacles to integration into American society. Focusing on the Nigerian community in DFW, this paper is a descriptive analysis of segmented incorporation. It first describes levels of educational and economic achievement. The essay goes on to survey Nigerian perceptions of discrimination and the obstacle posed by the differently accented English of many in the community. It concludes by comparing the Nigerian community in DFW with African immigrant communities elsewhere in the country, and with the experience of other immigrants from the African diaspora—notably people from the Caribbean—who arrived in the United States in the middle half of the twentieth century.

The essay is based on qualitative and quantitative data collected from a convenience sample of 100 households in the Nigerian community, supplemented by census data and field reports, all collected in the course of a recent National Science Foundation (USA) study.[1] Little of the very large literature on immigration has yet explored the "new" African immigration to the United States, a phenomenon that dates from the late 1970s and 1980s.[2]

DALLAS/FORT WORTH

Most of the Dallas/Fort Worth metropolitan area is included in Dallas, Tarrant, Collin, and Denton counties in north Texas. Dallas and Fort Worth

are the region's two largest cities. The four-county area has a current population of nearly 5 million inhabitants—4.6 million at the time of the 2000
census. The foreign-born totaled 753,000 in 2000, or 16.4% of the population of the four counties—507,000 of whom were born in Latin America
and 28,000 in Africa. About 1% of the foreign-born—or 7,300 people—
were born in Nigeria. They and their American-born children make up the
Nigerian community in DFW.[3]

In recent decades, the population of DFW has experienced substantial shifts in ethnic composition, largely as a result of immigration from
Mexico, but from many other counties as well. Thirty years ago, the foreign-born population numbered only 100,000 or 5% of the population.
At that time, 75% of the population was "white" or Anglo. By contrast,
in 2000, the white population made up only 56% of the population of the
four countries. This proportion has continued to decline, and is expected
to fall below 50% by 2010. Hispanics, including Mexicans, constituted
23% of DFW's inhabitants according to the last census. Now small at 4%,
Asians nonetheless comprise the fastest growing group. The African-origin
population, which includes African-Americans and a small black immigrant
population, hovers at 23%.

The principal focus of the NSF project was not racial or ethnic discrimination *per se,* but immigrant incorporation, and in particular the
socioeconomic, political, and cultural integration of newcomers in Dallas/
Fort Worth. However, given the new demographic context, characterized
by a much more complex ethnic landscape than in the 1970s, an analysis
of perceptions of discrimination in DFW seems timely and relevant. Before,
the numerical and political dominance of non-Hispanic whites led them to
expect that others would have to adjust to them. Blacks were the largest
racial minority in DFW, and were engaged in a struggle with whites for civil
rights and recognition that paralleled the white-black conflict in the rest of
the country. Mexican Americans were a small group struggling for recognition. The racial and political landscape has now changed.

Nigerian immigrants in DFW are of particular interest because they
clearly feel constrained by discrimination, and yet they enjoy high socio-
economic status. Moreover, they are fluent in English. Their experiences
challenge the popular notion that "successful" immigrant incorporation is
only a question of achieving high levels of education, speaking English with
ease, and making a significant income.

EDUCATION

Nigerians in DFW are highly educated. Virtually all of the 100 Nigerians
in our sample had a secondary school education when they arrived in the

United States. A large percentage had completed several years of university; many came with an undergraduate degree.

Table 1 summarizes the average number of years of schooling Nigerians in the sample had completed when they arrived in the United States, after their arrival, and at the time of the interview. They are grouped by period of arrival. Those who arrived before 1970—whose "average" arrival date we have pegged at 1965 since only a few Nigerians came to the U.S. before the Nigerian independence era in the 1960s—averaged 15 years of school. In the 1970s and 1980s, the average dropped to 12 and 13.4, respectively, probably because independence fueled the need for university-educated people. Even though numerous new universities opened in these years, they could still not meet the demand for post-secondary education. Moreover, a degree from an American university was (and remains) highly regarded. Nigerians arriving since 1990 averaged between 14 and 16 years of education, levels resembling those of the 1960s. This recent rise may well indicate that more Nigerians are staying home to complete their undergraduate educations, venturing abroad only for graduate work. It also suggests that more highly educated Nigerians are leaving their country in search of a better life in the U.S. Widespread corruption, insecurity, and the collapse of the Nigerian economy have pushed many people to leave their homeland. The U.S. visa lottery program granted permanent residence to a surprising 10 Nigerians of the 100 in our sample, which provided an impetus for some to immigrate.[4]

Table 2-1. Educational Attainment of Nigerian Immigrants at Arrival, After Arrival, and at Time of Interview (in Years)

Period of arrival	Education at arrival	Education after arrival	Education at interview
Before 1970	15.0	7.0	22.0
1970-1979	12.0	5.5	17.5
1980-1989	13.4	5.2	18.6
1990-1994	15.6	3.2	18.8
1995-1999	14.9	2.0	16.9
2000-2004	14.1	1.8	16.0

Source: "Immigrants in a Suburban Metropolis," responses of Nigerian immigrants to questions 11 and 13, Individual Immigrant Questionnaire

N=100 Nigerian Interviewees

In addition to arriving with substantial human capital in the form of education, Nigerians interviewed in DFW very frequently continued to invest energy and resources in education after coming to the United States. Table 1 also presents a summary of this investment. Men and women who arrived in the 1960s continued their education for an average of seven years following their arrival. Those who arrived in the 1970s and 1980s, went to school for another 5 to 5.5 years. Nigerians who came in the early and late 1990s and since 2000 have not gone to school in the U.S. for as long—3.2, 2, and 2 years, respectively—to some degree because they have not had as long to do so as their predecessors.

In many cases, Nigerians continued their studies to change fields, or to acquire credentials that are required by government agencies and professional associations here. Mr. X, for example, had a B.A. in English from the University of Benin when he arrived in 1985. Since he has lived in the United States, he has gone on to get a B.A. and an M.A. in Sociology, and is just now finishing his Ph.D. in the same field; he has specialized in criminology and has already worked for some years in a department of youth corrections. Nigerians also sometimes continue to study in the same field, aiming to get an advanced degree or higher level of certification. A graduate of a medical school in Nigeria, for example, came to Dallas for his residency and to specialize; he is now a professor at a medical school in the city. Another physician, trained in Greece, has had a more difficult time of it. She has worked in a medical lab for some years, and is studying for her medical certification exams in her spare time.

Finally, Table 1 summarizes the educational attainment of the 100 Nigerian interviewees at the time of their interviews. Immigrants who arrived before 1970, whose average date of arrival is pegged at 1965, had finished 22 years of schooling by the time they were interviewed (after 2001). Arrivals in the 1970s and 1980s had studied about 18 years, while those who came in the 1990s had finished the equivalent of an undergraduate degree. Even those who arrived after 2000, by and large a younger cohort, had studied 16 years! The dimensions of this investment in education—in time, energy, and resources—are quite extraordinary, and certainly debunk the common stereotype in the United States which portrays "immigrants" as poorly educated and unskilled. However, these characteristics resemble those of Nigerian immigrant groups elsewhere, such as the Igbo community in Chicago. Of this community, Reynolds writes," . . . the Igbo people I know resemble middle class, professional European and African-Americans in far more ways than other easily visible and coherent ethnic or immigrant groups. First of all, their educational achievements are immense, with all group members having completed post-secondary education (or they are in the process of doing so)."[5]

INCOME

Given their high levels of education at arrival, coupled with further investment in school and certification once in the United States, it is not surprising to learn that Nigerians in the DFW sample enjoy high levels of income relative to most other immigrant groups. Table 2 presents data on income collected in the interviews with 100 Nigerians in DFW. Even given the caveat that self-reported income data are subject to both under- and over-estimation, it seems clear that Nigerian interviewees are doing quite well. Many of them were interviewed at home, and their comfortable surroundings tend to confirm this conclusion.

Once again, these data are grouped and presented according to the period of arrival in the United States. Interviewees who arrived before 1970 report an average household income of $125,000 annually. Nigerians in DFW tend to live in single family residential units that are also filial and consumption units; therefore, this income represents household income. It is not the aggregate of the incomes of unrelated individuals who do not operate as a joint household. Incomes drop for those who arrived in the 1970s and the 1980s, but remain high at $110,000 and $96,000, respectively.

Table 2-2. Annual Household Income Reported by Nigerian Immigrants in Dfw, by Period of Arrival

Period of arrival	Income (in dollars)
Before 1970	125,000
1970-1979	110,000
980-1989	96,177
1990-1994	49,111
1995-1999	57,027
2000-2004	26,071

Source: "Immigrants in a Suburban Metropolis," responses of Nigerian immigrants to question included in Table A, Immigrant Household Questionnaire

N=100 Nigerian Interviewees

The average household incomes of men and women who arrived after 1990 are half those of those who came before, but still quite high, while those who have been in the United States only since 2000 have the lowest average income. Several factors contribute to these lower income levels. First, these members of the community tend to be younger, many are still in school, and many live by themselves or a roommate and have not yet established a household in the sense described above.

Given the data on education and income, how might the Nigerian experience in DFW be characterized? In immigration studies jargon, these high levels of education and revenue would probably be presented as a "positive incorporation outcomes." Education and economic success often serve as proxies for successful incorporation into American society. Other indicators of "successful incorporation," which cannot be presented here due to limitations of space and time, would be Nigerians' fluency in spoken and written English, and their more or less successful adjustment of immigration status—a very high percentage have moved from student visas to permanent residency and then citizenship over the years they have been in the United States.

However, the process of incorporation is more complex than the figure on a paycheck or a diploma. Incorporation also includes less tangible dimensions, such as the degree to which immigrants feel welcome, and whether or not they perceive that members of the host society treat them fairly. Indeed, Portes and Zhou's concept of segmented incorporation, mentioned in the introduction to this essay, speaks to this point.[6] They submit that the unequal treatment accorded domestic minorities in the US—indicated by continued *de facto* residential segregation, and substantive discrepancies in levels of education and income—is also visited upon immigrant co-ethnics and their children. The result, they suggest, may well be downward incorporation in the second generation, or integration into marginalized groups within American society that reject the mainstream American "success ethic."

To get at this set of issues, we asked Nigerian immigrants about their perceptions and experiences of discrimination since arriving in the US; we also asked them what they considered to be the major obstacle facing the Nigerian community in the United States today. We discuss the results here because they strongly suggest that Nigerians—despite their recent arrival—have quickly come to understand that their successful incorporation is at least partially conditioned and often limited by history and contemporary conditions in a society profoundly preoccupied by race and ethnic identity, and shaped by discrimination.

PERCEPTIONS OF RACIAL AND ETHNIC DISCRIMINATION

Perceptions of discrimination and racial or ethnic discrimination are, of course, not the same for all populations or for all individuals. The responses to the questions posed in the individual immigrant survey do not meet the definition of race and national-origin discrimination as defined by the courts in rulings growing out of the 1964 Civil Rights Act or the Fourteenth Amendment to the U.S. Constitution. Moreover, we did not define the terms racial or ethnic discrimination in our questionnaire. We used the terms in the questions and allowed respondents to interpret them according to their individual understanding of the concepts.

In general, respondents regarded discrimination as a measure of acceptance by other ethnic and racial groups in DFW; most also viewed it as an indication of unfair or inappropriate treatment based on origin or ethnicity. We have a better sense of how respondents understood discrimination from the individual immigrant survey,[7] because responses were open-ended, and because other questions not considered here shed additional light on their sense of rights, fairness, and how they get treated on the basis of their national origin, ethnicity, race, or immigration status. Some of what they described probably fits a legal definition of discrimination, such as decisions by employers to hire less-qualified, native-born employees over certain legal immigrants; actions of favoritism by supervisors on the basis of ethnicity or race; or, refusal to rent an apartment to particular national groups. Other instances that respondents characterized as discrimination are more appropriately classified as other types of abuses—for example, labor exploitation. In addition, some respondents complained of actions that, in fact, constitute lawful discrimination—such as denying unauthorized immigrants a job because they do not have a valid Social Security number or a means of identification.

As noted earlier, individual surveys were limited to Mexican, Salvadoran, Asian Indian, Vietnamese, and Nigerian immigrants. This essay focuses on the responses of Nigerians. They were asked first to decide if other members of their nationality faced "serious problems of ethnic or racial discrimination," and to provide concrete examples. Immediately thereafter, a second question asked them about their own experience with prejudice or discrimination "from any group." We added the words "from any group" to get beyond the black/white or Mexican/Anglo dichotomies that have prevailed in conventional conceptions of prejudice and racial discrimination in the U.S. In responding to the first question, about 70 percent of Nigerians said that they had heard about other immigrants who suffered discrimination. However, these figures, high as they are, underestimate the affirmative replies. Fifteen percent of Nigerians said that they did not think that their compatriots faced serious discrimination, but then elaborated on their answers in ways that really placed their responses into a "no-but-yes" category. Put together, then, 84% of Nigerians reported that members of their community have faced serious problems with discrimination. When asked about personal experiences with prejudice or discrimination, nearly three-quarters (73%) of Nigerians either replied in the affirmative or described situations that constituted an affirmative answer (see Table 4).

In their answers to the first question about what other Nigerians reported about their experiences, and in their answers to the second question about their own experiences, Nigerians offered opinions about the reasons for discrimination and the contexts in which it occurred. Tables 3 and 4 present these reasons and contexts ranked in order of frequency. Both other Nigerians and the Nigerian immigrants interviewed mentioned employment-related discrimination most often. Within that broad category, discrimination in hiring was most frequently cited, followed by hostility and unfair consideration for promotion once on the job. In the case of experiences reported by others, accent and ridicule ranked second, followed in third place by reports of being stereotyped as dishonest. As for personal experience, the second most common examples cited by the immigrants themselves were discrimination at school—usually related to their own educational experiences rather than to events in their children's classrooms—and poor treatment by African Americans. Generalized hostility, "simply being black," and accent ranked third among personal experiences described as discrimination. Nigerians reported that people often tell them to "speak English," when, in fact that is just what they were doing.

Fourth most common, among reports they had heard and from their own experience, came discriminatory actions or attitudes by the police. Problems with African Americans ranked fifth in discrimination reported by others, while immigrants themselves placed untoward social experiences in fifth place—experiences at church, for example, where several people said that people changed pews when they sat down, refused to speak to them, or to take their hands when the pastor asked members of the congregation to join hands. Finally, many other Nigerian immigrants reported discrimination that they believed stemmed from the fact that they were black—not necessarily because they were Nigerian. All in all, then, Nigerians describe high levels of discrimination—both in the cases of other Nigerians and themselves. It is clear that race and ethnicity are

Table 2-3. Experiences of Discrimination Reported by Other Nigerian Immigrants in Dallas/Fort Worth to Interviewees

Reasons/Contexts	Mentions
Rank 1	20
Employment	
Hiring	
Accent	
Overqualification	
On job	
Promotion	
Hostility/Harassment	
Firing	
Rank 2	16
Accent and Ridicule	
Rank 3	5
Dishonesty Stereotype	
Ranks 4 and 5	8
Police	*4*
African Americans	*4*
General Awareness	*30*
Black	
Denial/Minimization	*30*

Source: "Immigrants in a Suburban Metropolis," responses of Nigerian immigrants to question 73, Immigrant Household Questionnaire

N=100 Nigerian Interviewees

very problematic issues for Nigerians, despite their high levels of education and income.

As a way of measuring the importance that immigrants assigned to discrimination relative to other issues faced by the community, we finally examine what they identified as the "most serious problems" faced by Nigerians in Dallas/Fort Worth.

Table 2-4. Personal Experiences of Discrimination by Nigerian Immigrants in Dallas/Fort Worth

Reasons and Contexts (in order of frequency)	
Rank 1	
Employment	
Hiring	
Overqualification	
Accent	
Black	
On job	
Hostility/Harassment	
Promotion	
African Americans	
Firing	
Rank 2	
African Americans	School
Rank 3	
Accent	Hostility
Simply being black	
Rank 4	
Police	Church and Social
Denial or minimization of discrimination as a problem	

Source: "Immigrants in a Suburban Metropolis," responses of Nigerian immigrants to question 74, Immigrant Household Questionnaire

N=100 Nigerian Interviewees

NIGERIAN PERCEPTIONS OF THE MOST SERIOUS PROBLEMS FACING THEIR COMMUNITY

Table 5 dramatically illustrates the importance Nigerians attach to the issue of discrimination. Taken together, the 100 interviewees mentioned 186 specific challenges. In an effort to weight these responses somewhat differently, Table 6 classifies the "serious problems" identified by immigrants who listed only a single challenge—figuring that citing a single example may indicate that it really stands out as important to an interviewee. Once again, discrimination, and its subcategories of race and accent total nearly half of the "problems," or 16 of 38. The related problem of stereotyping weighed in as the single issue cited by 4 immigrants—for a total of 20 of 38 responses.

What is intriguing in both cases is how employment issues fall to mid-level among all the problems faced by the community—not surprising, given the high average income of Nigerians who were interviewed. Their issues with employment discrimination, then, appear to deal more with finding jobs commensurate with their skills and with promotion within an organization once they are hired. On the other hand, immigration issues rank quite high, just after discrimination and stereotyping. Once again, however, specific immigration issues do not have to do with getting admitted to the country or achieving some recognized legal status, as much as with status adjustment—and moving from student status to a more permanent status—and with getting visas for family members to come to the United States, either to visit, to go to school, or to join them.

A CAVEAT AND A CONCLUSION

However, before coming to a definitive conclusion about the experience and perception of discrimination among Nigerian immigrants, an additional important observation is in order. A significant number of immigrants tended to minimize or even deny the existence of discrimination. These kinds of comments were almost as common as complaints about discrimination related to employment. Moreover, some immigrants voiced impatience with African Americans who complained about discrimination and racism.

Nigerians explained these responses in several ways. Some said that they "did not believe" in discrimination, and that individual drive determined success. Others suggested that people who complained of discrimination needed to address limitations by looking within, rather than blaming others. Still others, for the most part "born-again" Christians and fervent members of Pentecostal churches, said that all people are the children of God, and that they "don't see color." In the end, these responses do not mean that Nigerians do not believe that discrimination exists. In one context or another in the course of their interviews, virtually all made reference to these obstacles. In responding to the direct question about discrimination, however, they meant to send two other messages. The first is that they intend to succeed despite the barriers in their path. This message echoes

Table 2-5. Nigerian Perceptions of Most Serious Problems Faced by Community in Dallas/Fort Worth

Reasons/Contexts	Mentions
Discrimination	68
General	12
Accent	26
Because of race	23
Other reasons	7
Stereotypes	32
General	5
Dishonesty, fraud	25
Savages	1
All wealthy	1
Immigration	23
Adjustment of status	21
Getting family in country	2
Adaptation and Incorporation	22
Adaptation to American Culture	11
Acceptance	2
Loneliness/Homesickness/Limbo/Divided Allegiance	6
Lack of confidence	3
Employment	15
Getting job commensurate with education	13
Transferring credentials	1
Unemployment	1
Financial problems	7
Credit too easy to abuse	

(continued)

Table 2-5. Nigerian Perceptions of Most Serious Problems Faced by Community in Dallas/Fort Worth *(continued)*

Reasons/Contexts	Mentions
Dishonesty of a few	
Loss of focus on reason for being here	
Access to loans and financial services	
Relations with African Americans	5
Corruption/competition in Nigerian community	5
Education	3
Getting education	2
Education of recent arrivals is inadequate	1
Police harassment	2
Poverty	1
Lack of health insurance	1
Loss of faith	1
Other Africans find Nigerians haughty	1
TOTAL MENTIONS	186

Source: "Immigrants in a Suburban Metropolis," responses of Nigerian immigrants to question 65, Immigrant Household Questionnaire

N=100 Nigerian Interviewees

West Indian reactions to racism in New York. As Nancy Foner notes, "West Indians tend to subordinate racial considerations to the overriding goal of achieving material success in America, and they believe that individual effort can overcome racial barriers."[8]

The second intent in denying the existence of discrimination is to set themselves apart from African Americans. Judging from comments made in many interviews, Nigerian immigrants clearly do not understand how forced immigration, the experience of slavery, and subsequent *de jure* and *de facto* discrimination have shaped African American society. The comments of some Nigerians about the alienation of African Americans and

Table 2-6. Nigerian Perceptions of Most Serious Problems Faced by Community in Dallas/Fort Worth by Immigrants Who Cited Only One Obstacle

Reasons/Contexts	Mentions
Discrimination	16
Race	13
Accent	3
Immigration issues	6
Stereotyping as not trustworthy	4
None	3
Adaptation and Incorporation ("culture clashes")	2
Competition and disorganization in community	2
Employment, job commensurate with education	1
Access to loans and financial services	1
Loss of faith	1
Don't know	1
No answer	1
TOTAL MENTIONS	38

Source: "Immigrants in a Suburban Metropolis," responses of Nigerian immigrants to question 65, Immigrant Household Questionnaire

N=100 Nigerian Interviewees

their lower educational and economic status in American society are often quite negative. They do not understand "why African Americans do not take advantage of the opportunities this society offers them." Some suggest that African Americans have a "slave mentality." At best, Nigerians who have sympathetic relations with African Americans admit that they simply cannot understand the situation of African Americans "because we weren't here" during the era of slavery, the period of legal discrimination that followed, and the civil rights struggle of the 1950s and 1960s. But all do want to make it clear that they are different. Again these comments are reminiscent of the statements of West Indian immigrants recorded by Waters in New York City:[9] "Indeed, one finds cultural distancing from black Americans among the immigrants we interviewed. They argued that West Indians merited inclusion in American society because of their strong work ethnic, the value they placed on education, and their lack of pathological behaviors. . . . West Indians make a case for cultural inclusion in American society based on being different from black Americans. . . . Cultural distancing may help individual black Americans and West Indians, but it leaves intact and reinforces stereotypes of blacks as inferior, thus harming other group members."

All of this taken together, what might we conclude about the incorporation of Nigerian immigrants into society in north Texas? First, they enjoy a high socioeconomic status. High levels of education and high incomes afford them more choices and greater security than many other immigrant communities. Second, Nigerians are very focused on economic success. For Nigerians such success promises a door to integration into American society. Their wealth allows them to invest in their standards of living here and to send money to extended family members in Nigeria.

Third, Nigerians, because they speak English, and are characterized by higher levels of education and income, connect with a greater diversity of people and groups in DFW. This is also due to the fact that Nigerians are a very small community. Their limited numbers compel them to deal with more people outside the Nigerian community.

Preliminary analyses of data concerning the people with whom Nigerian immigrants work and spend their leisure time also indicates that, apart from those who own small businesses where they tend to be joined by other family members and other Nigerians, their workplaces include all major ethnic groups in the Metroplex. While they do tend to spend much of their leisure time with other Nigerians, they also interact a lot with whites, African Americans, and other Africans.

There is a final irony in this tale of incorporation. Although Nigerian immigrants express impatience with hostility towards their native-born co-ethnics—which is to say African Americans—they interact with them as much as, if not more, than they do with other native-born groups. The relationship between Nigerians and African Americans is a very ambivalent one. At the same time, proximity means that for many Nigerian immigrants, native-born co-ethnics are both an avenue and an obstacle to incorporation into broader society in DFW.

NOTES

1. This chapter is based largely on data collected as part of a research project entitled "Immigrants, Rights, and Incorporation in a Suburban Metropolis," funded by a grant from the Cultural Anthropology Program of the

National Science Foundation (BCS0003938). The principal investigators were Caroline Brettell, Dennis Cordell, Manuel Garcia y Griego, and James Hollifield. In 2001–2005, the fours of us and our research assistants conducted approximately 600 face-to-face household interviews with Mexican, Salvadoran, Asian Indian, Vietnamese, and Nigerian-born immigrants. We also developed a telephone survey of 1,000 adult DFW residents, divided evenly between the native-born and foreign-born. While the results, opinions, and conclusions presented in this paper are mine alone, I would like to thank Manuel Garcia y Griego for stimulating conversation, and his collaboration on closely related projects.

2. Among the few book-length studies, see John A. Arthur, *Invisible Sojourners: African Immigrant Diaspora in the United States* (Westport: Praeger, 2000), and Adrian S. Capehart, "The Migration of Africans to the United States since 1960: Contexts, Responses, and Communities," Ph.D. dissertation, Department of History, The University of Illinois at Chicago, 2004.

3. www.census.gov. All data cited from the 2000 U.S. census come from this site. We use the terms "immigrant," "foreign-born," and "newcomer" interchangeably, thus including all persons born abroad.

4. For background, see Anna O. Law, "The Diversity Visa Lottery—A Cycle of Unintended Consequences in United States Immigration Policy," *Journal of American Ethnic History* 21, 4 (2002): 3–29.

5. Rachel R. Reynolds, "An African Brain Drain: Igbo Decisions to Immigrate to the US," *Review of African Political Economy* 92 (2002), 274.

6. Portes, Alejandro and Min Zhou. "The New Second Generation: Segmented Assimilation and Its Variants," *Annals of the American Academy of Political and Social Science* 530 (November, 1993), 74–96.

7. In documentation on this study, we often referred to this survey as the household survey, because individual immigrants were asked, among many other things, about other members of their household. For clarity, I use the term "individual immigrant survey" here, to emphasize that my researchers and I interviewed Nigerians face-to-face and one-to-one.

8. Nancy Foner, "Introduction. West Indian Migration to New York: An Overview." In Nancy Foner (editor). *Islands in the City: West Indian Migration to New York* (Berkeley and Los Angeles: University of California Press, 2001), 1–22. Foner cites here two other essays from her collection: Bashi Bobb, Vilna F. and Averil Y. Clarke, "Experiencing Success: Structuring the Perception of Opportunities for West Indians," 216–236; and Milton Vickerman, "Tweaking a Monolith: The West Indian Immigrant Encounter with 'Blackness,' " 237–256.

9. Mary C. Waters, "Growing Up West Indian and African American: Gender and Class Differences in the Second Generation." In Nancy Foner (editor), *Islands in the City: West Indian Migration to New York*, 193–215.

Chapter Three

Nigerian Exiles, Democratic Struggles and the Notion of Sacrifice: Interspatial Activism and the Proactive Discourses of Liberation

Anthony Attah Agbali

INTRODUCTION

The dialectical struggles for power and the contestations that took place within Nigerian territory during the Abacha dictatorial years is the subject of this chapter. The study explores the relationships and contestations of class, power, nationalism, and ethnicity, as rooted within certain historical configurations that define a certain kind of national and cultural habitus. Within such habitus, it is claimed that the despotic realties and contests under the military regime were embedded within the stripes of its origins, and amply reflect an elongation of the contradictory visions, influences, and agencies that predicated and sustained their formation processes.

Therefore, the Nigerian military is portrayed as masking a cultural thesis of colonial and imperial modalities and ways of acting. In the same mode of analytical reasoning, it is contended that the resistance imagination, depicted within the textured referential marker as pro-democratic struggle, represents another form of habitus that emerged and shaped the structural contours of the modern imagination of Nigeria, within the context of the earlier nationalism of self-determination, especially those of the anti-colonial contests.

Nigeria as a nation has gone through many traumatic political cycles out of which it has yet fully to emerge and find her true destiny. Since Nigeria gained political independence in October 1960, successive political leaderships, whether civilian or military regimes, have failed and proven to be a grandiose charade of delusive dreams. In spite of enormous potential and arrogant posturing, the Nigerian economic, cultural, and political landscape is in shambles. True development, due to misrule, poignantly eludes this nation of great people. Buried in deluded mirage and disillusioning rhetoric of self-aggrandizing notions of greatness, Nigeria's notorious fatal malaise rends the reasoning heart.

In spite of her great human potential and immense natural resources, Nigeria has remained a parasitic nation. Like a witch, it devours even its own, and like a vulture, it shreds its citizens on the slaughter slab in a display of abject indifference. Like the grasshoppers found within its savannah regions, hopping from one political experiment to another, every trial government has failed to establish any meaningful self-rule. Indeed, every attempt at new experimental governance has erupted into a nightmare. Nigerians in their resilience hardly intone dirges of disparagement—indulgently and resourcefully drilling through the mines of fatalities, envisioning hope in the sore of despair, anticipating that even in the worst case scenarios, salvation is possible, and that a *"Deus ex Machina"* will intervene.

Within these configurations, the Nigerian military evolved on the scene flagging messianic phraseologies, couched in regal "holier-than-thou" antics in pro-active rhetorical demarcations between themselves and the parasitic political class. However, the eventual unfolding of reality later proved such renditions to be predicated upon pseudo-rhetorical constructs and false, demented premises, incapable of reaching syllogistic conclusions. Such ramblings, matched with a pro-active appeal to force, did not often present logical fallacies, but farcical banditry that hijacked true political and social development, locking Nigerians in a closet supervised by Frankenstein-minted prototypes. Within the context of virulent struggles between these two segments of the ruling classes, Nigerians were stampeded. Many were imprisoned, others were exterminated; some fled into exile to save face and their lives, hoping to return to pick up from where they left off, or to get back into rhythm as forces of liberation or oppression.

The phenomenon of the later Abacha exilic experience, which forced many influential intellectuals and political activist Nigerians outside their native shores into foreign nations, especially in the West, and the tactics they employed, is situated within a different earlier consciousness that framed the cultural formations of the Nigerian political scene. Further, this view elicits and affirms the transformational transcendence of the earlier cultural resistance and nationalist culture, as configuring new forms of habitus. Such habitus serves the re-aligning plot that results from the state of hiatus within the dispossession, foreignness, and alienations occasioned by the processes of exile.

Within the strictures of such dynamics, I propose that the exilic experience of recent Nigerian exiles, though at the time painful and negative, possess durable structural qualities for producing the on-going transformation of the Nigerian nation-state, mainly given the different discourses and imaginative rhetoric such dispossessions initiated. In view of these, different trajectories derived from their reasoning and existential actions have been incorporated into the existential imagination of Nigeria, as positive consciousness, as pro-active schemes of liberation. Further, with a perceptive understanding of previous cultural antecedents—albeit disjointed and contradictory—we equally nuance the poignant impact of the then-charged political situation on the synchronic currents that configure other Nigerian cultural formations and spheres; namely, the ethical, the economical, and the social.

Such itemized schemes possess some present positive salience as the exploration of the archival field yields valuable perspectives. In this chapter, I engage in a diachronic referencing of these events, as much as possible engaging in ethnographical archeological drilling from the temporal archival storage. Ethnography of the archive, according to Jean and John Comorrof, supposedly incorporates qualitative properties that validly resonates ethnographic materials necessary for processing cultural phenomena.[1]

In arraying the Nigerian exilic situations, I explore different sources, especially scripted resources, mainly as encrypted by the Nigerian and international media, textual oral histories conveyed through various media interviews and other published sources, including the internet and other multimedia tools. There is no pretending that the quantitative dimensions of such archival resources relative to the period of the Abacha misrule or antedating military versions are exhaustive, given their vastness. Such usages utilize insightful analytical tools intending to bring to the surface hitherto repressed or unexplored trajectories such as are embedded in newspaper and magazine, including specific idioms within such materials such as cartoon graphics that creatively capture the popular imagination as it pertains to the period and the issues of brute domination.

NIGERIAN EXILES AND HISTORICAL IMAGINATION

Exile in the Nigerian historical experience, while rare, has nonetheless been a feature of the Nigerian political landscape. The experience of exile in the Nigerian consciousness can be traced back to the threshold period prior to full colonialism, but of heightened British territorial involvement within the areas of the protectorates of Southern and Northern Nigeria (including Niger Delta, Nupe, Kontagora, Sokoto) and the colony of Lagos, and other cultural areas that would eventually become the later jurisdiction of British Nigeria. The pronounced struggle for alien domination between the British and the indigenous leadership of certain African societies and communities, specifically between chiefs and agents of the colonizing authorities, led to antagonistic contests that often resulted in the exile of some chiefs outside their aboriginal communities.

Therefore prior to the emergence of Nigeria as a nation, British commercial interests, especially as centralized within the hegemonic desire of the Royal Niger Company, produced a modern Nigeria that had begun to initiate different political schemes that led to the exile of prominent African political actors. Essentially, the first exilic experience is rooted within a social movement of resistance and absolute disavowal of alien domination by the autochthonous leaders of different Nigerian cultural and ethnic communities. Thus, Kosoko (1851), King Pepple (1854), Jaja of Opobo (1887), Nana Olomo (1891), Oba Ovenramwen (1897), Attah Ocheje Onakpa (1900), among several others, represent this crop of Nigerian leaders who were deposed and exiled. Consequently, these constituted the proto-exiles within the emerging historical consciousness of the communities that now constitute Nigeria.[2]

Fundamentally, most of those who were exiled or deposed were indigenous political rulers and monarchs who controlled the political machinery and fortune of their kingdoms or sphere of political jurisdictions, entities whose protective interest of the traditional political sphere accentuated various struggles that antagonized and contested the intrusive British hegemonic political and economic interests intent upon decimating the traditional hegemonic order. Based upon their vested interest of domination and subjugation of the kingdoms and political territories that defined the traditional social structures, colonial forces sought to minimize or fragment these traditional institutions and elders. The case of Nana Olomu, the influential Itshekiri merchant and chief is instructive: "The power and influence of Nana thus represented an obstacle to the acceptance of British rule. It was in order to remove this obstacle that the Ebrohimi expedition was mounted against Nana in 1894. The charges of causing a breach of the peace, of breaking his treaty obligations and of engaging in the slave trade later levied against him were no more than a plausible excuse," (Obaro Ikime, 1971, 213).

Ironically, a similar historical replay would be simulated almost a hundred years later, with General Abacha's onslaught against the acclaimed winner of the annulled presidential elections and the Nigerian people in 1993. Interestingly, as a military despot, General Sani Abacha's tyrannical portraiture reflects a historical linearity within the British imperialist display of unwarranted military brutality predicated upon false and prefabricated notions to forge hegemony within an internalized urge for absolute domination. Abacha's brutal tyranny can best be understood within the direct alignment kinship framework that allied the contemporary Nigerian military class diachronically to its imperial progeny as an established continuum of the brutal tradition and representation of imperial colonialism. Such modalities lead to a better intellectual perception that illumines annotatively the military's vehement onslaught against democratic values as it crassly peaked with the truncation of Abiola's presidential ambition, and the overall hostage that the military has held Nigeria since 1983, within the determined attempt to sublimate and pacify all social order toward sanctioning the military's goals of misrule and overall despotic interests.

Few of the deposed African leaders were defined as constituting security risks and served their exile in foreign nations. Jaja of Opobo and King William Dappa Pepple are such instances. The exile of Jaja of Opobo began after he was manipulated and sent to Accra to stand trial, after which he was exiled to the Caribbean, where he eventually died in Tenerife, while returning to his Niger Delta homeland.[3] King William Dappa Pepple was exiled in 1854, spending time first in Fernando Po, then in Ascension, and later in London. Luckily, he returned alive in 1861 after seven years in exile restored to his throne, albeit a damaged personality. He died five years afterwards, succeeded by his son who spent the years of his fathers' exile in London, (Onwuka Dike, 1962, 144–47, 163–164).

Many others served their exile restricted to certain locations within Nigerian territories, devoid of contact with their homeland. Most died broken hearted in exile, never returning to their aboriginal homelands. Therefore, the primal experience of exile within the Nigerian consciousness is embedded within the contextual struggles for control between bipolar political forces, sometimes utilizing other multiple agents, but focally instantiated by the centered fixation upon structural control and political domination, framed around the realities and issues favoring the construction and emergence of the nation-state, and its unfolding ideology. On another level, objection to this intrusive and obstructive ideology upon already established pre-colonial political sovereignty and autonomous institutions generated determined conscientious reactions by the vested traditional authorities in protecting the structural dimensions of their customary boundaries and traditional purviews.

The consciousness of such sovereignty and equality with the British royalty is embodied in the 1841 statement of the Igala King, the Attah to the British expeditors.

> If your countrymen are glad to see me, they must believe what I say.
> The late King wished white men to come to his dominions, but he did

not care to see them. I am now the Attah, or King. If they intend to be true friends, they must not be in a hurry . . . The river belongs to me, a King, way up and down, on both sides, and I am King. The Queen of white men has sent his friend to see me. I have now seen a present, which is not worthy to be offered to me- it is fit for a servant. God has made me after his image; I am all the same as God; and he appointed me a King. "Can I send a messenger to the Queen of the Whites?" "You ask me to go on board of a ship. A king in this country never goes on board a ship. He never puts foot in a canoe. When white people were here before, the King never went on board. If any one desires to see me, he must come to me. If to speak privately, I will dismiss my people. If it be a public matter, then I shall allow them to remain; but the King never goes on board ship."[4]

In fact, Rev. Schon, a member of the same expedition, whose own text offered a somewhat corollary rendition, thus annotated, "Was not this a kingly answer?"[5] Of course it was, and more so, a statement sanctioning both royalty and referencing sovereignty.

Thus, the hegemonic contestations and arbitrary display of autocratic power by the alien British hegemonic order inevitably incensed social and cultural atrophy and anomie resulting from counter-hegemonic reactions. Colonial and imperialist rupturing, however, succeeded in engendering the pervading transformations of domination ordered through real structural, ritualistic, and symbolic devices of violence that rumbled through the foundational base of most traditional Nigerian societies.[6] Significantly, the militarized schemes rooting such possibilities would thence premise the heuristic display and ready appeal to paramilitary and terrorist schemes in trammeling Nigeria. As a result, the prefabricated foundations of Nigeria on farcical force would map a habitual referential base for future attempts at crude domination that would be depicted within the interplay of the contrasting contestations between the different segments of the powerful elite or ruling class.[7]

In colonial times, exile was utilized as a punitive measure against deposed chiefs and individuals considered as threats, capable of violating the norms of the *Pax Britannica* that theoretically underpinned the colonial order. Thus, many chiefs were dethroned, and usurpers enthroned in their stead, sometimes in acute violation of the traditional order of succession. The *Pax Britannica,* it was reasoned, nurtures a better civilized ideal. Hegemony defines what holds true, and the authority of force sharpens the perceptive images of falsehood as veracity within subjective mirror-framings.

The first modern experiences of exile in Nigeria can be traced to the political crises of the First Republic of an independent Nigerian state, following the accusation of treason against Chief Obafemi Jeremiah Awolowo and some of his cohort within the defunct Action Group (AG) political party, alleging their involvement in an attempted coup plot in 1964. Four persons fled the country, including S.G. Ikoku, who took an appointment at the Kwame Nkrumah Institute of Political Education in Ghana, and Chief Anthony Enahoro, who escaped to London in quest of political asylum following accusations that he was an accomplice to Chief Awolowo, concerning the speculative attempt to overthrow the Nigerian Federal government. Enahoro was later arrested and extradited to Nigeria from Britain, after much legal and political wrangling, to face trial.[8] Therefore, Chief Enahoro and his exilic cohorts became the first political exiles within the conscious imagination of post-colonial Nigeria.

The Nigerian-Biafran civil war occasioned the formation of another cohort of exiles. First, some Igbo were granted asylum in some countries of Africa such as Gabon, Tanzania, and Ivory Coast, including women and children. Shortly thereafter, following the decimation and surrender of the Biafran side, some elite members of the rebel forces transited into exile in different countries of Africa and in Western nations, especially Britain and the United States. It is significant to note that some Biafran citizens and sympathizers already resided in these Western nations and lobbied these governments and their public audiences, propagating and attempting to gain a favorable view for the Biafran agenda. Others were simply afraid to return home due to the televised horrors of the war and for fear of recrimination and persecution even after the war.

The most renowned exile of the post-war era was Colonel Emeka Odumegwu Ojukwu, the rebel leader of the ill-fated Biafran secessionist republican government and army, who departed Nigeria on an official visit to Côte d'Ivoire (Ivory Coast) during which his lieutenants surrendered on January 13th, 1970, to the Nigerian Federal Army. Thereafter, he became an instant exile, offered political asylum by the Ivorian government by the late President Felix Houphouet-Boigny. It was while still in exile that he was granted state pardon by the erstwhile democratic civilian administration of President Shehu Shagari in 1982, after determined lobbying by the Igbo, led by late Chief Chuka Okadigbo, then Special Adviser to President Shagari on Political Matters.[9]

Another prominent exile was General Jack Yakubu Gowon, Head of State, and war-time leader, who fled into exile in the United Kingdom, after he was dethroned in a military putsch on July 29th, 1975, while attending the annual conference of the defunct Organization of African

Unity (OAU) in Kampala, Uganda. His self-induced exile assumed political dimensions after he was implicated in the plots leading to the failed Colonel Bukar Sukar Dimka coup attempt on February 13th, 1976. He was eventually granted presidential state pardon by the civilian administration of President Shehu Shagari in 1982. In 1977, the renowned, and maverick, Afro-Juju Musician Fela Anikulapo-Kuti fled to Ghana as a result of his altercations with government security agents, but was forced to return because his pro-Nkrumah rhetoric provoked an inimical response from the Ghanaian government.[10]

The next generation of Nigerian political exiles occurred as a result of the military coup that dismantled the Second Republic led by the civilian President Shehu Shagari in the early morning of December 31st, 1983. This military regime held the dethroned politicians in apathy, detaining and treating them in ignominious and sub-human conditions. With the harsh and acrimonious state of affairs, some politicians like the former Senate President Joseph Wayas, Alhaji Uba Ahmed, a chieftain of the then ruling National Party of Nigeria, Chief Augustus Adisa Akinloye, Chief Ebenezer Babatope, the former Publicity Secretary of the disbanded Unity Party of Nigeria (UPN), Dr. Umaru Dikko, former Minister of Transports, and Presidential Liaison overseeing the importation of Thailand rice, and Presidential Re-election Chief Campaign Manager, and several others, went into exile mainly in Europe, and specifically in the United Kingdom.[11]

The most popular among the exilic cohorts of this era among the Nigerian political exiles was Dr. Umaru Dikko, forcefully kidnapped and caged in a diplomatic parcel awaiting shipment to Nigeria, but was detained at the Heathrow International airport, London, by the efforts of London's Scotland Yard Metropolitan police in 1985, after a tip-off. Many of these people remained in self-exile until the 1990s, when in anticipation of political transition, and with a more relaxed political atmosphere, they started filtering back into Nigeria, returning unmolested and without being persecuted for crimes which they were earlier accused. Today, almost all of these exiles are back in Nigeria and some of them, like Drs. Wayas, Dikko, and Chief Akinloye are still alive and continue to be somewhat politically active and articulate on national issues. Drs. Wayas and Dikko recently served as representatives to the National Political Reform Conference (NPRC) convoked by the current serving President Obasanjo, that took place in Abuja from February through April 2005. Dr. Dikko's vocal stance regarding the discussions on the issue of revenue allocation was prominently voiced as sanctioning the pro-Northern interests at the conference.

The next set of exiles followed in the immediate wake of the unsuccessful Major Gideon Orkar-led coup plot to remove the despotic government of General Ibrahim Babangida on April 22ⁿᵈ 1990. Prominent among these exiles were Chief Great Ogboru, and Col. Elias Anthony Nyiam who managed to escape to Europe, residing mainly in the United Kingdom, to avoid persecution and prosecution by the despotic Babangida government, given the torturous fate of most actors in the coup plot. Major Gideon Orkar and many of his cohorts were tortured, tried, and promptly executed.[12] In the hit of the crises resulting from the annulment of the June 12ᵗʰ presidential elections, Chief Abiola also escaped into exile, having been intimated in real threats to his personal security. While in exile he led frantic campaigns in many western capitals aggressively trying to drum up support for his mandate. He was persuaded by the Nigerian pro-democratic movements to return to Nigeria, during the troubled days of the Chief Ernest Shonekan's Interim Government.

In hindsight, Chief Abiola's return from his escape to the West was a miscalculation, eventually leading to his June 1994 incarceration by General Abacha, and his later death on July 8ᵗʰ, 1998, under suspicious circumstances a few weeks after the demise of General Abacha. Chief Abiola was an exile's exile in the sense that he was incarcerated and deprived of all sources of outside news and human interactions, as if indeed, he was in Weber's "iron's cage." In spite of all attempts at humiliation and denigration, he died upholding the beacon of the democratic ideal paying the ultimate price still clinging to his treasured prize—the desire to stand for a just cause and the sanctity of his electoral mandate. Sadly, he refused to heed to certain voices across the nation which urged him in the aftermath of the annulment and his escape from Nigeria to form a government of National Unity from his exile.

Perhaps the political outcome of such dynamics might have differently-orientated the directional course of Nigerian history. The attempt to reclaim his mandate and pronounce himself President at a pro-democratic rally led to his incarceration without resolution of the political crises and circumstances until his eventual death on the heels of General Abacha's demise. Abiola, who had earlier sworn by his resources of faith and inner strength that he would not die in jail[13] but would triumph over dictatorship, succumbed as an unsung hero of Nigerian democracy. Sadly, Abiola's son, Kola, later claimed after his father's demise, that the NADECO opposition misled his father into declaring himself as President without giving him serious backing.[14] The next group of Nigerian exiles, the focus of this chapter, would be the so-called "Abacha exiles" most of whom escaped to foreign and predominantly western nations.

"ABACHA EXILES" AND THE FALLACY OF TYRANNY: ACIDIC MILITARISM, PRO-DEMOCRATIC SACRIFICIAL ACTIVISM

The Abacha regime produced another exilic cohort, most of them political exiles fleeing Nigeria to different western metropolises seeking asylum. This cohort of exiles is herein referenced as the "Abacha exiles"—as marking the era and circumstances culminating in their self-exile. In this factual sense, these Nigerian exiles are more pro-democratic. However, though most were political exiles and pro-democratic, we need to assert *a priori* that some were exiles of convenience, given that they were tied to Abacha and the ruling military class, and though they fell out due to intra-class conflicts, their antagonism did not produce deep resentment against the military class, along whose crest they rode into political, professional, and economic prominence. Therefore, in spite of their dislocation, such scenarios hardly pushed their antipathetic turbine towards agitating against military rule in general, nor against Abacha, specifically. Within this antinomy of defining circumstances among these arrays of the Abacha exile cohort, we notably distillate between groups, since not all exiles of this era deserved the designation of pro-democratic exiles, as they never adopted such roles.

Further, certain groups of influential and echelon ranks of Nigerian entrepreneurs, civil servants and political appointees fled into exile following Abacha's belligerent but contradictory anti-corruption campaign targeting them. Such escapees, rather than becoming purely political exiles, were actually evading the law and hence feared the implications of their corrupt actions. In fact, many among these constituted a third-column of exiles as they maintained a low profile. Flying below the radar, they managed to elude notice, so as not to provoke a contest with the military regime or face repatriation procedures to force them back to Nigeria to face charges.[15] Additionally, many within this class hobnobbed with the ruling class at different levels, and some actually benefited as clientele of the state, through state patronage, within the reigning "politics in the belly." Thus, afraid of their own shadows they avoided any form of exuberant activism. In this way, they protected themselves against the moral shame of being unveiled by the military.

In this way, they attempted to secure their accumulated wealth and business interests in Nigeria from being frozen, pillaged, disbanded, and/or forfeited to the government. Therefore, while essentialized bifurcations existed between and among the exilic population that profiled differential class positions, such differences were minimized within their common fate occasioned by exile. Therefore, a new ethnicity emerged to unify and objectify all preexisting differential considerations and social positions into a field of shared identity. Such processes further delineated exile as disabling, and dislocated previous fields of identity definitions in nurturing the production of novel objectifications and dispositions. Nonetheless, such reductions do not totally eclipse these bifurcations given that at some level different *a priori* positions and social locations determined how and what productions individual exiles reinvented and disseminated.

Further, the variations within the exilic cohorts also helped to validate the reality of the Nigerian situation, in the sense that its anomalous operations diffusely and intensely affected diverse social groups. Therefore, these differentiations helped to underline the seriousness of the situation. Thus, the ranks of the exiles that consisted of erstwhile military officers, distinguished intellectuals, and prominent politicians, deriving from different ethnic and regional milieu, helped to emphasize to different Metropolitan authorities, especially western governments, the precarious predicament constituted by dictatorship. The Abacha exilic cohort reflected diverse sections of Nigerian society from the North, South, East, and West, including the intersecting territorial interstices of the Midwest and Middle Belt regions. It also included erstwhile military officers, members of the political class—and within this class, those of military backgrounds, journalists, intellectuals, academics, and even students. It was an inclusive array of the pro-democratic opposition actors singly or in collective actions, attempting to stem the pervasive and chronic diffusion of the Abacha strain of the dictatorship virus.

Such analytical consideration limits monolithic innocence and moral sympathy ascribed and elicited by the different members of this regime. In spite of Abacha's own moral and political deficiencies, in some respects, he appropriated some intellectual capital that laid claim to his veritable efforts at addressing the economic morass and the prevalent corruption devilling Nigeria. In this sense he appeared to have created a façade of virtuous moral leadership and economic probity.[16]

CARTOON IMAGERY OF THE OGRE GENERAL ABACHA STAMPEDING NIGERIA[17]

Given such inherent class demarcation, it must quickly be asserted that not all classes within the Abacha exilic cohort were morally innocent. Some corrupt Nigerians fled into exile rather than confront the consequences of their actions. For the most part, these were members of the ruling class and power elite, and many among them actively collaborated with the dictatorship at some level, until falling out of favor, hemmed in by their dishonest ethos, they escaped in cowardly fashion, unwilling courageously to con-

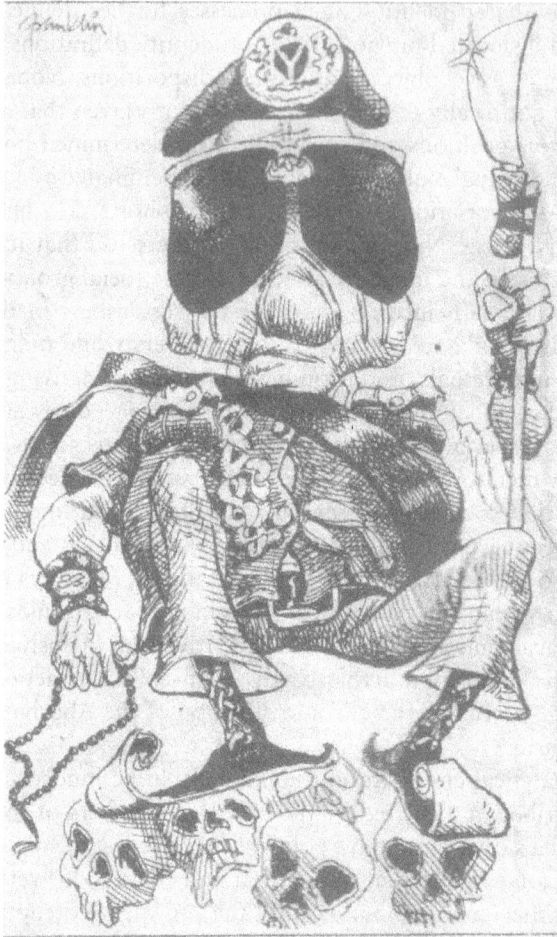

Figure 3–1. Exile Cartoon 1: Abacha Stampedes Nigeria

Franklin [Oyesikube], 1996 Cartoon illustration in Dare
Babarinsa, "Behold, His Military Majesty," *Tell*, October
7, 1996: 12.

test their situations. Therefore, while there is often a certain temptation
to assign moral probity and bravery to exiles, it must be underlined that
not all exiles deserved such heroic qualifications.[18] Such considerations also
typically apply to some political exiles that either played a subtle or active
part as collaborators in shaping the despotic military excesses foisted upon
the nation, but obstinately maintained a recalcitrant stance, appropriately

refusing to denounce dictatorship and terror in general, and specifically, the Abacha brand. Yet this collaborative class of Abacha exiles, due to the situation of exile, presented themselves as victims and ideologues of virtue. Abhorrently, such groups sought sympathy as they paraded themselves and laid claim to moral rectitude. Despicably, crowning themselves with the miter of sainthood, they had refused to purge themselves of their nauseating evil nursed against the Nigerian public.

Let it be understood, therefore, that the fact of exile, *in se,* is not and should not become the ethical referential canon for measuring and sanctioning the moral rectitude of some of the exiles, sheepishly and desperately questing after existential relevance. Rather, the canon of deferential relevance among the exiles must be sought within the capable transformation and pro-active stance each exile took against the pervading moral evil then represented by military rule and personified by Abacha—even when such choices placed them at personal and bodily risk. Such bravery as defined their position in perceiving dictatorship as aesthetically nauseous, marks the mode for appraising such exiles. Thus, the moral and intellectual quality that formed the basis of the moral aesthetics that defined such choices indicated that, in spite of the amoral and decimating character of the dictatorial ogre, Nigeria still possessed persons of qualitative character.

Linearly, historicity cogently marks an ironic condition that focally predicates the first notably Nigerian exile of the Abacha era as a military official with ties to that government. Thus, General David Mark, an army officer from the Middle Belt of Nigeria, of Idoma extraction, ironically became the prototype Nigerian exile, having escaped from Abacha's orgy of granulation and the pervading destructive onslaught that defined the period from November 1993 until June 1998, either in late 1993 or early 1994. General Mark had initially collaborated with General Abacha to topple the Interim National Government (ING) led by Chief Ernest Shonekan, the interregnum head of the weak political contraption that replaced General Babangida. Not long afterwards, fall-outs within the military climaxed in General Mark's flight into self-exile in London. Granting an interview to a Nigerian news magazine, the *Newswatch,* he insinuated General Abacha's determination not to relinquish power to any democratic government, until December 2000, after which it was thought he would transmogrify himself, shifting into a civilian "democratic" dictatorship, by using a charade democratic transitional process.[19]

General Mark claimed to have angered Abacha and was a direct target for elimination, the reason for which he fled into exile in London, where he sought political asylum. Such rhetoric would consequently become a popular refrain as the excuse for most of the later Nigerian exiles of the Abacha era. General Mark specifically notes his crime to be rooted within his close relationship with the erstwhile military leader, General Babangida. General Abacha, he claimed, was maliciously jealous and vehemently unhappy with this association. He plotted to humiliate, and even eliminate, the so-called "Babangida boys." Counting himself as one of the "Babangida boys," Mark saw the handwriting on the wall and fled.

Such plots are intriguing and remarkable as ironic historical accidents, whereby an actor critically involved within the different machinations activating the military siege and domination of Nigeria became the first Nigerian exile. Further, such contradictions would also manifest themselves in the emergence of the National Democratic Coaliation (NADECO) that was formed on May 15th, 1994, at the Ikeja residence of a retired army general, Adeyinka Adebayo, under the auspices of a Council for Unity and Understanding (CUU).[20] Interestingly, other retired military officers, in spite of the military's emphasis upon the norm of *esprit de corps* were vitally instrumental as pro-active agents within the Nigerian opposition, even from exile. The vocal stance of the erstwhile Chief of Army Staff, General Alani Akirinade, against the Abacha regime is also known, especially as the initial financier of the Radio Democrat (later Radio Kudirat International), the lethal anti-Abacha opposition radio established by Professor Wole Soyinka in 1996.[21] His vocal antagonistic stance against the regime from exile was reciprocated through dastardly reprisals of arson and bombing against his Lagos residence.[22]

Such varying forms of recriminatory and repressively dictatorial schemes unveil the raw inner and psychical operations predicating the irrational logic underpinning the Abacha dictatorship. Such encrypted dynamics inherently affirmed crude anti-human activities and the violation of civil rights, indulgently devoid of respect for human persons and interests. The only factual interests likable to the dictatorial instincts are those that are radically self-serving and oriented in perpetually limited monolithic and ego-centric vested interests. Cognizant of its deformity and instability, the Abacha dictatorship evolved diurnal and nocturnal schemes that eagerly intended to consummate the vitality of any perceived obstructive opposition, whether of persons, interests, or objects, against his misrule.

The dialectics of relationship within the military reflects a radical and unitary side-taking engagement that colors a scenario devoid of multiple options within the script of "you are either for me or you are against me." Those against are often marked for disgrace, humiliation, and even elimination, while collaborators and pro-actors are actively rewarded with material benefits. However, such modes are eternally unstable and temporary within

the environment of recurrent evaluative screenings characteristic of relationships and interactions of the dictatorial order. Therefore, the enjoyment
of such benefits are long lasting to the extent that collaborations are also
manipulated into masking their true feelings and conscientiously absorbed
in an eternal alliances of deception and lies.[23]

General Mark's interview from his London abode unmasked Abacha's
noxious agenda. This interview generated a storm regarding Abacha's supposed sincerity about his goal of democratic transition. Such a level of distrust among the Nigerian political elite and opposition groups occasioned
suspicion and raised questions regarding Abacha's integrity. Given that the
erstwhile military leader, General Babangida had indulged Nigerians on a
roller-coaster of political skating, the pro-democratic opposition raised their
antennae. Abacha was hurt, and without pretense, shamelessly detained
editors of the *Newswatch* magazine. Ray Ekpu and his other editorial colleagues particularly were targets of Abacha's veiled anger.

Not long afterwards on May 15, 1994, the National Democratic
Coalition (NADECO), formed a mosaic of cascaded political associations,
and pro-democratic activists interested in ensuring the enthronement of
Nigerian democracy. In view of this suspicion, they gave General Abacha
an ultimatum urging him to abdicate power by May 31st, 1994, by trans-
ferring leadership to a National Unity Government. This government, they
asserted, was to be headed by the presumed winner of the June 12th, 1993
Nigerian presidential elections, Chief M.K.O. Abiola, to whom General
Abacha and a cross-section among the military echelon were opposed, and
who had hitherto succeeded in pressuring the erstwhile military despot,
General Babangida to renege on his promise to hand over power to a democratically elected civilian administration.

Thereafter, Abacha turned his full bestial and recriminatory glare
against entire segments of the Nigerian political opposition using different antics, and frustrating tactics aimed at decimating their political base
or even physical annihilation. This set the stage that drove many Nigerians opposed to the dictatorship into exile.[24] This reign of state sponsored
terrorism led to the assassination of Chief (Alhaja) Kudirat Abiola, the
vocal wife of the jailed winner of the June 12th, 1993, Presidential election. Another prominent person exterminated was Chief Alfred Rewane,
a veteran politician, entrepreneur, and opposition chieftain. Committed to
the ideal of a free Nigeria, he was resolutely vocal against social injustice,
enough to irk Abacha. His suggestive views on the political impasse and
attempts at creative propositions toward resolution published as advertiser's announcements in the print media, seemed to have irked and flared the
Abacha regime's passion to get rid of him.[25]

Among his many plots was the accentuation of infiltration and divide-and-rule tactics, intentionally directed at fragmenting and heating up ethnic and political spaces.[26] Such antics also planted seeds of discord among family members, as was evident with the conflict regarding the battle for legal representation of Chief M.K.O Abiola, between Kola, Abiola's son, and his wife, Kudirat, thus fragmenting their relationship, with both pursuing alternative and opposing strategies. [27] Such artificially induced and incendiary conflicts were planned to cause distractions, shifting attention away from Abacha's infamy and misrule—intentionally aimed at diverting the people toward preoccupation with the crises of their immediate existential predicaments.

Most of the Abacha exiles dispersed into various nations in Europe, Canada, and the United States. A majority were political self-exiles, while a few were fugitives from the despotic version of lethal and fatalistic justice.

Figure 3–2. Exile Cartoon 2: NADECO the Villain

Moses Ebong [3bong], 1996, "Outlook," *The News* [Courtesy of the Punch], March 11: 4.

These exiles formed the National Democratic Coalition (NADECO-abroad), frantically mounting persistent pressure upon the regime, seeking resolutions to the political impasse, and furthering the idea of the enthronement of democratic rule. In this fight they used different tactics and munitions, including lecture circuits, pro-democratic rallies, delegated representations to different foreign governments, especially western governments, the use of the print media, and the beaming of signals from a renegade opposition radio.

The NADECO-abroad utilized the media greatly. They also ensured that their views were in the international press and Nigerian local newspapers and magazines, and favored radio broadcasts beamed to Nigeria. Thus, NADECO-abroad released in London a glossed monthly magazine edition, *Nigerian Liberation,* in February 1986,[28] while also beaming Radio Freedom (later renamed Radio Kudirate International) as the voice of democracy, through the agency of the opposition led by Wole Soyinka.[29] In Nigeria, traditional and alternative media forms such as music, theatre, and others were used toward achieving a similar goal as poignant instruments for denunciation and agitation against military rule.[30] In Nigeria, the intensity of such activism caused most crises or malfunctioning to be causally predicated upon NADECO's agency.

Many of these exiles resided in Europe and coalesced with different groups of Nigerian emigrant and diasporic communities to fan the ember of discontent against the military regime.[31] Their success in this area was not surprising given that most of the recent immigrants to many Western countries fled the Nigerian state directly or indirectly as the result of their despondent reactions to the disenchantment and confused atmosphere caused by the military. Among the exiles granted political asylum in the United Kingdom were influential Nigerians like Chief Ralph Obiorah, from Eastern Nigeria, Air Commodore Dan Suleiman, a former high ranking military chief from the Middle Belt; General Alani Akirinade, former Defense Minister, Senators Bola Tinubu, and Tokubo Afikuyomi from the Southwest; and Chief John Odigie Oyegun, former Governor of Edo State, and Chief Obadan, his former deputy, from Edo State in the former Midwestern Region.

The United States also offered sanctuary to some of the Abacha exiles. Wole Soyinka escaped from Nigeria into a neighboring African nation, and eventually came to the United States through France, after receiving information that marked him for elimination by state agents. Like Chief Enahoro, he had some exilic experience after leaving Nigeria in the aftermath of an earlier imprisonment by the Gowon regime, following his anti-civil war activism in the 1970s. This exile he tagged an "exile-of-despair," granting him the creative impetus for writing his prison notes; *The Man*

Died. During the Shagari administration, due to his scathing criticisms of the regime's anomalies, Soyinka was targeted for elimination by State security agents. Privy to highly reliable information, he fled clandestinely from Nigeria to Europe and then the United States.

Soyinka's escape from the Abacha regime greatly traumatized the dictator, who felt beaten at his own game over his inability to hunt down the Nobel laureate. Dismayed, but still tenaciously attempting to annihilate Soyinka, Abacha sought every avenue, sending his paid government spies and killer scouts into neighboring West African countries, like Benin, and presumably his assassin network to a hotel room where Soyinka had lodged in Washington, D.C, in the United States.[32] Chief Anthony Enahoro, a NADECO official and leader of the Movement for National Reconciliation (MNR) who had earlier had a foretaste of Abacha's gulag and bestial crudity, escaped and sought asylum in the United States.[33] Like Soyinka, he too had a foretaste of brief exile during the First Republic, when accused as an accessory to treason as an accomplice of the late Chief Obafemi Jeremiah Awolowo. Chief Enahoro fled first to Ghana then to Britain, but was refused asylum and returned to face trial in Nigeria in the celebrated case of the "Fugitive Offender."[34]

Another eminent political exile to the United States, escaping Abacha, was Professor Omo Omoruyi, the former Director of the Center for Democratic Studies (CDS) in Abuja, who collaborated in designing the political map toward the actual transition to civil rule of his friend, General Babangida, and who was a vocal critic of the June 12th election annulment. After a failed assassination attempt he sought and was granted political asylum and later United States' permanent residency, residing in the area of Boston, Massachusetts. Omoruyi was lucky to have survived the assassination attempt on his life after unknown assailants attacked him in front of his Benin-City residence in February 1994. This marked the first and definitive turn of political events, upon extermination strategies against Abacha's perceived opponents, (Babatope, 122).

The crackdown on civil society, especially the judicial murder of Ken Saro-Wiwa and eight Ogoni environmental justice activists by the Abacha regime, also encouraged escape from Nigeria into exile. Ogoni youths fled from the joint onslaught of Abacha and his devilish military reincarnations, Major Okutimo and Paul Etemahi Ledum Mittee. The latter was a lawyer and deputy leader of the Movement for the Survival of Ogoni People (MOSOP), and was miraculously acquitted by the lopsidedly partial military tribunal, headed by Justice Ibrahim Auta, upon the death of Ken-Saro-Wiwa. Upon his own release from prison, however, he fled Nigeria around May 1996.[35]

Such an array of exiles from all regions of the nation proved the regime's protagonists wrong in their assertion that the agitation for democracy in Nigeria was regional and obtusely Yoruba, spearheaded by politicians and influential personalities from the Southwest, Abiola's home area. While it was true that many from the Southwest were involved, noting the injustice involved as an affront against their membership in the Nigerian Federation, in fact the contrary was the case. The NADECO movement and its allies were constituted from all parts of Nigeria, even from the North whose voice was mostly coax and vitally weak. Many northern progressives like Alhaji Balarabe Musa, Alhaji Abubakar Rimi, the late Ambassador Jolly Tanko, Yohanna Madaki, and the radical ex-army and democratic advocate, Col. Abubakar Umar, who favored enforcing justice relative to the June 12ᵗʰ election, expressed solidarity and support for the opposition at one time or the other. Others would later, at various points, renege, recoiling or simply throwing their political weight behind the dictator.

The Abiola affairs also proved, unfortunately, that even among the Yoruba, he did not enjoy absolute support, especially among the Yoruba elites. Varying fissiparous individuals and groups, especially politicians and opportunists, were not enthused about the actualization of his acclaimed presidential yearnings. For instance Chief Bola Kuforiji-Olubi was presumed as having advised President Babangida to annul the June 12ᵗʰ election. General Olusegun Obasanjo and the National Unity Organization (NUO) varied with the Afenifere's stance regarding resolving the June 12ᵗʰ political imbroglio in Abiola's favor. Such contexts revealed a lot about the interactive effects, not only of ethnicity but equally of intra-class conflict within the unfolding political landscape. The Yoruba political and intellectual elite played along portraying the inherent centrifugal conflicts and contradictions embedded within their environmental purview, political matrix and historical consciousness.

Such discordant positions and centrifugal feuding within modern Yoruba consciousness, while not totally novel, revealed the crevices within its cohesive ethnic order. Diachronically, Yorubaland had been the scene of internecine warfare during the nineteenth century that decimated entire communities and radically altered the political fortunes of many Yoruba societies. Furthermore, within modern consciousness, these cleavages were reminiscent of the political altercations between Chief Obafemi Jeremiah Awolowo and Chief Ladoke Samuel Akintola in the 1960s. The June 12ᵗʰ issue and the struggle toward sustaining Nigeria's democratic aspirations, referenced by Abiola's presidential ambition, re-enacted the prior scenarios, indicating the cracks within Yoruba edifice that were affecting the delicate balance of a monolith Yoruba front, and equally characterized the different levels of sociopolitical, personal, and inter-group relations.

The accentuation of these varying political differences highlighted the profound crevices evident within contemporary Yoruba society. Individuals' personal ambitions equally frustrated and curtailed different efforts toward marshalling Yoruba energies in collectively representing their frustrations as it pertained to their assumed political relevance within Nigeria. As a result, these discordant positions eventually produced two extreme choices, either of acceding to dependency or of gaining their autonomy. The first demanded their choice either of compromising toward negotiating with the despotic hegemony, or of adopting the latter option that amounted to a virulent anti-dictatorship resistance. By June 1994, it was evident that bipolar, even multilateral, opinions were prevalent in Yorubaland, among different individuals and groups.

Thus, twenty prominent Yoruba elites meeting at the Hamdala Hotel in Kaduna became protagonists of the dictatorship. At this meeting, they secretly betrayed the political aspirations of Chief Abiola, empowering the government to invalidate him through incarceration. In reciprocation, according to their egocentric vested interests, most of these elites expected government pay-offs in the forms of plum contracts and political appointments. Among others, the participants at this meeting included the following: Lt. General Oladipo Diya, Chief Adisa Akinloye, Senator Afolabi Olambimtam, Chief Ebenezer Babatope, Dr. Olusola Saraki, Professor Wande Abimbola, Dr. Omolulu Olunloyo, Chief Richard Akinjide, Chief Lai Balogun, Chief Biola Akande, Chief Josiah Olawoyin, Mrs. Mobolaji Osomo and Alhaji Lateef Jakande. [36] Azeez Alao Ariseokola, another Yoruba, assumed Abacha as his political protégé, becoming his marabout.[37] A prominent Yoruba politician and the backbone of Ibadan politics, Alhaji Lamidi Aribiyi Adedibu also opted to sideline the claims of Chief Abiola's presidential reclamation bid, and denounced pro-democracy groups, especially NADECO. He became an avid stooge of General Abacha's dictatorship.[38]

Such dynamics also positively abetted the production of an intense political consciousness among the Yoruba. In spite of all intrigues, such feelings heightened Yoruba national awareness and cultural identity, framed around the consciousness of their perceived marginalization within Nigeria. As a result, such attitudes either gained sympathy or antagonism for the Yoruba. Even then, it situated and centralized the Yoruba question within the emergent rhetoric of the continuous survival of Nigeria and the overall Nigerian nationality question. Thus, the issue of Yoruba collective survival came to the forefront. Such consciousness underlined NADECO's formation and leadership structure as the foremost national opposition group, in spite of the fact that its meetings were held in Owo, Ondo State, and its leaders were preeminently Yoruba.

However, the accusation that NADECO served as a masked folder for advancing Yoruba interests can be aptly explained. The convocation of meetings in Owo was not to give primacy of relevance to Yorubaland. The choice of the venue rather involved some form of negotiations between the different groups who deferred to Chief Michael Ajasin's age and physical condition to host the meeting at his residence, without which traveling across the country to attend various important meetings would have been acutely difficult for the septuagenarian politician. Further, while it is true that many Yoruba featured enormously among the members of NADECO's core leadership, this was mainly due to the consideration that many of the initial actors who established the movement were Yoruba. Naturally, it was expected that some among these initial members would feature within its leadership, offering focus through their insightful visions and experienced perspectives. In spite of these, NADECO was actually representative of respectable and outstanding members of the political class and erstwhile military officers from across the diverse ethnic and regional spaces of Nigeria.

Significantly, most of those who criticized NADECO as preeminently Yoruba had failed to also note that many Yoruba actors within the pro-democratic movement overtly declined, in principle, to offer their support to another Yoruba personality—Chief Ernest Shonekan, the ill-fated head of the Interim National Government (ING) put in place upon the abdication of General Babangida from power in 1993. Should it have been the case that NADECO was a self-serving entity for the Yoruba, the Yoruba should rationally have been content with the choice of another Yoruba personality as leader of the interim government in place of Chief Abiola; but this was not the case, (Soyinka, 2006, 368). Therefore, it seems that NADECO nuanced its opposition on principles rather than simply reflecting an organized project out to secure all Yoruba interests within Nigeria.

Actually, some Yoruba members of different pro-democratic groups were instrumental in persuading Generals Abacha and Oladipo Diya to take the reins of power from Shonekan, a Yoruba, whom most Yoruba despised and considered as a weakling, (Babatope, 2000, 7–8). The overplaying of the Yoruba salience—primarily because many Yoruba were involved within NADECO, seemed too thin an argument to warrant the totalizing view in some quarters that NADECO was purely a self-serving Yoruba organization. Some Yoruba actually deviated and offered a different paradigm regarding the national conundrum and the political impasse, which differed substantially from the NADECO and Afenifere blueprints.

General Olusegun Obasanjo, a former Military Head of State, and his ally, Martin Kuye, were among many such renowned Yoruba personalities. Therefore, while the leadership of the Yoruba Cultural Group, Afenifere, almost exactly imitated NADECO's, we assume that the interjectory accusations that defined it as essentially a Yoruba political organization, masking as a national entity, was focally underlined by manipulative schemes, emphasized by the convenience of ethnicity distractively represented to pejoratively color the direction of the political discourse.

In spite of all perceptions and temporal shifts, the North and northerners were at various times vocal in their opposition toward General Sani Abacha's iron rule. The North was never outsmarted in the movement for resistance and social justice, constituted against General Abacha within the contextual struggle for the soul of Nigeria. In fact, even General Abacha's earlier protagonists and collaborators soon earned his antagonism and fell out of favor. Consequently, Abacha's popular Gestapo scheme was mercilessly unleashed against several such perceived opponents. Selectively, the regime went after different actors, including those who had collaborated in validating the goals of the regime, ultimately humiliating, hunting them down, and prosecuting them.

Many northern military officers, like Colonel Abubakar Umar and Lawan Gwadabe, were framed. They were accused of plotting coups and were accordingly removed from the army.[39] In spite of ties of regional and ethnic origin, northern military officers suffered as much as southerners during the despotic era of Abacha's dominion. Many northern officers were implicated and routed through self-serving intrigues designed by southern officers. For the dictatorship, ties of military and regional in-group solidarity meant little, thus dissipating the symbolical bond of *esprit de corps* that hitherto characterized the relationship between and within serving and erstwhile military officers. Rather, different military actors, including northerners, were consumed within the daredevil, narcissistic, and draconian passion for negating, decimating, and sacrificing fellow human beings. Vain ambitions won legions of disciples for the dictatorship, ever ready to devour their own kind.

Thus, General Shehu Musa Yar'Adua, a northern general and former Chief of Staff Supreme Headquarters, deputy to General Obasanjo whose military regime handed power to civilians in 1979, was arrested, tried and imprisoned over an alleged, but presumably pseudo-treasonable coup d'état. Later, he died in prison, succumbing to Abacha's brute cruelty and an illness that seems to have emanated from lethal poisoning by biochemical agents, possibly the HIV/AIDS virus.[40] Another prominent northerner, an eminent civilian and Sultan of Sokoto (the Spiritual leader of Nigeria's Islamic adherents), Chief Ibrahim Dansuki drew Abacha's ire. In spite of his highly revered traditional ruling position and sacred status within the imaginative consciousness of most northern Nigerians, Abacha unleashed his full wrath against him. Disgracefully dethroned and deposed, Dasuki was instantly internally exiled (within Nigeria) in Zing, Adamawa State.

The deposed Sultan's son, Sambo, a military officer, and a former Aide de Camp to the erstwhile President Babangida thus earned General Abacha's displeasure. General Abacha in his vendetta accused him of plotting his overthrow. Marked out for humiliation and possibly elimination, Sambo escaped into exile. Yet, the Dansuki family was not spared. The Sultan, even in exile, was hunted and humiliated, accused of financial mis-appropriations and graft.[41] Ahmed, another son of the deposed Sultan, was not spared the dictator's congenital public wrath and was equally marked for humiliation.[42] The irony is that many who later donned the hat of democratic activists were opportunists who actively collaborated with the military class at one point or another. Exile interrupted their social and personal convenience. As Edward Said notes, "exile is one of the saddest fates,"[43] and for some, it came with different prices—including depression. Given such prior alliances, certain members of this collaborator exiled class muted their voices even while in exile, preferring the backstage of history and privilege rather than agitating for social change or any significant transformation that would scuttle their class structures, revoke their social privileges, and/or risk their vested interests.

Challenging the dark goggled General Abacha and his military *confreres* was thus not an option. Many among such exiled collaborators had created and sustained their social relevance through pro-active collaboration with the military establishment, benefiting from state patronage mediated through pedantic channels of prebendalism.[44] In spite of all the crises, they calculatedly refused to cause any traumatic and critical situation that would further jeopardize their business and political interests. Among this silent class of exiles many yearned patiently for the time of their triumphant return and the social stabilization of events from the pervading national chaos, to enable them reclaim lost royalties resulting from their spatial dislocation.

Such an ironic twist is significant, as one relevantly distills the inherent contradictions embedded within the historical imagination. Thus, critically and ironically, other collaborators, saliently in steeled silence, muted their voices to project an ambivalent and/or indifferent face. Others, by prevaricating, became turn-coats, vehemently tidying their hitherto dirtied positions in favor of a new tidal outburst that completely contradicted or invalidated their prior positions. This led to political resolutions regarding the political crises that sprang out of the pro-June 12th election agitations. Flushed by the tides of tyranny, hemmed in by the raging Machiavellian tactics that diurnally became the cherished norm, and stilled by the steel of despotic violence, they too were victims of the non-actualization of democracy, an ideal whose operations would provide shade from the raw nerves of oppression and denigration.

Therefore, as subsequent events revealed, many who initially collaborated with General Abacha in his notorious schemes became seriously dented, and many were actually placed in situations of fighting for their dear lives. The initial array of Abacha's friends gradually and ignominiously became projected as politically risky fiends. To usurp their social and political relevance, they were continually hounded toward compartmentalizing their mental frame and fragmenting their acquired political, social, and economic capital. When such tactics failed, Gestapo methods were employed toward breaking them into total submission. At times, such processes were directed toward the physical annihilation of such perceived opponents. The list of this privileged class of personalities enlarged diurnally. Many among the crop of personalities that had fallen from grace licked their wounds, yet had suffered enormous humiliation. In a twist of fate, the protected class who had hitherto refused to rise up against oppressive systems and structures were caught by their own nemesis and given a dose of their own antics.

Those who failed to be involved actively in counter-oppressive schemes, in crying out in the face of the tyrannical display of power became consumed by the same entity they were helping to create, protect, or reinforce. Crushed by the fatality of inaction, by refusing to stand up for social justice, their avoidance or inaction became a tool of empowerment for the seal that would mark their fate. Refusing to sacrifice in favor of social justice, but more interested in vocally replicating government rhetoric and antics against so-called political dissenters, they empowered the dictatorship and its Gestapo tool, and obliquely mapped the path to their own hellish state—hitherto presumed as only meant for the so-called restless and noise-making dissenters.

Ironically, steeled by dictatorial tyranny, many were silenced through the same instrumentality of power that they nurtured and projected in refusing to proclaim their stance for social justice. Dictatorships are adept at utilizing the same sources of legitimation to damage those who grant such legitimation. Creating an alluring rope intended for roping its rivals, the inordinate ambition and inaction of many in positively effecting social and political change, offers a protective shield in conveniently unleashing the dictatorship's draconian onslaughts. These privileged few, though positioned to have acted credibly as a result of their earlier inaction, were also collaborators in unconsciously mapping their own fate and further empowering dictatorial antics. Their refusal to agitate for a democratic Nigeria became their nemesis—hemmed within the contradictory ecology of despondency, violence, and the culture of political collaboration and acquiescence that ensures or abets either the creation or viability of the forces of oppression.[45] Further, such fate also invokes feelings of guilt, regarding past but unutilized possibilities regarding action against dictatorial tendencies.

The foregoing dynamics offered two interesting insights. The first depicted the irrational struggles that pitched the different components of the ruling class against each other. The strategy of this vulgar witchery validated a vulturized "dog-eat-dog" syndrome. The Ogoni struggles, invoked appropriately, brought awareness to this idiom of vulgarized "vulture-culture." "The MOSOP campaign has thrown up an interesting bird, the vulture. Those opposed to the MOSOP approach were denounced as "vultures" who were presumably feasting on the blood of the community by being on the other side, the non-violent side, of the struggle. In a manner of speaking the federal government and Shell could also be seen as vultures who descended from time to time on Ogoni and carted away the oil proceeds and flew away like vultures, in their jets leaving a broken ecosystem behind."[46] This process revealed the intellectual porosity and frightening cowardice that configure the structural mindset of the ruling class. In fact, in line with such cognitive referencing, the Nigerian military dictatorships though referentially cavernous and noxious, are patently morally weak. Their weakness is amply compensated through condoning brute bestiality and shameless, atrocious exploitation as normative. This despicable weakness of moral character reveals the depth of their paranoia and the violence unleashed upon innocent civilians.

Such facts underlined the different struggles within the polity, including within the military establishment itself, dichotomized along considerations of region and ethnicity. These crises also led to the bifurcation of relationships within the various segments of the military establishment.[47] Abacha became panicky and started to further aggravate an already tensile situation by privileging ethnicity and regionalism. The framing of dualities and dissonance became tools by which raw power was amassed through cleavages and different forms of dispossession—fueling imagined suspicions that undermined the structural textures that are foundational to Nigeria's existence. Therefore, by bifurcating Nigerian citizens into different segmented and fragmented classes and positions, Abacha aspired toward perpetual sovereignty.

CARTOON DEPICTING THE STRUGGLE BETWEEN
GENERAL ABACHA AND DEPOSED SULTAN OF
SOKOTO, IBRAHIM DASUKI[48]

Figure 3-3. Exile Cartoon 3: Abacha-Sultan Tug of War

Franklin Oyesikube, 1996. "Graffiti," *Tell*, May 6: 8

Such fragmentations were vigorously pursued at different levels. Northern politicians were compartmentalized from their southern counterparts, the pro-Abacha from the anti-Abacha camps including NADECO, the serving military against the retired military officers. This movement, manifesting Abacha's antagonism against Generals Babangida and Mark, John Shagaya, Joshua Dongoyaro, the Babangida boys,[49] and later of General Olatunde Diya, his deputy, and General Adisa, protagonist of his presidential campaign, was historically unparalleled in Nigeria. Dynamics like this also undermined the military and almost destroyed the underlying philosophy and ideology of *esprit de corps* that structures its ranks. Consequently, General Abacha's tentacles entrapped General Obasanjo and Shehu Musa Yar'Adua, his former's deputy; they later trapped Abacha's own lieutenants, General Diya and General Adisa, the prime protagonist of the Abacha-Must-Stay presidential transmogrification, from Abacha's military rule into a civilian presidential scheme, among others.[50]

These military generals who fell out of favor were at various times implicated and alleged to be architects of different coup plots. Most were eventually detained, court-marshaled and sentenced to death. Other witch hunts included the fight against the ruling oligarchic and military leaders of his own aboriginal northern regions, of which the imprisonment and later extermination of General Yar'Adua was indicative, alongside the forceful antagonism directed toward Chief Ibrahim Dasuki, the Sultan of Sokoto.[51] His son, Ahmed Dasuki, also was also hunted, as the entire Dasuki family seemed to be haunting General Abacha, (Tijani, 24). Karl Maeir provides the reason for this witch hunting of such a prestigious northerner and personality, as rooted within intrigues pertaining to business dealings with Dasuki's late nephew, Aliyu, prior to the dictator's rise to power. The inability of the Sultan to provide the dictator with necessary financial information and documents fostered the mounting antagonism, whose culmination was the sultan's dethronement, (Maeir, 157–58).

Generals Abacha and Babangida were noted to be enraged at each other under the surface, and deeply entangled in different intrigues and power contests. Thus, it was rumored that General Abacha was intent upon combating and humiliating General Babangida.[52] Abacha turned against others who had been his personal friends, such as Ken Saro-Wiwa, whom he met and patronized during the Nigerian-Biafran civil war. Humiliated by Saro-Wiwa's refusal to accept a ministerial role after the November 1993 coup, Abacha nurtured a deep hatred against him, harboring the intention to humiliate and eventually to exterminate him. Abacha lived up to this ideal, when the killing of four Ogoni pro-government Chiefs, notably Saro-Wiwa's anti-government and anti-Shell environmental activists under the MOSOP platform, led to his arrest. This was followed by a political show trial, and Saro-Wiwa's "judicial murder" by hanging (with acid poured upon his body), along with eight other Ogoni activists on November 17th, 1995. Abacha's military lieutenants supervised the hanging, while he, while watching the video, was alleged to have been thrilled over Saro-Wiwa's demise.[53]

MILITARY POLITICS, CLASS STRUGGLES, AND CONTRADICTORY PLOTS

There has always been a contest for hegemony between various classes, characteristically shaped within the crucible of conflicting aspirations among the governing elite. At times, such classes are collapsed, yet there have often been crevices between them to form different delineations. Within the texture of this struggle between the governing classes we see the evolution of different intrigues and schemes. Even within the same class, mutual suspicion and conflicting ambitions toward hegemonic dominion underlie different motives and conflicts.

These conflicts were accentuated and reached their climax during the Abacha regime, which, given its dictatorial tendencies, was grounded on the mastery of manipulation, alertness to and suspicions of underground machinations, and was driven by the morbid centralization and privatization of power within the dictatorship. Within this interplay of class consciousness, conflict and political ambition, the Abacha dictatorship was virulently antithetical to any competitive tendencies capable of undermining its hegemonic potency and popularity. With such a recasting of essentially Marxist trends on the existential level, we consider this dynamic in the light of Nigerian political economy. Such dynamics are even grandly understood within the thematic notions articulated by Gramsci, relative to the intrinsic competitive struggles characterizing the nature of relationship between the intellectual class and subalterns.[54]

The Nigerian military originated at a low-level of public respectability, with a subaltern label. Within the dialectical replaying of its historical origins, the Nigerian army is a product of the colonial condition and imagination. Thus, within this context, as the fiery enforcer of the colonial regime that often willingly employs violence, the military is defined as alien, impersonal, and abstractly detached from the populace; the accidental ascent of the military to power provided it with a leverage to reinvent itself as a relevant, influential, powerful, and superior national force. However, caught within this primitive inferiority complex, it has been unable to transcend such constructs, no matter the efforts toward repudiating its repugnant antecedents and contemporary label. Therefore, the transformative quality of power is transposed onto a formal tool of violence and domination.

Within its inability to appeal to the populace, the military resorts to the use of certain intellectuals aligned to its hegemonic interests. Such intellectuals produce exactly the kind of oppressive outcomes that are directly appealing and related to the goals of praetorian domination. Such an analytic view reveals the recurring Nigerian experience, of constant reversion into a cyclical mode of invasive and retrogressive schemes of political oppression. The role and manipulative maneuvering of the military in Nigerian politics is well documented. It is the military that truncated the various experiments in democratic government, in the first republic, going further than their mandate; restoring peace and order, then abdicating by handing power back to the politicians after the failed Nzegwu coup in 1966, (Ojukwu). More than anything else, the military following their incursion into politics embodies a leprous faction, infecting every aspect of Nigeria's national life with a lethal virus that dislocates all entrenched modes of political and social linearity.

DICTATORIAL ANTICS, INTRIGUES, CONFLICT, AND OPPOSITION

Abdulazeez Ude, at the time, posited that the military had turned Nigeria into one huge army cantonment, where the whip and bayonet rather than reason was privileged and projected as the ideal norm of national social ordering.[55] Different military operations pervaded across the land using different code names such as *Operation Sweep,* with different military agents such as Col. Paul Okutimo and Kumo molesting and rampaging against the Ogoni. Further, within the Nigerian experience, the military has proven itself adept at developing and sustaining Gestapo tactics as tools of limiting human and civil rights.

In this way, they imprisoned people at will, utterly disregarding their humanity. Wole Soyinka notes, "Any system which allows for the machinery of secrecy against an individual is the method of the Gestapo. The Gestapo mind believes more in holding than releasing, in guilt than in justice."[56] Such Gestapo schemes reflect a strategic totalitarian overture against national sovereignty and human rights, solely intended toward domination and the engendering of a noxious hegemonic order. Michel Foucault powerfully illustrates this point regarding the relation between the instrumentality of punishment and the hegemonic political ritual.

> . . . in this liturgy of punishment, there must be an emphatic affirmation of power and of its intrinsic superiority. And this superiority is not simply that of right, but that of the physical strength of the

sovereign beating down upon the body of his adversary and master-
ing it: by breaking the law, the offender has touched the very person
of the prince; and it is the prince—or at least those to whom he has
delegated his force—who seizes the body of the condemned man and
displays it marked, beaten, broken. The ceremony of punishment,
then, is an exercise of 'terror.'[57]

Within the dictatorial design, such methods are intended symboli-
cally to expand Foucault's notion of "docile body" toward creating a
wider republic of docile bodies in society. Dictatorship privileges concerted
attempts directed at sublimating society to its whims. Rather than an individual, the object of creating a commonwealth of docile persons acting in
unison along command lines, exerted through the mechanism of militant
control, is to ensure structural control. Schematically, such processes entail
systematic and subtle displays that are gradually unveiled over time, leading toward a behavioral conditioning intended to create an order of social
uniformity, and an occult deference to the norms of dictatorship.

The intentionality of such modalities aims to create a public liturgy
of occult adoration that intones panegyric enchantment, which in turn
merges the teleological aim of the state with the paranoid dictatorship.
Given that a docile body is one that is subjected, used and transformed
(Foucault, 136–138), dictatorship intends to subject and use individuals
in a certain way toward altering behavioral consciousness, elevating the
demagogic dictatorship over one's own personhood. This mode of acting
envisages the necessity of achieving forced legitimation of hegemony and
dominant authority.

This process operates at distinct but mutually reinforcing bimodal
levels. Dictatorial schemata, at least as depicted by the Nigerian praetorian
despotic experience, affirms such a bimodal level of operations. First, by
making serial scapegoats of the bodies of real individuals through detention, torture, and even annihilation, dictatorships, in a mean spirited way,
often attempt to induce imaginary public fear regarding likely dissent and
opposition. Secondly, through accentuated programs of creating such fears,
through programmatic conditioning and high-handed control, dictators
aspire to minimize any reactionary tendencies from within the population
capable of rusticating their hegemony.

In this way, dictators utilize stoic coercion subtly and actually to legitimate symbolic, imagined, and even physical violence within the citizenry's
mental consciousness, as a tool toward constructing popular deference and
to induce the validation of imposed hegemony. Such self-serving frameworks are designed to be normatively implanted toward the goal of mass

self-policing and mental surveillance that conditions automaton behaviors intended to engender mass deference for the person and structure of the dictatorship, its sustaining intellectual order, and its rigid command systems. Concomitantly, while the dictatorship attempts forcefully to assert itself through such means it actually thwarts the underlying basis of its continuous survival. Tension often arises between dictatorship and certain intellectual classes since the later class's taste and their creative and rational inclinations generally tend to generate intuitive and sustained resistances against such primordial and prebendal forms of domination.

The intellectual class, driven by the ideas that merit and competition underlie social advancement and development, often feels a nauseating aversion toward any form of totalitarian and praetorian hegemonic ideology that seeks to create a structural political panopticon. Such perception represents the intellectual class as often initially opposed to the course of dictatorship. Insightfully driven by ethical considerations and humane aesthetics, most intellectuals are often averse, and, until decimated or seduced, attempt to counter the suffocating logic underpinning the pulsating rhetoric and turbines of dictatorial praxis. Most dictators recognize the possibility of opposition from among the radical intellectual class, and hence often attempt either to seduce, coerce, or decimate their ranks. Within the selection pool either to fight for survival, to compromise or to flee, members of the intellectual class are always among the first to hop into exile.

Historically, in most cases, the breeding ground for political exiles has always been the academic arena, and similar domains. Even when exiles derive from other social arenas, they are often the driving intellectual forces within such domains. Such non-academic intellectual exiles are often depicted as the rational motor-force and political horsepower within different societies. Therefore, most exiles are often among the best crops within their aboriginal home societies—distinctive, brilliant, and prominent.

As a result, dictatorships in attempting to extinguish the influence of such an intellectual class, emanating as it does from such diverse cross cultural and social strata—political, military, business, academic elites and ecclesiastical orders—create their own self-validating intellectual class as a tool of ensuring the success of their propaganda and power elongation, intended toward justifying their peculiar goals, idiosyncrasies, and ideologies of domination.[58] Such engendered formations often aim toward legitimating and elaborating the specific class modalities and processes that define their emergence and active functioning.[59] These minted intellectuals parallel the anti-dictatorship intellectuals in offering valuable services to the dictatorship, especially in acutely analyzing and validating his actions, whether morally sound or not. Such dictatorial protagonists also spend enormous amounts of time and resources in framing, challenging, and producing counter-polemics toward diluting the criticisms directed at the dictatorship.

Under such dialectics, granted social relevance by the dictatorial scheme, the minted pro-dictatorship intellectual class produces self-serving simulations that cast the dictatorship in a positive light, thus simultaneously and appallingly reifying, and even at times deifying, dictatorship. In replicating the logic and ideology of dictatorship, they self-indulgently ensure their own immanent relevance and continuous survival. Therefore, they are actively agile in producing intellectual modalities that would sustain the dictatorship, primarily toward favoring their own vested interest and survival, given that their peculiar existence hinges on a parasitic dependency on the existence of the dictatorship. The task of such intellectuals is intended toward assuaging and vilifying the negative effects of the diurnal, venomous and pejorative onslaughts that opponents direct at the dictatorship. Acutely alert, based upon their class dependency on the continuous survival of the dictatorship, the pro-dictator intellectuals accede toward ensuring the maintenance of its relevance by continually anchoring and sustaining the prevalent regime.

Such pro-dictator intellectuals thus deliberately magnify and inflame the ember of dictatorship through propaganda and terror, utilized within the varying attempts toward routinizing and evolving dictatorship into becoming a familiar reality in the popular consciousness. Devoid of ethical considerations, the pro-dictatorial intellectuals diurnally attempt to create the utopia that attempts to imbricate dictatorship with popular and nationalist aspirations.[60] Through such propaganda they mitigate the reality of oppression as necessary and rationalize it as innocuous. Inherently, the totalitarian class is significantly a fearful one at two critical levels. First, it is highly unstable and insecure. Hence, dictators are often afraid and paranoid, even of their own shadows. Secondly, the dictatorship is feared by the vast majority who are either passively controlled or actively mobilizing against it. In this way, as noted by Max Weber, the struggles for domination often privilege conflicts within the state and society, between the military and ruling class (the aristocracy).[61]

In any case, it is necessary to understand that military dictatorships, especially as manifested in the Abacha case, attempt vigorously to privatize the state within a patriarchal scheme, (Weber, 1028–1030). Hence, within this tendency, they relativize military discipline, which has been historically instrumental in the development of democracy and underlies capitalist activities in some cases, (Weber, 1152, 1155,-56). The dictatorial taste for absolute domination often sacrifices military discipline and hierarchy. Further, it is antithetical to capitalist pursuits in so far as it arms its opponents with the means for its dislocation. Thus, dictatorships are often given to arbitrary machinations, and devalue rational capitalist constructs as they pursue their governing goals through prebendal and patrimonial interests; they do not, therefore, acquiesce in considerations of merit, competence, and rationalization. Essentially, the military dictatorship, especially under Abacha, climatically reflects the lack of autonomy of the state, and is unable to resist becoming directly enmeshed in class struggles.[62] The Nigerian state, like other African nations, also has limited autonomy. The modality of limited autonomy has reflected the weakness of the state perpetually cycling as a peripheral formation.[63] Such dynamics have been responsible for various dictatorial regimes, schemes and conflicts, and real physical violence in Nigeria.

These contests highlight the bifurcated relationship that distinguishes the governing military class from other sections of the power elite that manifest themselves at different levels, thus fracturing and altering the dynamics of intra-factional relationships within the ruling class. It also abets the further stoking of the embers of discontent and intrigue even within the same military class Such tenuous intra-class struggles merely reflect the inferiority stigmata inherited by the Nigerian military as a result of its social status and colonial origin. "Soldiers had never been very popular in Nigeria. Because of its brutality to friend and foes alike, the Niger Coast constabulary was known in the nineteenth century as the 'Forty Thieves' . . . To some extent their low reputation may have resulted from the part they played in establishing British rule." [64]

> . . . this body of troops remained metropolitan. The army was isolated into the relative splendor of the barracks and the officers' mess. In pre-independence days, the army was answerable to powers which naturally were metropolitan not local. In training, the Nigerian Army was totally alienated from Nigerian society. It was a weapon closely guarded by the agents of imperialism to be unleashed whenever necessary on the native population. During this period the true criterion for judging the excellence of that force was its ability to serve the whims and caprices of the agents of imperialism: the more unquestioning the better. (Odumegwu-Ojukwu, 32–33)

Critics have often illustrated the colonial military as an imperial, alien, and brutal force, and have fundamentally observed how post-independence African soldiers attempt to elaborate and replicate fundamentally such modes of bestial behavior.[65] In the Nigerian case, even colonial officials and erstwhile members of the Nigerian military, such as Sir Frederick D. Lugard and Chief Emeka Odumegwu Ojukwu have alluded to the same sentiment. Lugard, Nigeria's presumed founding patriarch, and Ojukwu, a former colonel and Biafran secessionist war leader, respectively noted: "I have seen, alike among Indian troops in the Afghan war, and in Nigeria in the advance on Kano, how the native soldier identifies himself with the Government he serves, and will march against his co-religionists, and even against his own village. Mutinies may generally be ascribed to lack of touch and ignorance of causes of discontent."[66] " . . . a Nigerian soldier would proudly display on his chest medals won whilst 'pacifying' his own village; an action during which a number of his own relatives and childhood friends may have been killed or burnt to death. It was this that gave birth to the saying which read, *'Nne mulu soja amuro nwa'*- a soldier's mother is childless," (Odumegwu-Ojukwu, 33).

Further, the colonial attempt to alienate soldiers from their milieu of origin through outside posting away from their aboriginal homelands (Lugard, 577) further intensified the repressive military culture of arbitrary irresponsibility and unaccountability in trammeling over the citizenry. The Nigerian military has continued to internalize such brutality and has yet to shed itself fully of such a malicious behavioral accoutrement. The Nigerian army had a reputation for low social prestige and was unattractive to educated southerners in the 1950s and 1960s. In the North, it was despised as being a low-class establishment, born of peasantry and slaves, (Miners, 29–32, 41).

Conceptualized as a component of the ruling class through the colonial initiative, through the military incursion into political power, conscious attempts toward shedding and shredding such derogatory identities were pursued. Through their entry into the political realm, and amplified by their rhetoric of reflecting national aspirations as the constitutive marker embodying the nation, appealing to her discipline, honor, and decency, the military class secures the nation as the legitimating idiom for its forceful interjection into the political process. To cast this derogatory stigma related to its origins, the colonial officers attempted to update the military, thus co-opting it into a heuristic segment of the ruling class, (Odumegwu-Ojukwu, 32).

Such moves appealed to members of the traditional and established civilian ruling class. The colonial updating of the social status of the military class assured its members a privileged status that granted entry into the ruling class. The acquired privilege of respectability and governing capability, viewed as potentially necessary toward fostering the domination of the traditional and established ruling class within the pursuit of its political and economic interests, necessarily propelled it toward appropriating the military class fully into the colonial class structure.

Hence, the military, hitherto perceived as subaltern, all of a sudden was welcomed and reinvented as a space for furthering the hegemonic aspirations of the ruling class. Thus it was, that members of the traditional ruling class, initially from the North and then later throughout Nigeria, cognizant of the influential position of the military in furthering dominion, decided to appropriate the military by sending their children to be trained as officers. Through allying and associating the military class intimately with the ruling class interests, the former within the pursuit of hegemony and relevance definitively secured their vested interest.

However, in spite of this strategic facelift, the military's consciousness of the stigma of its historical subaltern identity; as a colonial and imperialist agent of a crude and brutal order, affected the nature of its relationship and the perceived utility of its violence against the populace. Thus, the military was perennially engaged in violent confrontation with civilians and even with different segments of the ruling class. Haunted by the stigma of alien origin and delineation as a brutal entity, it often appealed to the same source of brutality in asserting its power, relevance, and domination. In this, the military has continued to reinforce the notion of its indiscriminate utilization of brutal violence, therefore alienating itself further from real legitimacy. Such alienating perceptions further define its subaltern image and identity. Cognitively, the military feeds the popular imagination with distaste and discontent against its order. Cyclically, such internalized perceptions create mutual suspicions and ruptures the relationship between the military and civilian classes. These misgivings, it must also be noted, also extend into the sphere of politics, within the contest for relevance between these groups.

As a result, the military's relationship with the Nigerian civilian population is at best tenuous, and often couched in the symbolism of real and imagined violence, if not outright terror. Therefore, in spite of its alliance with the traditional ruling class though maintaining a semblance of cordial relations, the military remains a subject of veiled suspicion and morbid fear. Both the military and civilian ruling class are afraid of the capabilities of the opposite group toward divesting and dispossessing them whenever they are in power. Further exacerbating such tension is the fact that within the initial formation of the military hegemonic control, Nigerian military dictators have often delegated some of their powers to certain sections of the civilian ruling class, especially the traditional ruling class in hopes of achieving legitimation that would ensure the success of the government that they have imposed.

However, in the face of popular discontent, uncertain about how such delegated powers could be utilized in undermining the stability of their hegemony, they are always suspicious and fearful. As a result, the traditional ruling class and the allied civilian political class are intrinsically perceived as Frankenstein monsters capable of acting against their creators. Such morbid fears propel military dictatorships to consolidate their hold on power, through creating extensive networks of surveillance, and privatizing power toward patronizing their allied class more intimately, by arbitrary allocation of public goods and resources toward buying loyalties. In this way, traditional authorities in Nigeria come under the influence of patrimonial and prebendal schemes, which is also a double-edged sword as it can be used to blackmail the people in power. In this way, Nigerian military dictators have often been able to consolidate their aspiration of continuous domination, while muting popular grassroots resistance and uprisings against their rule.

Through such devices, both classes act symbiotically and yet parasitically upon each other, in legitimating their dual spheres and fields of functioning. In the case of the dictatorship, such antics further assure its absolute hegemonic control, while for the traditional ruling class, the military and allied political classes help to reinvent its public and social relevance. Problems arise when dictatorships are unable to subsume certain groups within their spatial borders. The fear of being relegated into an irrelevant and subaltern status ultimately justifies the dictatorship's disposition toward the perpetuation of its hegemonic domination, through the employment of acute violence.

Thus, the military class, within its exercise of political domination, is cognitively aware of its limited autonomy and ruptured power base. Brute force and diverse acts of violence become defined as the sustaining tools for enhancing absolute domination, in extending the duration of its ill-fated rule. Military dictatorships realize the instability of their hegemony, and so its actors lead a fearful existence. These fears are overcome only with violent tactics that are intended to scare the potential dissenter or opponent. Within such displays, the identity of the state is inverted: no longer as an abstract ideal that controls the use of violence but one that is really privatized and personalized within the occult hold of the dictator. Thus, the state becomes the sponsor of arbitrary and inordinate displays of state-terrorism.

Such an inversion paralyzes and invalidates the functioning of the state. The psychic paranoia of dictators nurtures arbitrary schemes, consistently ritualizing thematic inversions and reversions, in crystallizing propaganda and the amoral elongation of dictatorial hegemony, (Nwankwo, 34).

Paradoxically, such dynamics radically emaciate the dictatorial hegemony by substantively altering and puncturing its hegemonic control, metamorphosing the dictator into a subaltern position, mainly because these activities induce the population and various sectional and class formations toward reactionary antagonism. The evolution of contradictory forces emasculates the dictatorship, eventually dispossessing it of legitimacy.

The dictatorship's inability to enforce coercive control engenders further utilization of bestial and repressive force, which fuel further agitations that durably dispossess it of hegemonic domination, eventually leading to its decapitation. The utilization of brute force for crushing popular agitation also aggravates cleavages within the ruling military class. Such antics in enhancing centrifugal tendencies fuel cleavages, whose ripple effects further delegitimize the dictatorship and its associated cliques, in promoting their isolation and undercutting their hold upon power. This production of dialectical paradoxes handicaps the dictatorship, as popular denunciation against dictatorship destabilizes populations as well as governments.

Such intransigent intra-class contestations during the Abacha era, between members of the ruling class, within the civilian and military arenas, and between the ruling classes and their various civilian and military counterparts, represented dynamics that seemed to shatter the hitherto held assumption, of mythical dynamics that referred to the monolithic and overbearing significance associated with the enduring power of the Kaduna Mafia, toward shaping the structural dimensions and political direction of Nigeria.[67] Others, both serving and former military officers and civilians, would eventually fall out with General Abacha. The General, however, started subtly unleashing his lynching strategies against perceived opponents, adopting creative tactics to granulate Nigeria to a standstill. Poignantly, within the schemes assessed by Antonio Gramsci, tensile and subtle struggles occurred between the military class and their intellectual counterparts.

Furthermore, as these conflicts were occurring, Abacha also engaged in class re-alignment within his military and regional base in the north, thus further polarizing opinions and sentiments regarding his person and rule. Using Machiavellian tactics to fracture the old group of collaborators, in Gramscian sense Abacha utilized elements of the extant intellectual class to achieve his goal of fracturing their hitherto respectable social standing and their presumed political relevance. Thus, he fell back upon certain members of the civilian and military classes, especially those perceived as previously slighted, (Soyinka, 2006, 412–18). At this point, he appointed General Muhammed Buhari, a former military Head of State, overthrown by General Babangida in 1985, as Chairperson for the Petroleum Trust Fund. At the same time, he seemed to have contemplated using General Tunde Idiag-bon, Buhari's former deputy, to oversee his anti-fraud agency.

The economic arena and members of the commercial class are also often targeted by dictatorial force, simply because the dictator feels threat-ened by the capabilities attached to the accumulated wealth of certain per-sonalities, and corporate interests in acquiring power. Therefore, even within the ruling and entrepreneurial milieu, dictatorship induces fear, uncertainty, and paralysis. In Nigeria, members of this class are often the by-product of collaboration with the ruling military class. Hence, it is contradictory and ironic that under a military dictatorship they are not absolutely safe-guarded against its onslaughts. To the contrary, dictatorships often antago-nize this class, to invalidate their ability singly or collectively to marshal their resources toward truncating the conditions of their oppression.

In the case of Nigeria, in spite of collaboration with the traditional ruling class and the allied intellectual interests nurtured toward enhanc-ing its political stature and successful domination, often through means of patrimonial, prebendal, and clientele patronage, the dictatorship turned against these very same people. Massive investments and rapidly increasing wealth antagonize the dictatorship, which becomes afraid that such instru-mentalities can be put into use in challenging its hegemony. Such morbid fear of potential alternative sources of power and wealth strains the eco-nomic arena. In creating arid economic situations, dictatorships in turn put themselves on the firing line of popular outrage. Ironically, such outcries possess the same or higher capacities to induce what dictators fear most; their emasculation or their dispossession of hegemony.

The cognition regarding the unpredictability and instability of its rule, often unnerves the military class, and produces a Frankenstein effect. Frantically, the attempt toward accentuating its hegemonic hold and vested interests drives dictatorships to destabilizing the state's sources of economic power. Such actions also help to fuel antagonism from the subdued eco-nomic and allied ruling classes, as well as the trammeled masses. Within this sublimation of economic interests, in line with the dictator's aspirations, the owners of economic interests are pushed into subaltern status, when weighted against the dictator. Such dynamics escalate already existing intra-class antagonisms between the two interests, in a no-win struggle, leading either to compromise between the military and its allies, or to forging new social alliances and dynamically generating new social movements.

To the extent that such fights entail problems for the ruling military class, and even further split it, given that some members of the military have extended relationships and vested interests that are affected, the struggle for military hegemony transcends the immediate nodal purview, portending vitally dangerous troubles for the dictatorship. Dictatorships, by straining the economic arena further compound the level of popular reaction against their misrule, thus accelerating the reduction of their popular legitimacy, and hastening their demise.

Minimizing the goals of economic production and growth creates poverty and debilitating social chaos, such as unemployment, which propels sentiments of frustration and resistance, (Nwankwo, 25, 28, 37). The fear that underlies the contradictory attempt toward cutting allies in order to enhance tyrannical domination equally simulates the creation of the dialectics of intra-class destruction and counter-resistance. The Frankenstein thus becomes threatening to the dictatorship that created it. Crucially, this intra-class conflict also fuels new economic relationships, or a tightening of extant ones, focally directed toward sanctioning the interests of the dictatorship. Distrust for the economic class, accentuated by arbitrary dictatorial policies and direct interference in economic activities leads to an entrenchment of ties between the military dictatorship and international corporations. By this means, fortified by revenues from international businesses (who are also economically exploitative), the dictatorship feels empowered to counter any threat to his hegemony. Ironically, while most western countries were politically averse to the Abacha dictatorship, the Nigerian oil multinationals actively collaborated and supported his dictatorial aspirations. It was a case of balanced reciprocity, relatively described by the popular Nigerian parlance, "Rub my back, I rub your back."

In this sense, the interests of dictatorship and international business become aligned through a certain kind of exploitative logic that underpins the relevance of both internal and external domination, in scuttling true national development. Claude Ake asserts that, "The Nigerian State is constituted in such a way that it reflects a narrow range of interests, mainly that of the Nigerian bourgeoisie and metropolitan capital. The apparatuses of the state express the power and interests of labor in a limited way and that of the peasants and subsistence farmer, not at all. The significance of this has to be grasped to appreciate the trends in policy output and Nigeria's course of development," (The Nigerian State, 31).

The decimation of the local business arena in one sense favored global enterprises, whose sole production targeted foreign markets. Therefore, their basic market was never threatened. Rather, they aligned with the dictatorship, first as self-protection for their own business interests, and secondly because both interests pursued similar exploitative goals of domination, albeit within different spheres, casting aspersions upon the Nigerian people and nation. Such commonalities also reveal the deceptive

and dubious tactics employed in pursuing their polar but mutually integrated goals of acquisition, powers and wealth. In this way, they feverishly
enriched each other and burnished each party's ennobled yet insatiable
appetite for domination and the accumulation of wealth. In this way, both
interests engaged in mutual and balanced reciprocity. On these terms, Abacha laid claim to economic largesse and support for his political programs,
in exchange for the protection of his military for these foreign corporations.[68] Abacha therefore fulfilled his own part of the deal, toward ensuring the continuity of the multinational oil corporations—Shell, Mobil, and
other business operations—through the backing of his full military force
against raucous agitations by citizens of the Niger Delta oil communities,
(Agbali, 2002; Ake, Contemporary Africa; Saro-Wiwa, 1995).

    This scenario is generally true of the Nigerian context, in which rich
entrepreneurs, through the clientele state patronage they enjoyed, put their
wealth at the disposal of members of the military class toward plotting
coups. The late Chief Abiola was noted to have financed the coup that
brought Generals Buhari and Babangida to power in 1983 and 1985,
respectively. However, that fact was not enough in his quest to become
Nigeria's president in 1993, though ironically the June 12th presidential
election gave him a clean mandate. Some arguments attribute this fact to
Nigerians' exhaustion regarding military rule, and specifically the machinations of Abiola's friend, General Babangida. Another Nigerian entrepreneur, Chief Great Ogboru, also put his business establishment at the service
of the Major Gideon Orkar, for the latter's failed coup plot in April 1990.
Chief Ogboru was alleged to be mastermind-financier of that coup. It is in
such veins that influential civilian-owned economic enterprises were imagined as constituting a real and potential threat. Therefore, many incho-
ate and arbitrary economic policies ensure that many viable businesses
became insolvent. Thus, businesses owned by perceived opponents were
closed without notice, or any legal sanction or rational basis. In the aftermath of the 1993 election, many private media houses, mainly newspapers
and magazines, were arbitrarily shut. In fact, this was a well-entrenched
norm for countering the government's perceived media enemies through
1980s and 1990s.

    Political rivals who refused to "respect" the regime of the day risked
not only detention but also government targeting of their businesses. Similar punishment were meted out to the Concord Press publishers of the
National, Sunday, African, and Community Concord newspapers and magazine, owned by Chief M.K. O Abiola, following his agitation to claim his
presidential mandate. The government sealed his business property, thereby
starving production and financially liquidating his business empire.

THEORETICAL RATIONALIZATION AND REFLECTIONS UPON EXILIC DISPOSSESSION

Exile resembles a rite of passage in terms of the separation and attempts at reincorporation that occur. Initially, it would seem that there is no middle passage within the exilic processes, given that it is all about a sudden separation from the homeland and a rushed incorporation into a novel habitat, offered as adopted homeland and providing sanctuary. However, a critical look at the experience of exile reveals that it is actually a continuous liminal existence for most exiles, unlike most voluntary immigrants, as the former group subsists eternally in the fringe regions of their new adopted home society. The incorporation process of exiles is never finalized; it is open-ended, it leaves open the door of hope allowing for heuristic opportunities for return and reclamation, privileging the chanting of "Nunc Dimittis."[69]

Exilic liminality orders the hijacking of the completion of the processes of reincorporation or reintegration, into contexts considered as alien or unnatural. The entire existence of exile can be reified within the understanding of relative liminality, depicting the exile as dwelling within imaginative temporal and spatial interstices. The exilic experience often embodies the rupturing of a stable existential order, or is a reaction against the enthronement of an illegitimate hegemonic ideology in place of the non-realization of a subjective or collective utopian vision of a political paradise yet to occur. Political exile, in this sense, serves as an instrument of temporary counter-hegemony.

The vision of exile is often scripted in despicable and pejorative terms, but while true in most circumstances it does not have to be explicitly so. Often, however, the reality of exile is a metaphor in negativity and synchronizes hysteria, anger, degradation, uncertain hope and nostalgia: that of return. Hence, an "erosion of self-esteem is one of the commonest symptoms of dispossession."[70] Exile is a product of dispossession which also produces anomie that introduces the chain reactions that elongate the outward reaches and existential dimensions of dispossession. This dispossession, therefore, often internalizes the notions of displacement and dislocation. In fact, the Nigerian Nobel laureate, Wole Soyinka, reifies the situation of exile as "mimic death," (Soyinka, 2006, 23) while its reality "sinks into one as a palpable space of bereavement," (Soyinka, 2006, 387).

Exile occasions the mental state of being uprooted, and partially transplanted, revealing the scarifications of displacement and often the reality of the in-between, a monstrosity of hybridness, not within the imagination of the creolization processes that merges two purviews into an aligned synoptic codification. The exile "exists in a median state, neither completely at one with the new setting nor fully disencumbered of the old, best with half-involvements and half-detachments, nostalgic and sentimental on one level, an adept mimic or a secret outcast on another. Being skilled at survival becomes the main imperative, with the danger of getting too comfortable and secure constituting a threat that is constantly to be guarded against," (Said, 1998, 49, 52). In fact, Said compellingly notes that for the intellectual, exile in a "metaphysical sense is restlessness, movement, constantly being unsettled, and unsettling others. You cannot go back to some earlier and perhaps more stable condition of being at home; and alas, you can never fully arrive, be at one with your new home or situation," (Said, 1998, 52–53).

Exiles also sense acrid strangeness, experience arid torments that indulge hysteria regarding their sense of unsettled existence, as a hibernating outsider. "Exile is strangely compelling to think about but terrible to experience. It is the incurable rift forced between a human being and a native place, between the self and its true home: its essential sadness can never be surmounted. And while it is true that literature and history contain heroic, romantic, glorious, and even triumphant episodes in an exile's life, these are more than efforts meant to overcome the crippling sorrow of estrangement. The achievements of exile are permanently undermined by the loss of something left behind forever."[71] In spite of such notions, there is a positive value to the productions that exiles have generated on the template of their alienations and pain, often exhibited through their sonic intellectual contributions to cultural and social advancements. Said agrees that exiles and émigrés have made substantial contributions to the development of their exilic spaces, and even to the enrichment of modern culture overall, including those of their abandoned homelands, (Said, 2000, 173).

Thus, exile involves a necessary shift and repositioning in the world. As Paulo Freire notes in his *Letters to Christina:* "In the intimacy of these necessary repositionings in the world—in the world of those who had been to leave and in the original world of those who were able to stay—something I have been talking about a lot takes place: the drama of being uprooted. There is the need, lived out in anguish, to learn the great historical, cultural, and political lesson that, in attending to our business in a borrowed context, we create another context that we have not quite psychologically abandoned. And yet, we are forced physically to leave our preoccupation."[72]

Exile, though a place for cooling one's heels, is also a place of valuable personal and cognitive transformation possessing productive salience within the downloading of the transference of morbid solitude into vital translations. Therefore, the exile must be open to the process of reclamation of his lost ambience through the duration of the exilic process. The exile cannot despair so much as to exclude the readiness to reclaim, re-story, and transform his dented past. Achebe notes that the project of re-storying dispossession is a significantly indulgent venture, (Achebe, 59–60, 79–83).

THEORY OF HIATUS AND STRUCTURATION: REFLECTIONS ON EXILIC DISLOCATION AND PRO-ACTIVITY

The Nigerian exiles during the Abacha era referenced the mimesis of agency, creative rationalization, and reflexive engagements. Nigerian exiles were mainly political, and so their rhetoric and antics were vehemently counter-hegemonic toward military domination; they portrayed themselves as pro-active agents of democratic activism targeting the dismantling of the present military-hegemonic structure, in a struggle aimed at total disengagement from their previous public life, and their recoil by means of political disgrace into sanctioned roles as professional defenders of the Nigerian citizenry, rather than self-minted Frankenstein prototypes desiring to granulate and dissolve Nigeria. Such self-definitions, essentially derived from media tags, allocated the social agent an historic role in the struggle proactively to reclaim Nigeria and to institute democracy. The referential marker also imbued these actors with social relevance in the struggle toward Nigerian social and political transformations, specifically within the political arena.

The mission of pro-democratic revitalization defined their counter-hegemonic tactics, as embedded in dialectical opposition to the currency and vitality of military rule. In this fight, these activities utilized words as weaponry, abetted by their spatial dissonance that mitigated the power of hegemonic tyranny to use thundering and silencing ammunition in quenching this perceived opponent. It was a fight intended to create different perceptive visions of society, rooted in different cosmological positions. For Chinua Achebe, "strong language is in the very nature of the dialogue between the dispossession and its rebuttal. The two sides never see the world in the same light," (Achebe, 76).

Ironically, even the hegemonic power reflects a dispossessed consciousness. The exile, by his/her flight and emergent rhetoric, punctures its hegemonic hold and totalitarian pride. The tyrant finding its adversary out of reach, the exile is a more potent enemy. This introduces a new megalomaniac face-saving measure; a new dialectical struggle emerges. In this new contest, the tyrannical agent intones a new tirade in a reactionary war of words. Not yet dislodged, the dispossessed Frankenstein seeks victory at all cost, thus rhetoric is reinvented as a new kind of reactionary weapon: "In the war between dispossession and its nemesis civilization itself regresses into barbarism; words become weapons again rather than tools; plough-shares are beaten back into spears. Fear and suspicion take over from openness and straight conversation, (Achebe, 78)." As social actors, they engaged different reflexive schemes engaging the diachronic and synchronic rationales that defined the identity of the Nigerian nation-state.

However, this form of agency provokes another, initiating a novel layer of nationalism centered upon the cognition and elevation of different ethnic groups as the predicative constituent basis upon which the reality of Nigerian nationhood acquires its ontological essence. Despite differing visions and interests, the unified acceptance of the forged reality of Nige-ria reflects the dynamics and signification of Nigerian nationalism. Evi-dentially, such constructions embed a dual structural abstraction. Firstly, such nationalism hinges upon the resourceful resilience of ethnic tribalism as its underlying primordial source. Secondly, such a cognitive recognition of the framework of the reality of Nigeria points to the acceptance of the structural properties of the nationalism that is the outcome of the country's colonial and post-colonial essence.

Within these concepts we rationally sense the interactive and produc-tive impact of the dialectic processes of structure upon agency, and *vice versa,* in shaping the generation of consciousness, in this case political con-sciousness, and a shared nationalistic concept. The teleological impact of the dialectics of structure and agency appropriately enables agents to accen-tuate, within the conditions of their synchronic purview, their particular activities toward creatively shaping the norms for transforming Nigeria from mismatched notions of nationhood, transcendentally directing it away from the misnomer of nationalistic fatality. Agency working upon struc-tures could efficiently and analytically constitute itself as a relevant tool of development through helping the transformation of Nigerian social-politi-cal structures and spaces.

In this way, agency and structure interacting can ensure that the struc-tural properties of existential contexts and reflections possess qualitative dimensions necessary to translate theory into practice for realistic human and social development needs. In this way, agency can shape the positive processes of cultural transformations and development, through reflexive activities that reference and reframe the structural matrix toward propel-ling social advancement, using cultural variables and historical antecedents, especially in hermeneutically offering blueprints toward heuristic actions.

The exilic experience is theorized as rooted in the dislocation of hia-tus schemes, and thus shapes a new referential idiom as a habitus neolo-gism, ordering new historical and cultural trajectories that accrete as new processes and products of imagination. Further, this scheme of hiatus reflects spatial disconnection between the exilic self and its ecological niche, between one person's experience and another's. However, within the intellectual and reflexive dynamics distinguishing between the new and the old spatial existence, exile produces hybridized schemes that, through creolizing synthesis, attempt a synchronic "syntegration" formatting for new syndicated worldviews.

Often, the confused crises evident in the attempt to ensure social reincorporation induce social and self-alienation, due to the inconclusive mental objectification of such processes. The forced dislocation engendered by the realities of physical powerlessness makes adjustment critically challenging. At times such sentiments possess valuable opportunities that provoke consciousness and realizations that lead toward reinvention and mental reclamation projects, through inverted retrogression. Such conditions can foster different productive forms with extrinsic values, including the emergence of social and political activism, scholarship, religiosity, and other productive ventures. Therefore, the domain of exilic internalization and fixation possesses expansive and transformative characters.

Exiles, through existential focusing nurtured by their introspections, can transcend the limitations of hiatus as the reality of dispossession and severance from home, toward transcendental interlacing of bi-modal or multiple existential perspectives, and toward seeking the configurative revision of the conditions that created their exile. The exilic contest can be a transcendental and productive one, as it objectifies the hiatus experience, as well as the necessary conditions for the realignment of hiatus contexts; as a suturing of structural and historical bifurcations. Through reflective objectification and different subjective modalities, exiles activate transcendental delimitations of the boundaries of hiatus dislocations.

Such consciousness and methodic actions equally constitute the realignment of convoluted and spatially broken territorial linearity, which uses specific historicity to pierce the contiguous conditions of hiatus. The processes of realignment attempt to remedy and suture the conditions of dispossession and discontinuity as best as possible. The overturning of dislocations can engender the reification and production of certain essential values embedded within the dimensionalities of the spatial, temporal and mental dispositions that regulate the operational contours of human cognitive and territorial interactions. Such dimensional spaces can also extrinsically be modified for exiles, and constitute a market for cultural exchange and informational reciprocity, thus advantageously creating an arena for projecting ideational wares.

Therefore, the different domains where exilic viewpoints are articulated have different characters and multipurpose funding as the place where the exilic experience is shared, and other forms of exchange regarding the homeland and the new location occurs. Therefore, such ambience forms the domain of critical cultural interpenetration, where interceptions of different transnational views, "transpatial" ethos, and cultural idioms transcend spaces and bodies in order to promote interaction between intersecting idioms and cosmologies. In this sense, such spaces, physical or virtual, also represent zones of hybridized unity and spheres of social relations among actors. Such tenements constitute spiritual formations that unite and synthesize common humanity, transnational imaginations, cultural idioms, and social purviews.

Dislocation, notwithstanding, the exile is an articulate producer of meaning and a creative actor, whose experience of exile, in spite of the disruption of activities, can initiate salient meditations with profound effects for crucial reflections and the forging of new productive realities within the new context (exile), as well as the abandoned context (home). Within the context of exile, these revelations shed new meanings on certain social phenomena and events, including those hitherto taken for granted, and the translation of such revelations can be focally powerful, relative to the inventions they instantiate. Therefore, the exilic experience entails the cognitive transformation of self and social consciousness whose transcendental qualities diffuse into different spatial arenas. Therefore, such rational and epistemological frameworks challenge the exile to confront the ontological dispositions that define his being: his existential predication, psychic state, and symbolic mimesis, within his mnemonic and subliminal templates, as interjectory and intercepting distillations within which different modulated forms of experience makes sense, and to construct new frameworks toward contextual understanding of former environs and toward building new and possible significations as novel referential frames.

Exiles are differentiated from prisoners in one significant sense: their spatial freedom of mobility. They are not confined, they can engage in whatever they like, making real decisions about their lives. Yet even such freedom is not often as unlimited as one might imagine, since there are varying and mutating degrees of containment and limitations associated with the exilic state. Exiles, especially political ones, persistently watch their backs, suspiciously censoring the people they encounter. Such heightened sensitivities elevate their conscious sensors into roving antennae, often preoccupied with securing themselves, their families, and their surroundings. Many political exiles harbor and internalize the sense of recurrent danger.

Therefore, most exiles are highly insulated, protective and guarded—finding it difficult publicly to display information regarding their personal spatial and temporal locations and schedules. Such modes of acting affect and limit the exile's spheres of interaction with others, hence overtly privileging associations mainly with in-group members, while suspiciously censoring unfamiliar non-members of the group: "Because nothing is secure. Exile is a jealous state. What you achieve is precisely what you have no wish to share, and it is in the drawing of lines around you and your compatriots that the least attractive aspects of being in exile emerge: an exaggerated sense of group solidarity, and a passionate hostility to outsiders, even those who may in fact be in the same predicament as you," (Said, 2000, 178).

The feeling for most political exiles is that, while the space of exile is evidently more secure, there can be no certainty about potential dangers. The instinct of self-preservation introduces the notion of self-care, since the spaces of exile can be equally dangerous, with enemies masking their acts through anonymous channels and sources. Therefore, the invisible but real ghosts, acting for the enemy, can still be perceived as roaming intermediaries with looming machinations. Such fears are actually not totally false.

Among different cohorts of Nigerian exiles, this has been the case. Dr. Umaru Dikko, formerly Second Republic Minister of Transport, Presidential Liaison on Rice Importation, and campaign chief for President Shehu Shagari's 1983 re-election bid, was kidnapped by paid Israeli agents of the Nigerian government in broad daylight and caged in diplomatic baggage ready to be shipped to Nigeria. The plot was luckily aborted by the British authorities. Emeka Ojukwu noted that suspected assassins targeting him were dislodged and arrested during his exile in Ivory Coast, (Odumegwu-Ojukwu, 72). This manner of behavior was again apparent when the Nigerian intellectual, Nobel Laureate of Literature, and self-exiled pro-democratic political activist, Wole Soyinka, was targeted during the Abacha dictatorship for elimination in New York.[73]

Additionally the exile becomes an expert in witty self-adaptations and quick revisions, incessantly reworking and auditing the same statements in different forms, craftily reprocessing. He reviews his thoughts against certain selective aesthetics regarding their appeal, imagined sentimental effects upon the audience, the texture of their cultural and contextual reliability, and their significant hermeneutical and canonical implications as determined by the exile's personal aspirations in the host society. In varying degrees, the exile is engaged in vital decision-making, pre-testing his audition, negotiating, and selectively redacting certain vignettes within his postulated viewpoints.

The exile is, in essence, a dramatist. His or her performances invest and integrate varying plots toward satisfying the audience's taste. Hence, the exile is constantly self-engaged in self-monitoring and radically shifting modes of different interactions within the different forms of displays and utterances through self-censorship and the realization of uncertainty: "Time passed very slowly in exile. After a ten year confinement, the exile realizes with shock that only one year has passed. He waits but what appears most cruel is that he is not permitted to consider his travails in finite terms. An exile unlike a prisoner cannot say 'now I have spent three years, I have twenty-two more.' He could have one more, two more, or thirty years more, He could die in exile," (Odumegwu-Ojukwu, 2003, 72).

"The pathos of exile is in the loss of contact with the solidity and the satisfaction of earth: homecoming is out of the question," (Said, 2000, 178). Herein, the exile envies the non-exile. "Exiles look at non-exiles with resentment. They belong in their surroundings, you feel, whereas an exile is always out of place. What is it like to be born in a place, to stay, and live there, to know that you are of it, more or less forever?" (Said, 2000, 180–81). Understanding also clarifies the segmented barricade that markedly bifurcates the exile from the non-exile. Almost sounding hollow, General Ojukwu remembers the fatality of his exilic experiences, expressed in a repressed sentiment laden with pain that unveils his resentment against the non-exile: "I discovered that my predicament was not in the least unique—that many before me had suffered the same blackmail, the same betrayal, the same abandonment. I found that the fault was not with men, but rather it was the nature of exile. Soon it was clear that exile was not so much the separation from the kith and kin, rather it was an assault on the mind," (Odumegwu-Ojukwu, 72). The sealed reality of the fatality of exile dawns as non-exiles differentiate and treat the exile with derision, refusing to enthrone him with any undeserved celebratory crown. Such attitudes engrave more permanently the reality of dispossession and alienation already chiseled into the exile's consciousness:

> In exile, man is subject[ed] permanently to blackmail because he has been divested of every authority: aides revolt, staff revolt and even families revolt. The sympathetic effort of those intimate to pretend that nothing has changed soon wears very thin and any attempt by the exile to maintain authority appears grotesque. Soon the mere response 'yes sir' appears a term of abuse or ridicule. The exile shrinks, and hides. He treads wearily and begins to read faces and interpret and analyze every random gesture. All day, he sits and broods. The exile does not choose his friends—'friends' choose him. The exile cannot reject a proffered hand. He is permanently on view for approval or otherwise. His friends stay for only as long as it is convenient. (Odumegwu-Ojukwu, 71)

Therefore, the exile is the victim of alienation in a dual sense: victim of his moral decision or circumstances that drove the idea of exile, but worse still the exile is a victim of the betrayal of people, events, and more bitterly turn-coats, as they try to scapegoat, placing all outrageous mishaps upon the shoulders of the exile as the efficient cause of all tragic catastrophes and calamitous crises, whether natural, accidental, personal, national, structural, and/or systemic. Hence, everything gone awry is blamed upon the exile. Emeka Ojukwu, the former Biafran war leader and rebel, notes of his post-civil exilic experiences in Ivory Coast, following the sinking of Biafra' dream for self-determination. "The exile is blamed for everyone's misfortune around him. He does not fear death because death is preferable to remaining a non-person. The exile is a living dead; he is a sepulcher. While alive his property is acquired and shared by the very relatives whom he trusts to struggle for his return home. News filters in and out, each one another betrayal. In order to survive, associates turn Judas and deny him. Each denial is a nail hammered home on his invisible coffin. The exile has a choice; to survive or to succumb. I chose early to survive," (Odumegwu-Ojukwu, 71).

Such circumstances endorse the truism contained within the assertions of the Nigerian intellectual and novelist, Chinua Achebe: "What is both unfortunate and unjust is the pain the person dispossessed is forced to bear in the act of dispossession itself and subsequently in the trauma of a diminished existence. The range of aberrations and abnormalities fostered by this existence can be truly astounding," (Achebe, 70).

This dispossession therefore adduces new epistemological criteria, referential distillations and analytic processing, as reinvented skills necessary for dealing with people, situations, and events. Exile occasions new diluted meanings, constituted into hybrid cognition as an integration of bi-modal or plural views. Therefore, the experience of exile adduces a reasserting into novel learning, contexts, and productions: "When the reasons that push us from our context into another are ostensibly of a political nature, it does not matter why we woke up one day in a foreign land. Exile, over time, allows new situations to reinsert us in the world. The same thing happens to those people who stay in their own country, History does not stop for them, does not wait for our absence to end so that we can tell them upon returning that it was not really a reencounter. Things change, as we do."[74] "Much of [an?] exile's life is taken up with compensation for disorienting loss by creating a new world to rule. It is not surprising that so many exiles seem to be novelists, chess players, political activists, and intellectuals. Each of these occupations requires a minimal investment in objects and places a great premium on mobility and skills. The exile's new world, logically enough, is unnatural and its unreality resembles fiction," (Said, 2000, 181).

Exile therefore constitutes a school of dialectical learning, in which the exile is taught new modalities and perceptive frameworks, through active internalization, prompt processing, and quick reasoning. Such awareness also creates multiple novel visions of experiences and insights, resulting from the bi-modal contexts of internalized learning, as well as the ability creatively to intermesh, collapse, redact, and share those multiplex insights: "While it perhaps seems peculiar to speak of the pleasures of exiles, there are some positive things to be said for a few of its conditions. Seeing "the entire world as a foreign land" makes possible originality of vision. Most people are principally aware of one culture, one setting, one home; exiles are aware of at least two, and this plurality of vision gives rise to an aware-ness of simultaneous dimensions, an awareness that—to borrow a phrase from music—is contrapuntal," (Said, 2000, 186). This, at times, enables the exile to become a teacher, a respected iconic guru, whose reflections on his experiences are actively sought by individuals, social groups, gov-ernmental and non-governmental organizations, and often by competing forces affiliated with his homeland.

The Abacha regime and the consciousness it evoked marked the unin-tentional contributions of the Abacha legacy toward the development of Nigeria. Unconscious and unanticipated as those events were in their evolu-tion, they invoked a focusing on certain aspects of human existence, rela-tive to the meaning of homeland and dislocation, exile and displacement, and the meaning of nationhood, as understood within the context of the control of the means of violence balanced against the inordinate diminution of the rights of the citizen.

Therefore, the internal dislocations and demobilizations of civilized norms and values provoked critical re-locations and induced forced mobil-ity of persons across delineated borders, thus blurring the boundaries and the hold of an immoral nation-state over the existential and moral plenitude furnished by states ordered around sets of ethical values and polished struc-tures that respect human and civil rights. Such contradictory and exclu-sionary practices of the vampire state present despicable visions of reality that, though emotionally numbing, engenders the translation of the exilic experience toward intellectual and beneficial simulations, constructed into positive significations for both the individual and his community, in spite of his diurnal nostalgic yearning for familiar surroundings and the painful mnemonic realizations of his uprooting and displacement.

INTERSPATIAL ACTIVISMS AND PRO-ACTIVE LIBERATION

The activism of the Abacha exiles was carried out across vast territorial spaces. These exiles engaged in long distance nationalism and dual phases of international collaborations, in furthering their resistance against the Abacha regime. NADECO made significant in-roads in its campaigns and pro-democratic lobbying, and it seems that some foreign powers noticed their efforts. Abacha had helped their cause, since his own domestic actions also fanned the ember of foreign reactions against him.

International public opinion, mainly from the United States, Russia, Britain, and Germany, vented against the regime following the trials of suspected plotters of a phantom coup, involving Generals Obasanjo and Yar'Adua—a former Head of State and his deputy, respectively.[75] The first reactions came from foreign governments and pro-democratic institutions, groups, and individuals. Though Abacha was a Muslim leader, it was notable that Saudi authorities were averse to his modes of operation, and considered him a disgrace to the Islamic faith he professed. They were noted to be surprised as well at General Babangida, a Muslim, for annulling the June 12th election. In fact, the Saudis and other Middle Eastern governments aided the plot to ease Chief Enahoro's escape from Nigeria into exile, (Olorunfewa, "Escape from the Gulag," 10–14).

Interestingly, however, most Nigerian Muslims maintained public dissonance in their agitation, although both presidential candidates in that election, and the presidential candidate and his deputy of the winning Social Democratic Party (SDP), were all Muslims. Also, the greatest Islamic authority in Nigeria, Chief Ibrahim Dasuki, the Sultan of Sokoto, was deposed and internally exiled without much opposition. The only mild opposition among Nigerian Muslims against the Abacha regime derived from a riot by members of a radical and militant sect associated with the vocal anti-government leader Ibrahim El Zaky Zaky, a pro-Sharia agent.[76]

Different religious entities raised their voices against the prevailing dictatorial current. The Christian Association of Nigeria (CAN) was vocally critical of the dictatorship, especially its then president, Bishop Sunday Mbang, the head of the Methodist Church in Nigeria. As a result, the Abacha regime then sponsored a delegation of American missionaries? into the country, who eulogized his regime; a situation that highly irked CAN.[77] The body of Catholic Bishops' Conference of Nigeria (CBCN) denounced dictatorship during their annual meeting, advising the military to transfer power to civilians.[78] Individual Catholic Bishops, such as the Archbishop of Kaduna, Peter Jatau, cautioned Abacha against prolonging himself in power.[79] The Catholic archbishop of Lagos struck a similar chord.[80] The highest ranking Nigerian Anglican Archbishop of the day, Abiodun Adetiloye, voiced similar warning. Tagged by the regime as a "NADECO Bishop;" a euphemism for a political dissident, declared a *persona non grata*, he was incessantly targeted.[81] Primate Theophilus Olabayo of the

Evangelical Church of Yahweh was also critical of Abacha, and called for the release of Chief Abiola from detention.[82]

The Commonwealth Ministerial Action Group (CMAG) also recognized NADECO by inviting its delegation to a July 1997 meeting in London. This move enormously upset Abacha, with his government protesting the planned meeting.[83] The Americans continued to pound Abacha's government, especially his anti-human rights policies.[84] The late Pope John Paul II, during his second visit to Nigeria in March 1998, also called for national reconciliation:

> All Nigerians must work to rid society of everything that offends the dignity of the human person or violates human rights. This means reconciling differences, overcoming ethnic rivalries, and injecting honesty, efficiency into the art of governing.[85] Dear Nigerian Friends, in your own country you are all called to muster your wisdom and expertise in the difficult and urgent task of building a society *that respects all its members* in their dignity, their rights, and their freedoms. This requires an attitude of reconciliation and calls for the Government and citizens of this land to be firmly committed to giving the best of themselves for the good of all. The challenge before you is great, but greater still are your capacity and determination to meet it.[86]

He also pleaded with the regime to release political prisoners.[87] Then-President Clinton, while visiting six African nations, boycotted Nigeria despite mentioning the country consistently in his speeches. He urged the quick dismantling of military rule, release of political prisoners, and speedy democratization, (Agekameh, 28).

Such sentiments lucidly indicated that the Abacha regime was faced with dire crises of identity. The impact of such recognition and activism made Abacha desperate, and thus also extended the outreach of his networks fostering long-distance terrorism across transnational spaces. Both parties, the activist exile and the pro-Abacha groups also employed similar, yet distinctive patterns of agitation within the market of information and opinion exchanges, in their various attempts to capture the audience for their side. The pro-democratic group within this exchange utilized more refined and fine-tuned methods of confrontation. This observation, I confess, might not be defined as objective given that it is nuanced by my own subjective interpretations of reality, and predicated upon my "soft biases" due to my personal and class preferences and anti-oppressive social stance.[88]

The pro-democratic exiled activists fine-tuned their morally sound strategy, in furthering their agenda by sanctioning the logic of nurturing non-violent and democratic agitation. They utilized civilized norms of rhetoric, persuasive campaigns, political lobbying, lecture circuits, publications, and the global and local media, including their own radio and publication, as a form of symbolic anti-regime violence. For instance, the exiled political activists rattled the Abacha regime, following an insinuation of their desire to form a parliament in-exile, as a pressurizing tool against his dictatorship.[89]

The success of the global campaign waged by Wole Soyinka and NADECO-abroad shocked Abacha, making him perpetual jittery. Unable to curtail the proficient and effective tactics of the pro-democratic exiles, Abacha utilized different strategies at the international level. Failing to stampede the opposition and dazed by their successful activities, Abacha also changed tactics, and employed amorphous groups. Such groups are represented by the Committee of Patriots based in the United Kingdom, who engaged in smear campaigns attacking the moral integrity of prominent members of the opposition through printed literature.[90] Certain Nigerian diplomats in western countries, considered as "soft" to the opposition were also jilted by Abacha, and released from their jobs.[91] The Abacha regime also employed prominent Nigerian politicians, such as Chiefs Odumegwu Ojukwu, Anthony Anenih, Paul Unongo, Tom Ikimi, and Abiola Ogundokun, to cast off the regime's pejorative image abroad, and to lobby foreign, especially western governments, with the goal of acquiring positive acceptance. However, such delegations did not often meet with great success.[92]

Abacha jolted into action, fervently seeking the professional expertise of international lobbyist groups to salvage his regime's image by countering the efficient campaigns of the opposition. In attempting to gloss his image, Abacha reached out to certain segments of the American population, like Louis Farrakhan, of the Nation of Islam, and Senator Carol Moseley-Braun, whose previous public rhetoric suggested their support for African dictatorship, (Wilcox, "Battle for Washington," 13–17). Such stances induced a bellicose reaction against the vacillating and ambivalent perspectives of prominent African-American leaders dealing with African dictatorships.[93] In this fight, even the oil multinationals, like Mobil and Shell operating in Nigeria, took the regime's side, (Wilcox, US Plots to Invade and Battle for Washington; Olaniyan, 50–63). Herein was introduced one of the most important discursive productions of the exiled group and its allied interest groups in Nigeria.

Raising the issue of nationalism against the constitutive elements of Nigeria as shaped prior to, and as an outcome of colonialism, is a vital intellectual contribution toward accessing other allied issues related to the structural deficiency of its current constitution, as well as issues of social justice.[94] In fact, the exiled opposition nurtured the idea of the repatriation and reconciliation in the post-Abacha era.[95] Therefore, the eventual President Obasanjo's establishment of a handicapped similitude, the so-called Truth and Reconciliation Panel led by Justice Oputa, can be located within the ideas primed by the exiled pro-democrats. The pro-democrat movement led by Soyinka raised the bar on these critical rational frontiers as raised in his two books focusing on the Nigerian crises, (Soyinka, 1999 and 2000). Fundamental to these discussions is the relationship of the dictatorship and the ruling military class to the identity of the nation. Soyinka notes this relationship as non-extant: "Under a dictatorship, a nation ceases to exist. All that remains is a fiefdom, a planet of slaves regimented by aliens from outer space," (Soyinka, 1997, 158). Apparently, given the falsity of the foundational premise upon which the dictatorship hinged its claims of authority, it reveals the nature of its rhetoric as virulently self-serving and inordinately instinctual, within its illusory preoccupation with power and the accumulation of loot:

> Babaginda's love of power was visualized in actual terms: power over Nigeria, over the nation's impressive size, its potential, over the nation's powerful status (despite serious image blemishes) within the community of nations. The potency of Nigeria, in short, was an augmentation of his own sense of personal power. It corrupted him thoroughly, and all the more disastrously because he had come to identify Nigeria and her resources with his own person and personal wealth.
>
> Not so Abacha. Abacha is prepared to reduce Nigeria to rubble as long as he survives to preside over a name- and Abacha is a survivor. He has proved that repeatedly, even in his internal contests with Babangida. Totally lacking in vision, in perspectives, he is a mole trapped in a warren of tunnels . . . he charges to destroy every animate or inanimate object within the path of the vanished beam. Abacha is incapable of the faculty of defining that intrusive light, not even to consider if the light path could actually lead him out of the mindless maze.
>
> Abacha has no idea of Nigeria. Beyond the reality of a fiefdom that has dutifully nursed his insatiable greed and transformed him into a creature of enormous wealth, and now of power, Abacha has no notion of Nigeria. (Soyinka, 1997, 14–15)

The predatory class is incapable, as a result of its habitus, of far-sighted critical reflection. It is limited in its ability to transcend its immediate short-sighted purview in reflexive engagement with itself that would lead to social transformation. The dictatorial and praetorian class cannot look itself in the mirror. It would help to remind it of its despicable ugliness. Therefore, negating insightful reflections, social transformation and social structures become stunted. Thus, as already averred with reference to Gramscian principles, the dictatorship class appropriates the task of such reflexive engagement to its collaborating intellectual class.

However, these intellectuals are also caught up with the logic of dictatorship, which privileges arbitrary, irrational, and illogical arguments. Thus, even with the best of intentions, the dictator's intellectuals, perceptively captivated by dynamics of the subsistence, sustenance and relevance of its class, fake their intellectual production, confronted by the threatening logic and gimmicks of dictatorship. These intellectual allies of dictatorships are often an entrapped species, defined by the dynamics of the dictatorship's factual ignorance and demented megalomania and its demand for their utilization and production. Occupying a contradictory habitus, they relegate ethical considerations to the back burner, and thus crassly limit the visionary and perceptive thinking that would enable the dictatorship to transcend its limitations and favor true human development. Impulsive amoral preoccupations with the issue of survival and continuous self-relevance limit their capability for fervent rationalization and critical insights necessary for the development of society. This limitation hinders their transcendental ability to produce far-sighted insights and blueprints of adaptable changes that would rectify dictatorship, and vivify society.

Outright ignorance defines both the relationship between the intellectuals and the dictator, and the arbitrary and contradictory reifications that constitute the schemes of their intellectual production. Hence, through the reification of inappropriate and deceptive episteme, crucial toward nurturing true human development, society becomes stuck, as various degrees of scheming and falsehood predominate. The reasons motivating the sloppy intellectual production and deceptive rationalized schemes inhere within the critical drivers and assessments that grant relevance to these intellectuals within the dictatorial court.

Therefore, most intellectuals allied with dictatorship become royal court jesters and sycophantic voices, who, traumatized by their *a priori* context, fervently seek to transcend the limitations of past social irrelevance. Afraid of a reversion to their former state, they want to ensure their existential opulence and survival at all cost by perpetuating the dictatorship. Therefore, such allied intellectuals embody an infantile state of absolute dependency. Absorbed within the processes of self-perpetuation and survival they induce the symbiotic perpetuation of the ecology of dictatorship, in favor of their own class niche, elongated class utility, and existential relevance. Intellectuals allied to the military thus often indulge dubious protective schemes, as insulation against their dislodgement and even physical annihilation. Immersed in the participatory politics of their hierarchical niche, these intellectuals hardly produce refracted or substantial policies that would credibly sanction their potent capabilities, or that would favor cogent social transformations. Thus, both the praetorian class and its allied intellectuals relate within a cybernetic framework that promotes the synergistic production of mass deceit.

Essentially their production for and on behalf of the state is grounded in a field of deceptive logic that synonymously and simultaneously produces fraudulent political, social, and economic schemes. Hence, the repression of ethical principles, motivated by morbid fear of loss of class position and privileges, including personal damage or annihilation, motivates the allied intellectual class toward overt cautiousness in their social relationships and intellectual productions. This reality, true of the Abacha era, can be glimpsed from an inner reading of the cautious soft-treading and silences of cabinet members against the inherently deformed character of Abacha's regime. This scenery explains the limitations of the military and its intellectual class reasonably to resolve Nigeria's plethora of social problems.

CONCLUSION

In the Abacha era, exiled Nigerians were producers of meaning and creative social action, who took sacrificial risks on behalf of their fellow country men and women. In some senses, they were heroes, though such qualitative tagging would overall depend on a multiplicity of factors, mainly grounded in ethical considerations that may or may not be purely measured based solely upon the exilic context, but also on other sets of *a priori* pre-exilic ethical and social relationships and considerations. However, within the context of their moral audacity, their efforts to create a grounded Nigerian political democratic culture is worthy of commendation, within the synchronic freezing of their exilic pro-democratic risk-taking.

As reflexive actors, they pilloried their grounded understanding of the cultural norms that shaped Nigeria's *a priori* nationalist struggles and anti-imperialist resistance. Thus, in spite of the military appearing extrinsically as a Nigerian entity, its actions, proving otherwise as a repressive imperialist agency, necessitated the application of a resistance ethos that excited previous Nigerian anti- imperialists. This fact has been remarkably noted by different observers of the Nigerian military psychology and operations, (Ojukwu, 32; Lugard, 577; Miners, 29–44). However, one of the paradoxical ironies of history is that some of the same metropolises that anchored these pro-democratic exiles and their resistances were the same spaces where Nigerian nationalists began their agitation against colonial rule and imperialist dispositions. This time, it was a fight for a new form of national liberation from the tentacles of self-inflicted political death.

Since May 1999, Nigeria has made a significant though still troubled progression toward democracy. Different features of the present democratic arrangement continue to replicate certain elements of the Abacha era. These include the integration of certain nefarious military elements previously active in the Abacha fragmentation process, within the current processes of governance, without justice and sanction. Within this transformation, some former military officers who hijacked the political machinery in the pursuit of dictatorship are sadly still visible actors in the current democratic process. While national reconciliation and healing was sought in the post-Abacha era, the dismissive disregard for justice has continued to truncate viable national progress. Their antecedents would be used to support heuristic corrupt exercises by others. In spite of these, significant progress has been achieved.

The militarization of the Nigerian psyche is not fully over. In April 2003, the political space and positions were clogged by erstwhile military officers, intent upon once again hijacking the political process and machinery. Almost all of the presidential candidates of most political parties were pro-active erstwhile military officers, who in the past during military rule predominated national politics, as serving officers.[96]

The People's Democratic Party (PDP) presented General Obasanjo, a retired general and erstwhile Military Head of State, the All Nigerian People's Party (ANPP) presented former Head of State General Muhammed Buhari, and the All Progressive Grand Alliance (APGA) presented General Ojukwu, the erstwhile Biafran leader, as its own presidential candidate. In recent times, this militarization has become more refracted, as demonstrated by the current chair of the ruling PDP, Col (Chief) Ahmadu Ada Ali, a physician who was a former Military Federal Commissioner. However, to his credit, since 1979 he has been actively involved in politics as a tripartite elected senator, as elected member of the Abacha Constitutional Conference (1994–1995), and most recently as an appointed government nominee (elder) to the National Political Reform Conference (NPRC) (2005). General Babangida continues in his frantic efforts to reclaim relevance—this time through the ballot box, which in his distrusting actions, he diminished with his bullets in 1993.

The present political current in Nigeria is centered upon the saliently despicable looming campaign to alter the constitutional provisions, to enable President Obasanjo to prolong his second term. Thus, rather than winding down his current second term, he nurtures the diabolical idea of accreting another five year term. At the moment, different opposing voices are being silenced, and the political coast is clearing as different actors, mainly corrupt politicians and specifically the state governors and Federal legislators, beneficiaries of government financial largesse, endorse this manipulative scheme. Like the Babangida and Abacha's attempts, the same trends of self-serving sycophants and tactics of evil political machinations are being reinvented. Thus, the military habitus, embedded within its history of imperialist urges of annihilation, continues to manifest itself as a culture of death, directed by serving and retired military officers, thus vetting the truism in the Nigeria saying, *"old soldiers never die."* This fact is instructive given that General Obasanjo during the June 12th crises allied with Abacha, hell-bent upon safeguarding the military from being disgraced out of power.

Many Nigerians are currently not taking such claims seriously. However, Nigeria's recent experience indicates the truism in the statement, *"there is no smoke without fire."* The Babangida and Abacha self-succession schemes all began as rumors to which little attention was paid until after such plans were put into practice. Therefore, the recent military experiences of deception now alert Nigerians to a dangerous air whirling across the land. The culture of Nigerian resistance, which the Abacha exiles reinforced, should thus begin to arouse Nigerians from their collective amnesia, toward soliciting a ritual of ecological purification and purgation of the political niche, within the nocturnal outcry that characterized the end of the Abacha assault. This is significant, because in spite of consistent denial, history has proven many of those rumors true, including those of the sickening Abacha killer-squads, persistently denied at the time by that regime.

Though Nigeria currently operates under a semblance of democracy, the structural qualities of its democratic arrangement remain overtly militant and contradictory, latently undergirded by structures and schemes of repression and corrupt machination. Through such manifest logic, the military class continually attempts to remain in power, under different disguises. Apparently, this becomes the undoing of their heuristic hegemonic interests, as they ensure the emergence of new "armies" of democracy. Dictatorship propels, often unconsciously, the production of different autonomous logics, albeit differently defined in degrees and modulated by their respective claims of engagement, spheres of interest, and strategic pursuits of action.

Sad as this whole specter seems, there are positive historical lessons that emerged. One of these is the accentuation of the Nigerian culture of social movements of resistance and pro-active social activism, which provided a significant template toward countering despicable acts of tyranny and mass betrayal. The various sacrificial exilic experiences borne by pro-democratic activists during the Abacha era, richly conditioned the atmosphere that motivated the march toward democratic rule following Abacha's demise. This modern form of nationalist agitation, though reflecting as habitus of previous resistances, offers a new habitus whose referential contents would be valuable for future Nigerian counter-hegemonic oppositional stances, against political tendencies of arbitrary and despotic domination. Therefore, this historical trajectory manifests the spirited efforts that nurtured a political matrix and oppositional consensus that fought the Abacha despotism and his irrational and illegal attempts to manipulate Nigerians.

In this sense, the interspatial activism of these exiles had soteriological value for the identity of Nigeria, and its on-going attempts at self-definition. The very fact of the centering of the activism of exile around the political entity called Nigeria shows that in spite of their questioning of its elemental qualities and definition, there has been an acceptance of its reality as defined by alien forces. Therefore, while it is true that internally other local Nigerian activists were frantically also working against military rule, historical reversals again allowed the western space to function in the discourse of Nigeria's heuristic definition, as it did in the past, through the Colonial Office and the various London conferences. Such perspectives also vitally indicate the shared acceptance of the cultural embeddings that have, over the years, structurally defined Nigerian culture and social identity, even as signified by the unified opposition to the Abacha regime by individuals and groups that share differing political ideologies.

Nigerians, in exile despite the raging salience of ethnicity and different political stances, came together to work for a common Nigerian cause. In spite of the flaring of differences and pursuit of divergent agendas (Soyinka, 2006, 398–413), it proved the alluring fact that, in spite of all situations, Nigerians share a common sentiment regarding their nation. This sentimental preoccupation that articulates nationalism, references the identity of Nigeria, which, in spite of being a colonial creation, is somewhat accepted as a reality by the exiled anti-dictatorship opposition. The idea of Nigeria offers a common denominator for all cultural configurations, as various personalities from different geospatial niches colluded into a concentric entity toward assessing the issues of Nigeria, through pitched agitation on behalf of the revitalization of their nation. Drawing from the same cultural pool, they accessed *a priori* cultural repertoires, especially those of past nationalist movements, to define themselves and to vent their agitation. Therefore, a common Nigerian template served as a cultural referent for social action. Further, even the Nigerian military, in spite of its defective defining origin as an imperialist force, and its later malevolent scheming, constituted a part of the Nigerian phenomenon. In this way, culture was vital to the understanding of the events that produced the exilic situations in the first place.

NOTES

1. Jean and John Comaroff, *The Ethnographic and Historical Imagination*, (Chicago: University of Chicago Press, 1995), 10–11.
2. Michael Crowder, *A Short History of Nigeria*, (New York; Praeger, 1973). On Kosoko deposition see 150; Nana Olomo, 200; on Ovenramwen, 202–203; on King Pepple, see K.Onwuka Dika, *Trade and Politics in the Niger Delta, 1830–1885*, (Oxford: Oxford University Press, 1962), 142–143; Obaro Ikime, "Nigeria-Ebrohimi" book chapter in Michael Crowder (ed.). *West African Resistance: The Military Response to Colonial Occupation*, (London,, UK: Hutchinson and Co. Ltd., 1971), 205–232; Obaro Ikime, *The Fall of Nigeria*, (London: Heinemann, 1977).
3. Basil Davidson, *The African Slave Trade: A Revise and Expanded Edition*, (Boston, MA: Little, Brown, and Company [Back Bay Books], 1980), 260; P. Amaury Talbot, *The People of Southern Nigeria: Historical Notes, [Volume 1]*, (London: Frank Cass, 1969), 211–213; K. Onwuka Dike, 1962.
4. Captain H. D. Trotter, William Allen, and T. R. H. Thomson, *A Narrative of the Expedition Sent by Her Majesty's Government to the River Niger in 1841*, (Volume 1). (London: Frank Cass, 1968), 287–288.
5. James Frederick Schon (Rev.) and Samuel Crowther (Mr.), *Journals of the Rev. James Frederick Schon and Mr. Samuel Crowther [Accompanying the Expedition up the Niger in 1841]*. (London: Frank Cass, 1970), 85–87.
6. Urs Bitterli, *Cultures in Conflict: Encounters Between European and Non-European Cultures, 1492–1800*, (Stanford, CA: Stanford University Press, 2002 [1986]), 22–23. Bitterli makes similar point, noting that while the initial contacts between Europeans and non-Europeans are normally peaceful and decorous, it later acquires a turbulent dimension with the aim of stamping their finality of domination and authority upon the encountered people.
7. The term "power elite" is sometimes referred to the notion of "ruling class." On this distinction or parallel usage see C. Wright Mills, *The Power Elite*, (New York: Oxford University Press, 1969.), 277.
8. [Chief] Anthony Enahoro, *Fugitive Offender: An Autobiography*, (London: Cassell, 1965), 205–246; Richarld L. Sklar, "Nigerian Politics: The Ordeal of Chief Awolowo, 1960–65," book chapter in Toyin Falola (ed.), *African Politics in Post-Imperial Times: The Essays of Richard L. Sklar* (Trenton, NJ: Africa World Press, 2002), 305; Lateef Jakande, *The Trial of Chief Obafemi Awolowo*, London: Heinmann, 1966.

9. Emeka Odumekwu-Ojukwu, *Because I am Involved*, (Ibadan, Nigeria: Spectrum Books Limited, 2003 [1989]).

10. Nats Agbo, "Cages Again," *Newswatch*, April 28 (1997): 12.

11. Kayode Soyinka, "Diplomatic Baggage; MOSSAD and Nigeria: The Dikko Story," *Newswatch*, February 6 (1995): 36–40.

12. Anietie Usen, "The Treason Trial," *Newswatch* June 4 (1990): 217–1

13. Oscar Iguisi, "'I Won't Die in Jail'-Abiola," *The Winner*, June 21 (1995):3.

14. Oma Djebah, "NADECO Misled My Father-Kola Abiola," *ThisDay News* (Online.com), July 13 (2003).

15. Seye Kehinde, "The Fear of Abacha," *The News* [Nigerian Newsmagazine], June 2 (1996): 9–11.

16. Joseph Ode, "In? Out?" *Newswatch* September 23 (1996): 12–21,

17. Dare Babarinsa, "Behold, His Military Majesty" *Tell*, October 7 (1996):12.

18. Such was the case of Alhaji Ismail Isa Funtua a second republic junior minister and then publisher of the *Democrats* newspaper, prior to being charged at the Failed Contracts and Parastatals Tribunal, he fled to London. See Demola Abibomye, "On the Run," *The New*, March 31 (1997): 20.

19. "Hope Betrayed: Interview with General David Mark," *Newswatch* [Nigerian News Magazine], April 11, 1994. Later renditions by military officers intimately involved and informed within the processes that produced General Abacha seem to counteract General David Mark's assumption that he was targeted for being a "Babangida Boy." Rather, such accounts note the active role played by General Mark in the attempt to co-opt the support of different military actors to wrestle power from Babangida, whom some of these military elements saw as vacillating toward handing power to Chief Abiola, whom some of them in turn despise absolutely. Therefore, it is sound to assume that General Mark and others were consumed by the same military cliques with whom he was initially allied, within the pervading atmosphere of crude intrigues that characterized the military, with different officers outplaying one another in the interplays that aimed at grabbing raw power, and in that aspect granulating the Nigerian nation and people. This interpretation derives mainly from my reading of different *a posteriori* accounts following the death of the dictator Abacha by some engaged inner operatives and military actors. See, Lawan Gwadabe, "The Genesis of My Ordeal: The Prison Notes of Lawan Gwadabe," *The News*, September 21 (1998): 17–25; Abubakar Umar, "Vagabond in Power: The Story of Abacha's Coup against Babangida, Shonekan, and Abiola, *Tell*, August 10 (1998): 14–28.

20. Ebenezer Babatope, *The Abacha Years: What Went Wrong?* (Ikeja, Lagos, Nigeria: Ebino Topsy Publishers [CSS Limited], 2000), 18

21. Wole Soyinka, *You Must Set Forth at Dawn: A Memoir*, (New York: Random House, 2006), 452.

22. Uche Maduemesi, "A Bomb for the General," *Tell*, May 13 (1996): 26–27; Soji Akinrinade, "Interview with [General] Alani Akirinade: Our New Battleground," *Newswatch*, January 31 (2000):8–21;

23. This dynamic is given a cogent analytical and grounded treatment in Arthur Nwankwo, *African Dictators: The Logic of Tyranny and Lessons*

from History (Enugu, Nigeria: Fourth Dimension Publishers, 1990). Page 21 specifically marks this aspect of self-serving deception and manipulation although the entire breadth of the book- each line, sentences, and page reference such behaviors among dictators.

24. Ade Olorunfemi, "Red Card for NADECO," *Tell,* January 13 (1997): 21–22. In a recently published book, released after this chapter was first written- presented at the March 2006 conference at the University of Texas at Austin- Wole Soyinka provides vivid and detailed chronicles of these events, his pro-active stance as an opposition icon, and the exiled oppositional activisms which favored varying forms of international lobbying, national civil disobedience, and the possibility of armed struggle. See Part VII- Nation and Exile in' Wole Soyinka, *You Must Set Forth at Dawn: A Memoir,* (New York: Random House, 2006), 344–644.

25. One such advertiser's announcement of his is entitled: "The Link with the Past: The Quest for Nigerian "Unity in Diversity" Statement by A.O. Rewane, published in the *Nigerian Tribune,* in three full pages. Ironically within the same newspaper and directly opposite one of Chief Rewane's paid ad is a feature article edited by Paul Wale Ademowo and Bayo Alade, entitled "The Scourge of Hired Assassins: Five Thousand Naira for a Life," *Nigerian Tribune,* Thursday June 29, (1995): VT 1–2, which would relate to the later fate of Chief Rewane, who would be coldly murdered by the instruments his tax helped procure, given that, as we would later become aware, this amoral act was carried out by security agents and military personnel of the Nigerian State and monitored from Abuja—Abacha's centre of government. One naturally would be tempted to wonder whether such an occurrence was a chance coincidence or whether it was a coded and symbolic warning to Chief Rewane that couldn't be passed directly.

26. Ayodele Akinkuotu, "The General's Hatchet Men," *Tell,* January (1997): 10–16; Mike Akpan, "Who Speaks for the North?" *Newswatch* [Nigerian Newsmagazine], April 13 (1998): 8–15.

27. Victory Omuabor, "Uneasy Search for Freedom," *Tell,* March 4 (1996): 16–18.

28. Dayo Ajigbotosho, "New Arrow from NADECO's Quiver," *Tell,* June 10 (1996): 6.

29. John Okafor, "Battles of the Airwaves," *Tell,* June 10 (1996): 31; Wole Soyinka, *You Must Set Forth at Dawn,* 2006, 384, 401, 407, 452–53.

30. Ayo Olukotun, "Traditional Protest Media and Anti-Military Struggle in Nigeria 1988–1999," *African Affairs* 101 (2002): 193–211.

31. Kole Ahmed Shetimma, "Nigerian Pro-Democracy Movements in the Diaspora," Paper pared for the Diaspora Panel at the ISA Conference, Washington, D.C., February 1999; http://www2.hawaii.edu/~fredr/shet. html=NADEC; Wole Soyinka, 2006, 398.

32. Ade Olorunfemwa, "Abacha's Most Wanted Man," *Tell,* March 4 (1996): 8–12; "Wole Soyinka Tells His Exile Story," Pan-African News Wire, October 18, 1998; Soyinka, 2006, 385–86.

33. Ade Olorunfewa, "Escape from the Gulag," *Tell,* May 13 (1996): 10–14.

34. [Chief] Anthony Enahoro, *Fugitive Offender: An Autobiography*, (London: Cassell, 1965), 205–246.

35. Wole Adeyemo, "Swelling the Ranks of Exile," *Tell*, June 17 (1996): 22.

36. Ahamefula Ogbu and Lilian Okenwa, "Kuforiji-Olubi Advised IBB to Annul June 12 Election-Counsel," December 10 (2001) available at http://www.thisdayonline.com/news/20011012news13.htm; Sola Shittu, "Secret Document Exposes Yoruba Betrayal of MKO," Daily Independent Online, October 03 (2003)- http://www.dailyindependentng.com/dailyindependent/news/nnoct030301.html; Wale Akin Aina, "An Exercise in Futility: Bringing the Various Yoruba Groups Together is Still a Tall Order," *Newswatch*, March 13 (1995): 18–19; Theophilus Olabayo [Primate] (Interviewer-Kehinde Bemighetan), 1995, Interview: "Abiola Must Not Die," *The Week*, June 19:30–31.

37. Dare Babarinsa, "Abacha's Menacing Seriki," *Tell*, October 9 (1995): 7; Soyinka, 2006, 445–446.

38. Adeolu Adeyemo, "Interview with Alhaji Lamidi Aribiyi Adedibu: 'I will Support Abacha,'" *The News*, March 31 (1997): 18–19.

39. See, Lawan Gwadabe, "The Genesis of My Ordeal: The Prison Notes of Lawan Gwadabe," *The News*, September 21 (1998): 17–25; Abubakar Umar, "Vagabond in Power: The Story of Abacha's Coup against Babangida, Shonekan, and Abiola, *Tell*, August 10 (1998): 14–28.

40. Yar'Adua's death was associated with illness in almost all the media accounts, but no one is sure what it is that killed him. Ade Olorunfewa, "Death in Abacha's Gulag," *Tell*, December 22 (1997): 12–17; Anietie Usen, "Death of an Icon," *Newswatch*, December 22 (1997): 8–21. This point is make alluringly in an interview granted by the incumbent Nigerian Vice President, Alhaji Abubakar Atiku, "No Threat to Nigeria," *Newswatch*, March 27, 2000: 12. Other accounts have similarly insinuated the same possibility that General Yar'Adua was wasted after being injected presumably with the AIDS virus by then army physician, Lt. Col (Dr.) Yankassai, the Nigerian Dr. Death. See accounts in Dotun Adekanmbi, "The Death Doctor," *The News*, September 28 (1998): 14–17. It is apparent that General Yar'Adua was poisoned, and indicators pointed to having being injected with the AIDS virus; also Soyinka, 2006, 383–84.

41. Jonah Achema, "Not Out of the Woods," *Newswatch*, September 9 (1996): 22.

42. Karl Maeir, *This House Has Fallen: Midnight in Nigeria*, (New York: Public Affairs, 2000), 157–59.

Ima Niboro, "The General Hangs Tough," *Tell*. October 9 (1995): 14; Ademola Adedoyin, "Who Wants Dasuki's Throne?" *The Week*, March 25 (1996): 10–15; Ayodele Akinkuotu, "Fall of a Sultan," *Tell*, May 6 (1996): 12–20; Aminu Tijani, "Fresh Travails of the Dasuki Clan," *Tell*, May 18 (1998): 24.

43. Edward Said, *Representation of the Intellectual*, (New York: Vintage Books [Random House], 1998), 47.

44. Prebendalism as used here reflects somewhat a derivation from Max Weber's usage within the terms of patrimonial dominations that utilizes

a patron-client relationship in which patrons disburse favors and material resources freely to specific clients, either due to their social status, kinship relationship, and political inducement intended toward ensuring balanced reciprocity of present and future favors. In Nigeria, terms such as "settlement" vividly describes this relationship, where leaders typically bride individuals and groups, especially members of the same class, political organization, traditional chieftains, military cohorts in furthering favors and ensuring loyalty in return. Weber states: "We wish to speak of "prebends" and of a 'prebendal' organization of office, wherever the lord assigns to the official rent payments for life, payments which are somehow fixed to objects or which are essentially economic usufruct from lands or other sources. They must be compensations for the fulfillment of actual or fictitious office duties; they are goods permanently set aside for the economic assurance of the office" (H. H. Gerth and C. Wright Mills, 1958, *From Max Weber: Essays in Sociology,* (New York: Oxford University Press, 1958), 207). Derived from this Weberian ideal is the context in which within the operations of the Nigerian state, government leaders and officials offer economic and material inducements to clients under obligations to be reciprocal in their loyalty to the patrons (often the hegemonic leaders of the Nigerian modern state). In fact, even more than prebendalism, Nigeria has been perceived as accentuating predation within its political economic order that locates its national economic decline (see Peter Lewis, "From Prebendalism to Predation: The Political Economy of Decline in Nigeria," *Journal of Modern African Studies* 34(1) (1996): 79–103).

45. Olayinka Oyegbile, "The Stew and Juice Parable," *Third Eye Daily* [Nigerian Newspaper], May 12 (1995):9.

46. Ray Ekpu, "Man of the Year: Frankenstein's Monster," *Newswatch,* January 15 (1996): 21, also See Anthony Agbali, "Politics, Rhetoric, and Ritual of the Ogoni Movement," book chapter in Toyin Falola (ed.), *Nigeria in the Twentieth Century,* (Durham, NC: Carolina Academic Press, 2002), 524, 530–31. Witchcraft, as it is noted among many African ethnic groups, is a malevolent spiritual force that engages in spiritual cannibalism, and they also in this mysterious form engage in the phrase "vulgar vulturized," which derives from the name of the eagle-like vulture bird found in most parts of West Africa, notably detested by most within the cultural and popular imagination within the observed depiction of its cannibalistic tendencies in devouring its dead peer, an activity regarded as "dirty," "noxious" and "despicable." Hence, the vulture becomes here an antithesis of culture. Further, even when fighting their brutal usage of their beaks against each other can have lethal effects. The Ogoni of Nigeria used this term to refer to Shell in their environmental agitations against the International Multinational and the Nigerian government. In the same manner, dogs' fighting among themselves manifests similar brutality, leaving deep and traumatizing wounds.

47. Wale Akin Aina, "Making Matters Worse," *Newswatch,* March 13: 26 (1995); Obiora Nwosisi, "Hitting Back," *The News,* March 11 (1996): 12–16.

48. Franlin Oyekusibe Ogo, "Graffiti" *Tell,* May 6 (1996): 8
49. Abraham Useh, "Generals at War," *Tell* [Newsmagazine], June 10 (1996): 8–14; Odia Ofeimun, "The Jungle and the Rumble," *The News,* July 29 (1996): 13–16; Obiorah Nwosisi, "The Grand Deception, "*The News,* July 29: 16–21 (1996).
50. Obasanjo was initially detained but released following pressure upon General Abacha both from within and outside Nigeria- cf. Chukwuemeka Gahia, "Free in Chains," *Newswatch* April 3, (1995): 10–13. Later, together with his former deputy, General Yar'adua, General Obasanjo was rearrested and court-martialed—see Sam Olukoya, "Now, in the Dock?" *Newswatch,* July 3 (1995): 10–14; Generals Oladipo Diya, Abacha's deputy, and senior officers in Abacha's government such as Major Generals Tajudeeen Olarenwaju, Abdulkarim Adisa, Major Olusegun Fadipe, and Adebola Adebayo were arraigned and sentenced to death by firing squad—see Mike Akpan and Dotun Oladipo, "Facing the Firing Squad," *Newswatch,* May 11 (1998): 8–18
51. Maeir, 157–59; Ima Niboro, "The General Hangs Tough," *Tell.* October 9 (1995): 14; Adedoyin, 10–15; Ayodele Akinkuotu, "Fall of a Sultan," 12–20.
52. Abraham Useh, "Generals at War," *Tell* [Newsmagazine], June 10 (1996): 8–14; Odia Ofeimun, "The Jungle and the Rumble," *The News,* July 29 (1996): 13–16; Obiorah Nwosisi, "The Grand Deception, "*The News,* July 29: 16–21.
53. Dare Babarinsa, "Behold, His Military Majesty," *Tell,* October 7, 1996: 12–13; Tunji Adeyemi, "How Abacha Watched Saro-Wiwa's Hanging," *Post Express* [Nigerian newspaper online edition], April 19 (2000); Mustapha Ogunsakin, "Komo Supervised Hanging of Ken Saro-Wiwa, says Witness," *The Guardian Online,* January 30 (2001)- http://ngrguardiannews.co.
54. Antonio Gramsci, *Selections from the Prison Notebooks,* (New York: International Publishers, 1973), 10–14; Said, 1996, 52.
55. Abdulazeez Ude, "The Nation as a Huge Army Cantonment," *Tell,* December 14 (1992):38
56. Wole Soyinka, *The Man Died,* (New York: Harper and Rows, 1972), 39.
57. Michel Foucault, *Discipline and Punish: The Birth of the Prison,* (New York: Vintage Books, 1995 [1977]), 49.
58. My reasoning has been supportively reinforced by Professor Wole Soyinka in his recently released memoir, *You Must Set Forth at Dawn,* which came out after I already made this point. Noting the roles of Chief Abiola Ogundokum and Major R.O.A. Salawu within Abacha's mechanism of state-subversive-madness, we see how dispossessed intellectuals can acquire potency within the perimeter of dictatorial rule. See Soyinka, 2006, 412–18.
59. Antonio Gramsci, *Selections from the Prison Notebooks,* (New York: International Publishers, 1999 [1971]), 5.
60. cf. Anthony Giddens, *The Nation-State and Violence,* (Berkeley, CA: University of California Press, 1987), 303.
61. Max Weber, *Economy and Society,* (Los Angeles, CA: University of California Press, 1978), 1160.

62. Claude Ake, "The State in Contemporary Africa," in Claude Ake, ed., *Political Economy in Nigeria*, (London, UK: Longman, 1985), 1–8; Claude Ake, *A Political Economy of Africa*, (England: Longman, 1981), 126; hereafter cited in text as Contemporary Africa

63. Claude Ake, "The Nigerian State: Antimonies of a Periphery Formation," in Claude Ake, ed., *Political Economy in Nigeria*, (London, UK: Longman, 1985), 9–32; hereafter cited in text as The Nigerian State.

64. N. J. Miners, *Nigerian Army 1956–1966,* (London: Methuen, 1971), 29.

65. Frantz Fanon, *The Wretched of the Earth: The Handbook for the Black Revolution that is Changing the Shape of the World*, (New York: Grove Weidenfeld, 1991 [1963]), 38; Ali Mazrui and Donald Rothchild, "The Soldier and the State in East Africa: Some Theoretical Conclusions on the Army Mutinies of 1964," in Ali Mazrui, *Violence and Thought*, (Longdon: Longman, 1969), 3–23.

66. Lord [Frederick] Lugard, *The Dual Mandate in British Tropical Africa*, (Hamden, CT: Archon Books, 1965), 577.

67. Bala J. Takaya and Sonni Gwanie Tyoden, *The Kadina Mafia: A Study of the Rise, Development, and Consolidation of a Nigerian Power Elite,* (Jos, Nigeria: University Press, 1987).

68. Danielle Knight, "US Oil Giant [Chevron] Admits Role in Nigeria Killings," *Electronic Mail and Guardian,* [South African newspaper online], October 6, 1998 available at http://www.mg.co.za/mg/news/98oct1/6oc-chevron.html; Geoffrey Lean, "Shell 'Paid Nigerian Military," 2000 available at http://wwww.greenpeace.org/'~comms/ken/opay001.html; Associated Press, February 2, 2001, "Shell Acknowleges Arms Purchase"; "Oil Companies Complicit in Nigerian Abuses," Lagos February 23, 1999 available at http://www.hrw.org/hrw/press/1999/febnig0223.html; John Wilcox, "Battle for Washington," *The News,* July 14 (1997): 13–14; hereafter cited in text as Battle for Washington. Years later, a former energy minister and special adviser on Petroleum, Alhaji Rilwanu Lukman, would accuse the oil multinationals of sabotage- see Sanya Adejokun, "Lukman Accuses Multinationals of Sabotage," *Daily Independent Online,* February 25 (2003); Nigerian democratically elected President, and also erstwhile military leader, Olusegun Obasanjo would accuse the foreign oil multinationals as fueling corruption. See Chinwe Maduagwu, "Foreign Firms Fuel Corruption," Daily Champion [Nigerian newspaper online], March 18 (2005). Available at http://odili.net/news/source/2005/mar/18/611.html; also Gbenga Oguntimehin, You are Dishonest, Corrupt, Obasanjo Tell Oil Firms," *Daily Times* [Nigerian Newspaper] March 18 (2004). The American Halliburton Oil firm also recently acknowledged bribing Nigerian officials for about $180 million for award of the construction contract for the Nigerian Liquefied Natural Gas (NLNG) plant in Bonny Island during the decade that Abacha ruled. See Hector Igbikiowubo, "$180m Alleged TSKJ Bribe: Halliburton Filing Indicts Nigerian Officials," *Vanguard* [Nigerian newspaper online], November 9 (2004).

69. This is the song of hope and praise sung in the Christian Bible- New Testament- Luke 2: by a man named Simeon. It connotes the joyful emotional

rendition that points to the finality of purpose. "Now, at last I have seen the end," thus referencing the finality of anticipatory yearning, the fulfillment of nostalgic expectation.

70. Chinua Achebe, *Home and Exile,* (New York: Anchor Books [Random House Inc.], 2000), 81.
71. Edward Said, *Reflections on Exile and other Essays,* (Cambridge, MA: Harvard University Press, 2000), 173.
72. Paulo Freire, *Letters to Christina: Reflections on My Life and Work,* (New York: Routledge, 1996), 7–8.
73. Olorunfemwa, 8–12; "Wole Soyinka Tells His Exile Story," *Pan-African News Wire,* October 18, 1998; Soyinka, 2006, 385–86.
74. Freire, 7; also see Said, 1998, 59.
75. Sam Olukoya, "The Trial," *Newswatch,* June 19 (1995): 10.
76. Tunde Asaju, "A Bloody Week," *Newswatch,* September 30 (1996): 16–17.
77. Tajudeen Suleman, "Activist Priests," *The News,* February 5 (1996): 8.
78. Ima Niboro, "A Time to Go," *Tell,* March 18 (1996): 10–12.
79. Isaac Shobayo, "'Why Abacha Must not Succeed himself,'" *Nigerian Tribune,* May 1 (1997): 1–2.
80. Abiodun Fagbemi, "Moral Rot: Okogie Doubts Govt., Lauds Fela's Crusade," *The Guardian* [Nigerian newspaper], August 8 (1997): 1–2.
81. Abiodun Adetiloye, "Parable of the Evil Shepherd," *Tell,* April 29 (1996): 8–10; Abiodun Adetiloye, "Special Interview: 'I pray for a Bloodless Revolution," *Tell,* April 29 (1996): 11–15.
82. Theophilus Olabayo [Primate], "Interview: 'Abiola Must not Die," *The Week,* June 19 (1996): 30–31.
83. Joel Gure and Churchhill Umoren, "FG Protests C'Wealth [Commonwealth], NADECO Meeting," *The Punch,* July 10 (1997): 1–2.
84. Yinka Oduwole, "US' Stance on Nigeria Confounds Abacha," *The Punch,* July 10 (1997): 1–2; Joel Gure, "I've no Apology-Carrington [US Ambassador to Nigeria]," *The Punch,* July 10 (1997): 1–2.
85. Pope John Paul II, Homily at Holy Mass of Beatification, March 22, 1998 at Oba, Onitsha *Nigeria: Be Reconciled! Exhortation of the Holy Father Pope John Paul II on the Occasion of his Second Visit to Nigeria for the Beatification of Blessed Cyprian Michael Iwene Tansi* (March 21–23, 1998), 14.
86. Pope John Paul II, "Arrival Ceremony Speech, Nnamdi Azikiwe International Airport, Abuja, March 21" in *Nigeria: Be Reconciled! Exhortation of the Holy Father Pope John Paul II on the Occasion of his Second Visit to Nigeria for the Beatification of Blessed Cyprian Michael Iwene Tansi* (March 21–23, 1998), (Lagos, Nigeria: Catholic Secretariat of Nigeria), 7.
87. Dele Agekameh, "Always a Brick wall" *Tell,* April 20 (1998): 28.
88. Carol J. Greenhouse and Davydd J.Greenwood, "Introduction: The Ethnography of Democracy and Differences," in Carol J. Greenhouse (with Roshanal Kheshti), *Democracy and Ethnography: Constructing Identities in Multicultural Liberal States,* (Albany, NY: State University of New York Press, 1998), 1–24.

89. Tayo Ogunlewe, "Democrats in Parliament," *Tell,* July 1 (1996): 21; Wole Soyinka, Interview with Wole Soyinka "Abacha Has Wasted my Generation," *Tell,* July 14 (1999): 8–14; John Oyegun [interviewer-Soji Akirinade], "Interview: "We want a New Nigeria," *Newswatch,* March 2 (1998): 34–38.

90. Dayo Ajigbotosho, "New Arrow from NADECO's Quiver," *Tell,* June 10 (1996): 6; Austin Uganwa, "Smear Campaign," *The News,* July 29 (1996): 22; Soyinka, 2006, 413–18.

91. Ade Olorunfewa, "Abacha's Most Wanted Man," *Tell,* March 4, 1996: 8–9.

92. Soji Akinrinade, "Battle for Foreign Ears," *Newswatch,* July 3 (1995): 15–16; "The Stranded, Ex-Officio Envoys," *Tell,* October 9 (1995): 34; John Wilcox, "US Plots to Invade Nigeria," *The News,* July 14 (1997): 10–12; hereafter cited in text as US Plots to Invade.

93. Keith Richburg, *Out of America: A Black Man Confronts Africa,* (San Diego, CA: A Harvest Book [Harcourt Bruce] 1998), 138–145; Tejumola Olaniyan, "The Return of the Native Son," *Transition* 0 no. 72 (1996): 50–63.

94. Wole Soyinka, *The Open Sore of a Continent,* (New York: Oxford University Press, 1997).

95. Wole Soyinka, *The Burden of Memory, The Muse of Forgiveness,* (New York: Oxford University Press, 2000), 34.

96. Critically, the Nigerian military officers, whether serving or retired, perceive themselves still as members of the armed forces. This fact was revealed when a news magazine reporter, Seun Sonoiki, went to the present Nigerian President, for an interview for a story on retired generals, he was abusively hounded out. He was blatantly told, "I still draw my full salary. I am a full General. Now out. Out you go." See "Temper at 'Temperance,'" The African Guardian [Nigerian news magazine], April 10 (1986): 13. It is in that vein that the present determined efforts by the retired generals must be critically evaluated. The various insinuations that they intend to hold on to power must be met with suspicion and critical resolve, especially by the electorate, in scuttling any devious attempt subtly to dominate lives once more. See Dele Sobowale, 2000, "Military Conspiracy against Civilians: Ex-General to rule till 2050," *Vanguard* [Nigerian Newspaper] Online edition, October 1st available at http://www.vanguardngr.com/01102000/fs108100. html; "Obasanjo is Babangida's Surrogate in Aso Rock- Sunny Okogwu," Daily Independent Online, November 22, 2004 available at http://odili.net/ news/source/2004/nov/22/402.html. In another interview, Okogwu sounds averse to civilian democratic rule, and critical of President Obasanjo, though horning the virtues of military dictatorship, but sounds contradictory, when he averred: "Any time a non-democrat comes to democratize, in the beginning it tastes good, sounds good, but at the end, it is what is referred to in literature as 'full of sound and fury signifying nothing.' Failure all the way." see Ben Agande, 2006, "Sunday Interview: Obasanjo Altered Nigeria's Ruling Pattern-Sunny Okogwu," *Vanguard,* June 11, 2006.

Chapter Four

Immigrants' Pilgrimage and Imaginations: The Cinematic Portrayals of African Immigrants in Movies

Raphael Obotama

This chapter examines the salient discourse on immigration using four very different cinematic representations and taking an in-depth analytical view of how the cinematic genre represents and discourses on issues of immigration. In order to unveil relevant insinuations that under-gird the imagery and discursive depictions significant to an understanding of immigration and spatial mobility, especially from the African cinematic perspective, I have selected certain vignettes for analyzing the trajectory of African immigration. Firstly, I construct my analyses around three movies that deal with immigration from the African continent (*Coming to America, Dirty Pretty Things,* and *The Secret Laughter of Women*), and secondly, I analyze one movie (*Coming to South Africa*) that deals with immigration within the African continent. This comparative approach helps to visualize the cinematic framing of the reality, stereotypes, and popular imagination dealing with the existential realities of African immigration.

THE MOVIES

For the benefit of those who have not seen the movies or as a refresher for those who watched them a long time ago, I provide brief insights into the different movies in the form of synopses.

Coming to America

I must say here right away that the target audience of this movie is not African but American. I picked the movie because the cinematic depictions reflect the trajectory of African immigration. This is a 1988 movie, directed by John Landis and produced by Eddie Murphy. Eddie Murphy plays the African prince, Akeem, the sole heir to the throne of the fictitious Zamunda kingdom. Akeem lives in a lavishly furnished palace and has scores of servants of both sexes waiting on him. Young damsels toss petals of roses at his feet as he walks along. On his 21st birthday, as tradition demands, Akeem meets with his would-be wife, who had been prepared since birth to be his obedient wife. She happens not to meet his taste, not because of her beauty but because his idea of a wife is more than just a romantic partner. After some discussion with his father, he is given a 40-day grace to go out and sow his royal oats.

Akeem and his aide-de-camp, Semmi (Arsenio Hall) set out to New York. On arrival, they are robbed in front of an apartment on Queens street. They get a job in a fast food restaurant, McDowell, where they work incognito. Here he meets and falls in love with Lisa McDowell (Shari Headley), the daughter of the proprietor of the fast food place, and refuses to go back to his parents without her. The movie ends with his return to Africa where he celebrates a high-class wedding with Lisa McDowell.

Dirty Pretty Things

Directed by Stephen Frears and produced by Robert Jones and Tracy Seaward, the movie is set in a hotel in London. The plot deals with an interesting urban legend which is revealed as the plot unfolds. Interestingly too the movie has an all-immigrant cast. The filmmaker brings out the inhuman treatment of illegal immigrants in the hotel. The protagonist, Okwe (Chiwetal Ejiofor), is a Nigerian medical doctor, an illegal immigrant who doubles as a cab driver in the day and a hotel porter at night. Okwe, as he narrates in the movie, left Nigeria because of persecution by the government, because he refused to commit atrocities on their behalf. They set him up, vandalized his house, killed his wife in the process and accused him of the crime, so he fled the country into exile. In the hotel, he lives with his friend Senay (Audrey Tautou), a Turkish immigrant who was admitted conditionally into the United Kingdom. Her immigration status does not permit her to engage in any paid job for at least six months and she is not supposed to rent a space in her room to anybody. She not only takes a job but also shares the room with Okwe in defiance of the law.

In the hotel, Okwe discovers a human heart in the lavatory of one of the guests' rooms which he reports. He is surprised at the reaction of the hotel manager (Sergi Lopez), whose nick-name in the movie is "Sneaky." He later discovers to his chagrin that the hotel manager is running a dirty business, trafficking in human organs, which he removes from the illegal immigrants, and in return, he gives them traveling documents. "Sneaky" tries to recruit him into the business but he refuses. Okwe, who is faced with a moral dilemma, decides to play along with Sneaky. His decision to work for him is not for any of those illegal benefits, but to save lives. He wants to use his expertise to perform a skilled surgery on the donors.

Coming to South Africa

Of the four movies under discussion here, this is the only one that is produced within Africa. This movie is produced by Emmanuel Emeka Okpara, a Nigerian living in South Africa. It is directed by Paul Louwrens. In the movie, Edward (Ramsey Nouah) and Mike (Hakeem Kae-Kazim) set out from Nigeria to visit Chris Ndubuisi, Edward's classmate living in South Africa, who will help them to get jobs. On arrival they discover that Chris has been arrested and is in jail. In their frustration they move around looking for a place to go. In front of a hotel they are manhandled, robbed and left with nothing. They go into a night club where they meet and introduce themselves to one Makelle (Thulani Mengdo). To their delight, he introduces himself also as a Nigerian. He later introduces them to Igwe (Sonke Buthelezi) a drug baron, who recruits them into his business.

Edward, not being so comfortable with this job, quits and gets another job in a parking lot. In a bid to save a lady being attacked in the parking lot by armed robbers, he gets shot. Mike continues with the drug trade and lives a flamboyant lifestyle. The long arm of the law soon catches up with him and he is arrested by the South African police. He is taken to court where he is convicted for drug trafficking and sentenced to 25 years.

The Secret Laughter of Women

This movie is set in France. It was produced by O.O. Sagay and Jon Slan and directed by Peter Schewabach. It portrays a Nigerian community in France as they re-construct and re-enact African identity outside the shores of Africa. They have an African Church where they all worship together in the African rhythm. The principal character is Nimi, played by Nia Long. The community wants her to marry the pastor, the Reverend Fola. She has a son, Sammy (Oluwafisayo Roberts), who is friendly with Matthew (Colins Firth), a comic book author. Sammy's desire, contrary to the wish of the community, is to see his mother married by his friend, Matthew. The community spends time gossiping, while Sammy teaches his friend, Matthew, about traditional African table etiquette. His friend picks up food from the common dish with his left hand and Sammy tells him that using the left hand to eat is neither hygienic nor traditionally sanctioned.

There are some cinematic parallelisms in the movies. Produced at different locations and in different time frames, three outstanding depictions cut across the plots: Robbery, the City of New York, and Inquiries of Intent. In *Coming to America* and *Coming to South Africa*, certain depictions are quite similar. The filmmakers present robbery on arrival. The city of New York comes into display in both *Coming to America* and *Dirty Pretty Things*. In *Coming to South Africa* and *Coming to America*, two ladies pose similar questions to two different characters. Both movies deal with the questioning of intentions through migration and movement. These parallel questions pilot the theme of this chapter as they relate to immigration and immigrant depictions.

The movies are produced trans-continentally but they all pertain to African immigration. This helps us to engage comparatively and discursively on the African immigration evoked in the cinematic mimesis pertaining to the theme. Further, such representations also fuel the whole issue of cinematic constructs of identity, referentially touching on the polemical issue of what constitutes African cinema, in terms of the possibility of whether an African cinema can be defined as such even if produced by non-Africans, or are they those that are produced by Africans-even if, at times, they do not occupy themselves with themes defined as African?

Theoretically, the phenomenon of global immigration also presents critical issues of African cinematic definition. For instance, although *The Secret Laughter of Women* centers on issues within a certain African immigrant community in France, it relates to religion, marriage, child rearing, the struggle for survival, gossip and the re-creation of an African immigrant community, and was produced by a Western director. Does such a movie, capturing and integrating the hybrid context of new immigrants' struggles, remain excluded as not pertaining to African realities? Do the imagery and images that define African immigrant communities non-resident on the African continent sever ties with African identities, even when these same immigrants through their remittances contribute toward the development of the continent and still consider Africa as home? How do the transnational realities frame African identity quintessentially and dynamically? It is a looming question that is also tied to the mode of the definitions of Africans who reside in the West. Are they westerners or Africans, sojourners or settled?

Professor Wole Soyinka addresses these questions with a pack of rhetorical questions. In an essay in *African Culture: Rhythms of Unity*, he asks, "How can we, intelligent beings, submit to self-imprisonment of a "saline consciousness" which insists that, contrary to all historical evidence, Africa stops where the salt water licks its shore? Or that conversely all that is bound by the salt water on the African continent is necessarily African."[1] On the strength the above, therefore, I can say that Africanity is not limited to a geographical space. Movies that have authentic African themes, whether produced within or outside Africa, should be considered African movies. In saying this, I am not losing sight of the movies that were produced by imperialists and detractors to humiliate Africans. Following what Sekou Tall suggests, movies with African themes but with distorted facts are not African. Writing about African cinema, he says, "An authentic African cinema is that where each spectator can recognize himself through the attitudes and behavior of the actors who express the struggles of the individual with himself or with Nature, and in a language that he can understand."[2]

The movies I have selected for analysis here, despite their trans-continental production, share certain immigration themes. African immigrants face some cultural shock in their new host communities. They are no longer the same; hence, this transformation affects their ethical, spiritual and religious values to the extent that they either compromise or reinforce their original beliefs.

MOVIES IN PERSPECTIVE

Two scenes in two of the movies introduce the main issues to the viewer. The first is the scene at a restaurant in *Coming to America,* where Lisa queries Akeem:

> *Lisa:* Why did you come here?
> *Akeem:* To find something special.

The second similar question is at the house of Tessy. In a scene in *Coming to South Africa,* she asks Edward, who claims he has a B.A. in Business Administration:

> *Tessy:* Why did you leave Nigeria and come here?
> *Edward:* It's a long story, a sad and long story.

Edward has made a perfect statement here, "It is a long story." Any type of movement entails a change which comes with a lot of decision making. Sometimes it needs the counsel of others to be able to make a decision. Migration is not an on-the-spot decision. It entails a much longer intellectual process, weighing the ups and downs of such a movement.

Immigrants ask themselves questions, exploring the reasons why they want to leave their homelands, and replay these reasons within themselves in their cognitive operations, and even revisit them in their sleep. Immigrants are also asked questions. Within the modern construction of the nation-state, mainly at the Visa sections of national embassies and consulates, there especially they have to lay themselves bare through questions and answers. Here they must present various documents that interweave individual histories, reasons, and narratives, with national ones such as passports, visas, and other documents that are in-between such as letters of invitation, employment and religious bodies' letters, proper and authentic documents from accredited academic institutions. Within this intermeshing of realities, narratives, and documents, the aspiring immigrant is an in-between personality, whose motive has to be unmasked through the powerful idiom of verbal texts and the genre of questions and answers, determining the definite future of the aspirant—to stay or to go. Yet that is not all. As the immigrants continue on their journeys, all kinds of questions are asked by different people, principally the ones asked by the gate-keeper, the immigration officer, at the entry port. Again, answers are vital and must be deemed appropriate, because even at the port the immigrant can be turned back. Even after immigrants have safely arrived at their destinations, people continue to ask different questions relative to their accents, language skills, appearance, or some instrument of differentiation betraying them as "other." Such questions are constant, and in some cases, may abate after a long while, when the immigrant is deemed to have blended in—but then such questions can still surface intermittently and under unpredictable circumstances.

Therefore, there is a relation between the questions asked of the individual and the self-perception he has in the new place of residence. After all is said and done, the intensity of these questions are defined by the level of the differentiating variations that contrast that the immigrant from his or her new home environment, such as his/her biological outward appearances (phenotype) and social constructs such as language, dressing, hair-style etc. Thus, existentially, the answers to the above question often go beyond the cinematic space as they mimic real life situations that immigrants find themselves, and which they struggle to answer, sometimes elaborately or cryptically, depending on who is seeking the answer. At every turn, they need to wear their consciousness-hat and refine their answers in relation to the same questions asked time and time again within different settings. The immigrant learns how to frame his/her reality using notions and instances that are both real and at times mythical. These questions may look simple on the outside but they can cover a whole range of issues bordering on immigration, which is as old as history itself.

Immigration is an ancient phenomenon as it pertains to humans, ever since the *homo sapiens* became fully developed and walked the face of the earth.[3] Humans and animals, even birds have engaged in mobility from time immemorial in search of sources of survival. They scout different boundaries traversing space and time in their quest for comfort and livelihood. In some places humans settled, making such places their homes and engaging in agriculture and animal husbandry. Migration therefore is, indeed, "a long story."

Today, human migration continues unabated across diverse spaces, still in search of better opportunities or of sanctuaries away from ecological or political turmoil. According to the United Nations, "around 175 million persons currently reside in a country other than where they were born, which is about 3 per cent of world population."[4] The area of immigration studies has become one of the vast arenas of human scholarship, cutting across academic disciplines and areas of interest in anthropology, history, sociology, public policy, political science, medicine, and different existential spheres such as politics, economics, ethics, and others. Given the issues related to immigration, the United Nations General Assembly Article 13 stipulated that, "Everyone has the right to freedom of movement and residence within the borders of each state." In the same vein, it further declares that "Everyone has the right to leave any country, his own and to return to his country."[5] Hence, given the significance of the issues of international migration, the United Nations General Assembly has called upon relevant organizations to address the issue of international migration and development, in order to provide appropriate support for processes and activities.[6]

Migration of Africans across boundaries of their original homelands began in prehistory. Writing on the historical perspective of migration, William McNeil (1984) portrays how African ancestors left tropical Africa behind and moved into temperate zones. This was the beginning of the movement that led human beings to spread across the face of the earth. Today, migration is discussed principally in relation to developing countries. Nonetheless, immigration seems to be couched within the hegemony of imperialism, as it seems to be imagined that immigrants are only seeking homes in the rich and developed nations of the world, when in point of fact, citizens of rich nations of the developed world are also emigrating to other, less developed nations of the world, as missionaries, multinational corporation executives, and even as mercenaries. The safe name for such people is often "expatriates" rather than "immigrants." Often, the nuanced emphasis on immigration as presented by the global media and hegemonic interests of the developed world is on non-Western peoples immigrating to the West in search of better livelihood.

The movie, *Coming to America* validates the fact that at times, not all immigration to the West is predicated upon economic interests. Sometimes it is based upon the sentiment of exploration of the world, and venturing into a place where one can discover oneself and one's aspirations. This was the case of Akeem in the statement he made to Semmi. Akeem remarks; "I want a woman who can arouse both my intellect and my loins." To this Semmi asks "and where can you find such a woman?" Akeem promptly replies, "In America." Such sentimental portraiture depicts that certain rich and comfortable Africans in the quest for nurturing their intellect and nourishing their physical comfort can also migrate in search of the proverbial "golden fleece." This search for the proverbial "golden fleece" might not be interpreted in a monolithic way, as such quests can be rooted in the desire to acquire American education, which many Africans find to be pragmatic and intensely scientific. Hence, factually, it is not surprising that according to the US Census, African immigrants to the United States have consistently possessed the highest level of educational attainment of any group, including native-born Americans; the same has been reported in Great Britain.[7]

Given the global salience and trans-spatial and cross-continental networks that define the trajectory of African immigration, I base my considerations of African immigration mainly on cinematic representations as enacted in four movies. Primarily, I examine the nature of portraiture of the African immigrants within these movies, and outline their basic plot within an analytical, hermeneutical and theoretical framework as it underlines the issues and context of African immigration across the globe. I intentionally attempt to utilize specific vignettes and segments of specific plots from each movie rather than the entirety of the movies. I also direct attention to relevant and salient scenes pertinent to the consideration of the theme of African immigration.

African immigration, like most of the "New Immigration" (post-1965) to the United States, is mainly an urban phenomenon, and like other immigrants, African immigrants are highly concentrated in the same urban American destinations. They are like other new immigrants, except that they are noted to be more diverse in their mode of their spatial distribution and diffusion. New York continues to stand as the choice of most immigrants to America, regardless of origin. Among African immigrants, New York equally stands out as their prime destination. Therefore, New York features strategically in two of these movies that engage the theme of African immigrants to America, thus dually possessing a strong magnetism and offering a symbolic signification within the popular and immigrants' imagination, as well as within the dual cinematic representations of the phenomenon of American and African-to-American immigration experiences.

NEW YORK

New York has appeared in two of the movies as a kind of El Dorado for the immigrants. In *Coming to America,* Akeem and Semmi, in deciding to leave their home town to America, specifically target New York which they think would satisfy their yearning. Also in *Dirty Pretty Things,* Senay frantically looks for a visa and heads to New York. Why in all the cities in the world have two filmmakers decided to use New York as a port of call for the immigrants? New York and Los Angeles constitute the major immigrant destinations in the US. Multiple studies depict New York as a global and strategic urban attraction for various groups of American, including African, immigrants.[8] New York is notably considered as being immigrant friendly. In a scene in *Dirty Pretty Things,* while both Okwe and Senay are eating, in Senay's room, Okwe regrets: "I sometimes wish that London would be like New York." There are of course many reasons why Okwe would have loved London to be like New York. In comparison, New York is more liberal than London and more receptive to immigrants. It offers prospects for better life, a vital factor associated within the construction of the reasons for immigration. Francois Weil says of New York that "hundreds of thousands of men and women converged on New York with the hope of improving their living conditions. . . ."[9] New York's alluring significance is embedded within American history and identification as a "nation of immigrants." New York embodies America in some unique senses, as a center of global business and popular culture, as a major tourist attraction, as the "Big Apple"—an expression that situates this city virtually as the central nerve of the American identity (William Pencak, Selma Berrol and Randall M. Miller).[10] François Weil asserts that New York City grew 50-fold during the 19th century, principally because of immigrants and their children . . . these migratory movements profoundly reshaped the New York ethnic landscape. Father Joques is quoted by Weil to have noted in 1643 that "on the island of Manhattan and its environs, there may well be four to five hundred men of different sects and nations and eighteen different languages," (Weil, 2004, 55). New York is therefore essentially the reflection of American heterogeneity and expression of cultural diversity

In a scene in the movie *Coming to America,* while Akeem and his father are having a conversation in a garden, he tells his father: "I have yet to experience what the outside world has to offer." Such ambitions to discover and explore the world propelled his relocation to New York, a city which accommodates such personalities and interests. "Today," asserts Elizabeth Bogen, "New York City shares its role as refuge of the oppressed, the ambitious, the seekers of the world."[11] New York stands out as a beacon of hope that attracts immigrants to the new world.

It is not surprising that these two filmmakers utilize the idiom of New York as a spatial icon of emotional and self-liberation. New York is therefore crystallized as a focal dream place for many immigrants to America. In *Dirty Pretty Things,* Senay, who was ready to do anything, including giving up her vestal dignity to "Sneaky" the Hotel manager, as a ploy toward acquiring traveling documents to New York, could not understand the reason for Okwe's migration to London from New York, which is considered as the utmost desirable destination of most immigrants. In ecstasy and disbelief, she asks Okwe, "You've been to New York and came back here?" The two filmmakers' utilization of New York as an ultimate icon for immigrants' notion of El Dorado, through their mimetic representations, is therefore not accidental.

THE WAVES OF THE NEW ENVIRONMENTS: SHOCK, ASSIMILATION AND ACCULTURATION

Two of the movies posit dual cinematic parallelism in their portraiture of immigrants arriving in their new host communities. The two movies present the arriving immigrants being welcomed with robbery. In *Coming to South Africa,* Edward and Mike are robbed on their arrival in South Africa. In *Coming to America,* Akeem and Semmi are robbed in front of an apartment on Queens Street as they go inside to inspect the room they intend to rent. In the two instances, these arriving immigrants are dispossessed and left virtually empty handed.

These dispossessions have critical implications in the cinematic representations within my cogent perception. I posit certain interpretations as I define such cinematic representations, within two considerations. Of these two, one is moral or ethical, and the other lies within the mode of personal reconfiguration and reordering of certain constructs of self-internalization within this hermeneutic script. The prime interpretation posits that as the immigrant arrives at their new community; they are dispossessed not just of their material possessions, as a symbolic loss of their former artifacts of their homeland, but actually and affectively, involving a profound dispossession of certain imaginative perspectives regarding their host destination. Such perceptions seem to be rooted in their principles, values, and notions of their new host destination as a virtuous land, and even with the additional possible referential notion of visualizing it as paradise on earth; these are views that are often encrypted as contrasting delineations of novelty that demarcate their new destinations from those regarding their aboriginal homelands.

This process of dispossession occurs within their first imagination of their new host destination, and helps to begin, even though inducing traumatic dispositions, a process of adaptation to new concrete rather than imagined visions of their new context and locality. It entails the shedding and shredding of some "metaphysical" notions and divesting of certain regal vestiges of the imagined meanings and attractions imputed into their encrypted notions of the reality of immigration, sometimes constituted within the strictures of false consciousness. Therefore, despite the negative re-imagining of previous mental constructs, this shock produces real and vital outcomes that thrust the immigrant into the lived reality of his/her situation rather than allowing deal continuously with a utopia as their frame of reference.

Such traumatic experiences can also lead to unfortunate interpretations for some African immigrants who then try to adapt negatively. With a lack of imagination, they adopt negative moral scripts as the guiding texts for their lives within their new domains. Casting off certain ethical preconceptions and traditional codes that define them, they adapt criminal perspectives, perceiving freedom to mean carelessness and anonymity, therefore engaging in acts that hitherto they imagined as noxious and abhorrent. In the case of Mike and Edward, the trade in drugs dominated their interests. Thus, casting off the "shackles" of their *a priori* codes of ethical imperatives, within the distillation of good from bad, they jumped into the drug trade, without delimiting boundaries of any customary or religious ethics.

Secondly, such dispossession, in transcending the moral sphere, might actually shatter and fragment hitherto held assumptions and imaginative constructs, absorbed as value-schemes of self-internalization. A Nigerian-American and feminist academic, Dympna Ugwu-Oju in her autobiographical work, attests to such experiences. Following her first arrival in the United States, at the New York airport, seeing scavengers rampaging through garbage, she became disillusioned and almost thought of herself as daydreaming, of having landed in a third world nation rather than in New York. Upon the approach of a man soliciting her for a quarter (a mere twenty-five cents), she mused: "I thought to myself 'surely this cannot be America. How could there be beggars in America?'" The "culture shock" confronts immigrants with a new perspective and new evaluative reality, that initially is virulently dispossessing and destabilizing, but which in fact serves to rupture a demented vision or imagined fantasy. In this way, such imaginations of the immigrants, especially if they are first-timers, turn out to be illusive and disappointing. Such confrontational oddities, in fact, raise the nostalgic antennae that nurture feelings regarding the comfort zone that their homeland offers.

This phenomenon of culture shock is framed by Alan Richardson; "the immigrant begins to realize more fully the difference between his old community and his new one."[12] Dympna Ugwu-Oju, experiencing such a culture shock, further notes regarding her own ordeal, "I held my breath, believing that I was probably caught up in a nightmare and that I would wake up and find myself in the real New York." [13] Immigrants' experience of culture shock is embedded within their expectations and referential notions of the structural parameters of their new destination, in a way that can over-impute certain aspects of their host communities, while undervaluing other equally real aspects. Qualitatively, even when conscious of such pejorative aspects of their new destinations, often mentally juxtaposing it alongside the utopia of novelty, and novelty represented as masking the haven of paradise experience, the reality of the immigrant's destination country becomes suppressed or even repressed. Such attitudes are mainly underlined by the fact that new or adopted homelands are often invested with the comparative and contrasting ascription that often denotes "better."

As the filmmakers present these new immigrants entering new spaces in their life pursuits, logically, the experience of robbery entails a follow-up rooted in the acquisition of new material properties. Hence, the immigration experience indicates dispossession and displacement that often is associated with new accumulation. For the immigrants this involves the acquisition of new material things, but it is not limited to the materials alone; it verges on the acquisition of new forms of meaning, geographical locations, spiritual values, social worlds, and the creation of a novel ecological niche that helps to engender the ideal of "transplantation." Hence, the notion of immigration involves being "uprooted"[14] and being "transplanted."[15]

By their uprooting and transplanting, they learn to cope with their new ecological and social niche, while also putting down roots following their transplantations within their new spatial domain and host destination. The acquiring of new properties represents their level of social and structural assimilation. In a scene in *Coming to America,* as Akeem and Semmi come out of a store after they have bought themselves new clothes and dress in them with a matching baseball cap, Akeem tells Semmi, "We are now, let's behave like New Yorkers." Through the dynamic processes of immigrants' heightened interaction with members of the host community, they become acculturated, acquiring the cultural norms, ethos, values, and social *élan* of their new community, and with time through blending and cultural reduction of structural differences—language acquisition, intermarriages, acquisition of citizenship, and other elements of social "naturalization"—they would have become assimilated with their host community becoming a home to them, in a virtual, real, and imagined sense. This point also comes across in the movie *Dirty Pretty Things,* as Ivan, the gate keeper at Baltic Hotel, cognitively notices this about Okwe, and thus comments, "You stay here too long, you start dressing like an Englishman, uh."

Any arriving immigrant into a new country faces an uphill task. The newcomer has to work his or her way into the new community. Paul Elivitz provides a tangible clue as to how the immigrant is seen by the host community, specifically writing about the American community though his writings could also apply to other host communities globally. Offering four perspectives, he notes that "The immigrant can be seen as a cultural hero, an outsider, a dangerous alien, and as a human being" He enunciates upon the meaning of these terms: 1. *A Cultural hero:* The immigrant represents the dramatic story of the outsider who becomes an insider usually through economic, cultural, or political success. 2. *An Outsider:* The immigrant is perceived as someone suitable to do tasks in the society that others are not willing to perform. 3. *An Alien:* The immigrants is viewed as a dangerous parasitic organism that hurts the body of the nation, This takes the form of a welfare cheat, a criminal or a subversive foreign agent. 4. *A Human being:* The immigrant is accepted as a fellow American, and can be a suitable marriage partner.[16] An immigrant can be seen through two or more sides of the prism in a given host community. The ultimate picture however will be presented by the individual as he lives his daily life in the community.

FACING STEREOTYPES

In this age of the media, it is possible to see, hear and learn about a people without physically interacting with them. It is possible to internalize the images presented to us by various media about some people. This is what happens when a negative image of a people is shown around the world. Africans are among the most negatively stereotyped people of on Earth. African immigrants bear the brunt of these negative portrayals at one point or another in their new spaces. The colonial cinema which had the sole mission of showing Africans in bad light did a great harm to the African image. This is depicted in the movies here under discussion. In the basketball game scene in *Coming to America,* Daryl, (Eric La Salle) derides Akeem, who is being asked to pull off his jacket, "wearing clothes must be a kind of a new experience for you." *Coming to South Africa* is a movie produced by a Nigerian. This movie presents a different perspective, in the sense that it portrays immigration within the African continent. The stereotypes presented here raise a different type of question. All the drug traffickers in the movie are Nigerians. Not just that they are Nigerians but they represent a particular ethnic group. This raises a question: what makes a Nigerian producer in South Africa to portray his country in such a bad light? Is this filmmaker trying to tell the world that there are no good Nigerians in that country? In the court scene, after Mike has been sentenced, a television news reporter in a Live Report outside the court concludes his report with, "Currently there are about 13 Nigerians in jail on drug trafficking convictions."

MAKING A DIFFERENCE IN THE HOST COMMUNITY

In *Dirty Pretty Things,* a film set in a Hotel in London. Okwe is a Nigerian physician turned cab driver. At the airport addressing his two would-be passengers, he underlines his real mission with this statement: "I am not here to see you. I am here to rescue those who are let down by the system." The import of this statement is not revealed in Okwe the cab driver or in Okwe the hotel porter, but in the global contribution of African immigrants in their host communities. He lives with Senay a Muslim girl from Turkey, who, unlike Okwe, was admitted conditionally into the country. He cooks for the girl and cares for her but he does not exploit her sexuality by engaging in any form of intimate relationship with her. In the hotel, he discovers a human heart in the toilet of one of the hotel rooms.

The heart is the center of human life. The hotel business here is an icon of capitalism. The discovery of the human heart in a toilet portrays the abuse of human life through some inhuman ideologies. The hotel manager is in a dirty business, as Okwe discovers. He refused to be dragged into the business by rejecting the money offered to him by the hotel manager. The devouring power of the system is highlighted through the hotel manager as he challenges Okwe to call the police if he dares. Herein, we sense how within the stricture of the illegal—even at times the legal—immigrant, dominant powers attempt to cajole and blackmail and eventually ensure the attainment of control over the moral person, through subordinating means. This statement goes a long way to portray the despicable existential situations in some of the developed countries that attempt to compromise the values and principles of African immigrants. While many African immigrants rationalize that employment would better their lives and ensure their valuable contribution toward the development of their host communities, they are at times compromised and subjected to physical abuse and moral indignities. Further, the very fact of their spatial dislocation and powerlessness often conspire to reduce many African immigrants to sources of cheap labor in the morbid hands of the instrumentality of capitalist exploitation and hegemonic domination, even within the nations to which they migrate in the expectation of gaining freedom and bettering their lives. Often caught between the ambiguity of starvation in standing up to these values and surviving in a foreign land, many immigrants come to the realization of the cross-spatial force of evil, inherent also within the structural and systemic component of their host societies that at times run counter to their own ethical formations and internalized norms.

In general, immigrants are in many ways agents of cultural enrichment within the societies where they reside, and they constitute instruments for capitalist economic advancement within many nations. Regarding this relationship between brain gain and brain drain, the United Nations International Migration Report points out that "migration also has the potential of facilitating the transfer of skills and contributing to cultural enrichment. The vast majority of migrants are making meaningful contributions to their host countries." [17]

African immigrants are making enormous material and spiritual contributions toward the advancement of their host societies. Though often unacknowledged, African immigrants are helping the transformation of many Western societies. Given their noted industry and high educational attainment, they are agents of social and economic transformation within the discrete locales, and the ecological and occupational niches that they occupy. For instance, African immigrant physicians, pharmacists, religious ministers, attorneys, and small business owners are making remarkable contributions to the development of American cities and even the revitalization of many inner cities through their economic acumen and spending.

A critical look at religion reveals the contribution of African immigrant religious congregations or social entities dotting various American urban domains.[18] Nigerian Catholic priests, for instance, have become replacements for those of European and Hispanic descent in many Catholic parishes in American inner cities, saving some of these from foreclosure as a result of the dismal paucity in American priestly vocations. In Detroit for instance, a news feature on the contribution of foreign priests to the sustenance of the faith in American Catholic dioceses observed "The priest who runs St. Anthony's and Annunciation, two parishes on the Detroit's East side, is a Nigerian. . . . Throughout the United States, there is a growing influx of foreign born priests in Catholic dioceses." [19] The Redeemed Christian Church of God (RCCG) is rapidly expanding in North America, and even intends to build its international headquarters in Floyd, on the outskirts of Greenville, near Dallas, Texas.[20] This church is an off-shoot of the Nigerian church. Most of the leaders of the church are African immigrants.

In academia, a very good percentage of educators in the American colleges are immigrants from foreign lands, Africa inclusive. The health sector is replete with African physicians, nurses, pharmacists, physician

assistants, respiratory therapists, nurse practitioners, and medical techni-
cians that either have their private practice or work within different medical and health centers. Therefore, Okwe's statement, "I'm here to rescue
those who are let down by the system," can yield representational ramifi-
cations to mean that African immigrants are here to support those let down
by the systems within inner city communities, among others. Such a fact is
represented by a Nigerian immigrant and pharmacist in the Boston area,
Dotun Diyaolu, who opened Plaza Pharmacy and Home Care in Downtown Brockton, specifically with the intention of catering to the pharma-
ceutical needs of the elderly and low income families in the vicinity.[21] Such
risk-taking and industriousness are characteristic of African immigrants as
they utilize the different opportunities they find amidst struggles against
different systemic barriers. Many African immigrants own their own
businesses, often making enormous progress. Cheitah Babou relates the
example of the Mudrid immigrants, around 116th street in New York and
Malcolm X Boulevard, creating a "sort of economic and cultural enclave
which is now known as Little Senegal. Senegalese immigrants own 80 percent of businesses located in this area." [22] West African street vendors in
New York are noted to be enterprising in the midst of their alienation. As
Paul Stoller notes, "The traders are, for the most part, culturally alienated from American life. To combat this alienation, they have used their
various networks to construct an array of community forms that provide
the potential for economic, political, and cultural integration. In the end,
this economic agility and cultural dexterity teach us a great deal about
the complex texture of social life in contemporary urban worlds."[23] In the
same vein, Elizabeth Bogen, writing about the influential role of immigrants on the garment industry in a New York area, notes: "The garment
trade was dependent on immigrant labor," (Bogen, 1987, 17).

The trait of African immigrant industriousness is noted in *Coming
to America*. Akeem works tirelessly and scales to relevance in the fast food
restaurant based upon a set of work ethics, sheer determination, and industry. In the face of his work-place being robbed, he manifested courage in
striking the robber (Samuel Jackson), using only a mop, and with the help
of Semmi, knocks the gun off the robber's hands overpowering the assail-
ant in the process, thereby disrupting his plans. Such risk-taking in the face
of danger to ensure the safety of others in his workplace depicts not just
his valor but also is indicative of his concern for the welfare of his fellow
workers and the frightened customers. Therefore, he was recognized appropriately, when the restaurant proprietor, Mr. McDowell, in a statement of
appreciation noted: "I'm really proud of what you're doing, you see, that
guy has hit us three times in the past. Now he will not come again thanks to

my African connection." He then invites them to a party. "Leave your Sunday night open. I'm having a get-together in my house." Akeem observes by remarking to Semmi "you see it's working, he has accepted us as equals." At this party, Akeem and Lisa start a relationship. Here, the theory of Paul Elivitz as narrated above comes alive. In a similar encounter, in *Coming to South Africa,* Edward saves the life of a lady being robbed in a parking lot, though unlike Akeem, he is shot in the process. The robbery victim, Tessy, visiting him in the hospital room, says, "You saved my life," to which he replies, "I did what I had to do." Through her connection, Edward gets a job, and of course they end up dating.

In *The Secret Laughter of Women,* Nimi, a Nigerian immigrant living with her mother, turns out to be a very successful landscape architect. She takes care of Matthew's garden. Her hard work is praised by Matthew, and at the end they get married. African immigrants have made waves in their host communities. The above analysis considers some of their contributions.

The above analysis shows cinematic portrayals of African immigrants and how they cope in their new environments. Akeem finally returns to Africa to celebrate his wedding with Lisa. This is not the case any more with immigrants. Some, because of the economic situation in their countries of origin, prefer to remain in foreign lands. In a most ungrateful way, some of them denigrate their homelands in the presence of foreigners, sometimes to curry favor, or to justify why they cannot go back to their homeland. While we sympathize with the likes of Okwe who were forced by the powers that be to leave their fatherland, only to become a nonentity in a foreign land, there are many political exiles from Africa like Okwe in many foreign lands. Some, even in the foreign land, still guard jealously the cultures and traditions of their homeland and even transmit such to their kids, as we see in the *Secret laughter of Women.* A good number of the immigrants still maintain their links with the homeland by providing financial support to families at home, like Edward. From the above discourse we can see that movies are a reflection of human societies. They help us to see ourselves in a way that some other disciplines may not have been able to reveal.

NOTES

1. Wole Soyinka, "The African World and the Ethnocultural Debate," *African Culture: The Rythms of Unity,* (Molefi Kete Asante and Kariamu Welsh Asante: Africa World Press, Inc., 1995).
2. Sekou Tall, Seminar on "The role of the African Film-Maker in Rousing an Awareness of Black Civilization," Ougadougou, April 8–13, 1974. in M.

Martin (ed.), *Cinemas of the Black Diaspora: Diversity, Dependence and opportunity,* (Detroit: Wayne State University Press, 1995),480.

3. William H. McNeil, "Human Migration in Historical Perspective." *Population and Development Review* 10 no. 1 (1984): 1–18.

4. United Nations International Migration Report 2002.

5. United Nations Universal Declaration of Human Rights, Article 13.

6. United Nations General Assembly, Resolution 56/203, December 2001.

7. "African Immigrants in the United States are the Nation's Most Highly Educated Group," *The Journal of Black in Higher Education* 26 (1999/2000): 60–61; "African-Born US Residents have Achieved the Highest Level of Education Attainment," *The Journal of Backs in Higher Education* 4(1994):10–11; "African-Born Blacks in the United Kingdom are Far More Likely than Whites to Hold a College Degree," *The Journal of Blacks in Higher Education* 34 (2001/2002): 29–31; Marie Nathali LeBlanc, "Process of Identification among French speaking West African Migrants in Montreal," *Canadian Ethnic Studies* 34 no. 3 (2002); 121–136.

8. Nancy Foner (ed.), *New Immigrants in New York,* (New York: Columbia University Press, 2001); Robert Anthony Orsi, *The Madonna of 115th Street: Faith and Community in Italian Harlem, 1880–1950,* (New Haven: Yale University Press, 1988); Paul Stoller, *Money Has No Smell: The Africanization of New York City,* (Chicago: University of Chicago Press, 2002); Paul Stoller, *Jaguar: A Story of Africans in America.* (Chicago: University of Chicago Press, 1999).

9. François Weil, *A History of New York,* (Columbia University Press, 2004), 202.

10. William Penack, Selma Berrol, Randall M. Miller, *Immigration to New York,* (Philadelphia: The Balch Institute Press, 1991), 175.

11. Elizabeth Bogen, *Immigration in New York,* (New York: Praeger, 1987), 4.

12. Alan Richardson, "A Theory and A Method for the Psychological Study of Assimilation," *International Migration Review* 2 no.1 (1967), 3–30.

13. Dympna Ugwu-Oju, *What Will My Mother Say? A Tribal Girl Come of Age in America,* (Chicago: Press, 1995), 250.

14. Oscar Handlin, *The Uprooted: The Epic Story of the Great Migrations that Made the American People,* (Boston: Little Brown and Company, 1979 [1951]).

15. John Bodnar, *The Transplanted: A History of Immigrants in Urban America,* (Bloomington, IN: Indiana University Press, 1987).

16. Paul Elivitz, *Immigrant Experiences,* (Madison: Fairlegh Dickson University Press, 1997), 11.

17. The UN International Migration Report 2002.

18. David J. Wakin, "Where the Gospel Resounds in African Tongues," *The New York Times* April 18, 2004.

19. Lekan Oguntoyinbo, "Foreign Priest Fills Needs," *Detroit Free Press,* April 4, (2000), A1; Stephen Innes, "3 New Priests from Nigeria Reflect U.S. Catholic Trend," *Arizona Daily Star,* August 28, 2004.

20. Laolu Akande, "Redeemed Christian Church of God Buys Multimillion Dollar Property in Dallas" April 9, 2003 available at www.nigeriaworld.com

co; Simon Romero, "A Texas Town Nervously Awaits a New Neighbor," *The New York Times* August 21, 2005.

21. Jennifer Kovalich, "Boston: Risk Pays Off in Downtown Brockton for Dotun Diyaolu, Five Years after Opening his own Pharmacy," available at www.nigeriaworld.co, February 16, 2004.

22. Cheihk Anta Babou,"Brotherhood Solidarity, Education and Migration: The Role of the *Dahiras* among the Murid Muslim community of New York." *African Affairs* 101, (2002); 151–170.

23. Paul Stoller, *Money Has No Smell: The Africanization of New York,* (Chicago: University of Chicago Press, 2002), 10.

REFERENCES

"African Immigrants in the United States are the Nation's Most Highly Educated Group," *The Journal of Black in Higher Education* 26 (1999/2000): 60–61.

"African-Born US Residents have Achieved the Highest Level of Education Attainment," *The Journal of Backs in Higher Education* 4 (1994): 10–11.

"African-Born Blacks in the United Kingdom are Far More Likely than Whites to Hold a College Degree," *The Journal of Blacks in Higher Education* 34 (2001/2002): 29–31.

Akande, Laolu. "Redeemed Christian Church of God Buys Multimilion Dollar Property in Dallas." April 9, 2003 available at www.nigeriaworld.co.

Babou, Cheihk Anta. "Brotherhood Solidarity, Education and Migration: The Role Of the *Dahiras* among the Murid Muslim Community of New York." *African Affairs,* 101 (2002), 151–170.

Bodnar, John. *The Transplanted: A History of Immigrants in Urban America.* Bloomington, IN: Indiana University Press, 1987.

Bogen, Elizabeth. *Immigration in New York*. New York: Praeger, 1987.

Elivitz, Paul. *Immigrant Experiences*. Madison: Fairlegh Dickson University Press, 1997.

Foner, Nancy. (ed.) *New Immigrants in New York*. New York: Columbia University Press, 2001.

Handlin, Oscar. *The Uprooted: The Epic Story of the Great Migrations that Made the American People.* Boston: Little Brown and Company, 1979 [1951].

Innes, Stephen. "3 New Priests from Nigeria Reflect U.S. Catholic Trend,"*Arizona Daily Star,* August 28, 2004.

Kovalich, Jennifer. "Boston: Risk Pays off in Downtown Brockton for Dotun Diyalou, Five Years After Opening His own Pharmacy." (2004) Available at www.nigeriaworld.co.

LeBlanc, Maria Nathali. "Process of Identification Among French Speaking West African Immigrants in Montreal. *Canadian Ethnic Studies*. Calgary. 34 no. 3 (2002), 121–136.

McNeil, William H. "Human Migration in Historical Perspective." *Population and Development Review*. 10 no. 1 (1984), 1–18.

Oguntoyinbo, Lekan. "Foreign Priest Fills Needs." *Detroit Free Press,* April 4, 2000.

Orsi, Robert Anthony. *The Madonna of 115th Street: Faith and Community in Italian Harlem, 1880–1950.* New Haven: Yale University Press, 1988.

Penack, William, Selma Berrol, Randall M. Miller. *Immigration to New York*. Philadelphia: The Balch Institute Press, 1991.

Richardson, Allan. "A Theory and Method for the Psychological study of Assimilation." *International Migration Review*. 2 no. 1 (1967), 3–30.

Romero, Simon. "A Texas Nervously Awaits a New Neighbor." *The New York Times*, August 21, 2005.

Soyinka, Wole. "The African World and the Ethnocultural Debate." Asante, M.K.; & Asante, K.W. (eds.). *African Culture: The Rhythms of Unity*. African World Press, Inc., 1995.

Stoller, Paul. "Money Has No Smell: The Africanization of New York City" Chicago: University of Chicago Press, 2002.

———. *Jaguar: A story of Africans in America*. Chicago: University of Chicago Press, 1999.

Tall, Sekou. "The Role of the African Film-Maker in Rousing Awareness of Black Civilisation." Martin, M. (ed.). *Cinemas of the Black Diaspora: Diversity, Dependence and opportunity*. Detroit: Wayne State University Press, 1995.

Ugwu-Oju, Dympna. *What Will My Mother Say? A Tribal Girl Comes of Age in America*. Chicago: Chicago Press, 1995.

Wakin, David J. "Where the Gospel Resounds in African Tongues." *The New York Times* April 18, 2004.

Weil, Francis. *A History of New York*. New York: Columbia University Press, 2004.

Part II

Migration, Labor Conflicts, and Development

Chapter Five

"The Uprooted Emigrant": The Impact of Brain Drain, Brain Gain, and Brain Circulation on Africa's Development

Godwin S.M. Okeke

SYNOPSIS

Worsening economic conditions in many African countries have uprooted many of its people from their home countries, voluntarily and involuntarily, in search of the "golden fleece" abroad. This has led to brain drain, brain gain and brain circulation. Brain drain is synonymous with knowledge loss or drain. Brain gain is the reverse side of brain drain, in which Africans in the diaspora return to their various countries with high skills to contribute to their countries' development. Brain circulation entails a continuous and counter-balancing in-flow of highly skilled personnel. The nature of most economies in Africa today has warranted this jigsaw puzzle. The outcome of bad management of the economy and the generalized violent conflict on the continent has not helped matters. Some survivors in war-torn countries, both skilled and unskilled, look outside of their countries for a better life. In some African countries people run away from economic hardship to improve their lives abroad where things are expectedly better. This phenomenon cuts across all manners of people, including professionals and other skilled labor.

This situation is true of many countries in Africa, including Nigeria, Angola, Mozambique, Zimbabwe, Niger, Senegal, Togo, Cameroon, Ghana, Liberia and Sierra Leone, to mention just a few. Some of those who are not well educated travel and get educated and develop and acquire better skills and make positive contributions to those societies. These movements do not take place only outside Africa, but also within Africa.

The consequences of these developments are many and varied. Aside from the image problem it creates for Africa, it portrays Africans as people who are not serious and their governments as irresponsible and corrupt, especially Africa south of the Sahara. There are also those who have made Africa proud in various fields of human endeavor. But the problem remains that the recipe which made them succeed abroad never works at home. Against this background, this chapter investigates the impact of this type of crisscrossing migration on Africa's development, and how far the benefits or otherwise can go to assist in the sustainable development of Africa.

INTRODUCTION

Africa's development is not experiencing the best of times due to worsening economic conditions. The largest proportion of the poorest countries in the world today is found in Africa. This condition has led to the flight of human capital, otherwise called brain drain. This entails knowledge loss, whereby highly skilled professionals including doctors, engineers and university lecturers among others emigrate abroad for greener pastures. It has been noted that Africa spends an estimated USD 4bn annually to recruit some 100,000 skilled expatriates, while her own professionals (some of whom are trained by the government) are abroad contributing to the development of those places.[1] Some of these professionals do not come back, but the positive side of this movement is that there is also brain gain, where some of the professionals in the diaspora return to their home countries with the acquired skills to contribute to its development. The cumulative effect of brain drain and brain gain is brain circulation, which is a continuous and counter-balancing flow of highly skilled personnel.

Across Africa, especially Africa south of the Sahara, the story is the same. From available facts based on studies conducted by the International Organization for Migration (IOM) and the UN Economic Commission for Africa, between 1960 and 1975 an estimated 27,000 highly qualified Africans left the continent for the West. Subsequently, this number increased to approximately 40,000 between 1975 and 1984, and then almost doubled by 1987, representing 30% of the highly skilled manpower stock. It was also discovered that Africa lost 600,000 professionals between 1985 and 1990 and has continually lost 20,000 on average per annum.[2] Each of the countries involved has virtually the same stories to tell in this regard. Nigeria, Angola, Mozambique, Zimbabwe, Niger, Senegal, Togo, Cameroon, Ghana, Liberia, Sierra Leone and South Africa all display the same scenario. The consequences of this phenomenon are many and varied. The whole issue of sustainable development in Africa will continue to be a mirage if the problem is not properly addressed. The African people will be regarded as not being serious and as people with irresponsible and corrupt governments, incapable of managing their own affairs.

Against this background, this chapter investigates the impact of this crisscrossing migration on Africa's development, and how far the benefits or otherwise can go to assist in the sustainable development of Africa. The chapter defines the following terms: brain drain, brain gain, brain circulation, development and uprooted emigrant. This is followed by analysis of the issues and the nature of migration in Africa, brain drain, brain gain and brain circulation and Africa's development. In this chapter therefore, we define brain drain as "human capital flight," which is the emigration of trained and talented individuals (human capital) to other countries as a result of conflicts, lack of opportunity or health hazards where they were living. This has also been likened to "capital flight" which is financial capital that is no longer invested in the country where its owner lives and earns it. With regard to human capital flight, the investment in higher education is lost when the trained individual leaves, often not coming back to the country of origin. The result is that what ever social capital the individual was part of is reduced by their departure.

In Nigeria, the Presidential Committee on Brain Drain defines brain drain as, "The loss, indeed an exodus, of highly trained and often experienced individuals from their country to other nations in pursuit of higher paying jobs, as well as more conducive working environments within which to express and utilize their hard-earned specialized talents and skills."[3] A reverse situation whereby trained and talented individuals migrate to live and work in a country is called brain gain. The effect of this is that a condition of brain drain is created in the country that the individuals are leaving. In other words, the migration is detrimental to the country of origin because the labor force is depleted by the departure of its most productive and/or qualified manpower.

By brain circulation we mean the movement, to and fro, of skilled manpower from the countries of origin to the countries that absorb these skills and vice versa. It involves a continuous and counter-balancing in-flow and outflow of highly skilled manpower. This may involve staff exchange and visiting scholarships or fellowships. This movement could be found both within and outside Africa. Among Africans, the Technical Aid Scheme of the Nigerian government could be a typical example of the way brain circulates among African countries. Under the scheme Nigerian professionals go to work for one or two years in other African countries. The focus of development in regard to this chapter is that people by their own efforts will carry their destiny, and as participants, stakeholders and beneficiaries. Therefore, human resource development and capacity building are priorities in addition to promoting equitable development, social integration, good governance, and environmental protection and regeneration.

With regard to migration and development, the relationship is close, yet complex. With proper management, international migration is bound to contribute more positively to the development of both countries of origin and destination. There is great potential in international migration to contribute to sustainable development through investments, skills transfer, remittance, brain circulation (by also reducing the impact of brain drain) and diaspora networks. There could be favorable and positive migration policies which deal with the migration—development nexus, which could facilitate voluntary return and reintegration either temporary or permanent, with special emphasis on the highly skilled, while facilitating the transfer of remittances and reducing transfer costs, and also encouraging investment in the country of origin by migrants and diasporas.

The issue of uprooted emigrants involves the young, educated and highly skilled and talented who constitute the core of the manpower and/or workforce who should make significant contributions to a country's development. Some people also travel without skill, but due to dint of hard work they were able to get a good education and acquire skills. In my estimation, therefore, they form part and parcel of the uprooted emigrant, and their skills and knowledge cannot therefore be discountenanced.[4]

CONCEPTUAL ISSUES AND THE NATURE OF CONTEMPORARY MIGRATION PATTERNS IN AFRICA

Scholars have tried to make explanations on the causes of migration. In the introduction to an edited scholarly work, Zegeye and Ishemo incorporated a neatly summarized paper on the causes of migration by J. Clyde Mitchell, in which he situates the causes within a colonial context, and most of the debates operate within a "colonial ideological framework and sought to explain migration in a Durkheimian theoretical mould."[5] However, theoretical developments after this period saw forced labor and migration, on the contrary, as major "components of colonial capitalist development and their reproduction in the post-colonial era as a colonial legacy," (Zegeye and Ishemo, 1–2). They contend that the precise form of the origin of forced labor and migration is incontestable. The problem is rather with the timing. With reference to Namibia, the origins are to be sought in the pre-colonial period and not as an African tradition as the earlier theorists contend. It is rather as a consequence of the pre-capitalist state's response to the penetration of European merchant capital. Therefore, "With the development of colonial capitalism, the pre-capitalist aristocracy became transformed into agents of the colonial state and with the introduction of taxation, forced labor and migration proliferated," (Zegeye and Ishemo, 2).

There is however caution to the effect that migrant labor was not a simple outcome of capitalist manipulation. It was instead an outcome of struggle rather than structure. As a starting point also, it is situated in the way colonial capitalist development disrupted indigenous production processes, among other reasons. This is why some scholars who have interrogated the socio-political nature of economic production rooted in historical analysis, based their theories on the problematic of conflicts of interests between different global actors in the struggle for expropriation and appropriation of global resources. The leading theorists in this regard are Paul Baran , Samir Amin, Andre Gunder Frank, Immanuel Wallerstein, among others.[6] This very fact could equally be said to have affected the pattern of migration in contemporary times, especially in Africa. More so, Makinwa-Adebusoye concludes that the migration system in West Africa results from both long-standing historical and economic forces, as well as recent developments, and geographical factors which also play a significant role in determining the direction of migrant flows.[7]

    In an important sense Amin has argued that the conventional approach to the migratory phenomena can be contextualized within a theoretical framework based on the hypothesis that the 'factors of production (labor, capital, material resources and land) are given *a priori* and geographically distributed unequally. He contends also that this is the basis of conventional marginalist economic theory. He argues further that, "The unequal geographic distribution of the available 'factors' of production also determines the unequal remuneration of each one of these. In certain regions labor is relatively more abundant and capital is scarcer; in others it is the opposite. Labor moves in the directions where it gets the highest remuneration: this is the basis of the conventional explanation."[8] We shall find out later in this discourse if this is the general explanation in reference to the issue of brain-drain in Africa.

    It has been acknowledged that, "before European colonization, Africa was the scene of mass movements of peoples. Since then, marked movements of labor have taken place and continue today," (Amin, 1974, 66). This is an affirmation of Wallerstein's position that "there has been considerable movement of peoples in West Africa for a long time . . . the movements have generally been recognized to have political significance, and as such have attracted the notice of persons in authority."[9] As Toure has observed, "During the colonial era, the dominant feature of population dynamics was a series of internal and international migrations all over the continent. Judging by the evidence, the migrations were responses to development policies based, for the most part, on the exploitation of raw materials and on the need of the colonial countries to find outlets

for their manufactured goods in the colonies."[10] This is why in numerous places there was the exploitation of natural resources such as minerals in Zambia; the development of plantation agriculture, featuring coffee
and cocoa among others, in Cote d'Ivoire, Nigeria, Congo and the Central
African Republic, and the single-crop agricultural regimes such as in the
groundnut-dominated country of Senegal. These developments stimulated
population movement, urban areas and immigration zones. In countries
like Senegal, Central African Republic, Zambia and Lesotho, some regions
were drained of their populations. Other areas in Côte d'Ivoire and Nigeria
became immigration zones, while others became labor pools; for instance,
Lesotho supplying South Africa, Zambia feeding Zimbabwe, and Burkina
Faso supplying Côte d'Ivoire and Ghana.

   This trend continued, even after independence, and from available
facts the countries studied maintained the basic guidelines of colonial development policies, with Tanzania as the only exception. As Touré also stated,
" . . . export crops were developed and diversified, as in Côte d'Ivoire, mining was intensified, as in Zambia and the Central African Republic, and
everywhere the practice of concentrating infrastructural facilities in the
urban and the better-developed areas continued. Old causes produced the
same old results, and the implementation of neocolonial developed policies
inevitably accentuated internal and international migrations," (Toure, and
Fadayomi, ii). There was therefore growth in both the rural exodus and
the old international migratory circuits. New ones also developed on the
continent itself, leading towards South Africa, the Central African Republic, Zimbabwe and Cote d'Ivoire, as well as towards countries and continents abroad, mostly Europe and America. Our North African brothers
(the Maghreb region) have the tendency to migrate, mainly towards the
Middle East, to assert their Arabness. The flow in this region is therefore
more towards the Middle East than Europe and America. However, the
point here is that the nature of the migration then was mainly internal, i.e.
within and among Africans. This migration of labor has been classified in
several ways including rural to rural migrations; rural-urban, urban-urban,
and urban-rural, (Amin, 1974, 67). To him, these developments later led
to the exodus of Africans towards Europe in the sixties for some regions
(especially the Sarakolle country in Senegal) and later that of intellectuals
(brain-drain) of which the effects were felt, and of which the volume of
flow has increased tremendously.

   There was also a kind of emigration that we had during the period of
colonization among the educated; those who traveled abroad and acquired
western education. Some of them came back and joined the struggle for
the liberation of the African peoples. In this category could be found

people like Nnamdi Azikiwe, Obafemi Awolowo, Kwame Nkrumah, Houphouët-Boigny and more recently, Nelson Mandela, among so many others. Outside this cadre, the nature of migration especially during the colonial period was inspired by the nature of the occupation at that point in time. As it were, the colonial masters forced the Africans to shift from food crop production to cash crop production of which the development created plantations, and subsequently oases of agricultural prosperity and the demand for labor. There were also the settler farms which existed side-by-side with peasant agriculture. This required land alienation from indigenous populations, and out grower schemes involving the cultivation of plantation crops in contiguous set-ups.[11] As a result of these changes, the direction of migrations was affected especially with the settler farms, including plantations, and out grower schemes which depended on migrant labor.

As Makinwa-Adebusoye has argued, "Thus began voluntary, seasonal movements (during the dry, slack season) of agricultural labor from the dry sahel interior to plantations of cocoa and coffee in better-watered areas of Ghana, Cote d'Ivoire (Ivory Coast) and southern Nigeria. Similar migrations took place to the tea, sisal and cotton plantations in Kenya and Tanganyika (now Tanzania)."[12] Other migration inducing policies during the colonial era also include the designation of new or old settlements as administrative headquarters coupled with the opening up of mines which consequently attracted migrant labor. It is noted that the South African mines attracted a lot of migrant labor from Zambia, Zimbabwe, Botswana, Lesotho and Swaziland. The infrastructural facilities available in these new administrative centers and other social amenities also attracted migrants. In most countries and cities in Africa, later developments showed that rapid development could be achieved by shifting perceived "surplus" agricultural labor to urban-based industry where it was expected that labor could be more productive. This development was expected in time to provide the much needed economic stimulus for the African continent. By the early 1970s it became obvious that this strategy was not working as the development which was expected to 'trickle' down by that effort adversely led to continued unemployment, under-employment and low-productivity, especially in the rural areas.

The gender factor has been raised in early migrations in Africa. During this period, it was usually men who used to migrate, leaving the women and children behind. For instance, the South African mines were the throb for countries like Zimbabwe and Zambia. The men migrated to seek for jobs in the mines leaving their wives behind. The implication of this is that the women now became the heads of the family. The remittances by their husbands also empowered them the more as they were placed in positions to make important decisions for the family. It has to be noted that there are also health implications for the long absence of the husbands, as there is always the temptation of patronizing women of easy virtue with the attendant possibility of contracting sexually transmitted infections, and also the fact that the wives at home are exposed to infidelity.

This trend in migration later changed when single ladies started traveling out. As Adepoju has observed, "Internal migration in Africa, as in other developing countries, is functionally linked with a variety of demographic and socioeconomic factors. Female migration has been strongly influenced by the structure of economic activity, socio-cultural factors which define sex roles, and the impact of education on spatial and occupational mobility. Men have often tended to migrate alone, leaving wives behind. Since employment in the formal labor market is highly correlated with education, women in general and Moslem women in particular, are disadvantaged by their low levels of formal education."[13] The trouble here is that they also started facing the same difficulties with men. The problems of a change in environment, such as encountering a different culture or coping with the problem of assimilation, among others, constitute some of the issues that the migrant has to contend with. For a Nigerian who travels to Europe, it would be inconceivable to wear "Agbada" during winter. So their perception about life will change, the personality will also change in order to be accepted in that society. In general terms this leads to the feeling of low self esteem and debasement. This identity crisis is accentuated by the fact that in as much as the foreign society does not fully accept them, back home they feel 'superior' to the people they left behind who do not equally accept them as such, and re-integration becomes a serious problem. For the men, it is easier to assimilate. Some of them get married easily in their new location to the ladies there. But for the females, the problem of choosing the right partner and settling down properly, among other things, makes the problem of assimilation gradual and very slow.

With the attainment of independence by most African countries, the patterns of migration variously changed. As Makinwa-Adebusoye has observed, " . . . the emigration of professionals from west African countries to other countries of the region, but mainly to developed countries (also known as the "brain drain") and, more recently, to the Middle East, appear to be on the rise and has been a source of concern for many governments since the 1970s," (Makinwa-Adebusoye, 1992, 69). Some of the emigrants who went abroad to acquire western education came back to support the task of nation-building. Some came back when the economies of their countries were booming. There is evidence to show for instance that most Africans who traveled abroad to acquire western education came back when the economy was booming. A study of Tom Mboya's "students" airlift organized from Kenya before its independence in 1963, which carried more than 1,000 students in chartered aircraft to the US, and another 100 to Canada showed that almost all went back, "for this was an exciting time to be in Africa."[14] In the case of Nigeria, for instance, problems started when the economy began to collapse. As Egbe and Ndubuisi state, "During the decade of the 1970s, tens of thousands of Nigerians entered the United States of America to study. The overwhelming majority of these students came on students' visas, with the expectation of returning home after their studies. When the oil boom ended in the mid 1980s, from about 1984, the Nigerian economy stagnated, and actually went into decline. Economic opportunities disappeared, and living standards declined sharply. As a result of the adverse changes that took place in the Nigerian economy, these former students decided to remain in the United States after they completed their studies."[15]

This could equally be applicable to most countries. This is largely because there is the tendency for the professionals to stay in a more favorable environment, where they are well treated and their skills given due recognition. This major factor among others has shaped the pattern of brain drain in Africa over the years. This assertion has been confirmed in what a perceptive observer has termed the (internal) push and (external) pull factors in the consideration of the causes of brain drain. The push factors which are mainly formed in the countries of origin of the emigrants include the following:

- Low and eroding wages and salaries;

- Poor and unsatisfactory living conditions, lack of transport (and when sometimes it is available, it is chaotic, and poor) and inadequate housing and accommodation;

- Under-utilization of qualified personnel, coupled with unsatisfactory working conditions and low and discouraging prospects of professional development;

- Lack of research and research facilities, including support staff, inadequate research funds and lack of professional equipment and tools;

- Continuous decline in the quality of the educational system, including an unstable academic calendar which is often disrupted as a result of strike actions by staff unions, violent student demonstrations, cult activities and general break down of law and order, reinforced by political instability;

- Discrimination in appointments and promotions which results in frustrations among qualified and skilled personnel; and

- The vexed issue of bad governance and corruption among many African countries. These also create major problems for leadership and governance, with the attendant policy inconsistencies, and these create an inharmonious working environment for skilled professionals who have no other option(s) than to look elsewhere, to where the conditions are more attractive.

Contrariwise, the (external) pull factors include the following:

- Higher remuneration and standard of living;

- More favorable working conditions, including job and career opportunities and professional development;

- Substantial and readily available research funds, advanced technology, modern facilities and availability of experienced support staff,

- Assured political stability that encourages a modern educational system coupled with the prestige of advanced foreign training; and

- Emphasis on meritocracy, transparency, hard-work and intellectual freedom.

Ibidapo-Obe (2005, 8) has also identified some other factors as "internal pull factors" and "external push factors," and both of them contribute to brain-gain. The internal pull factors are those restraining factors within Africa which exert pressure on the individual to stay back and contribute to the development of his or her country. These include:

- Strong family ties/attachment;

- High frustration tolerance level, and

- High optimism about the prospects of success and improvement, (Ibidapo-Obe, 2005, 8).

The external push factors are those factors that tend to repel the highly skilled professionals from the receiving countries, pushing them back to their countries of origin. As he argues, the expectations of some of the skilled professionals are not realized on getting abroad because, " . . . many realize that the promised jobs are not readily available and are not for everyone. Many suffer discrimination, alienation and isolation. There are situations in which some of the highly qualified emigrants condescend to do various forms of odd jobs (cab driving, cleaning, and security personnel) which are not in any way related to their training, in order to make ends meet, while they could be more useful in their countries of origin," (Ibidapo-Obe, 2005, 8). It would then be an aspect of brain-gain when this set of people return to their countries of origin and assist their country's development with their skills. The extent of this impact and other factors shall be the subject of our next discussion.

BRAIN DRAIN, BRAIN-GAIN, BRAIN CIRCULATION AND AFRICA'S DEVELOPMENT: AN ANALYSIS

There is a problem with conflicting figures among the data available on brain drain in Africa. From statistics made available by the International Organization for Migration (IOM), Africa has already lost one third of its human capital and has continued to lose its skilled personnel at an ever increasing rate, and an estimated 20,000 doctors, university lecturers, engineers and other professionals have left the continent annually since 1990. There are also currently over 300,000 highly qualified Africans in the diaspora, out of which 30,000 have Ph.Ds. Ironically, with these abundant human resources, Africa spends USD 4.0 billion per year (which represents 35 per cent of the total official development aid to the continent) as remunerations for some 100,000 western experts who perform functions that are generically described as technical assistance. This dilemma is represented in the table below, based on the estimates from the International Organization for Migration (IOM) and the United Nations Economic Commission for Africa, (UNECA).

The depressing fall-out from the above figures is that in Gabon, for instance, an estimated 90 per cent of the private firms are managed by expatriates, and the whole of Africa counts only 20,000 scientists (which represents 3.6 percent of the world total) following from which its share in the world's scientific output has fallen from 0.5 percent to 0.3 per cent, with the continuous suffering from the brain drain of scientists, engineers and technologists. This has resulted in serious human capital alarm in Africa, with Ethiopia, Nigeria and Ghana, ranked in that order, leading the human capital loss.

The breakdown of IOM's statistics shows that in Ethiopia, over the past 10—15 years, about 50 percent of their people who went abroad

Table 5-1. Emigration of Skilled Africans to Industrialized Countries (Based on IOM and ECA Estimates)

Time Period	Average Annual Rate	Total Number
1960–1974	1,800	27,000
1975–1984	4,000	40,000
1985–1989	12,000	60,000
Since 1990	20,000	—

Source: Brain Drain in Africa: Facts and Figures; available at internet:@http://www.ncf. ca/~cp129/factsandfigures.pdf

for training did not return after completing their studies. Again, Ethiopia lost about 74.6 of its human capital from various institutions between 1980 and 1991. It is so bad that while Ethiopia has one (1) full-time Economics Professor, they have more than 100 Economists in the USA alone. In the case of Nigeria, the estimates from the Presidential Committee on Brain Drain, set up in 1988 by the Babangida administration; show that between 1986 and 1990, Nigeria lost over 10,000 academics from tertiary education institutions alone. It is also estimated that over 30,000 highly skilled personnel left the country including the public, industrial and private organizations. More so, 64 per cent of Nigerians in the USA aged 25 and older have at least a bachelor's degree. With regard to Zimbabwe, in 1997 alone, more than 1,000 professionals left Zimbabwe, and the Zimbabwe National Association of Social Workers estimates that 1,500 (50 percent) of the country's 3,000 trained social workers left the country for the UK in the last 10 years. In Kenya, it costs about USD 40,000 to train a doctor and USD10,000—15,000 to educate a university student for 4 years. In essence, the African countries generally fund the education of their nationals only to see them end up making contributions to the continual growth of advanced and developed economies with little or no return on their investment.

From all indications, the worst hit is the health sector. Kenya, for instance, loses an average of 20 medical doctors per month. Ghana lost 60 percent of its medical doctors in the 1980s, while between 600 and 700 Ghanaian physicians are currently practicing in the US alone, and this figure represents roughly 50 per cent of the doctors in Ghana. In 1993, the UNDP Human Development Report showed that over 21,000 Nigerian medical doctors were practicing in the USA alone, while Nigeria has an acute shortage of doctors. When we add the other Nigerian doctors in diaspora e.g. in Saudi Arabia, the Gulf States, Europe, Canada, Australia and those scattered all over other African countries, the figure could be 30,000. In Ethiopia, one-third of its medical doctors have already left the country. As Randal Tobias, the US Government's Global AIDS Coordinator, states, "there are more Ethiopian-trained doctors practicing in the city of Chicago alone than in Ethiopia. In Zambia the situation is not better off, as only 50 out of the 600 doctors trained in the country's medical school from 1978—1999 could be retained by the public sector. According to a story focused on Ghana which is generalized to the whole of the continent, the medical staff have been "lured" away to work in the USA and Britain thereby crippling Ghana's health service. As it were, "Its (Ghana's) training school turns out almost 100 nurses a year—to be sucked up by the West, lured by the ten-fold salaries. Almost 1,000 nurses and 150 doctors have left Ghana for the UK in the past six years, and the flow is accelerating. Hundreds more have gone to the US, Australia and other countries in a mass migration fuelled by the worldwide demand for medical staff."[16]

It has also been observed that 30 per cent of doctors and nurses in the UK trained outside the country. In France and Germany, the figure is only 5 per cent. Again, half of the 16,000 medical staff recruited in Britain come from outside Europe. Almost all the 2001 class of medical students in Ghana have left and those who remain are preparing to leave the country. The net effect of all these is that the loss of large numbers of medical staff and other skilled professionals is compromising the local health care provision and other relevant sectors where their services are needed in their countries of origin.

In general terms, people have argued about the positive impact of the remittances made to the home countries by these professionals in diaspora. It has been stated that Africans working abroad send home some USD45 billion every year. The other positive impacts include:

- The remittances inject new skills in the system when the migrants return to their countries;

- The remittances boost household welfare;

- The remittances also support balance of payments.

These have been countered by the fact that they do not make up for the social costs and adverse effects of the losses on developing economies of the flow of skilled personnel in the form of brain drain. The other negative impacts include,

- The further reduction of the already low quality of skilled man-power available in African countries which is needed for their development;

- Increases in the continual dependence on foreign technical assistance;

- Gradual but steady slow-down of the transfer of technology and the widening of the gap between African and industrialized countries;

- The continent's scientific and development outlook is negatively skewed; and,

- The loss of money in income tax revenues from the brain drain which would have been counted in potential contributions to gross domestic product.

It becomes clear then when Amin opines that, "We begin to understand then why no single region of emigration has ever developed either in Africa or elsewhere. The transfer—which is more than considerable—is virtually a "gift" from the poor source areas to the rich areas which benefit from it and this is sufficient in itself to explain the stagnation of the regions of origin of the migrants. And, because of their stagnation, the conditions for the reproduction of the pattern of unequal development are perpetuated; because inequality in the 'allocation factors,' far from being 'natural,' is produced and reproduced socially," (Amin, 1974, 106).

These hard facts have put African countries in very serious jeopardy. Aside from the fact that Africa suffers from various problems, some of which are self inflicted, the negative effects of brain drain have worsened the chances of the continent's rapid development. There is also another source through which Africa's manpower continues to be depleted. The introduction of the 'visa lottery' by the US and more recently Canada has continually and quietly been removing the moderately skilled manpower from the states of Africa. Some may see this as an opening to run away from jobless-ness and unemployment and other frustrating conditions in Africa, but the fact remains that these skills if properly trained and harnessed could make some meaningful contributions to the development of the continent.

It is however good that effort is being made by African governments at various levels to stem the tide of brain-drain. These include the following:

- There is effort in the direction of what has been called the "dias-pora option" or "virtual participation," which entails encouraging the skilled personnel "lost" in brain-drain to participate in nation-building of their countries of origin without physically relocating there. This effort therefore sees brain-drain not as a loss, but a potential gain, as the highly skilled expatriates are seen as a pool of potentially useful human resources for the country of origin.

There is also the option of "virtual linkages," which are independent, non-political, and non-profit networks which facilitates skills transfer and capacity-building. The essence is that these networks mobilize skilled diaspora members' expertise for the development process in their countries of origin. It is on record that about 41 virtual networks in 30 different countries have been identified, six of which are African, and including the South African Network of Skills Abroad (SANSA), with members in 68 countries: there is also the Nigerians in Diaspora Organisation (NIDO), among so many others.[17] There are also contributions through virtual networks by individuals of the diaspora, as visiting scholars, by investing in companies, and also by assisting in joint ventures between host and sending countries. The NIDO has been used mainly for political, rather than economic purposes.

- There is also the special effort by the African Union (AU) which shows that African governments have begun to pay serious attention to the menace of brain-drain. The effort was given the breath of life when in 2003, both the New Partnership for Africa's Development (NEPAD) and the AU formally recognized the African Diaspora as a key player in the development agenda of the continent. Accordingly, the AU amended its charter to, " . . . encourage the full participation of the African Diaspora as an important part of the continent."[18]

- There are also so many other efforts in various parts of the world to encourage the exploitation of the positive gains of brain drain. For instance in 2004, the Association for Higher Education and Development (AHEAD) in collaboration with International Development Research Centre (IDRC) organized an international Stakeholder Roundtable which was held in Ottawa, Canada, and brought together key stakeholders, including IOM, Canadian government agencies, African missions, non-governmental organizations, and Diaspora groups to discuss brain-drain in Africa and the potential strategies for mobilizing the African Diaspora. Their discussions yielded positive results which included the need to recognize the African Diaspora as a Key stakeholder in the on-going dialogue and efforts aimed at addressing the issues of brain drain and capacity building in Africa. The importance of sustained diaspora engagement was emphasized, and this will require policy and resource commitments by key stakeholders, including international organizations, African governments, and host countries. They agreed that there was urgent need for the emerging Diaspora movement to become more involved in Africa's development efforts, the growing political will in Africa to recognize the diaspora's potential contribution, and the possibilities created by information technology show the negative impression about brain drain, is not after all, a total loss to the African continent. (Tebeje, 2006)

It has to be acknowledged that various governments are currently in dialogue and are making efforts to curb the negative impacts of brain drain.[19] On this note, it would suffice for us to make an evaluation and to conclude this discussion.

EVALUATION AND CONCLUSION

From our discussion, we could find out that brain drain is only another type of migration, which involves highly skilled personnel who are lost to the developed world because of the several disequilibria at their countries of origin which we have articulated in our discourse. Apparently brain gain and brain circulation, for obvious reasons—are heavily skewed against the countries of emigration from Africa, and what we see as positive contributions are "mere gifts" rather than anything that can engender any meaningful development in Africa. Migration flows indicate that there is circulation within Africa, Europe, Australia, etc. In as much as Nigerians aspire to go to other places, people also want to come to Nigeria, Europe, South Africa, Australia, Senegal and Côte d'Ivoire, among others.

The facts available to us show that there is still serious work to be done. Researchers have discovered that among other things, Africa has already lost one-third of its human capital, an estimated 300,000 skilled professionals are outside Africa, Africa continues to lose 20,000 skilled professionals every year, there are 30,000 Africans with Ph.D. degrees outside Africa; one can go on and on.[20] The solution to this problem does not lie in bemoaning our fate, but in adopting dispassionate and pragmatic approach(es) toward turning the tables in our favor. As Amin has observed, "History has shown elsewhere that a rectification of the situation is possible if an appropriate effort of voluntary planning is carried out to deal with the rules of the market and the 'allocation of factors,' resulting in a development which then, and only then, can stop the impoverishing flow of emigration," (Amin, 1974, 106). Despite the ideological bent of his conviction, the message cannot be ignored if we actually want any meaningful and sustainable development in Africa. The new momentum toward this effort should be sustained in order first and foremost to break some of the major barriers, which also include the sour relationships between African governments and the African Diaspora. African governments should also look inward and develop skills that will take care of their development needs and stop producing manpower for the West. The emphasis on remittances has only produced oases of rich families but poor governmental institutions to take care of the people's problems. The African Diaspora can still contribute genuinely when the conditions are ripe in so many ways, including skill transfer, resource transfer, and transfer of technology, strengthening of civil society and complementing foreign aid, among others.

In as much as poverty is mainly driving people out from Africa, it has to be noted that the advanced countries also need Africa. The fact remains that they have an aging society and their youth are not prepared to take up the challenge of adequately replacing the manpower for which Africans are needed. This is why qualified immigrants take over the skilled jobs. People also emigrate for other reasons, including ecological factors (landslide, desert encroachment), and conflict. These are the reasons why the developed world should invest in Africa. They should invest in education, health, agriculture and give grants for other development purposes. This is to counter-balance what they are taking away from Africa. Today, even with the fact of globalization which sees the world as a global village, Africa has no say on whom it receives and the type of people that emigrant countries accept. The USA and European Union continue to tighten their visa requirements, thereby making things more difficult for Africa. The solution does not lie only in debt forgiveness. They should also assist in stopping the sale and flow of small arms and light weapons into Africa. This is because it fuels conflict and destabilizes the economy and political stability of the continent. They should know that the world cannot be at rest until Africa has peace.

We in Africa must realize the essence of good governance which entails, among other things, greater transparency, effective public sector management, increased government responsiveness to the citizens including the poor, credible institutional mechanisms for monitoring and redressing human rights violations, equity in representation, including gender and social group representations, and zero tolerance for corruption. This will create confidence in the system and rekindle the hope of the African Diaspora that they are not investing in vain.

Finally, we can understand that though the relationship between migration and development tends to be a complex one, especially international migration in the mode of brain drain, if properly managed it could contribute to the development of both countries of origin and destination, and perhaps create the necessary harmonious relationship towards a more stable world order.

NOTES

1. 'Brain Drain,' in "Africa: Facts and Figures," available at http://www.nct.ca/-cp129/factsandfigures.pdf; Accessed last on January 8, 2006.
2. "The Brain Drain: Africa's Achilles Heel," available on the internet at http://www.worldmarketsanalysis.com/InFocus2002/articles/africa_braindrain.html
3. O. Ibidapo-Obe, "Brain Drain, Brain Gain and Brain Circulation: What Chances for Africa?," a paper presented at the National Workshop on "Technical Cooperation and Economic Integration: A Development Paradigm for Breaking the trans-Boundary Divide in Africa," organized by the Directorate of Technical Cooperation in Africa; Federal Ministry of Cooperation and Integration in Africa, (Abuja, Nigeria, February 15–16, 2005), 2. As cited in, O. Ibidapo-Obe, "Brain Drain, Brain Gain and Brain Circulation: What Chances for Africa?, a paper presented at the workshop on Technical Cooperation and Economic Integration: A Development Paradigm fot Breaking the Transboundary Divide in Africa" 2 (1989); 42, organized by the Directorate of Technical Cooperation in Africa; Federal Ministry of Cooperation and Integration in Africa,(Abuja, Nigeria, February 15–16, 2005).
4. The issue was noticed in South Africa, when the Super Falcons (the Female Football players of Nigeria) were not fairly treated in South Africa after winning the championship. Their allowances and match bonuses were not paid. It was discovered that the bulk of Nigerians living in South Africa who had come to give the female football players the necessary financial support (on their refusal to come back home unless their allowances are paid) are Nigerians who left Nigeria after facing various forms of frustrations. Some of them left with GCE ordinary level certificates and some with first degrees. As a result of their determination to succeed in life some of them now have Ph.D. Degrees from South African universities and are contributing meaningfully to the growth of the South African economy. The same could be said without fear of contradiction about Nigerians and other Africans who now reside in other countries both in and outside Africa as a result of similar circumstance(s).
5. A. Zegeye, , and S. Ishemo, (eds.), *Forced Labour and Migration: Patterns of Movement within Africa* (London, Munich, New York: Hans Zell Publishers, 1989), 1–27.

6. P. Baran, *The Political Economy of Growth*, (Harmondsworth: Beacon, 1973); S. Amin, "Underdevelopment and Dependence in Black Africa: Origins and Contemporary Forms," *Journal of Modern African Studies*, 10 no 4, (1972); A.G. Frank, *On Capitalist Underdevelopment*, (Oxford: Oxford University Press, 1975); I. Wallerstein, *World Inequality: Origins and Perspectives on the World System*, (Montreal: Black Rose Books, 1975).

7. P. Makinwa-Adebusoye, "The West African Migration System," in M.M. Kritz, L.L. Lim, and H. Zlotink (eds.), *International Migration Systems: A Global Approach* (Oxford: Clarendon Press, 1992): 76–77.

8. S. Amin (ed.), *Modern Migrations in West Africa* [Studies Presented and Discussed at the Eleventh International African Seminar, Dakar, Senegal]. (London: Oxford University Press, 1974): 85.

9. I. Wallerstein, "Migration in West Africa: the Political Perspective," in H. Kuper (ed.), *Urbanization and Migration in West Africa,* (Berkeley and Loss Angeles: University of California Press, 1965): 148.

10. M. Toure, and T.O. Fadayomi (eds.), *Migrations, Development and Urbanization Policies in Sub-Saharan Africa,* (CODESRIA Book series, 1992): ii.

11. A.L. Mabogunje, "Agrarian Responses to Out migration in Sub-Saharan Africa," in Geoffrey McNicoll and Mead Cain (eds.), *Rural Development and Population: Institutions and Policy*. Supplement to Population and Development Review 15, (New York: Oxford University Press, 1990).

12. P.K. Makinwa-Adebusoye, "The African Family in Rural and Agricultural Activities," in A. Adepoju (ed.), *Family, Population and Development in Africa,* (London: Zed Books Ltd., 1997): 103.

13. A. Adepoju, "Migration and Urbanization in Africa: Issues and Policies," in Van de Walle, E., Sala-Diakanda, M.D. and Ohadike, P.O. (eds.), *The State of African Demography,* (Belgium: International Union for the Scientific Study of Population, 1988), 124.

14. Clyde Sanger, "A Diaspora and its Good Deeds," A University Affairs at: http://www.universityaffairs.ca/issues/2005/feb/opinion_01.html: last visited on January 8, 2006.

15. C. Egbe, and C. Ndubuisi, "Institutional Factors and Immigrant Investment in Homeland: Nigerians in the USA," in, A.N. Nwaneri (ed.), *Nigeria's Visions for the Future* (Nigeria: Macmillan, 1997): 42–43.

16. Black Looks: Africa's brain drain; available at http://okrasoup.typepad.com/black_looks/2005/05/a_worrying_stor.html; last visited on October 29, 2005.

17. Another one is,Association of Nigerian Physicians in the Americas (ANPA);And the Imo State-USA Association, which visited Nigeria in December 2006, and was solely responsible for sourcing and equiping the Imo State University Teaching Hospital, Oru, in Imo State, Nigeria.

18. A. Tebeje, "Brain Drain and Capacity Building in Africa: International (Development Research Centre, IDRC); 2, available at http://www.idrc.ca/en/ev-71249–201–1-Do_TOPIC.html (last visited January 8, 2006).

19. This writer was a participant in the National Workshop on "Technical Cooperation and Economic Integration: A Development Paradigm for Breaking the Trans-Boundary Divide in Africa" organized by the Directorate of Technical Cooperation in Africa (DTCA), Ministry of Cooperation and

Integration in Africa, February 15–16, 2005. One of the paper presenters, Ambassador Joe Keshi, "The Nigerians in the Diaspora Organization, (NIDO)," emphasized the need to encourage Nigerians in the Diaspora with special skills to come home with special incentives, concessions and other necessary enabling environments to invest their talents in the country. He also admonished the 'entrenched interests,' not to feel threatened, as if those in Diaspora are coming home to take their jobs. This could be one of the positive ways of 'luring' the Diasporas back home to assist in the development of their various countries.

20. Brain Drain in Africa: Facts and Figures, It is noted that these figures represent a gross under-estimation of the facts on the ground.

REFERENCES

Adepoju, A. "Migration and Urbanization in Africa: Issues and Policies." in Van de Walle, E., Sala-Diakanda, M.D. and Ohadike, P.O. (eds.), *The State of African Demography*. Belgium: International Union for the Scientific Study of Population, 1988.

Amin, S. "Underdevelopment and Dependence in Black Africa: Origins and Contemporary Forms," *Journal of Modern African Studies*, 10. 4. (1972).

Amin, S. (ed.) *Modern Migrations in West Africa* [Studies Presented and Discussed at the Eleventh International African Seminar, Dakar, Senegal]. (London: Oxford University Press, 1974.

Baran, P. *The Political Economy of Growth*. Harmondsworth: Beacon, 1973.

Black Looks; Africa's Braindrain available at http://okrasoup.lypepad.com/black_looks/2005/05/a_worrying_stor.htm

Egbe, C. and Ndubuisi, C., "Institutional Factors and Immigrant Investment in Homeland: Nigerians in the USA," in, Nwaneri, A.N. (ed.) *Nigeria's Visions for the Future*. Nigeria: Macmillan, 1997.

Frank, A.G. *On Capitalist Underdevelopment*. Oxford: Oxford University Press, 1975.

Ibidapo-Obe, O., "Brain Drain, Brain Gain and Brain Circulation: What Chances for Africa?," a paper presented at the National Workshop on "Technical Cooperation and Economic Integration: A Development Paradigm for Breaking the trans-Boundary Divide in Africa," organized by the Directorate of Technical Cooperation in Africa; Federal Ministry of Cooperation and Integration in Africa, Abuja, Nigeria, February 15–16, 2005.

Mabogunje, A.L., "Agrarian Responses to Out migration in Sub-Saharan Africa," in Geoffrey McNicoll and Mead Cain (eds.), *Rural Development and Population: Institutions and Policy*. Supplement to Population and Development Review 15, New York: Oxford University Press 1990.

Makinwa-Adebusoye, P., "The West African Migration System," in Kritz, M.M.; Lim, L.L. and Zlotink, H. (eds.), *International Migration Systems: A Global Approach*. Oxford: Clarendon Press, 1992.

Makinwa-Adebusoye, P.K., "The African Family in Rural and Agricultural Activities." in Adepoju, A. (ed.), *Family, Population and Development in Africa*. London: Zed Books Ltd., 1997.

Tebeje, A., "Brain Drain and Capacity Building in Africa: International Development Research Centre, IDRC; available at: http://www.idrc.ca/en/ev-71249–201–1-Do_TOPIC.html last visited January 8, 2006.

Toure, M., and Fadayomi, T.O. (eds.) *Migrations, Development and Urbanization Policies in Sub-Saharan Africa*. CODESRIA Book series, 1992.

Wallerstein, I. *World Inequality: Origins and Perspectives on the World System*. Montreal: Black Rose Books, 1975.

Wallerstein, I. "Migration in West Africa: the Political Perspective." in Kuper, H., (ed.) *Urbanization and Migration in West Africa*. Berkeley and Loss Angeles: University of California Press, 1965.

Zegeye, A., and Ishemo, S. (eds.). *Forced Labour and Migration: Patterns of Movement within Africa*. London: Munich, New York: Hans Zell Publishers, 1989.

Chapter Six

Walking for Land, Drinking Palm Wine: Migrant Farmers and the Historicity of Land Conflict in Brong Ahafo, Ghana

Isidore Lobnibe

In Ghana, as elsewhere in Africa, disputes over the boundaries of chieftaincies and fields are not only widespread, but in constant flux.[1] Berry for instance, notes in her study of southeastern Asante that conflicts over farmlands, which commonly lack precise boundaries, are continually "enacted, renewed, and redefined through numerous daily dramas of assertions, contestations, and debate," (2001:157) in which the parties involved are forced to make representations of the past to legitimate claims in the present. Even among members of the same family disputing over succession to office or stool land boundaries, conflicting claims often have to be interpreted and constantly reaffirmed through narratives of the distant past or tradition. Lentz has recently made similar observations in the Black Volta region where alternative "first comer" and "late comer" narrative accounts are proffered by rival claimants to disputed land or earth shrine boundaries, providing discursive content for contestation and counter-contestation.[2] It has long been recognized, however, by both historians and anthropologists of Africa, that the past or tradition upon which such narratives draw can be very recent and invented.[3] However, the means by which self-professed outsiders, viz. recent migrants, fit into this terrain have not generally been a focus of investigation.

In the land dispute between two chieftains, namely, the Dormaa and the Wenchi, located on the fringes of the southern Akan forest of Ghana, which I discuss in the following pages, the parties similarly draw on different versions of the past: each different in terms of its depth and connections with the colonial past rather than in terms of its substantive detail.[4] In this chapter, I explore the dynamics of historical production in the context of the present day struggle over one case of a colonially demarcated land boundary, but one of my main aims is to show how the narratives of the dispute both feature in the daily public discourse of migrant farmers, and also shape and reshape their livelihood and interactions with their hosts.

In West Africa more generally, debates over the effect of colonial rule on African property relations have sought to reveal how colonialism, and the capitalist accumulation that came with it, generated conflicts of interest among Africans. Such conflicts have continued to be shaped not just by the material and political resources, which different groups can marshal in support of their interests, but also by the terms in which people understand their interests and express them.[5] Building on these insights, I argue that conflicts between landowners in the food production frontier of Ghana,[6] in northern Ashanti and the Brong Ahafo regions, are commonly staged as intermigrant conflicts by the actors involved, in order to conceal age-old conflicts of a quite different nature. It can even be maintained that landless migrants from the North are drawn into these confrontations to help protect the interests of the local disputants.

INTERMIGRANT CONFLICT AT AHYIAYEM: A SPARK TO A LAND BOUNDARY DISPUTE

In 2003, a local tension involving two immigrant households in a farming community in the Brong Ahafo region of Ghana (see fig.1) quickly escalated, degenerating into an open conflict, according to sources in a village called Ahyiayem. A teenage girl informed her parents in December of that year that a young man in the village was responsible for her pregnancy. Her parents sent the case to a village court to find out the truth of the allegations and what to do next, but the young man refused to appear before it to answer the allegations leveled against him. Frantic efforts were made by the village headman (himself a migrant) to resolve the matter at his level, but realizing that the issues involved were beyond his control, he referred it to his superior, the Omanhene (Paramount chief) of the Wenchi traditional area, under whose authority he was made head of the village. Tensions peaked when the relatives of the girl, angered by lack of cooperation by the young man and his father's subsequent failure to pay an initial fine of 200.000 (two hundred thousand cedis) for the upkeep of the expectant mother, decided to take matters into their own hands: the young man was declared a *persona non grata* in the village and his father, Dozie, was almost lynched in the village market. Dozie was therefore summoned to the Wenchihene palace. There, he was fined an unspecified sum of money and, in addition, ordered to leave the village immediately after he finished harvesting his food crops.

When news of Dozie's expulsion from Ahyiayem spread to the nearby Dormaa town of Chiraa, the citizens of that town, in an apparent defiance of the Wenchi paramount chief, rallied to the support of the expelled migrant farmer; one of the town's elders, Agya Badu, is said to have even gone personally to invite Dozie to come and settle on his piece of land under exceptionally generous terms: "He [Agya Badu] has shown me a place to build a house, adding that I could even put up a zinc house if I have the means to do so. He has also shown me a more fertile and 'bigger' piece of land on which to farm than my previous farmland. My farm is close to my house and the town; I do not have to walk a long distance as before. Besides, I am no longer in the middle of houses as in Ahyiayem which is good for the safety of my animals."[7]

The land on which Dozie was resettled by Agya Badu lies in between Chiraa and Ahyiayem (lit "a meeting place" in the Akan language), and is less than 100 metres south of the disputed boundary (see figure 2). Given that migrants are generally considered "strangers" (*ahoho*) and marginal with respect to land rights and other resources in this Akan controlled territory[8], it is interesting that a domestic squabble between two immigrant households should receive the attention of the host community the way it did, and even ignite an invitation from a village elder in support of the stranger. What was at stake here?

From Dozie's new settlement one sees a giant signboard erected a few meters from the disputed boundary with the words boldly written: "New Wenchi, "Ahyiayem," "Ohenekoko" to welcome visitors to Ahyiayem(see figure 3). Villagers I interviewed explained to me that the signboard has been put there by the Wenchi paramountcy, to substantiate her claims that Ahyiayem is the location where a British colonial officer marked the boundary between the states of Wenchi and Dormaa in the early days of colonial rule, after a walking contest was conducted between the chiefs and peoples of the two, in which the former emerged victorious.

Since the 1930s, the boundary in question has, however, been the subject of multiple interpretations and representations, not only by the rival claimants, but in recent times, also by the migrant farmers resident on the boundary. These interpretations are the subject of this chapter. Before going into the historical representations of the disputed boundary and a discussion of how and for what purpose migrants became inserted in these debates, a few remarks on the settlement of the village and on how I came to be familiar with its history will be useful.

THE SETTLEMENT OF AHYIAYEM AND THE LAND DISPUTE

Ahyiayem is one of the numerous villages inhabited mainly by farm migrants from northern Ghana, a group among many who have established themselves between the ecological transition zone of the northern savanna and the fringes of the southern Akan forest. Labor migration from northern Ghana to the south dates back to the turn of the 19th century when the British colonial administration carved out the "North" as a labor reserve from which laborers were recruited to work in the mines, cocoa plantations and government public works.[9] The phenomenon has continued in the post-independence era, with farmers leaving the dry savanna region of their own volition in search of more fertile lands in the south.[10]

Many villagers still remember the days when they started settling the area in the mid-eighties, a few years after the massive bushfires that swept through the entire forest of southern Ghana. In 1982/3 these fires decimated large sectors of food crops and cocoa farms. The devastation resulted in widespread shortages of food and basic supplies in the Ghanaian local markets. Lacking the hard currency from the cocoa exports to import food from elsewhere, the country was plunged into a severe food crisis. The forced repatriation of over a million Ghanaian migrants from Nigeria in the same year, amid continuing political instability in the country arising from the 1981 military coup d'état by Flight. Lieutenant, J.J Rawlings, exacerbated the food crisis.[11] Most landowners, cocoa farmers, and even some traditional rulers in rural southern Ghana responded to the emergency by giving out on contract their ruined cocoa farms and bush fields (koya) to landless northern migrant farmers. These migrants settled and started producing food crops on a share-crop basis (Dominyenkye).[12]

During the 1980s, the political and economic conditions described above may have precipitated the founding of several settlements such as Ahyiayem, but in the case of this area there was an additional factor, a *longue durée* context that made the landowners welcome the migrants: a dispute over a colonially demarcated boundary.

I visited the market of Ahyiayem in February 2005, while conducting field work, and was warmly welcomed with calabashes of sorghum beer (pito). As we chatted over the drink, my host–called Dozie—commented on his recent expulsion from the village, as if to inform me that he was no longer a resident there. When pressed, he explained that he was expelled from the village by the Omanhene (i.e. paramount chief) of Wenchi (now deceased) because of the incident described above. I offered a few words of sympathy, but Dozie assured me that he felt much happier to be relocated within Chiraa's territory which is under the Dormaa traditional authority.

Given that Ahyiayem is very close to Chiraa(less than 3 miles), I asked why Ahyiayem is under the traditional authority of Wenchi- which is twelve miles away. My hosts first appeared amused at my question; then he told me what I later found out to be a popular narrative in communities neighboring Chiraa: " . . . the landowners have told us that the people of Chiraa were busy drinking palm wine at the time when they were asked to walk for the land to determine the boundary. . . ."[13]

THE HISTORICITY OF THE DISPUTED BOUNDARY

It is hardly surprising that the past should be invoked in conversations on traditional boundaries.[14] What is interesting, however, is that our conversation got enmeshed in a local popular history that widely associates the people of Chiraa with the drinking of palm wine.

In recent times, historically-minded anthropologists have increasingly turned their attention to analyzing the lived past of informants with a view of gaining insights into how the past created the present.[15] Others ask the question differently, being mindful also of the fact that the past is "selectively appropriated, suppressed, or invented."[16] For this reason, scholars such as Tonkin (1992) and Trouillot (1995) prefer to ask how the present is mobilized for the past, even as they draw their analysis from oral traditions and the people's lived past.[17] In appraising the narratives of the Ahyiayem dispute, therefore, one needs to be guided by insights from Michel-Rolph Trouillot's discussions about the power dynamics inherent in moments of historical production. In his seminal essay on analysis of the events of the Haitian Revolution of 1791, Trouillot observes that the production and consumption of historical knowledge entail both mentions and silences of the past, which in his view, occur at multiple sites, (26). He insists that because the boundaries between these moments are quite fluid, careful attention needs to be paid to both "the socio-historical process, or what happened" (historicity 1), and "the historical narratives, or what is said to have happened" (historicity 2) of a given event, (Trouillot, 3). In what follows, let me start by providing the historical context within which the boundary dispute over Ahyiayem was produced.

THE BRITISH COLONIAL ADMINISTRATION AND THE AHYIAYEM BOUNDARY

Although conflicts, especially those over land, must have existed among Africans before colonial rule, their proliferation in the postcolonial period has been observed to flow largely from the changes wrought by the colonial administrative structures that were established to regulate property and land administration on the continent.[18] In Ghana, students of colonial land policy have attributed most of the current disputes over land to what they thought was a flawed ideological base upon which the British colonial administration built its indirect rule system. As Berry citing Ranger notes: "Many Europeans assumed that African communities consisted of mutually exclusive socio-cultural units-tribes, villages, kin groups-whose customs and structures had not changed over time. Officials could see, of course, that there was conflict among Africans at the time of conquest, but they assumed they could restore order by reconstituting what they believed to have been the 'closed, corporate, consensual systems' of the past (Ranger, 1983). Accordingly, colonial administrators set out to discover the boundaries and customs of traditional societies, and the 'original' relations between them in order to use tradition as the basis of their own administrative structures and practices," (Berry, 1992, 331). Indeed, the administrators, in building what later came to be known as Native Authorities based on local custom, found allies in chiefs who often interpreted the custom to fit their interests. No wonder the colonial administration ignored the dynamic and conflictual nature of local land rights. Indirect rule was thus erected on a foundation of conflict and change based on the assumption that customary land rights constituted a coherent, homogenous, and stable system of rules and beliefs. The result was the proliferation of claims and counter-claims to rights over land and people rather than creating a social order.[19]

In the Gold Coast (now Ghana) the early decades of the British colonial administration coincided with the emerging cocoa economy, a process in which large areas of the forestland were brought under cultivation.[20] The increasing demand for, and pressure on land drove most southern Ghanaian chiefs into making accessible tracts of land to foreign interests for mining or logging, and to subjects of other permanent stools for cocoa production, in return for attractive land rents.[21] The evolving land tenure regime, when viewed against the backdrop of previously permeable or even non-existent land boundaries (Berry, 2001, i-xviii; Lentz 2003, 274), provided fertile grounds for tensions over access and control over land between communities or chiefs. Such tensions caused more problems and conflict over land than could be resolved by the colonial administration.

The emergence of a new cocoa frontier in the Brong Ahafo region, for instance, did not immediately inform the need to define stool boundaries with precision.[22] But that soon changed as disputes over boundaries with neighboring chieftaincies arose because of the new value that the introduction of the crop accorded the land, (Austin, 2005). The colonial administration may have facilitated the quickening pace of agricultural commercialization based on cocoa production, but they were soon confronted with the intense competition it generated between local communities or among chiefs over control of land. Such is the context in which the Ahyiayem boundary dispute needs to be situated.

THE DISPUTANTS

The Wenchi and the Dormaa are among several Akan-speaking peoples who live in what is the present day Brong Ahafo region of Ghana. Before the arrival of Europeans, they were both characterized by long traditions of polities. The Dormaa were among some of the Akan clans that founded the Kingdom of Akwamu. They later migrated from the Eastern Region to the Brong Ahafo region after the disintegration of the Akwamu at the hands of Akyem.[23] The Wenchi, for their part, are among the earliest Akan-speaking people to have lived in the northern edge of Ghana's southern forest.[24]

THE CONTESTED NARRATIVES OVER AHYIAYEM[25]

Oral accounts from Buoku, the Wenchi village with authority over Ahyiayem, recount that in pre-colonial times, Ahwene koko was the seat of the kingdom of Wenchi. It was from there that the people of Wenchi escaped to settle in the present location further north as victims of the Asante wars of expansion. The decisive conquest and occupation of Asante by British forces in 1896 stopped that kingdom's aggression, allowing the Wenchi to head back south to regain control over their lost territories. When they arrived, however, they ran into the Dormaa who had by then settled the area to farm around Abesim, New Dormaa, and Chiraa[26] (see fig.2). A struggle ensued between the two states over territorial boundaries which dragged on until the Whiteman arrived to intervene.

A Wenchi version of how the disputed boundary was demarcated suggests that in the absence of courts and other historical precedents, a colonial administrator in the early colonial period decided to settle the issue with a contest. He instructed the chiefs and people of both Wenchi and Dormaa states to walk from their respective settlements toward each other starting at dawn. Nana Addai of Buoku boasted that the Wenchi chiefs and subjects were determined to cover as much space/distance as possible; hence, they endured in the contest and outpaced their rivals, walking almost into Dormaa territory, near Chiraa, to meet their opponents at what is the present location of Ahyiayem. This story thus explains the etymology of the village name, "meeting place" (Ahyiayem).[27] According to him, the victory of the chiefs and people of Wenchi over the Dormaa in the contest was possible because, while the former were walking, the latter lounged around drinking palm wine, and then having ingested too much of the beverage they were not in a condition to walk further. But whereas the Wenchi's claims to the territory lie in the victory won in this contest, the claims of the Dormaa are based on forceful occupation of the area before European rule.

Some Dormaa informants in Chiraa admit there was a call to a walking contest on the part of the colonial administration, but they maintain that their ancestors refused to participate in it, since the disputed land had been occupied by them by defeating the Wenchi, long before the Whiteman arrived. Agya Badu, for example, cited the well-known military prowess of the Dormaa and argued that it was their ancestors, and not the Asante, who evicted the Wenchi from Ahwene koko.[28] This explains, according to him, why the Dormaa refused to participate in the walking contest, which they saw as an attempt by the colonial officer to impose an arbitrary boundary between them and the Wenchi whom they had expelled from this land in pre-colonial times. In his view, the walking contest was a ploy designed by the late Dr. Busia, a close confidant of the colonial administrator, and also a son of the Wenchi, to win back for his native group land that the Dormaa had seized. Agya Badu rejected the palm wine drinking story, saying that because the Dormaa traditionally love to live life to the full, other people have taken advantage of common shows of conviviality to fabricate stories in order to claim a territory, which the Dormaa had won by right of military conquest.

THE ARCHIVE

The records held in the Sunyani Regional Archives (referred to henceforth as BRG) on the dispute suggest that it first came to the attention of the colonial government agent in Sunyani on 23 May 1935. On that date, the Dormaahene and the elders petitioned the then chief commissioner of Asante, asking him to return to the Dormaa the lands north of Chiraa that they had previously occupied, in accordance with the restoration of the Asante confederacy by the British colonial administration.[29] They started the petition with both a history and the description of Dormaa boundary with Wenchi (Western Province of Ashanti) which they claimed was marked "by a stream known as "Tromo."[30] The petition, included among other things, a complaint that:

> Your humble petitioners peacefully enjoyed the right and privileges of the said lands up to the time of the Yaa Asantewaa war, when a certain unknown European of the Government department accompanied by

soldiers came and altered the said ancient and natural boundary about two and half miles from Chiraa our last village on the Sunyani-Wenchi road . . . that this change took place with unknown reason and when the Ohene of Chiraa and his people asked the cause, they were mal-treated by the soldiers, and as Government was concerned, we feared to take any action thereby the Ohene of Wenchi got the access of taking the land up to this time. (BRG, 1932)

The colonial administration did not cede the land to Dormaa as requested in the petition, but the request necessitated the colonial resi-dent at Kumasi to revisit the boundary issue between the two states. He declared that all lands east of the Fan-palm tree, including Buoku, still belonged to Wenchi-sub district, in line with the earlier decision reached by Sir Stewart.[31] This was vehemently contested by the Dormaahene. In fact, the implementation of the redemarcated boundary was tested in 1949 when Chiraahene brought a complaint before the Sunyani District Com-missioner (DC), challenging Wenchihene's attempt to collect land tributes from his subjects in the disputed territory. The DC directed Chiraa to send the matter to the Asantehene Court A in Kumasi to obtain clarification on how the 1924 colonial boundary book, which in his opinion was supposed to be final, defined the boundary.[32] The Chiraahene was unimpressed with this response and continued to press for recognition of his rights to the disputed territory.

In 1955, he objected to the collection of stones near Buoku by one J.D Adomah who was contracted by the Public Works Department to supply it with materials.[33] This move by Chiraa infuriated the Sunyani District Com-missioner, but it was well calculated because there were concrete develop-ments at that point toward granting political independence to the people of the Gold Coast. Already, elections had been held in 1951 and 1954 and some key sectors of administration were handed over to a government headed by an elected local official in the person of Kwame Nkrumah. Moreover, dur-ing the 1954 campaigns for the impending elections, the CPP and its leader, Kwame Nkrumah had promised to create a new region out of what was then the Western Province of Ashanti, and Chiraahene may have been keen to extend the territory under his jurisdiction in the new region.[34] What the government agent at Sunyani considered Chiraa or Dormaa's intransigence intensified, compelling him to refer the matter to Kumasi, with the expla-nation that his office "held an arbitration to mediate over the matter but time did not allow."[35] It is possible that the people of Wenchi feared that the election of a CPP government in the coming election would dim the prospects of resolving the boundary issue in their favor because of a bitter rivalry between Busia (a native of Wenchi) and Nkrumah. They therefore filed the case in the Asantehene Court A for the first time on behalf of a Plaintiff by the name of Kwaku Amoako, with Kwame Ntoa acting as Dormaahene and others of Chiraa as Defendants.[36]

When Ghana's independence came in 1957, the Dormaa-Wenchi land boundary dispute was still unresolved. Between 1960 and 1962, a flurry of exchanges in the form of presentations was made by both the Wenchi and the Dormaa to the Regional Commissioner at Sunyani. This official initiated a number of meetings between the rival chiefs to settle the dispute "once and for all."[37] In 1962 a breakthrough seemed to have been achieved when the two parties agreed to the hiring of a Kumasi-based surveyor, Mr. E. L. Minta, to demarcate the boundary. But no sooner had he set to work than objections were raised by Dormaa, ordering him to stop the work. Dormaa's action infuriated Wenchi and led to an escalation of tensions. In a letter to President Nkrumah, the then Wenchihene, Nana Abre Mborhre Bediatuo VI sought to dismiss Dormaa claims to the territory. Returning to the colonial past, he explained in his letter that the conflict resulted from a "misunderstanding between Wenchi and the Dormaa traditional authorities as to the exact meaning of the description of 'Chiraa boundaries' as spelled out in the provincial Boundary Book, Western Province of Ashanti by Sir Stewart."[38] The Wenchihene explained that as far back as 1924, Sir Stewart, the first government resident of Kumasi, had fixed the boundary between Chiraa and Wenchi, allocating Buoku to the state of Wenchi. But that "the only portion of land in dispute is that to the east of the Sunyani-Techiman road, i.e. from the fan-palm tree on the Sunyani-Techiman road to the River Tano," (BRG Sunyani 1962). To support his claims to this territory, portions of the colonial boundary book delimiting the boundary between the two states were quoted extensively: "The Fan Palm tree three miles north of Chiraa has been defined as the centre from which to mark the boundary (3). From the Fan tree the boundary can be marked straight to the River Sisi, thence to the Bisi River and on the River Tain on the West. It appears also that a line drawn straight from the Fan Tree to the River Tano on the East (a natural obstacle) would be a fair and equitable determination of what by the only evidence available should constitute the boundary between the two states."[39] From this brief overview of the archival records, it is clear that there was indeed a long standing land boundary dispute between the Dormaa and the Wenchi which both the colonial and post-colonial governments attempted to resolve. However, the records present the land boundary dispute from the 1930s to Ghana's independence in a different light from the narratives that have wide currency today. A search in the colonial archive has so far not produced any record of the walking contest as recounted in the oral accounts. It is possible that the omission is either the result of an invented story by the Wenchi to help legitimate their claims to ownership of the disputed territory, or the colonial authorities' deliberate expunging the incident from their records.

It is beyond the scope of this paper to analyze the origins of the conflict or determine the relative merit of the different accounts. Suffice it to say here that the rival claimants' accounts of the demarcation of the boundary in dispute, and their past relationships with each other are to a large degree informed by their respective present day interests in the disputed territory. The oral narratives and archival records also help illustrate how African relations to land and to each other were significantly reshaped with the agricultural commercialization of the early decades of the colonial regime. New strategies were designed in struggles over access to land and a new meaning of land rights emerged. It is the strategic use to which the disputants have put the migrants resident on the colonial boundary at Ahyiayem, in their struggle to control the disputed territory, that I now bring up for an appraisal.

MIGRANTS AND THE DISPUTE: AN APPRAISAL

To assess the issues at stake in the Ahyiayem land dispute requires a closer look at the behavior of the two major actors involved, the Wenchi and the Dormaa, in the conflict involving the migrants, and the different interpretations and meanings they ascribe to the colonial boundary. In particular, there is a need to examine the motive behind the urgency with which the Wenchihene expelled Dozie; and the reason for the swift response of Agya Badu to resettle the expelled migrant on his field. These are taken up in the rest of the discussion to help illustrate the broader argument that migrants may have been invited to reside on the boundary, or even drawn into its narrative representations by the rival claimants in order to strengthen their respective political and economic positions with respect to the disputed territory.

In the past few years, scholars of African borderland populations have provided new insights, which seek to challenge conventional views of the arbitrariness of African colonial borders.[40] They argue that although national borders, which were drawn during colonial rule, disrupted the economic and social lives of local populations, their effects should not be viewed purely in terms of the constraints they present or as impositions on hapless and unwilling Africans, as was previously the case. In his study of smuggling strategies adopted along the Anglo-French border separating Ghana and Togo, Paul Nugent, for instance, argues that far from being victims, the local populations across this border negotiated and renegotiated with the colonial authorities for its precise location, (Nugent, 1999, 8–11). Thereafter, smugglers of goods and litigants of land disputes, depending on the context, were able to turn the border into a political and economic resource; the former often evaded custom duties by escaping across the border, and in court cases, litigants of land disputes invoked the presence of the border to nullify the competing claims of their rivals.

Although we are dealing here with a boundary over farmland, this nuanced view of African reaction to national boundaries has some relevance. In both their discourses and practices, the disputants have tried either to subvert the boundary to advance their interests, or to use it as a weapon to nullify the claims of their rivals.[41] We have already seen how the Wenchi consistently draw on the colonial past to support their claims, relying on the act of the boundary-making by the colonial administrator to nullify the Dormaa claims to the territory. On their part, the Dormaa have sought to subvert the boundary, referring to it as an arbitrary imposition by the colonial authority. It can be argued, therefore, that the involvement of migrants in this century-old land dispute was necessitated by the chiefs' desire to adopt a new strategy to give more concrete legitimacy to their respective claims.

Since the 1980s, one effective strategy deployed by landowners in Wenchi territory has been to invite farm migrants to settle on the disputed boundary to help boost their claims to the territory. Some informants in Chiraa explained that although the land dispute has been in existence over a century, it remained dormant for the most part, erupting only intermittently. As a result, they had been able to farm on the disputed territory until the mid 1980s when the migrants were brought to settle in the area. The presence of these farmers, they claim, was the reason for their rights to the farmlands in the area being taken away and given to the strangers. It is even alleged that the early settlers of Ahyiayem initially lived near Buoku. As landless migrants, they were recruited by the Wenchi to help the local youth to erect the signboard that now stands as public reminder of Wenchi success in asserting the disputed boundary. In return for supporting the people of Wenchi, it appears that the early migrants were then granted settlement rights, and one of their leaders was given an additional limited authority to run the village affairs.

The above background may explain the urgency with which the Wenchihene expelled Dozie while settling the pregnancy dispute. It further clarifies the purpose for which the migrants were allowed to settle on the disputed boundary. By inviting the migrants to settle on the disputed boundary, the Wenchihene brought into existence a category of subjects whose presence should give practical legitimacy to his claims. He also expected them not only to profess their subordination and loyalty to him, but also to recount the Wenchi version of the narrative legitimizing his claims to the territory as a shared history.

Dozie was not part of this shared history. He was a latecomer to the village whose loyalty could not be counted upon by the Wenchihene. Dozie was a retrenched migrant laborer who had arrived from the Obuasi mines where he had worked over twenty years. In 1999, he went to settle at Ahyiayem at the invitation of his mother's brother, instead of returning to his native village in the north. Unlike most villagers, Dozie was clearly exposed to city life. He understood the local politics in which he and other migrants have been situated and therefore could exploit the ongoing dispute to his own personal advantage. He told me that even before his son's affair with the young lady, his frequent visits to Chiraa were a matter of concern to land owners at Ahyiayem. But whether he actually struck a deal with the Dormaa of Chiraa before his expulsion and had anticipated their support in the unfolding tension is unclear to me.

At any rate, Agya Badu was fully aware of the strategic use to which the early migrants were deployed by the Wenchi to advance their interests. By offering to resettle Dozie on his own piece of land, he courted his allegiance and perhaps reframed the domestic dispute in terms of the age-old land dispute. This move could also lend him the support of other late comers in the village beside Dozie. As Anderson has observed, land disputes are ongoing political struggles and rival claimants seize on the least opportunity either to reassert or to renew their control over a disputed territory (as in the case of the Wenchi), or to contest the control of a rival claimant over a territory that may already have been lost (as in the Dormaa case).[42]

Writing of the intense political culture that characterized property relations of nineteenth century Asante, McCaskie observes that throughout that period, certain individual chiefs of the outlying communities in the kingdom struggled for control over subjects and land. According to him, these were viewed more as socio-political rather than economic resources, which the individuals used to mark achievement and status, (McCaskie, 176). Anderson came to a similar conclusion in a situational analysis of one land dispute in contemporary Zimbabwe when he argued that the process of allowing people to settle, or to remain on disputed territory, already suggests that the dispute centers more on the political control of that piece of land rather than on its productive economic value, (Anderson, 574). These insights are useful to the present discussion in that they illuminate both the current local land struggles between the Wenchi and the Dormaa, and the political dimension of the boundary dispute.

There is no doubt that the influx of migrants in the area, who are searching for farmlands in lieu of the hitherto seasonal wage labor, has placed new demand for access to land, intensified conflicts and debates over community citizenship, including the issue of who in the host communities has the right to allocate use rights to the individual migrant. Several migrants at Ahyiayem actually stated that they prefer to lease land annually or on a short-term lease basis. But most landowners, they complain, often insist on share-cropping, and charge them exorbitant leasing fees in order to compel them to take the latter option.

Despite these complaints, the land situation in Ahyiayem cannot be reduced to one of shortage causing tension between the migrants. Moreover, inter-household conflicts such as the one described in the beginning are common in all farming villages and not unique to Ahyiayem. That this particular tension escalated, and generated so much interest among members of the host communities has more to do with the strategic use to which migrants have been put by the disputants than the particulars of the paternity disagreement. At one level, the involvement of the members of the host communities in the dispute serves as a "diagnostic event," to use Moore's phrase that allows us better to understand the particular way in which conflicts among migrants and between them and their hosts are staged, and the substance of these conflicts.[43] In areas of Ghana with sizeable migrant population with claims to land, or new groups wanting to be integrated, their response to calls by the local traditional rulers for them to recognize their authority and meet certain demands often ignite ethnic tensions which easily degenerate into open conflict. Moreover, new possibilities have opened with the creation of the District Assemblies in the 1990s that entail local revenue mobilization from local or village resources from which payment of royalties are drawn by chiefs. Consequently, chiefs more than ever before are determined not to lose control over certain villages that are supposed to fall under their control.

This is not to suggest that migrants do not have vested interests in the ongoing land dispute. As strangers whose access to land depends on their ability to pay the ever increasing land rents, many of them look for landowners to guarantee continuous access and would readily participate in narrative discourses in support of the hosts in situations of land conflict, in order to consolidate their own access and or status in the host community, (Mikell, Peasant Politicization; Chauveau, 2006). But from the casual manner in which I observed the walking contest narrative to feature in the public discourses of most migrants in the Ahyiayem market scene, it is doubtful that they have assimilated their role in the historical production of the disputed boundary as a shared history. Furthermore, whether such accounts will not be turned around in the future by the migrants themselves, to modify or solidify their own mode of access to farm land remains to be seen.

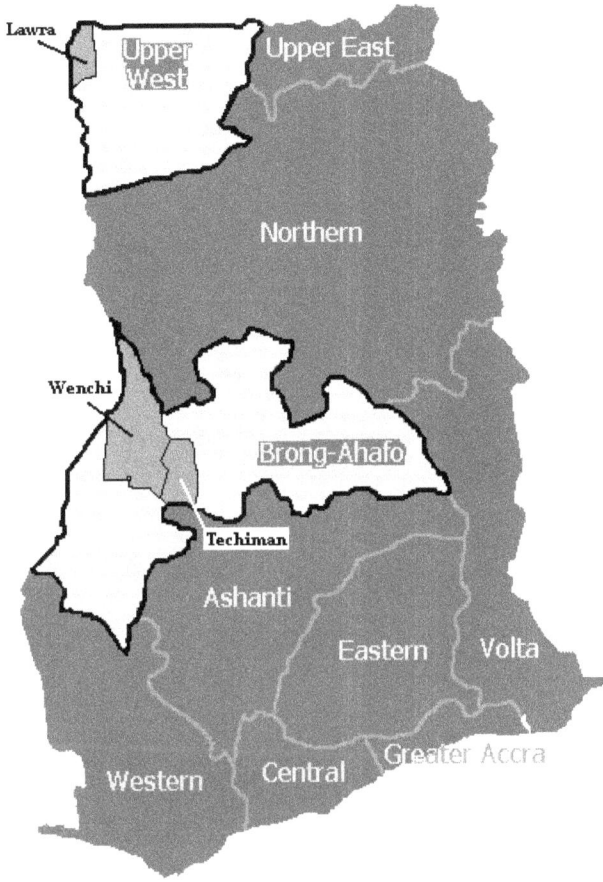

Figure 6-1. Map of Ghana

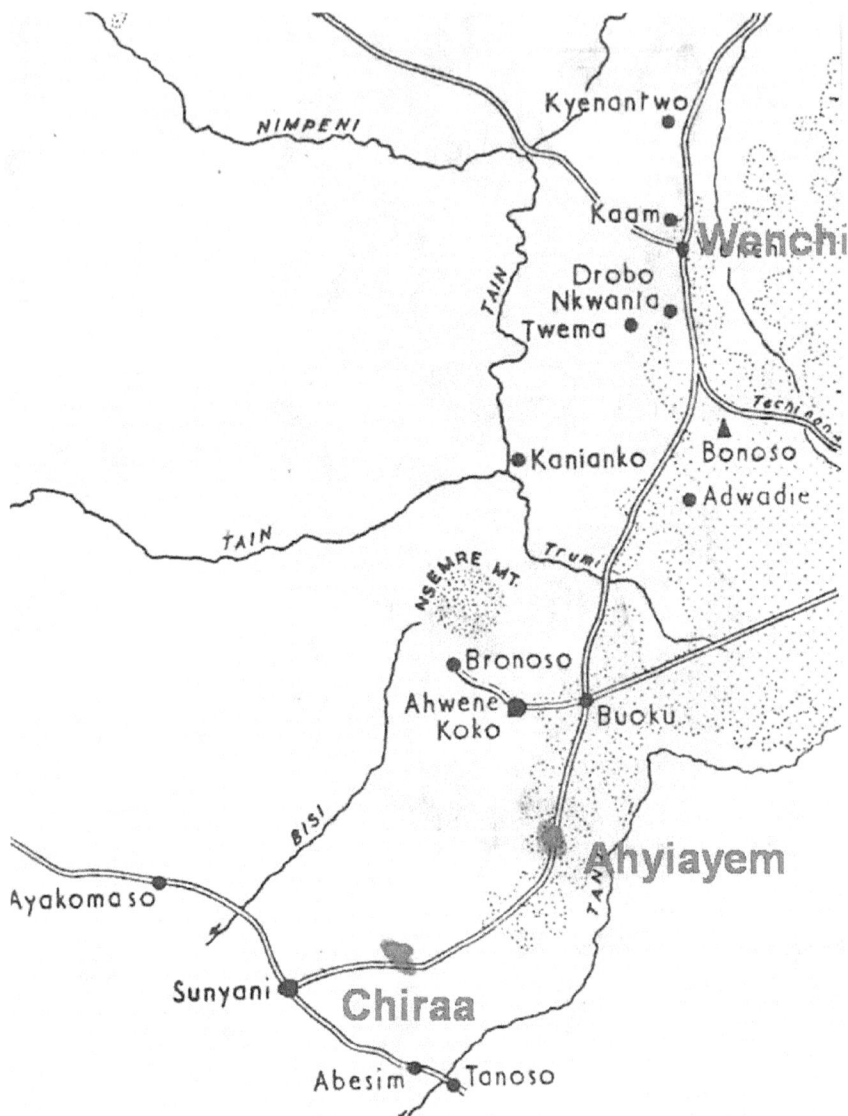

Figure 6-2. The Wenchi State Showing Relief and Important Sites (Adopted from Boachie-Ansah 1986)

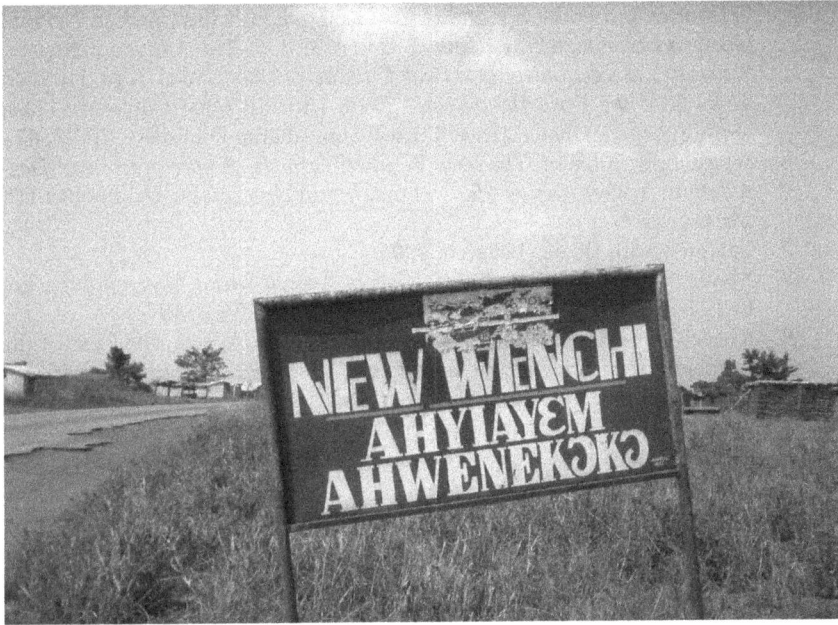

Figure 6-3. Ahyiayem Signpost

NOTES

1. Sara Berry, *Chiefs Know their Boundaries: Essays on Property, Power, and the Past in Asante, 1896–1996,* (Portsmouth, N.H.: Heinemann, 2001); Carola Lentz, "This is Ghanaian Territory!: Land Conflicts on a West African Border," *American Ethnologist* 30 no. 2 (2003): 273–289.
2. Lentz, 2003; see both Carola Lentz, "Land Rights and the Politics of Belonging in Africa. An Introduction," In *Land and the Politics of Belonging in West Africa* Ed. by Richard Kuba, and Carola Lentz. (Leiden, Boston: BRIll, 2006, 1–34); hereafter cited in text as Introduction, and Carola Lentz, "First-Comers and Late-Comers: Indigenous Theories of Land-ownership in West Africa," In *Land and the Politics of Belonging in West Africa.* Ed. by Kuba, Richard , Carola Lentz. (Leiden, Boston: Brill, 2006, 35–56); hereafter cited in text as First-Comers and Late-Comers.
3. Terrence Ranger, "The invention of tradition in Colonial Africa," In *The Invention of Tradition* Ed. E. J. Hobsbawm and T. O. Ranger, (Cambridge: Cambridge University Press, 1983).
4. Sean Hawkins, "Disguising Chiefs and God as History: Questions on the Acephalousness of Lodagaa Politics. . . ." *Africa* 66 no. 2 (1996): 202.
5. Sara Berry, "Hegemony on a Shoestring: Indirect Rule and Access to Agricultural Land," *Africa* 62 no. 3 (1992): 327–355, 328; Carola Lentz,

"Histories and Political Conflict: A Case Study of Chieftaincy in Nadom, Northwestern Ghana," *Paideuma* 39 (1993): 177–215, 180; Paul Nugent, *Smugglers, Secessionists & Loyal Citizens on the Ghana-Toga Frontier: The Lie of the Borderlands since 1914*, (Athens: Ohio University Press; Oxford; Legon, Ghana: James Currey; Sub-Saharan Publishers, 2002), 62.

6. Sebastian K. Amanor, *The New Frontier: Farmers' Response to Land Degradation: A West African Study*, (London and New Jersey: Zed Books LTD, 1994).

7. Interview with Dozie, 3 March, 2005.

8. Meyer Fortes, "Strangers," In *Studies in African Social Anthropology*, Ed. by E. Fortes and S. Patterson. (London, Academic Press, 1975).

9. Roger G Thomas, "Forced Labor in British West Africa: The Case of the Northern Territories of the Gold Coast 1906–1927," *Journal of African History* 14 no. 1(1973): 79–103; Carola Lentz and Viet Erlmann, "A working class in formation? Economic Crisis and Strategies of Survival among Dagara mine workers in Ghana," *Cahiers d'etudes africaines*, 113, 1989.

10. Isidore Lobnibe, "Forbidden Fruit in the Compound: A Case Study of Migration, Spousal Separation and Group-Wife Adultery in Northwest Ghana," *Africa 75*, no. 4 (2005).

11. George. J. Sefa Dei, "The Renewal of a Ghanaian Rural Economy," *Canadian Journal of African Studies*, vol.26 no.1 (1992): 24–53; Nicholas Van Hear, New Diasporas: The Mass Exodus, Dispersal and Regrouping of Migrants Communities, (Seattle, WA: University of Washington Press, 1998); Berry, 2001.

12. For the settlement dynamics of migrant villages in the Kumawu area in the Ashanti region see Berry, 2001, 180–183.

13. Interview with Dozie and others, 3 February, 2005.

14. See Nugent 2002; Berry, 2001; Lentz, First-Comers and Late-Comers, 2006.

15. Ann Brower Stahl, *Making History in Banda: Anthropological Visions of Africa's Past*, (New York: Cambridge University Press, 2001) for a review.

16. Stahl, 8 original emphasis.

17. Elizabeth Tonkin, *Narrating our Pasts: The Social Construction of Oral History*, (Cambridge: Cambridge University Press, 1992); Michel-Rolph Trouillot, *Silencing the Past: Power and the Production of History*, (Boston, Massachusetts: Beacon Press, 1995); cf. Stahl, 8.

18. Berry, 1992; Berry, 2001; J. Thomas Bassett and Donald Crummey, *Land in African Agrarian Systems*, (Madison: University of Wisconsin Press, 1993); Jean-Pierre Chauveau, "How does an Institution Evolve? Land, Politics, Intergrational Relations and the Institution of the Tuorat Amongst Autochones and Immigrants," (Gban Region, Cote D'Ivoire), In *Land and the Politics of Belonging in West Africa*, Ed. by Richard Kuba and Carola Lentz, (Leiden, Boston: Brill, 2006), 213–240; Lentz, Introduction, 2006.

19. John Dunn and A. F. Robertson, *Dependence and Opportunity; Political Change in Ahafo*, (Cambridge, England: University Press, 1973), 73; Berry, 1992, 333; Lentz, Introduction, 2006, 1.

20. Polly Hill, *The Migrant Cocoa-Farmers of Southern Ghana; a Study in Rural Capitalism,* (Cambridge England: University Press, 1963).

21. (Hill, 1963; Gwendolyn Mikell, *Cocoa and Chaos in Ghana,* 1st ed. (New York: Paragon House, 1988); Sebastian K. Amanor, *Global Restructuring and Land Rights in Ghana: Food chain, Timber and livelihoods,* (Research Report, vol.108), (Uppsala, Nordiska Afrikainstittutet, 1999); Berry, 2001; Gareth Austin, *Labour, Land, and Capital in Ghana : From Slavery to Free Labour in Asante, 1807–1956,* (Rochester, NY: University of Rochester Press, 2005).

22. Dun and Robertson 1973; C. Okali, *Cocoa and Kinship in Ghana: The Matrilineal Akan of Ghana,* (London; Boston: Published for the International African Institute by Kegan Paul International, 1983); Mikell, 1988.

23. Ivor Wilks, Forests of Gold: Essays on the Akan and the Kingdom of Asante, (Athens: Ohio University Press, 1993); Ivor Wilks, Asante in the Nineteenth Century: The Structure and Evolution of a Political Order, (London / New York: Cambridge University Press, 1975).

24. K. A. Busia, *The Position of the Chief in the Modern Political System of Ashanti; a Study of the Influence of Contemporary Social Changes on Ashanti Political Institutions,* (London / New York: Published for the International African Institute, by the Oxford University Press, 1951); J. Boachie-Ansah, *An Archaeological Contribution to the History of Wenchi,* (Calgary: University of Calgary, 1986).

25. I conducted oral interviews over a period of three months (from February to April, 2005) gathering information on the land dispute in Chiraa, Ahyiayem, Buoku and Sunyani. The interviews have been complemented by the colonial records relevant to the topic held at the Sunyani Regional Archives.

26. Interview with Nana Addai II, Odikro of Buoku, 3 March 2005.

27. Compare with Ahyiamu in T. C. McCaskie, "Ahyiamu—'A Place of Meeting:' An Essay on Process and Event in the History of the Asante State," *Journal of African History* 25 no. 2 (1984): 169–188.

28. An archaeological excavation has been conducted at Ahwene koko and 1715 is suggested as the date for the sacking of the ancient settlement. There is also a general agreement that the Asante were responsible for its destruction. For detailed discussions (see Boachie-Ansah 1986).

29. Petition of Nana Yeboah Afari II and elders 382/s.1/32 BRG/1/4/2. The disintegrated pre-colonial Ashanti conferederacy following the British conquest was restored in 1935.

30. BRG, no.96/P.12/ 1932; hereafter cited in text as BRG, 1932.

31. Sir Stewart was the first colonial resident officer at Kumasi. It is interesting that the Dormaa referred to him in the petition as an "unknown European."

32. Letter in response to Chiraahene BRG, Sunyani, /2/3/2

33. BRG, Sunyani /0065/sf.2/55

34. The present day Brong Ahafo region was created by the CPP government under Kwame Nkrumah in 1959. Before 1961 its inhabitants paid tributes to Ashanti and Kumasi chiefs and agitated for regional autonomy see Gwendolyn Mikell, *Cocoa and Chaos in Ghana,* 1st ed. (New York:

Paragon House, 1989); Gwendolyn Mikell, "Peasant Politicization and Economic Recuperation in Ghana: Local and National Dilemmas," *The Journal of Modern African Studies,* vol.27, no.3 (Sep. 1989), 455–478: 462; hereafter cited in text as Peasant Politicization.
35. BRG. Sunyani, Reference letter No.B.00133/44 of 12/10/56
36. BRG. Sunyani, Reference letter No.B.00133/44 of 12/10/56 the Dormaa-hene, Agyeman Badu was on study leave in Britain at the time.
37. BRG. Sunyani,2/3/2 Memo by Regional Commissioner S.W.Yeaboh to Osagyefo
38. BRG, Sunyani Wenchihene Abrefa Mbrohre VI's letter of request to Osa-gyefo, 23 April, 1962; hereafter cited in text as BRG Sunyani 1962.
39. BRG, Sunyani 2/3/2 ; Wenchihene Abrefa Mbohre Bediatuo VI's letter of request on the Wenchi-Dormaa Boundary Dispute.
40. K Danna Flynn, "We are the Border: Identity, Exchange and the State Along the Benin-Nigeria Border," *American Ethnologist* 24, no. 2 (1997): 311–330; Nugent, 1999; Lentz, 2003.
41. Paul Nugent and A. I. Asijawu, *African Boundaries: Barriers, Conduits, and Opportunities,* (London / New York: Pinter, 1996).
42. Jens A. Anderson, "The Politics of Land Scarcity: Land Disputes in Save Communal Area, Zimbabwe," *Journal of Southern African Studies* 25, no. 4 (1999): 553–578, 556.
43. S. Falk Moore, "Explaining the Present: Theoretical Dilemmas in Proces-sual Ethnography," American Ethnologist 14 no. 4 (1987): 727–736, 730.

REFERENCES

Anderson, Jens A. "The Politics of Land Scarcity: Land Disputes in Save Commu-nal Area, Zimbabwe." *Journal of Southern African Studies* 25, no. 4 (1999): 553–578.

Amanor, Sebastian K. *The New Frontier: Farmers' Response to Land Degradation: A West African Study.* London and New Jersey: Zed Books LTD, 1994.

Amanor, Sebastian K. *Global Restructuring and Land Rights in Ghana: Food chain, Timber and livelihoods.* (Research Report, vol.108), Uppsala, Nordiska Afri-kainstittutet, 1999.

Austin, Gareth. *Labour, Land, and Capital in Ghana: From Slavery to Free Labour in Asante, 1807–1956.* Rochester, NY: University of Rochester Press, 2005.

Berry, Sara. *Chiefs Know their Boundaries: Essays on Property, Power, and the Past in Asante, 1896–1996.* Portsmouth, N.H.: Heinemann, 2001.

Berry, Sara. "Hegemony on a Shoestring: Indirect Rule and Access to Agricultural Land." *Africa* 62, no. 3 (1992): 327–355.

Boachie-Ansah, J. *An Archaeological Contribution to the History of Wenchi.* Cal-gary: University of Calgary, 1986.

Busia, K. A. *The Position of the Chief in the Modern Political System of Ashanti; a Study of the Influence of Contemporary Social Changes on Ashanti Politi-cal Institutions.* London / New York: Published for the International African Institute, by the Oxford University Press, 1951.

Bassett, J. Thomas and Donald Crummey. *Land in African Agrarian Systems*. Madison, Wisconsin: University of Wisconsin Press, 1993.

Chauveau, Jean-Pierre. "How does an Institution Evolve? Land, Politics, Intergrational Relations and the Institution of the Tuorat Amongst Autochones and Immigrants." (Gban Region, Cote D'Ivoire). In *Land and the Politics of Belonging in West Africa*. Edited by Richard Kuba and Carola Lentz. Leiden, Boston: Brill (2006): 213–240.

Cordell, D., J W Gregory, and V. Piche. *Hoe and Wage A Social History of a Circular Migration System in West Africa*. New Jersey: Westview Press, 1996.

Dei, George. J. Sefa. "The Renewal of a Ghanaian Rural Economy." *Canadian Journal of African Studies*, vol.26 no.1 (1992): 24–53.

Dunn, John, and A. F. Robertson. *Dependence and Opportunity; Political Change in Ahafo*. Cambridge, England: University Press, 1973.

Fortes, Meyer. "Strangers." In *Studies in African Social Anthropology*. ed by E. Fortes , and S. Patterson. London, Academic Press, 1975.

Flynn, K Danna. "We are the Border: Identity, Exchange and the State Along the Benin-Nigeria Border." *American Ethnologist* 24, no. 2 (1997): 311–330.

Hawkins, Sean. "Disguising Chiefs and God as History: Questions on the Acephalousness of Lodagaa Politics. . . ." *Africa* 66, no. 2 (1996): 202.

Hill, Polly. *The Gold Coast Cocoa Farmer: A Preliminary Survey*. London: Oxford University Press, 1956.

Hill, Polly. *The Migrant Cocoa-Farmers of Southern Ghana; a Study in Rural Capitalism*. Cambridge England: University Press, 1963.

Kopytoff, Igor. *The African Frontier: The Reproduction of Traditional African Societies*. Bloomington: Indiana University Press, 1987.

Kuba, Richard, and Carola Lentz. *Land and the Politics of Belonging in West Africa*. Leiden: Boston: Brill, 2006.

Kuba, Richard, Carola Lentz, Claude Nurukyor Somda, Universität Frankfurt am Main, and Université de Ouagadougou. *Histoire Du Peuplement Et Relations Interethniques Au Burkina Faso*. Paris: Karthala, 2003.

Lentz, Carola. "First-Comers and Late-Comers: Indigenous Theories of Landownership in West Africa." In *Land and the Politics of Belonging in West Africa*. Ed. by Kuba, Richard , Carola Lentz. Leiden, Boston: Brill, 2006, 35–56.

Lentz, Carola . "Land Rights and the Politics of Belonging in Africa. An Introduction." In *Land and the Politics of Belonging in West Africa* Ed. by Richard Kuba, and Carola Lentz. Leiden, Boston: BRIll, 2006, 1–34.

Lentz, Carola . "Histories and Political Conflict. A Case Study of Chieftaincy in Nadom, Northwestern Ghana." *Paideuma* 39 (1993): 177–215.

Lentz, Carola. "This is Ghanaian Territory!: Land Conflicts on a West African Border." *American Ethnologist* 30 no. 2 (2003): 273–289.

Lentz, Carola and Viet Erlmann. "A working class in formation? Economic Crisis and Strategies of Survival among Dagara mine workers in Ghana," *Cahiers d'etudes africaines,* 113, 1989.

Lobnibe, Isidore. "Forbidden Fruit in the Compound: A Case Study of Migration, Spousal Separation and Group-Wife Adultery in Northwest Ghana." *Africa* 75 no. 4 (2005).

McCaskie, T. C. "Ahyiamu—'A Place of Meeting': An Essay on Process and Event in the History of the Asante State." *Journal of African History* 25 no. 2 (1984): 169–188.

Mikell, Gwendolyn. *Cocoa and Chaos in Ghana.* 1st ed. New York: Paragon House, 1989.

Mikell, Gwendolyn. "Ghanaian Females, Rural Economy and National Stability." *African Studies Review* 29 no. 3 (1986): 67–88.

Mikell, Gwendolyn. "Peasant Politicization and Economic Recuperation in Ghana: Local and National Dilemmas" *The Journal of Modern African Studies,* vol.27, no.3 (Sep. 1989), 455–478.

Moore, S. Falk. "Explaining the Present: Theoretical Dilemmas in Processual Ethnography." *American Ethnologist* 14 no. 4 (1987): 727–736.

Myers, Gregory W. "Competitive Rights, Competitive Claims: Land Access in Post-War Mozambique." *Journal of Southern African Studies* 20 no. 4 (1994): 603–632.

Nugent, Paul. *Smugglers, Secessionists & Loyal Citizens on the Ghana-Toga Frontier: The Lie of the Borderlands since 1914.* Athens: Ohio University Press; Oxford; Legon, Ghana: James Currey; Sub-Saharan Publishers, 2002.

Nugent, Paul, and A. I. Asijawu. *African Boundaries: Barriers, Conduits, and Opportunities.* London / New York: Pinter, 1996.

Okali, C. *Cocoa and Kinship in Ghana: The Matrilineal Akan of Ghana.* London; Boston: Published for the International African Institute by Kegan Paul International, 1983.

Ranger, Terrence. "The invention of tradition in Colonial Africa." In *The Invention of Tradition* Ed. E. J. Hobsbawm and T. O. Ranger. Cambridge: Cambridge University Press, 1983.

Stahl, Ann Brower. *Making History in Banda: Anthropological Visions of Africa's Past.* New York: Cambridge University Press, 2001.

Tonkin, Elizabeth. *Narrating our Pasts: The Social Construction of Oral History.* Cambridge: Cambridge University Press, 1992.

Thomas, Roger G. "Forced Labor in British West Africa: The Case of the Northern Territories of the Gold Coast 1906–1927." *Journal of African History* 14 no. 1(1973): 79–103.

Trouillot, Michel-Rolph. *Silencing the Past: Power and the Production of History.* Boston, Massachusetts: Beacon Press, 1995.

Van Hear, Nicholas. New Diasporas: The Mass Exodus, Dispersal and Regrouping of Migrants Communities. Seattle, WA: University of Washington Press, 1998.

Wilks, Ivor. *Forests of Gold: Essays on the Akan and the Kingdom of Asante.* Athens: Ohio University Press, 1993.

Wilks, Ivor. *Asante in the Nineteenth Century: The Structure and Evolution of a Political Order.* London / New York: Cambridge University Press, 1975.

Archival Materials

File BRG. Sunyani, 1/4/2.

File BRG. Sunyani, 2/3/2.

File BRG, Sunyani, no. 96/P.12/ 1932.

Oral Interviews

Interview with Dozie and others. Ahyiayem, 3 February, 2005.

Interview with Dozie and Wife, Ahyiayem, 3 March, 2005.

Interview with Agya Badu, Chiraa, 3 March 2005.

Interview with Linus and Simon, Chiraa, 2 March 2005.

Interview with Regional Stool Land administrator Brong-Ahafo, Sunyani , 3 March, 2005.

Interview with Suzzie Nana, Chiraa, 6 March, 2005.

Interview with Nana Addai II, Buoku, 2 March 2005.

Interview with Remy and others, Buoku Junction, 2 March 2005.

Chapter Seven

Migrants in French Sudan:
Gender Biases in the Historiography

Marie Rodet

When I first began this study on West African female migration a few years ago, some important studies synthesizing scholarship on gender and migration had just been published, suggesting that the field emerged from decades of disregard for female migration.[1] The 1990s were actually a central decade in the rediscovery of female migration and in the recovery of female migration experiences. To date, a great deal of African migration scholarship had taken the masculinity of the labor force for granted and tended to confine women to the subsistence economy. Women were primarily described as being left behind in the rural areas, embedded in the domestic sphere, or were seen as "passive migrants" who accompanied their husbands who had wage-labor jobs in urban centers. Studies were therefore focused on male labor migration, which ultimately became synonymous with migration.[2]

A growing body of feminist scholarship within African studies has challenged this gender-biased approach to migration by showing that African women were not actually "passive migrants," and by analyzing the degree of agency in decisions about migration. Contemporary African female migrations have now largely been analyzed, while African female migrations prior to the 1970s remain understudied, especially in the history of the former French West African colonies.[3] It would appear as though the new gender awareness would only be applied to the study of contemporary African migrations. The historical discourse about African migration appears to remain very much influenced by the old masculinist colonial discourse and is ultimately unable to break free from the gender bias of such categories as "labor migration," which excludes the complexity and variety of female and male migrations.

In this chapter, I aim to relocate West African historical scholarship in a non-gender biased dynamic and show how African historians can gain a more detailed understanding of African migration through the examination of female migration in particular. Here, I specifically examine one pattern of female migration that has been, until now, largely neglected by historical migration scholarship: the participation of women in the slave exodus in French Sudan at the beginning of the twentieth century.[4] This study is specifically concerned with the larger region of Kayes, situated in the western part of the Colony of French Sudan (now known as Mali), at the border with Senegal, and usually called Upper Senegal.[5] It focuses on women because I am still convinced that if they are not explicitly studied, African women tend to be largely forgotten by African historical scholarship. However, it is not my intention to focus on women and therefore to carry out a reverse exclusion of men. My study links women closely to their own households, family, and environment; and therefore to men. Ultimately, this chapter attempts to integrate women into the narrative of African migratory history.

AFRICAN MIGRATION SCHOLARSHIP AND COLONIAL AND MASCULINIST DISCOURSES

The importance of women in the African economy was largely overlooked until the 1980s. Women were described as non income-generating family members, and therefore not as concerned by migration (understood as labor migration). When female migrations were recorded, they were largely described as insignificant, since female migrants were merely "accompanying spouses and daughters." Women were in most cases viewed as "passive" migrants dependent on the willingness of their husbands to bring them along.[6] Women were not believed to have a major influence over the choice to migrate. Thus, female migrations were regarded as irrelevant to understanding why migration occurs.

When scholars did note independent African female migrations, they were often described as marginal and deviant, also being linked to prostitution. When it became impossible to deny the importance of female migrations, they were then analyzed as the main consequence of the male labor migration: women were said to have began taking part in labor migration to alleviate the absence of the male workers who did not send remittances to the community of origin. This approach subscribed once again to the underlying notion that men were the first migrants into the colonial cities and that women began migrating only in the last decade of colonialism when African colonies began to experience rapid urbanization.[7]

The gradual acknowledgment of the importance of women's economic role in African societies from the 1970s[8] has allowed the questioning of this gender-blind approach to migration in the 1990s. However, African female migrations have been solely taken into account from the moment they became visible to Western eyes, i.e. from the 1970s when the main African cities started experiencing a so-called "population explosion" and when Western countries were gradually facing the increasing participation of African female migrants in international labor migration networks. African female migrations were a fact and they could no longer be denied. Contemporary African regional and international migrations have now been largely analyzed, while regional African female migrations prior to independence remain understudied.[9] This neglect is largely due to the fact that West African historical scholarship is still biased by the colonial approach to African women and African migration.

THE COLONIAL FOCUS ON MALE LABOR MIGRATION

One of the main reasons for the colonial neglect of African women and female migrations is the focus of the French colonial administration on male labor migration. French colonial archives were essentially produced by male colonial civil servants and politicians, who, in their project of domination, were ultimately rarely interested in African women's migrations or in African women in general. African women's tracks are generally hard to find in the colonial archives.[10]

The question concerning African women which seems to have been most particularly of interest to the French colonial administration was that of the legal aspect of women's status. Numerous reports were produced on this issue between 1920 and 1960.[11] However, this concern about African women's status gives little information about the life of these women and their participation in any migratory movements. The problem with such purely legal sources is that they tend to present women only and entirely within a legal framework, which would define the limits of their existence. The archives suggest that colonial authorities especially understood women through the legal framework of marriage. Any matters regarding women outside this particular framework are hardly visible in the archives. The colonial legal texts about marriage in particular and women's status in general tended to imprison them in a legal history which is not their own, one in which they did not appear as historical actors with their own lives outside their status as married women. They were discussed in stereotypical reproductive roles as wives, concubines, and mothers. African women were also regarded as responsible for securing some ancestral customs and the integrity of the community, therefore appearing as transhistorical creatures living outside the dynamics of historical development.[12]

The scarcity of colonial documents on African female migrations shows that the category of female migrants was considered irrelevant by the colonial administration: women could not be "labor migrants," since they were not supposed to supply any labor to the administration within the framework of forced labor, for example.[13] They were neither head of the family nor did they pay any head tax of their own. If they migrated to colonial cities, they were regarded as constituting an insufficient number to be taken into account. Labor migrations were further regarded by the colonial administration as the symbol of the introduction of capitalistic modernity into African colonies. In the colonial mind, women could not be concerned by this modernity, since they did not "work." They remained, therefore, in the backwardness of their home and traditions.

These assumptions were based on Eurocentric and androcentric binary oppositions between "wage-labor jobs" and "female domestic duties." In reality, the French colonial administration tended to impose the distorting framework of the nineteenth-century bourgeois family onto their approach to work in Africa, while taking into account the local traditions and customs.[14] The language often used in the colonial documents underestimates women's work and their experiences.[15] The masculinity of the labor force is taken for granted and women's work is placed in the same category as "family labor,"[16] As one colonial document noted, "Wage-earning women will remain for a long time the exception, compared to the vast majority of those who in the country as well as in the city are solely demanded by the family duties."[17] The way in which these sources were produced integrated sexual inequalities, and the marginalization and depreciation of women's work.

Unfortunately, these considerations on African women are still prevalent in African migration scholarship. The view of African female migrations seems to be even further embedded in a colonial and masculinist approach. Most researchers still do not think of looking for tracks of women in the archives[18] because they continue to assume that before independence African women were never really concerned by the social and economical changes experienced by their male counterparts.

AFRICAN MIGRATION HISTORIOGRAPHY BASED ON SEXUAL DICHOTOMIES

The 1990s saw the development of important feminist scholarship in migration studies, which has questioned the common gender-blind approach towards African migration. However, even if feminist studies attempted to restore female migrants to history by fighting against the image of the "passive accompanying female migrant," these studies continue to use implicitly the same dichotomy of "passive vs. active migration:" They try to prove that female migrants are actually "active migrants" but without questioning the existence of this "sexual dichotomy."[19]

In the dichotomy "active vs. passive migration," the referent, which allows one to know whether a migratory movement has to be considered as passive or active, is always the "labor migration" pattern. Female migrations are taken into account only if they fit into the same criteria as patterns of male labor migration. It is crucial therefore that scholars working on African female migrations stop using sexual binary oppositions such as reproduction/production, domestic/wage-paid work, rural/urban areas, private/public sphere, subsistence/capitalistic economy, and tradition/modernity, in order to be able to analyze the complexity of African migration. Because of the lack of questioning of these sexual dichotomies, scholars continue to refer implicitly to "labor migration" as the central/neutral/universal reference, where the referent is actually a male one. As with Halfacree and Boyle, I therefore view "labor migration" as a masculinist concept.[20]

While few in number, some important existing studies of women and African migrations exist, which attempt to disrupt the centrality of "labor migration" in the discourse on African migration and to decolonize the discourse on African women.[21] They question the scholarly focus on economics as the underlying cause for voluntary migration flows. They suggest that women migrated for a variety of complex reasons and as early as the beginning of colonial times. The focus on labor migration and economic factors as well as the general invisibility of African women in history led to the neglect of the diversity of migration experiences lived by both women and men. African migration history scholarship therefore still provides an incomplete and inaccurate picture of African migrations.

Scholarship on female migrations in the larger region of Kayes is rare, even for the most recent period, whereas there exists an extensive literature on male migrations out of the area.[22] The Kayes region is a typical example of the neglect of female migrations in African studies, where women when they migrated have been considered as "accompanying spouses" or as too insignificant in number to be taken into account.[23] Manchuelle assumes that women became urban migrants only in the late 1950s, (Manchuelle, 191). It is actually his sole comment on female migration in his study of Soninke migrations for the period 1848–1860. He describes them as being brought to Dakar by their husbands who had already been labor migrants in this city for many years. I have been able to locate only one study on contemporary female migrations from the Kayes region.[24] But this study by Findley and Diallo analyzes once again only the female labor migrations. Their analysis remains therefore within the dualistic conceptual framework of "active vs. passive" migration.

Closely examining one instance of female migration will reveal the complexities of women's migration: the participation of women in the slave exodus in the larger region of Kayes in French Sudan. Most scholars have regarded the slave exodus in this region as insignificant and the participation of women in this exodus as even more insignificant. This exodus has furthermore never been considered in historical scholarship as a "proper migration pattern" since it was not a noteworthy "labor migration."

"THE COMMANDANT HAS CATEGORICALLY REFUSED TO GIVE ME MY WIVES BACK": FEMALE SLAVES, THE SLAVE EXODUS, AND THE POPULATION INCREASE IN THE COLONIAL CITY OF KAYES

The slave exodus in the larger Kayes region was often presumed to be insignificant, and has therefore been largely neglected in historical studies of French Sudan,[25] whereas the Banamba exodus has been extensively analyzed.[26] African historical literature has neither regarded this exodus as a proper migration pattern, nor has the literature ever seriously considered a significant participation of female slaves in this exodus. The historiography of these migratory movements has been inclined to presume that these migratory movements were mainly male ones and had only occurred in regions where most slaves were not born within the household (i.e. not "*captifs de case*") or where they were barely integrated in the community.[27] In Upper Senegal, the "slave population" was estimated at the end of the nineteenth century at a rate varying from 30 to 60% of the total population, depending on the district.[28] In French Sudan, an average of one third of the slaves would have left their master with the gradual introduction of the French emancipating legislation.[29]

SLAVE EXODUS OR FEMALE SLAVE EXODUS?

With the gradual end of "slavery" in French Sudan at the beginning of the 20th century, newly emancipated slaves began to leave their former masters.[30] Some of them came to the "liberty villages" funded by the French administration in the first years of the conquest of French Sudan. These liberty villages were an attempt by the French administration to control the increasing slave flights in the region and to create permanent settled communities in the deserted surroundings of the colonial posts and along the main conquest and trade routes. They were also a first response to the lack of a labor force faced by the colonial administration. They enabled the administration to organize a cheap labor supply, as the inhabitants of the liberty villages were the first target for colonial labor requisitions and *corvée* labor. The liberty villages are also said to have played an important role in populating colonial urban centers such as Kayes or Bamako.[31] Since in rural areas access to land, seeds, and agricultural tools for "ex-slaves" remained restricted because of their former status, emancipated slaves were inclined to migrate into the newly developing colonial cities. The cities provided them with the opportunity to make a living by working, often on a temporary basis, for the trading houses or on various colonial building sites. Former slaves slowly formed a so-called "floating population" in these colonial cities.

Some scholars assess that it was easier for men than for women to leave their former masters, as female slaves had often children born in the community, and were therefore said to be more integrated (whether or not the children were from their masters). The integration of female slaves was actually encouraged as it was thought to prevent male flight. According to Clark and his oral informants, most women remained with their former master, as there were very few alternatives for female slaves, (Clark, *From Frontier to Backwater,* 169, 200, and 207). The slave exodus would have been confined to male slaves. Does this mean that because they were women, female slaves had no access to any resources, and were as a result "weaker" than male slaves and unable to migrate?

A closer examination of the colonial archives actually shows that former female slaves, alone or with their family, even if they were the wives or the concubines of their masters, did participate to a great extent in these migratory movements. Several archival documents even attest of the numerous attempts made by female captives to leave their masters each time they had the opportunity.

In September 1900, the Délégué in Kayes of the Governor-General received a complaint from Beydy Couloubaly asking for the return of his three wives who sought refuge in the "liberty village" of Kita: "I have the honor to address you this letter in order to inform you that my three wives have escaped to the liberty village of Kita . . . A fellow that I did not know has captured these three women who went to trade in several villages. In July, I went to Kita to take them but these women having more than three months stay in the liberty village, the Commandant categorically refused to give them back to me."[32]

His "wives" had actually left the liberty village one month earlier. In this story, the "husband" said he considered his "wives" as free, even if he had bought them as slaves, while the women had declared themselves as slaves when entering the liberty village. Finally, he was unsuited and the women were now declared to be free; as a result, it was now a divorce case that had to be brought to the Colonial court.

Bouche assumes that women could leave the liberty villages only if they married *"tirailleurs"*[33] or colonial agents, (Bouche, 155). This view underestimates the capacity of women to choose how they wanted to rebuild their lives. According to Miers and Kopytoff, freedom was certainly linked to the fact of belonging to a family group and being the client of a powerful patron. In the Western sense of its acceptance, the law was not actually powerful enough to protect individual freedom and autonomy. Therefore, freedom depended mainly upon the capacity of protection. The slaves were un-free because they were without any social or family ties to protect them in the society where they were captive. Thus, the antithesis of slave was not "freedom" or autonomy but rather "belonging."[34] It was extremely difficult for women in patrilineal and patrilocal societies like those of the Upper Senegal to remain unmarried because they would remain unprotected, especially when they were of former slave status, and therefore lacked extensive kinship. The acquisition of a new source of protection through remarriage was obviously one of the strategies female slaves adopted to "emancipate" themselves from a socially difficult situation. Women often attached themselves to men linked to the colonial administration (colonizers, *"tirailleurs,"* railway workers etc.) who could secure them a certain degree of freedom/protection. But does this really mean that they had little chance to obtain "success" on their own, which would have helped them to reduce their marginality as Miers and Kopytoff presume? (Kopytoff and Miers, 28).

The Beydy Couloubaly case and some following examples show how women were far from being the "victims" that Bouche assumes. Even if there might have been a limited range of opportunities available for female slaves to obtain their freedom, some documents have shown that women simply settled on their own, even if this option was less common.[35] In 1905, the colonial administrator of Bafulabe noticed that since he had been in the region, he had received numerous complaints about the fact that many female captives, who had been sent by their masters to cook for the railway workers, did not return at the end of the engaging period.[36] Most of these female slaves tried to stay permanently on the railway building sites, where they could live free. Other complaints in the Cercles of Kita and Kayes attest to the flights of female slaves to settle on the railway building sites.[37] Numerous women fled therefore without coming to the liberty villages, and started rebuilding their lives in colonial cities such as Kayes, Bamako or Saint-Louis. In 1899, Matada Diakité sought refuge for the first time at the liberty village of Medine. Her "husband" came to claim her and she was given back to him. One month later, she fled again but this time she disappeared without going to the liberty village, so that she could not be returned to her "husband." The population of the liberty villages was actually essentially "floating." Most of the former slaves stayed in the liberty villages only for the time necessary to obtain the liberty certificate, since life in the liberty villages was not that different from the one they had when they were still living in their master's household. They were often abused by the colonial administration, systematically recruited for forced labor, and simply treated again as slaves.[38]

Two further cases show that female slaves often decided, on their own, to leave their masters in order to secure their freedom in the colonial cities. They also tried to recover the freedom of their relatives who were still living in the masters' villages. In 1905, Nioumou Sakiliba, a former slave from the Cercle of Kayes, came from Kayes to Saint-Louis in order to present her grievances directly to the Governor-General, since she was unable to see the Commandant in Kayes because the interpreter would not allow her.[39] She actually wanted to set free her still enslaved family. The end of slavery meant the acquisition of an important new power for former slaves: the power over their families. Until their emancipation, slaves had actually always been prevented from having any control over their offspring who automatically belonged to the master. The struggle for control, not only over family life, but also over land tenure, was a very important consequence of "emancipation," (Klein, *Slavery and Colonial Rule*, 207). A second example confirms the importance of the struggle led by former slaves in gaining control over the family and above all over the children: In 1907, Makan Coulibaly asked the prosecutor's office in Kayes for her children who, she claimed, were still enslaved in the Cercle.[40] Seven years earlier, she had obtained her freedom in Kayes after having come to the city for work. She had then left the Cercle for Senegal.

Unfortunately, the archival documents mentioning the flight and exodus of female slaves are not sufficient to determine the exact number of female slaves who effectively left their masters, and whether those who left were, in the majority, slaves acquired by purchase or capture, or slaves born within the household (*"captifs de case"*). However, it is uncertain that the distinction between born-in-the house and purchased slaves played an important role in the lives of female slaves, since they were indistinctively forced to carry out the hardest duties, working in the fields as well as managing numerous domestic tasks. They then had to work both day and night during the rainy season.[41] As female slaves were in the majority in the slave population,[42] and as they had to perform the hardest work in the household, it is no surprise that they formed the majority of those who left their masters. Some archival documents record the monthly number of male and female slaves asking the colonial administration for permission to leave

their masters, and in these accounts, as in the accounts of the liberty villages, female slaves appear to have been in the majority.[43]

FORMER FEMALE SLAVES: THE "FIRST SEX IN TOWN"

Despite the clear participation of women in the slave exodus, former male
slaves are still assumed to have been the first migrants in the colonial cities and women to have been "the second sex in town."[44] However the sex
ratio in the liberty villages, as well as in Kayes, was always far from being
unbalanced to the disadvantage of women.

It would surprise more than one scholar if I were to say that the
sex ratio in Kayes between 1904 and 1908 was pretty unbalanced to the
disadvantage of men: in 1904, the sex ratio in Kayes attested to 93 men
per 100 women, the difference becoming even more pronounced in 1908
with a rate of 80.8 men per 100 women.[45] In the liberty village of Kayes,
this rate oscillated between 62 and 76 men per 100 women from 1900 to
1909.[46] It demonstrates that the arrival of female slaves to Kayes largely
contributed to the sex ratio imbalance in Kayes. The census of 1904 shows
that, per neighborhood, the sex ratio was not only to the disadvantage of
men in the liberty village but also in other neighborhoods where former
female slaves may have settled permanently after having obtained their liberty certificate.

The accuracy of the census on which these rates are based is certainly
questionable. The methods used to take the census in the French African
colonies at the beginning of the twentieth century were only approximate.[47]
However for a city such as Kayes of around 6,000 inhabitants in 1908, it is
uncertain that they would have been so inaccurate. Kayes was, at this time,
the capital of French Sudan, where the number of colonial agents might
have been sufficient enough to take an accurate census.

Thus, the liberty villages contributed greatly to the population increase
of colonial cities such as Kayes. In this context, women ultimately appear
to have been "the first migrants in town." They also formed a major part of
the "floating population." Even in the census of 1936, the imbalance seems
to have been maintained in neighborhoods such as Kayes-Liberté or Legal-
Segou with a sex ratio of 84.8 men per 100 women in Kayes-Liberté and 83
men per 100 women in Legal-Segou. This imbalance strongly diminished in
1941 with 99.5 men per 100 women in Kayes-Liberté (with a diminution of
69 women in this latter neighborhood between 1936 and 1941) and 95.5
men per 100 women in Legal-Segou. This imbalance may be explained by
an outgoing male migration at a time when the peanut migrations towards
Senegal were still significant in the region. However, the report specified that

the floating population had largely diminished in these two neighborhoods after the colonial administration took severe purging measures, which provoked the departure of around 300 to 400 persons; possibly explaining a change in the sex-ratio imbalance. In the case of Kayes, a closer examination of the colonial documents shows that women represented a significant part of the "floating population." Therefore, the picture that emerges is far from the usual image of the colonial city where solely male labor migration contributed to the formation of the so-called "floating populations."

CONCLUSION

The historiography of African migration has been eager to assert that the colonial towns were mainly shaped by male labor migrations. The analysis of the neglect of the prevalence of women in the slave exodus in Upper Senegal and in the population of the city of Kayes at the beginning of the twentieth century demonstrates how important it is to take into account every form of human mobility in order to have a more complete understanding of the history of African migratory movements and of colonial towns. It is actually the focus on male labor migration by both the colonial administration and African historical scholarship that has excluded the diversity of the migratory movements experienced by Upper Senegal at this time. These assumptions resulted in complex migration patterns being assimilated into a simplified pattern of labor migration, entailing a homogenization of views over both male and female African migrations. In order to make female migrations visible again, it is important to interrogate the centrality of "labor migration" to this question and to abandon gender dichotomies, which fundamentally prevent an analysis of the mobility of African women. Female slaves migrated from rural areas into the colonial cities, which enhanced their opportunities to gain a new kind of colonial "protection," and, ultimately, their "freedom." They took advantage of the new opportunities offered by the colonial environment as much as possible; colonial posts and newly developing colonial cities becoming places of refuge. The different examples of female slave migratory movements demonstrate the degree of agency that women may have used, even those whose range of opportunities originally appear to have been restricted.

NOTES

1. Among others: Paul Boyle and Keith Halfacree, eds., *Migration and Gender in the Developed World* (London: Routledge, 1999); Sylvia Chant, ed., *Gender and Migration in Developing Countries* (London: Belhaven Press,

1992); Jan Fairhurst, Ingrid Booysen, and Philip Hattingh, eds., *Migration and Gender: Place, Time and People Specific* (Pretoria: University of Pretoria, Faculty of Science, 1997); Pamela Sharpe, ed., *Women, Gender, and Labour Migration: Historical and global Perspectives* (London: Routledge, 2001); Caroline Wright, "Gender Awareness in Migration Theory: Synthesizing Actor and Structure in Southern Africa," *Development and Change* 26, no. 4 (1995): 771–791. Katie Willis and Brenda Yeoh, eds., *Gender and Migration* (Cheltenham, UK: Elgar, 2000); Gregory A. Delaet and Debra L. Delaet, eds., *Gender and Immigration,* (London: MacMillan, 1999).

2. Manchuelle defines "labor migration" as the following: " . . . *labor migration* designates an economically motivated, *temporary* form of migration. Labor migrants are generally young men from rural areas, often unmarried. They have no plans to settle abroad but shuttle between their villages and places of employment (cities and more developed agricultural areas), as a movement often described as 'return' or 'circular' migration." François Manchuelle, *Willing Migrants, Soninke Labor Diasporas, 1848–1960.* (Athens, Ohio: Ohio University Press, 1994), 2.

3. One rare exception is the book by Dennis D. Cordell, Joel W. Gregory, and Victor Piché, *Hoe and Wage: A Social History of a Circular Migration System in West Africa,* (Boulder: Westview Press, 1996). To my knowledge, it is the only book dealing with female migrations in a colony of French West Africa.

4. This study is based on colonial documents collected in Bamako (Archives Nationales du Mali, subsequently ANM), Dakar (Archives Nationales du Sénégal, ANS) and Aix-en-Provence (Centre des Archives d'Outre-mer, CAOM).

5. It refers in the French colonial archives to the *Cercles* (Districts) of Bafulabe, Kayes, Kita, Nioro and Satadugu.

6. Sally E. Findley, "Les migrations féminines: une revue de leurs motivations et expériences" in *L'insertion urbaine des migrants en Afrique,* Actes du Séminaires CRDI-ORSTOM-URD, Lome10–14 February 1987 (1989), 55.

7. Teresa Barnes, "Virgin Territory? Travel and Migration by African Women in Twentieth-Century Southern Africa," in *Women in African Colonial Histories,* ed. Jean Allman, Susan Geiger, and Nakanyike Musisi, (Bloomington and Indianapolis: Indiana University Press, 2002), 165.

8. A milestone publication in that sense has been the book published by Ester Boserup, *Woman's Role in Economic Development* (London: G. Allen and Unwin, 1970), in which she attempted to prove that women played a central role in the African economy. However, as colonialism and modernization had disrupted the gendered division of labor and favored men for gaining access to money and resources, women remained in poverty with an increased work load.

9. The lack of attention to women in studies of the history of African migration is by no means unique to this issue. In general, the field of African history has treated women as if they were insignificant actors. Tiyambe Zeleza "Gender Biases in African Historiography" in *Engendering African Social Sciences,* ed. Imam Ayesha, Amina Mama and Fatou Sow (1999), 82.

10. On the problem of finding the tracks of African women in the French colonial archives, see Marie Rodet "C'est le regard qui fait l'histoire. Comment utiliser des archives coloniales qui nous renseignent malgré elles sur l'histoire des femmes africaines" *Terrains et Travaux* no. 10 (2006), 18–35.
11. See in particular: FR CAOM GGAOF 17G160 (FR): Politique indigène. Questions politiques diverses; 17G381: Rapport Savineau; 23G12: Mariages indigènes; CAOM, FM AFF POL 541: Civilisation locale. Mariages indigènes 1934–38. Condition de la femme indigène 1936–39; AFF POL 2201: Politique indigène. Conférence de Brazzaville; AFF POL 2295: Administration Générale. Conférence de Brazzaville. Rapports; AFF POL 3349: Situation politique de la femme africaine; AFF POL 3658: Mariages coutumiers en Afrique. Statuts coutumiers. 1949–1951; SE ANS GGAOF (FR) K89 (26): Enquête du département sur la main d'œuvre aux colonies. 1926–1929.
12. Tiyambe Zeleza, "Gender Biases," 82.
13. For a discussion whether women were recruited by the colonial administration of French Sudan for forced labor, see Marie Rodet "Les femmes sur les chantiers coloniaux du Soudan Français: de simples 'accompagnatrices' des recrutés du travail forcé? (1900–1946)." *Ultramarines* (forthcoming).
14. In order to set up an alliance with the traditional power and to consolidate their own power, the colonial administration decided to make the respect of local customs one of the central features of their domination policy. See Marie Rodet "Frauen im Spannungsfeld des 'Droit colonial' in Afrique Occidentale Française. Zwei Fallbeispiele aus der Region Kayes, Soudan Français (1918 und 1938)." Stichproben 7 (2004), 89–105.
15. On the colonial non-consideration of women's work, see Marie Rodet "C'est le regard qui fait l'histoire" (2006).
16. Cheryl Walker "Gender and the Development of the Migrant Labour System c. 1850–1930," in *Women and Gender in Southern Africa to 1945*, ed. Cherryl Walker, (Londres: James Currey, 1990), 177–178.
17. SE ANS GGAOF (FR) K192 (26): Circular 629 concerning female and children work, 4 November 1936.
18. Michelle Perrot, *Les Femmes ou les silences de l'Histoire* (Paris: Flammarion, 1998), iv.
19. According to Eichler, a "sexual dichotomy" consists of treating the sexes as two discrete, rather than overlapping groups. This sexual dichotomy actually tends to appear when researchers want to avoid gender insensitivity, as in the case of the feminist scholarship which attempts to rehabilitate the importance of female migration. Margrit Eichler, *Nonsexist Research Methods: A Practical Guide,* (New York, London: Routledge, 1991), 119.
20. Keith Halfacree and Paul Boyle "Introduction: Gender and Migration in Developed Countries," in *Migration and Gender in the Developed World,* ed. Paul Boyle and Keith Halfacree, (London: Routledge, 1999), 10.
21. See among others: Sean Redding, "South African Women and Migration in Umtata, Transkei, 1880–1935," in *Courtyards, Markets, City Streets, Urban Women in Africa,* ed. Kathleen Sheldon (Oxford: Westview Press,

1996), 31–46. Christiana E.E. Okojie "Female Migrants in the Urban Labour Market: Benin City, Nigeria." *Canadian Journal of African Studies*, vol. 18, no 3 (1984), 547–562. Jean Allman, Susan Geiger, and Nakanyike Musisi, eds., *Women in African Histories* (Bloomington & Indianapolis: Indiana University Press, 2002). Imam Ayesha, Amina Mama, Fatou Sow, eds., *Engendering African Social Sciences* (Chippenham, Wiltshire: Anthony Rowe Ltd., 1999). I was unfortunately unable to find any literature on francophone West Africa, which interrogates the centrality of "labor migration" to this question. Even *Hoe and Wage* by Denis D. Cordell, Joel W. Gregory, and Victor Piché (1996) on migrations in the Upper Volta, adopts the position that virtually all mobility is labor migration in one form or another, and therefore does not question this concept.

22. See among others: Adrian Adams, *Le long voyage des gens du fleuve* (Paris: Maspero, 1977). Jean-Yves Weigel, *Migration et production domestique des Soninké du Senegal* (Paris: ORSTOM, 1980); François Manchuelle, *Willing Migrants* (1994).

23. You can read in *Migration et production domestique des Soninké du Senegal* by Weigel (1980), 84: "The migration rate of the male active population oscillates between 30 and 50%; female migration is insignificant."

24. Sally E. Findley and Assitan Diallo "Interactions Between Household Structure and Female Migration in Rural Mali" in *Women's Position and Demographic Change in Sub-Saharan Africa*, ed. Paulina Makinwa and An-Magritt Jensen (Liege: International Union for the Scientific Study of Population, 1995), 271–289.

25. Manchuelle argues that the Soninke slave exodus was never very significant in the region because Soninke slaves were not interested in running away. Manchuelle, *Willing Migrants,* 133–134. Andrew F. Clark, *From Frontier to Backwater. Economy and Society in the Upper Senegal Valley (West Africa), 1850–1920* (Lanham, NY: University Press of America, 1999), 133.

26. See in particular, William Klein and Richard Roberts, "The Banamba Slave Exodus of 1905 and the Decline of Slavery in the Western Sudan." *Journal of African History,* no. 21 (1980), 375–394.

27. Martin Klein, *Slavery and Colonial Rule in French West Africa* (Cambridge: Cambridge University Press, 1998), 197–198, 205–208; hereafter cited as Slavery and Colonial Rule.

28. Eric Pollet and Grace Winter, *La société Soninke (Dyahunu, Mali)* (Brussels: Institut de Sociologie de l'Université de Bruxelles, 1971), 238. Majhemout Diop "Etude sur le salariat (Haut-Sénégal-Niger, Soudan, Mali) (1884–1969)." *Etudes Maliennes,* no. 14, special issue (1975), 9. Manchuelle, 29. Andrew F. Clark, "The Fulbe of Bundu (Senegambia): From Theocracy to Secularization." *International Journal of African Historical Studies,* vol. 29, no.1 (1996), 14. In the French colonial archives, the main quantitative sources concerning slavery in French Sudan are the two series of inquiries on captivity that were conducted in the different Cercles of the colony in 1894 and 1904: FR CAOM GGAOF (FA) K14 and K19. However, it is important to be cautious towards the accuracy of this kind of statistics,

which were often merely gross estimates. Some administrators even refused to give any detailed figures because they assumed that such estimates were very questionable. These reports, however, show certain constancy in the importance of the slave population between 1894 and 1904. Slaves would have represented around 40% of the total population of Upper Senegal, but this number could be as high as 60% in some parts of the region.

29. Klein, *Slavery and Colonial Rule,* 197. In the Cercles of Kita and Bafulabe, where the slave population was particularly important because of the Samorian wars (probably 50% of the population at the beginning of the twentieth century), half of the population would have left in some villages. FR CAOM GGAOF (FA): Reports on the captivity in the Cercles of Bafulabe and Kita. 1894. MA ANM Koulouba (FA) 1E17: Census tour report by Teramond. May-June 1911. FR CAOM GGAOF (FA) 2G10/17: Upper-Senegal-Niger, Political Report, 1st quarter 1910.

30. The first attempts to restrict the slave trade in French Sudan began with the nomination of Albert Grodet as Governor of French Sudan (1893–1895): in 1895, the slave trade was officially forbidden on the territories of French Sudan (FR CAOM Soudan XIV: General Order n°273, 17 May 1895, and general Order n°301, June 19 June 1895). However, the Commandants in charge of the administration of the Cercles did never strictly apply this measure. The slavery abolition politics took a new impulse when William Ponty became the representative (Délégué) in Kayes of the Governor-General in 1899. It is under his administration that slaves were gradually "emancipated" and that the Decree of 12 December 1905, abolishing the slave trade in French West Africa, was promulgated. However, this decree did not explicitly abolish the system of *"captivité de case."* It was solely with the circular of 20 December 1906, specifying how the 1905 decree had to be enforced, and with the circular of 24 April 1908, that the administrators were clearly instructed to put an end to any form of slavery, by not recognizing the slave status.

31. Denise Bouche, "Les villages de liberté en A.O.F. (suite et fin)." *Extrait du Bulletin de l'Institut français d'Afrique noire,* vol. 12, no.1 (1950), 192.

32. In this chapter, translations of the colonial archival documents from French into English are mine. MA ANM IE201 (FA): Political Affairs, Correspondence Cercles. Kayes. 1882–1921.

33. The *"tirailleurs"* were colonial soldiers recruited by the French Army in the French African colonies from the 19th century.

34. Igor Kopytoff and Suzanne Miers, "African 'Slavery' as an Institution of Marginality" in *Slavery in Africa. Historical and Antropological Perspectives,* ed. Suzanne Miers and Igor Kopytoff (Madison: The University of Wisconsin Press, 1977), 17.

35. SE ANS GGAOF (FA) 2G4/13: Nioro, Monthly Political Report, December 1904.

36. MA ANM Koulouba (FA) 1E17: Bafulabe, Monthly Political Report, June 1905.

37. SE ANS GGAOF (FA) 15G140: Kita, Outgoing-Correspondence Commandant of Kita. 26 August 1900—31 December 1902.

38. FR CAOM GGAOF (FA) K14: Report on the captivity in Medine, undated but probably 1894; K24: Maurice Gamon, "Kayes—Le village de liberté. 8 novembre 1904" *Au Soudan*. Poitiers Universitaires (1905). See also Denise Bouche, *Les villages de liberté*, 183–184)

39. MA ANM Koulouba (FA) 2M279: The Nioumou Sakiliba Case.

40. MA ANM Koulouba (FA) 2M279: The Makan Coulibaly Case.

41. FR CAOM GGAOF (FA) K14: Report on the Captivity in the Cercle of Nioro, undated but probably 1894.

42. Female slaves had a greater value than male slaves. Female slaves gave new dependents to their masters, but above all, female labor was predominant in production (Claude Meillassoux, *Anthropologie de l'esclavage: le ventre de fer et d'argent* (Paris: PUF, 1986), 49). Their domestic labor was also essential to the family economy (FR CAOM GGAOF (FA) K14: Report on the Captivity in the Cercle of Bafulabe, undated but probably 1894). Their value was therefore attached to their reproductive role, as well as to their productive role. Margaret Strobel. "African Women's History." *The History Teacher*, vol. 15, no.4 (1982), 511). The Bafulabe Report on captivity of 1894 assumed that female slaves represented 60% of the adult slave population. The report 1904 presented a similar rate: 4825 males for 6540 females (FR CAOM GGAOF (FA) K19). The Nioro report of 1894 gives the rate of 25 males, 40 females, and 35 children per 100 slaves, i.e. a female rate of around 60% of the adult slave population. Similar estimates are to be found in the Medine report of 1894. Klein assumes that these rates may have been underestimated (Martin A. Klein, "Women in Slavery in the Western Sudan" in *Women and Slavery in Africa*, ed. Claire C. Robertson et Martin A. Klein (Madison: The University Press of Wisconsin, 1983), 68–70). A closer examination of the Bafoulabe report of 1894 may confirm this point. It suggests a colonial underestimation that would have been inherent to the colonial gender-biased census methods. The Bafulabe report uses the census sheets of the districts of Kentella and Tomora to attest to the number of slaves in the region. However, it is clearly specified that these rates do not take into account the number of women and children.

43. See among others the political reports and tour of inspection reports of the Cercle of Kayes, 1891–1910. MA ANM Koulouba (FA)1E44. These monthly reports clearly show the participation of women in the slave exodus.

44. Josef Gugler, "The Second Sex in Town," *CJAS*, vol. 6, no.2 (1972), 289–301. This prejudice seems to have originated in the abusive extrapolation of data collected in Central and South Africa. Odile Georg, "Les femmes, citadines de deuxième plan? Réflexion sur le *sex ratio* dans les villes en Afrique sous la colonisation." in *"Mama Africa" Hommage à Catherine Coquery-Vidrovitch*, ed. Chantal Chanson-Jabeur and Odile Georg (Paris: L'Harmattan, 2005), 148. However, in the latter case, a growing body of feminist scholarship within African studies has challenged this assumption with case studies on African female migrations. They demonstrate that this imbalance, even in South African towns, was not as marked as it has often been said. See in particular: Belinda Bozzoli, *Women of Phokeng*.

Consciousness, Life Strategy and Migrancy in South Africa, 1900–1983 (Portsmouth, NH: Heinemann, 1991). Caroline Wright, "Gender Awareness in Migration Theory: Synthesizing Actor and Structure in Southern Africa," *Development and Change*, vol. 26, no.4 (1995), 771–791. Cherry Walker, ed., *Women and Gender* (1990). Teresa A. Barnes, *'We Women Worked so Hard.' Gender, Urbanization and Social Reproduction in Colonial Harare, Zimbabwe. 1930–1956* (Portsmouth, NH: Heineman, 1999). Teresa A. Barnes, "Virgin Territory? Travel and Migration" (2002).

45. MA ANM Koulouba (FA) 5D29: Census of the population of the District and the City of Kayes, 1904. FR CAOM GGAOF (FA): Table VII, Population of the main cities, 1908.

46. The liberty village was geographically a neighborhood of Kayes with, however, a special status: the inhabitants did not have to pay the head tax. It was later integrated into the rest of the city under the name of "Kayes-Liberté." SE ANS GGAOF 15G145 (FA): Letter n°13.142. William Ponty, Lieutenant Governor of the Upper-Senegal and Niger Colony to Commandant of Kita, 10 February 1908.

47. On the limits of the usefulness of colonial censuses and demographic quantitative data for the demographic History of French West Africa, see Raymond Gervais, "Contribution à l'étude de l'évolution de la population de l'Afrique occidentale française, 1904–1960" *Les dossiers du Ceped*, no. 23 (1993). See also Raymond Gervais "Etat colonial et savoir démographique en AOF, 1904–1960" in *AOF: réalités et héritages. Sociétés ouest-africaines et ordre colonial, 1895–1960,* ed. Charles Becker, Saliou Mbaye, and Ibrahima Thioub (Dakar: Direction des Archives du Sénégal, 1997), tome 1, 961–980.

Chapter Eight

The Impact of the Relationship between Migrants and Traditional Authorities on South African Mining Communities

Charity S. Chenga and J. Freek Cronjé

INTRODUCTION

In recent years the South African mining industry has been faced with new constraints on its operations. Through the Mining Charter (2002)[1] as well as the Mineral and Petroleum Resources Development Act (MPRDA—2004)[2], the mining industry has had to look at more than the usual two "Ps," namely "profit" and "planet," but also have to consider the third "P," namely "people" in their operations. In terms of "people," the MPRDA (2004)[3] has put pressure on mining organizations in South Africa to start behaving like corporate citizens, to begin to accept social responsibilities, and to work towards sustainable development in the areas in which they operate.

In response to this, mining corporations have "rushed" in to set up community development projects without really understanding or taking account of the dynamics within communities that may impact their success and sustainability. This chapter focuses on the impact that the relationship between migrants and traditional authorities may have on communities in terms of the sustainability of developmental projects.

OBJECTIVES

Against the above mentioned background, the main objectives of this chapter are:

- To give a brief background of migration and the role of traditional authorities in the mining industry

- To explore the relationship between migrants and traditional authorities and the effects thereof

- To analyze the relationship between migrants and traditional authorities and indicate the ways forward with regard to this issue

RESEARCH METHODOLOGY

This chapter is based on qualitative longitudinal research[4] undertaken at two South African platinum mines—one located in the North-West Province (semi-urban) and the other in the northern Limpopo Province (rural), which was commissioned by a local mining company. More specifically, the data collection entailed focus groups, personal interviews, observations, and case studies. The longitudinal survey was undertaken over a period of two years. Data collection was carried out over two periods. The research design for the two surveys was the same in terms of sample techniques where purposive and snowballing sampling methods were used. The sample selection included: local community members, migrants, members of the traditional authorities, mine management and employees, and government officials. Focus groups (eight to twelve people) and interviewees were selected to take account of gender, race, migrant or local status, age, and specific interest groups (e.g. local business people). In total, seventy focus groups and seventy eight personal interviews were conducted; it is estimated that nearly five hundred people participated in the survey. The researchers aimed to use the same participants for the two survey periods, but this was difficult because some people had moved. Consequently, when the same respondents could not be used, the researchers involved people with similar characteristics. The data was analyzed by using the thematic interpretive method.

MIGRATION THEORY OVERVIEW

Migration in South Africa needs to be considered in terms of the macro and micro perspectives. The historical background of migration in the South African mining industry has been predominantly macro driven. The origins of the migration process in the South African mining industry can be explained by the historical-structural perspective. This theory stresses the unequal distribution of economic and political power in the world economy. Migration is seen as a way of mobilizing cheap labor for capital. It perpetuates uneven development, exploiting the resources of poor countries to make the rich even richer.[5] This theory is illustrated by the exploitative bilateral labor agreements governing the movement of contract migrants to South Africa.[6]

The neo-classical economic equilibrium perspective also takes account of the micro factors in migratory movements; this approach is often known as "push-pull" theory. This theory argues that on a macro basis migration is caused by the supply and demand of labor and the resulting wage differentiation based on a country's economic condition; on a micro level individual actors migrate after making cost-benefit analyses, and migration is ultimately a form of investment in human capital.[7] This theory closely resembles other micro migration models that are associated with South African migration patterns. These migration models include circulatory migration, oscillation migration, and gravity flow migration. The similarities between these models and the push-pull theory are that these models are closely tied to the notion that jobs and income dominate people's reasons for moving. The problem with these theories is that they fail to take account of other reasons for migration aside from the economic reasons; these theories do not explain reasons such as asylum seeking and refugee movements.

The migration systems perspective is a more comprehensive approach that takes account of the macro as well as the micro factors in the migration process. The migration systems perspective can be defined as migratory movements that generally arise from the existence of prior links between sending and receiving countries based on colonization, political, trade, investment, or cultural ties, (Castles and Miller, 1998). The migration systems perspective implies that any migratory movement can be seen as the result of interacting of macro-and micro- structures. Macro-structures include the political economy of the world market, interstate relationships, and the laws, structures and practices established by the sending and receiving countries to control migration settlement. This theory may provide a more comprehensive explanation of the post-*Apartheid* migration pattern in the country and how that impacts on the mining sector and communities.

A BRIEF BACKGROUND OF MIGRATION IN THE MINING INDUSTRY

The roots of migrant labor recruitment in the mining industry in South Africa go back to the colonial era. At this stage it is important to state that the background of migration in the South African mining communities has to be considered both in terms of external (people from outside the borders of the country) and internal migration (people from within the borders of the country).

To maintain profitability, the mining industry required cheap labor and consequently looked outside its borders.[8] In terms of external migration, most of the workers recruited during the Apartheid period from Mozambique, Botswana, Lesotho, Swaziland, and Malawi worked in gold mines, with less than 10% in agriculture and other non-mining industry, (Castles and Miller, 1998). In addition, white laborers who were imported for their mining skills and experience shortly after gold was discovered in 1886 saw blacks as a threat to their relatively high wages. To combat this threat, the white unions, among other things, forced the industry and then government to adopt the "color bar," banning blacks from skilled jobs, and preventing black families and black workers from settling permanently in mining towns. These policies were the forerunner of the *Apartheid* system, (Schoofs, 1999). Recruitment to South Africa was highly organized; people were subjected to physical and aptitude tests and those who were successful were transported by air, rail, or bus to the mines where they lived in hostels. One of the consequences of this highly organized system was that not only the migrants, but also the sending countries became very dependent on the mining industry in South Africa. Contracts were set up between the private mining houses in South Africa and some of the sending countries and even some colonial powers (e.g. Portugal), to pay a certain amount over to the sending community or the colonial power. According to Bohning, South Africa paid at some stage 15 % of Mozambican mine workers' salaries, valued at US$42 per fine ounce, over to the government in Lisbon.[9] In addition, Crush states that in the case of Mozambique and Lesotho, home country legislation compelled South African mining migrants to remit 60% and 30% respectively of their earnings home. The amounts involved are large and constitute a significant proportion of the foreign exchange earnings of Mozambique and the Gross National Product of Lesotho.[10]

In terms of numbers, by 1910 there were already more than 100,000 laborers working on the South African mines, and according to Curtis (in Gungwu), more than half of this figure were migrant laborers from outside the country's borders.[11] The numbers of the labor force peaked in the 1970's at around 600,000; migrant laborers constituted about 60% of the mine labor force in South Africa.[12] Despite legislation and efforts by the post-1994 South African government to promote employment of local people and to reduce the level of dependency on migrant labor, the level of migrant employment within the mining sector remains relatively high, ranging from 40 to 55%, (Crush, 2003).

In terms of migrant presence in the mining communities, the levels appear to be rising. This is reflected by the cross border migration between South Africa and its neighbors after 1994 and the relaxed laws with regard to spousal visits to the mining industry. Indications are that in the post-1994 regime, there has been a change in the numbers of people entering South Africa legally on visitors' permits for purposes of visiting, tourism, or business. The numbers rose from 3.7 million in 1992 to 9.9 million in 1999. Fifty percent of those entering gave "holiday" as the purpose of entry. What is important to note, specifically in relation to mining communities, is that small entrepreneurs involved in cross-border trade use visitors' permits to enter the country. These small entrepreneurs constitute a significant percentage of migrants in the mining communities, (Crush, 2003). It would appear that the economic status of South Africa's neighbors and the rest of the continent have had an impact on the migration patterns in the mining environment. It would appear that despite migrants coming in to work as miners, migrants have become more creative in their survival techniques compared to the host population, (Crush, 2003).

Internal migration has also had a significant impact on the mining communities. Restrictive movement under the Pass Law meant that there was strict control of movement into the mining environment. The principle of the Pass Law was first introduced to control the movement of slaves in 1760 by the settlers of the Cape. The principles of this system were later used by both the Republican and Colonial governments and were one of the most important techniques to create an economy, not only of forced cheap labor, but also of migratory labor. This system was designed to serve two purposes: firstly to continue, in the case of black Africans, to force them into the chains of farm and mine owners and to keep their wages down forever at the lowest possible level. Secondly, to entrench the *"herrenvolk"* policy (superior race) by classifying each section into a racial group for the purpose of discriminating against and oppressing certain people.[13] In practice this meant that black people had to carry pass books on their person at all times. These pass books indicated areas where the carriers thereof were allowed to travel and live. To go beyond the boundaries set in these pass books, the individuals required permission from their employers or government officials. When the Pass Law was dismantled in 1986 and citizenship IDs were issued to black people for the first time, the impact on the mining communities was significant. People from employment disadvantaged areas, such as the rural areas in the Eastern Cape, took advantage of this free movement and "flocked" into perceived employment rich areas such as the mining industry in the vicinity of Johannesburg. The overwhelming response to this newly found freedom significantly impacted various communities, specifically mining communities, in several ways, e.g. economically, socially, and politically. This tendency disturbed the nature and hierarchical order of formerly closed communities. As these communities became multi-ethnic melting pots, the hierarchical structures had unwillingly to take account of other South African ethnic groups and cultures.

A BRIEF BACKGROUND OF TRADITIONAL AUTHORITIES IN SOUTH AFRICA

The historical roots of the traditional authority system in Africa date back to the pre-colonial era. During the colonial period the British formalized existing local authority structures to facilitate indirect management and control of colonies in Africa and Asia. Traditional leadership of indigenous people was based on inheritance; that was the key element of this approach. This structure basically continued throughout the different stages of South African history, namely the Colonial era and the *Apartheid* era (which included parts of Unification as well as the Republican era) until 1994. The main functions and powers of the traditional authorities included management of tribal land, and common law (cultural and family) issues.[14] The traditional authorities played a key role in the establishment and maintenance of the former Bantu homelands. The Bantu homelands system was an *Apartheid* creation for separate development for black people. The traditional authorities were perceived as the agents of maintenance of the *Apartheid* system during the struggle. Consequently, their role and position post *Apartheid* (after 1994) has been substantially revised.[15]

The post-*Apartheid* Government's position on the role of traditional leaders did not come about spontaneously; there were intense negotiations between the two parties that eventually culminated in the Framework Act for Traditional Leadership and Management (2003).[16] In essence the Law disempowered the traditional authorities by taking away their independent rule of the "chieftainships" in exchange for "grand" titles (Kings and Queens, Senior Traditional Leaders, and Headmen), better and more formal remuneration, and an advisory role, (van Wyk, 2004). Many traditional leaders were not happy with this, but there was no other way out for a new democratic state. It was difficult to merge the functions of the new constitutional structures that included provincial and local government with the hereditary role of the local chief. A further issue is that traditional authorities and communities are not commonplace in all areas of South Africa; therefore legislation relating to administration of traditional authorities has been delegated to the Provincial Government level. The law is carefully phrased so that traditional authorities, in negotiations with the Provincial Premier, take on an advisory role on issues relating to culture, land issues, health, application of common law, the environment, safety, and tourism at both national and provincial levels, (van Wyk, 2004).

Some traditional authorities in the mining environment experienced their role differently from other authorities. One of the most significant differences was that some of the traditional authorities in the mining industries enjoyed additional income from rentals of the land being mined and royalties from the minerals. It is difficult to estimate how much some of the traditional authorities were granted as royalties because most of them are quite secretive about the amounts. However, in some cases the royalties amounted to one percent of the pre-taxable income of the mining company.

The implied purpose of the income from the royalties was to contribute towards the development of the surrounding mining communities. Historically, there was no formal checking system that monitored the use of these royalties. The consequence of this has been that there have been some cases of traditional authorities who have earned themselves a reputation of being an example of good governance, (Mohale, 2001). But for most the call for foul play has been the order of the day, as in the case of a chief who has been accused of mismanaging millions of rand in royalties paid to the community by the surrounding mines. The impoverished community members claim that they did not benefit from the mine royalties. In this case in point the mine claims that it paid more than ZAR100 million (US$16.7 million) between 2000 and 2003.[17] On the other hand, whilst some traditional authorities enjoyed this additional income, some complain that they did not get anything at all, (Mohale, 2001).

In line with other legislation relating to the traditional authorities, the MPRDA (2004) states that the nation will be the sole owner of mineral rights; in effect this legislation takes away traditional authorities' access to the royalties, (Mohale, 2001).

All these changes have come about at a time when the traditional authorities have had a change of attitude about the high numbers of migrants in their communities. This background information sets the scene for the discussion on the relationship between the migrants and the traditional authorities.

THE RELATIONSHIP BETWEEN MIGRANTS AND TRADITIONAL AUTHORITIES

Theoretically the relationship between the migrants and the traditional authorities can be analyzed in terms of the theories of integration. Integration in this case relates to how the migrants choose or forced to integrate into the mining communities. At the same time it is also about how the traditional authorities expect and facilitate the integration of migrants into their communities. For the purpose of this paper, the researchers are going to explore how integration models impact on the relationship between these two groups. Although not all-inclusive, this paper is going to focus on only three of the integration models, namely the differential exclusionary, the assimilation, and the multi-cultural models, which will be applied in structuring and explaining the findings. Basically, the differential exclusionary model is where the dominant definition of the nation is that of a community of birth and descent. The dominant group is unwilling to accept immigrants and their children as members of their nation. This unwillingness is expressed through exclusionary and restrictive practices towards immigrants. The assimilation model may be defined as the policy of incorporating migrants into society through a one-sided process of adaptation: immigrants are expected to give up their distinctive linguistic, cultural or social characteristics and become indistinguishable from the majority population. Lastly, multi-culturalism implies that immigrants should be granted equal rights in all spheres of society without being expected to give up their diversity, although usually with an expectation of conformity to certain key values, (Castles and Miller, 1998).

The basis of this section is going to be on the findings of the relationship between the migrants and the traditional authority. Although the findings reflect a predominantly negative picture of the relationship between the two groups, it is important to also highlight the positives as well as some of the explanations behind some of these views. In view of this, the structure of this section will be as follows:

- Migrants' experiences

- Traditional authorities' experiences

MIGRANTS' EXPERIENCES

It is important to note that most of the findings relate to external migrants. However, there were occasions in which internal migrants by virtue of the treatment received from the traditional authorities identified with the external migrants. Migrant communities are not homogeneous and not all immigrants form communities. The structure and migration pattern to mining communities has changed over the years. Consequently, different migrant groups will have different experiences with the traditional authorities depending on their relative needs within these communities. The researchers endeavor to reflect this in the findings. The following are the main themes that came out of the research in relation to the migrants' experiences:

- Culture

- Employment

- Housing

- Development/Community projects

CULTURE

There are many definitions and approaches to the concept of culture. Henslin's broad definition of culture which includes the language, beliefs, values, norms, behaviors, and even material objects that are passed from one generation to the next, covers the essence of the issues raised in this study.[18] Since this study is based on an emic research approach—the way the members of the given culture perceive their world, this paper is going to use the approaches given by the respondents with regard the definitions of culture.

Culture has become a central theme in debates on new ethnic minorities. As an explanation of some of the issues raised in this study, Castles and Miller offer four dynamic characteristics that occur when new ethnic minorities integrate into an environment. They suggest,

> "(Firstly,) . . . that cultural difference serves as a marker for ethnic boundaries. Second, ethnic cultures play a central role in community formation: when ethnic groups cluster together, they establish their own neighborhoods marked by distinctive use of private and public spaces. Third, ethnic neighborhoods are perceived by some members of the majority group as confirmation of their fears of a "foreign take-over." Ethnic communities are seen as a threat to the dominant culture and national identity. Lastly, dominant groups may see dominant cultures as primordial, static, and regressive. Linguistic and cultural maintenance is taken as proof of inability of come to terms of an advanced industrial society." (Castles and Miller, 1998)

In terms of the cultural significance of language, both internal and external migrants reported difficulties at initial contact with the communities. These difficulties manifested themselves in the form of difficulties in accessing service provisions and social interactions. Internal migrants suffered from this aspect despite being of South African origin. South Africa has eleven official languages which can differ from province to province. In the communities surrounding the mining operations in the North-West Province, Tswana, Afrikaans, and English are the languages spoken. In the communities in the Limpopo Province, Pedi, Venda, Ndebele, Afrikaans, and English are the languages spoken. Consequently, they suffer the same way as the external migrants on this issue. In the mining work environment the migrants interact by using *Fanagalo* (a "mixed" vocabulary from different languages of about 500 words, most of which are mine operations related). However, this is not extended to community interactions. Some migrants over time have adopted the assimilation approach and have mastered the local language to overcome these difficulties and gain acceptance. Others, e.g. those from Lesotho, have adopted the differential exclusionary model; they have isolated themselves as a group and indicate that they have no interest in mixing with the communities. Consequently, few can speak the local language.

With regard to the normative component of culture, the question of values and norms comes to the fore. According to Coreno, values are defined as broad guidelines for "right and wrong" and for desirable and undesirable behavior. Norms are derived from values, are more specific, and can be described as behavioral rules; norms can be formal (written) or informal (unwritten).[19] Against this background, one of the major contentious issues related to values and norms is the creation of second families by the migrants. There are two important components underlying this practice: firstly, the circumstances migrants find themselves in whereby they cannot bring their spouses and families to the mining environment; consequently they start new families; and secondly, some of the migrants, such as the Mozambicans, come from cultures where the men can have more than one wife. This contradicts the local value system and has resulted in conflict within the communities and amongst the women involved. In addition to this, even where the issue is not about a second family, the migrants have complained that where they marry and have children with local women, they find it difficult to convince their local wives to return home with them. This has an impact on child rearing in that the children and the wife remain in South Africa when the husband returns home; the result is an incomplete family that is left behind. The social, economic, and psychological effect on the family and communities are immense. The welfare of the children and the women has been the cause of conflict between community leaders and migrants, because community leaders feel they have to carry the burden when migrants leave without taking care of the families they leave behind.

Other practices that impact on the value and norm system of the local communities and the migrants relate to burial and help seeking behavior. Most migrants interviewed expressed that they would like to be buried in their own home land following traditional customs. However, there were no indications of the existence of a burial society or money put aside by migrants to facilitate this practice in terms of transportation and details about families in the sending communities. In terms of help seeking behavior, most migrants, especially Mozambicans, indicated that for psychological and other health related problems they prefer to consult traditional healers from their own country. The ability to practice and to establish these values and norms amongst the migrants is dependent on how cohesive the migrant communities are. Some migrant groups are more cohesive than others, e.g. the migrants from Lesotho appear to be more cohesive than other groups. Consequently, they have maintained their cultural values and norms. However as indicated above, this is also reflected by their choice of integration model.

Some of the following quotations may offer a better understanding of the above mentioned issues: "I first came to this community twelve years ago. When I first came, the local community treated me well, but the treatment changed when my business picked up. They think that I am taking away their business; they have even thrown a brick through my window," (Mozambican Migrant).[20] "They [people from Lesotho] don't mix easily; they like to stick to themselves," (Mine Hostel Official).[21] "We do not mix in the communities; we don't know the locals. We only have friends from Lesotho; we want to mix with the local people, but we do not know how," (Lesotho Migrants).[22]

EMPLOYMENT

As indicated above, mine work has been associated with migrants at the expense of local people. As a result some myths have been going around about the capabilities of certain migrants working in specific departments, e.g. that the Xhosa are adept at drilling. From the migrant's point of view, the reason why there is a high rate of migrant employment in the mining sector is that migrants are hard working, reliable and do not fear working underground. They argue that the local people do not like them because of the above mentioned reasons, but they have to work hard because they say there is poverty where they come from and their families and other people back home depend on them. Currently, few countries in Africa are experiencing economic growth; consequently, migrants from all over Africa are migrating to South Africa and the few other African countries where economic growth is positive. Most migrants feel that the local people do not want to work because they are getting social grants and label them as lazy. Against this background, it would appear that migrants are in an advantageous position to find employment because they have experience of working in the mining environment and they also have the contacts in the mining industry to help them get jobs. In addition to this, the informal recruitment network is very strong among migrants, e.g. the traditional practice of replacing an injured or deceased employee with a relative and the domination of labor unions by certain ethnic groups.

In addition to mine employment, migrants have also established themselves as business people and entrepreneurs in the communities. What is also important to note is that this has also impacted the gender mix of migrants into the mining communities; more women are now constitute the mining communities. Migrants from Mozambique have set up small informal engineering businesses while Zimbabweans and Somalis have been involved in informal rag trade and general service industries (e.g. hairdressing).

It is also important to note that immigrants from outside Africa (e.g. from China, Pakistan, etc.) are setting up businesses and living within the mining communities. Despite living within these communities, their integration approach is the differential exclusionary model.

In terms of integration, most migrants have indicated that they are using the multi cultural and assimilation approach, especially for those who want to settle in South Africa. However, despite some acceptance from the general communities, migrants are still "ear marked" in terms of police raids, accusations of "taking the work and the women" by the traditional authorities, etc.

Quotations to support the above mentioned are the following: "This may sound silly, but there is a perception that migrants have a special aura which helps them to sense danger; consequently they are better mine workers," (Policeman).[23] "We bring skills to this community that we would like to share, but all that the traditional authority does is to report us to the police," (Cross Border Migrant Sales Woman).[24]

HOUSING

Accommodation in the mining environment is generally very poor, both for local communities and mine employees, as well as migrants. Housing problems are not unique in South Africa, but the lack of coordination between the mining company, local government and the traditional authorities has exacerbated the problem. Consequently, the enactment of the MPRDA, which requires that the mine company work in collaboration with other stakeholders to improve the infra-structure, includes housing in the communities surrounding the mine. In terms of the migrants working on the mine which employs up to 27, 000 people, of which 55% are migrants, the accommodation supplied was inadequate for several reasons. Some of these reasons include lack of married quarters and overcrowded hostels—sometimes 8 to 10 men in one large room. With the dismantling of the Pass Law as well as the relaxation of immigration policies, the result was the inevitable mushrooming of informal settlements to accommodate spouses, relatives, and other job seekers into the area.

The above mentioned factors plus the resistance of traditional authorities to allocate land to migrants has become a major stumbling block in the migrants' ability to integrate into the communities. The major discriminatory factor relates to the ID-system; according to the respondents, the Department of Home Affairs is refusing to grant them IDs despite living and working in South Africa for over 5 years. Most of the respondents in this study have been living and working in South African mines for over ten years. According to the Department of Home Affairs regulations, an individual can apply for citizenship if they have worked and lived in South Africa for 5 years and over. An official of the mine confirmed the difficulties that the migrants were experiencing with regard to accommodation and IDs.

In some cases migrants rent rooms or *shacks* (poorly constructed corrugated sheds) from local communities. This has helped the local community members and migrants to integrate in a less artificial way. To a certain extent this has made local communities become more tolerant of migrants due to the economic gains from this relationship. Migrants living in rented accommodation within the communities were positive about their integration into the communities despite complaints about high rents.

Migrant groups complained of poor relationships with the traditional authorities. Some groups complained that the traditional authorities frustrated infra-structural development in the areas where migrants resided as a way of chasing them away. One group complained that one of the traditional authorities had instructed the electricity and water companies to stop infra-structural work being undertaken in an area which was predominantly occupied by migrants. This is despite the fact that the work was part of the local government's development plan. According to the migrant group, the efforts to negotiate and discuss with the traditional authority have been ignored. This makes the migrants feel unwanted and excluded despite their efforts to integrate.

Some of the quotations regarding housing are the following: "Some of the migrants are here for over 15 years without IDs—I don't understand it," (Mine Hostel Official).[25] "Although I'm a South African [from the Eastern Cape] the traditional authorities continue to frustrate development in the area I live because I'm living amongst [external] migrants. They have called me aside to discourage me from living there; they told me that they would give me better accommodation elsewhere," (Internal Migrant).[26]

DEVELOPMENT/COMMUNITY PROJECTS

The few community developmental projects in the area are being undertaken by the Development Trust of the mine as well as the government. Generally, migrants are not included in most developmental projects. Exclusion from participation in these projects is usually because of lack of information, non-invitation to participate, and generally lack of interest on the part of some migrant groups.

Where they have participated, migrants have reported that the traditional authorities made it clear that they don't want migrants to be involved. In a case study of an agricultural project where migrant participation was high, conflict between the project members and the traditional authorities resulted in non-support from the mine and the stagnation and deterioration of the project that had been successfully progressing for a number of years. Migrants expressed feeling hurt and dehumanized by being referred to as aliens. Internal migrants felt equally discriminated against by the traditional authority despite being South African.

This is exemplified by the following quotations: "They [traditional authorities] disrupted the electricity supply; this affects the water supply for our garden project. When we asked them for help to reinstall the electricity, they tell us that this will be done when we get rid of the 'aliens,'" (Garden Project Leader).[27] "Our plan was to invest substantially to the garden project so that it can be sustainable, but the traditional authorities would not give us support, because the project is full of 'aliens,'" (Mine Manager).[28]

TRADITIONAL AUTHORITIES' EXPERIENCE

In the research setting in the North-West Province there is one traditional authority while in the research setting in the Limpopo Province, there are three. Generally, the integration strategy used by all four authority figures leans towards the differential exclusionary model. Although this integration strategy is mainly directed to the external migrants; they express the same sentiments towards internal migrants with regard to certain issues.

The major issues of contention include:

- Culture
- Employment
- Service provision
- Land issues

CULTURE

As indicated above, the traditional authorities are the custodians and gate keepers of the cultural values and practices of the community. Therefore, when migrants come into their communities, they are viewed as people who come in to challenge and destroy their cultural heritage. As a result of this, traditional authorities tend to be generally negative towards migrants and can experience cultural shock with regard to certain cultural issues.

Traditional authorities' main problems with regard to cultural issues in the mining environment are that migrants are coming in and using their economic power and worldly views to influence young people. The traditional authorities claim that they lost control of the young in the communities because of the temptations that the migrants placed upon the youth. Migrants are accused of using money to sleep with young girls. According to the traditional authorities, young girls have lost the values of their heritage by not respecting marriage and sleeping with men before they are of age. The traditional authorities argue that the local population, specifically the youth and the women, are blinded by the migrants' perceived "flashy/artificial" lifestyle to the extent that they undermine their own culture. They feel that what the community members do not realize is that, despite behaving artificially in the mining communities; migrants maintain their own cultures in their homelands. "All they do is to destroy our cultures and communities and we don't want them here."[29]

Traditional authorities expressed that their community members are the victims and not the migrants. They feel that migrants are able to introduce things that community members do not understand and the community members latched on to them without really understanding the impact of what they are doing. The traditional authorities feel that poverty makes the local community members "ignorant" and unequal partners in any relationship with migrants. In addition to being responsible for the loss of traditional values and moral codes, migrants are also accused of spreading HIV/AIDS, STDs, crime, and degeneration in the communities. They also feel that they have to carry the burden of all this and take responsibility for bringing up the children of migrants who either die from HIV/AIDS or leave their children behind and return to their homelands.

The major concern for the traditional authorities regarding culture is that, according to them, the migrants are destroying the local culture and heritage from the roots because they are targeting the most vulnerable groups, namely the women and the children. The traditional authorities have expressed feeling helpless and powerless to remedy this situation. As a way of dealing with this situation, some traditional authorities have indicated that they want the mine to build appropriate accommodation for migrant workers that is secured and away from the rest of the communities; they do not want them to mix with the local people.

The following quotations will shed light on the above mentioned: "We are in principle against migrants; we want these outsiders to be kept out of our communities. The mine should ensure that the hostels are locked that the migrants stay inside," (Traditional Authority).[30] "We can't control our children, because they are taking the ways of the migrants," (Traditional Authority).[31]

EMPLOYMENT

Traditional authorities are aware that local people used to shun mine work and associated it with migrants. However, the challenges of poverty, the realization that mine work is no longer a "dead end job," globalization and the liberalization of the political economy have broadened their views and made them appreciate that they are now able to control their own destiny unlike under the *Apartheid* regime. Consequently, traditional authorities are now calling the mines to stop employing migrants and increase employment of local people. In the Limpopo research setting, the traditional authorities demanded that all recruitment for mine work be undertaken and controlled by the traditional authorities. This way, they can ensure that only local people are employed. Reports are that this strategy was once tried, but it did not work for three main reasons: firstly, it is said to have continued to "underhandedly" employ migrants by bringing them in under the "cover of darkness" (at night); secondly, the traditional authorities were accused of nepotism by the general community and thirdly, local people were said to be too scared to work in the mine, because they fear death and felt that they were not skilled enough to work safely in the mine.

The issue of mining skills is a matter that baffles the traditional authorities. On the one hand, the general view is that migrants have mining skills that local people do not have, but on the other, they don't really know what these skills are. As a result of this "mystification" one tribal leader went to the mine to investigate what these skills are. The result of the investigation found that most migrant laborers are rural folk just like them. In view of this, the traditional authorities are now challenging the mine to set up training programs that sensitize and equip the local population to work in the mine just like the migrants do. As far as they are concerned, migrants are only getting jobs because of their historical links. The reason why the traditional authorities feel so strongly about the employment of local people is that they feel that technically the land and minerals belong to the local tribe. They find it difficult to accept that people from outside should benefit at the expense of the owners of the minerals who remain riddled in poverty. They feel that during the *Apartheid* era they did not have much choice or control. But now, with the democratization of the South African economy and society, they should benefit from the resources of their heritage. It is worth noting that the MPRDA states that the minerals belong to the nation and not to one company or tribal group; the Act requires that companies or individuals need a mining license to mine the resources. Therefore, technically, the owner of the mining rights (license) has more rights to the minerals than the owner of the land. To a certain extent, the Act could be perceived as "weakening" the power of the traditional authorities. However, the Act appears to compensate the traditional authorities, in its requirement that companies provide an acceptable Social and Labor Plan as part of the license application. The Social and Labor Plan is a document that commits the applicant to develop the human resources and the communities and to manage downscaling for the eventual closure of the mine.

The traditional authorities expressed mixed views with regard to migrant entrepreneurship and migrant employment in other sectors within the mining communities. On the one hand, they welcome what they perceive as the boosting of the communities by the Asians and North-Africans who revamp run down businesses previously owned by local blacks. At the same time, they feel that this development is only face value, because most of these businesses only employ their family members and adopt the differential exclusive integration strategy. According to the traditional authorities, these business owners do not plough back anything into the communities and consequently are viewed as "economic parasites." Despite these perceptions about the Asian and North-African migrants, the traditional authorities appear to be more tolerant of them compared to migrant entrepreneurs from neighboring countries who adopt a more assimilative integration strategy.

Quotations in this regard are the following: "Because of the migrants our local people are not employed," (Traditional Authority).[32] "These migrants are taking the jobs that our children should be getting," (Traditional Authority).[33]

SERVICE PROVISION

In terms of service provision and infra-structure, there are three main stakeholders, namely the mine, the government, and the traditional authorities.

The mine's responsibilities have been specified under the MPRDA. Accordingly, government is mandated to provide services and infra-structure development according to policies, plans, and budgets reflecting the needs of the community. The traditional authorities' responsibilities are based on two factors, namely their role as custodians of culture and land, and the payment of royalties to them. According to traditional authorities, both external and internal migrants create complications in the planning and implementation of service provision and infra-structure in the communities.

When government and other stakeholders are planning for service provision and infra-structure, they make them in accordance with the demographics of the communities. Uncontrolled migration impacts negatively on service provision and infra-structure; throughout the survey there were consistent reports of overcrowded public services such as health clinics, schools, provision of electricity and water, etc. This state of affairs in turn impacts the relationship between the stakeholders responsible for providing these services, the relationship between the traditional authorities and their people, and the relationship between the traditional authorities and migrants. A tug of war among the stakeholders responsible for service and infra-structure provisions relating to who is responsible for correcting the imbalance of supply and demand has been the result. Traditional authorities feel that the mine should correct this imbalance, because if it wasn't for the mine, the migrants would not be so overwhelmingly attracted to the area. In terms of the relationship with the local communities, the traditional authorities are blamed for not playing their role as custodians of culture effectively and misappropriating the royalties. In view of this, it negates the relationship between traditional authorities and migrants.

The following quotation reflects the above sentiments: "The migrants are overcrowding our services, especially our clinics. One of our babies died in the queue whilst waiting to be seen," (Traditional Authority).[34]

LAND ISSUES

As indicated above, the traditional authorities own some of the land that is within and surrounds the mine activities. As a result of this situation in terms of residential land, the traditional authorities have a responsibility to allocate land for housing and businesses. Each specific traditional leader therefore determines his or her conditions for qualifying for land allocation. Generally most traditional authorities' primary condition for qualifying is that the individual must have a South African ID, which poses a problem for migrants without South African IDs. This situation is one of the underlying causes of conflict between traditional authorities and migrants with regard to land allocation.

The traditional authorities say that the establishment of informal communities impact greatly on their development plans. They argue that migrants set up temporary structures on land that is planned for other developmental projects. Legislation prevents the traditional authorities from removing them and taking over the land. Legislation states that if a person settles on a given piece of land for a specific length of time without being removed, there comes a point beyond which the person cannot be removed without a high court ruling. The traditional authorities state that they are unable to look for support elsewhere, because the law states that it is the responsibility of the landlords to ensure that their land is not invaded. One traditional leader reported that he had identified some land that he wished to use for economic development, but because of the inflow of migrants into the land, he cannot develop the land for economic purposes. He indicated that he has been struggling for four years to try and resettle the migrants, but the migrants are not keen to move elsewhere.

The following quotation is significant with regard to the above mentioned: "Informal settlements are now not only housing mine employees, but also people from local areas, and other migrants coming to do farming in the surrounding areas. These informal settlements are infested with unsocial behavior such as crime, prostitution, and anarchy. We have to carry the burden of all this," (Traditional Authority).[35]

DEVELOPMENT/COMMUNITY PROJECTS

In most of the mining communities the traditional authorities play a big role in the coordination of who participates in the community development projects. Regardless of who initiates the projects, the traditional authorities generally ensure they have some input. Most development projects undertaken did not include many migrants; when migrants get involved in projects conflict and tension arise between the migrants and the traditional authorities. This conflict and tension adversely impacts the success of the projects.

The traditional authorities state that migrants do not participate in local community activities. They feel that migrants are only here for economic activities. In view of this, migrants do not attend meetings and therefore do not know what is going on in the communities. If they do attend, it is just for show; because once they get citizenship they become less interested. The traditional authorities argue that, as an example, migrants mix at work and even get involved in union issues, but in the communities this is not reflected.

The following quotation reflects the above mentioned: "Few migrants use the skills that they have to help in the community development projects. So, why should we involve them?" (Traditional Authority).[36]

ANALYSIS

The relationship between traditional authorities and migrants is a key component underlying developmental efforts in mining communities. As a way of acknowledging the significance of the traditional authorities in these environments, it is important to note that mining companies come and go once the minerals have been depleted, governments come and go through the electoral system; however, traditional authorities remain throughout. They are the ones who have to pick up the pieces after the damage that the communities have endured. At the same time, it could be argued that the traditional authorities and the migrants are the victims of the prosperity that South Africa has gained from the mining industry. Consequently, the two parties' actions reflect their response to this victimization.

In terms of the power relations in the mining communities, it is not only the economic relations that play a crucial role in shaping inequalities (Marx, Weber in Bilton et al.[37]), but also racial and ethnic factors (Gumplowicz, Gobineau, Chamberlain in Fulcher and Scott[38]). The analysis of the relationship between the traditional authorities and the migrants seem to follow similar underlying trends. The migrants in this relationship have the economic power in the sense that they earn money that they use to "buy" the communities' admiration over the traditional authorities. At the same time, the traditional authorities use the power stemming from ethnic domination over the migrants. In summary, it can be argued that the migrants have economic power while the traditional authorities have status and communal power (power associated with important social positions, customs, and practices of a particular social group, Weber in Fulcher and Scott, 2003). What is interesting, but important to take note of in terms of resolving the conflict between the two parties, is that they are displaying the same form of power that is being used to oppress them. The migrants are economically being oppressed by the mine in terms of the draconian working conditions that they have to endure. Consequently, when they find themselves among those with less economic power than them (unemployed local community members), they boast and to a certain extent victimize the underdogs. By the same token, traditional authorities had their land forcibly taken away by the mining companies (Mohale, 2001), and are now using the reduced power they have over access to land to exploit and oppress migrants. This behavior concurs with Freire's analysis of the oppressed in that " . . . the oppressed instead of striving for liberation, tend themselves to become oppressors or "sub-oppressors." The very structure of their thought has been conditioned by the contradictions by the concrete existential situation by which they were shaped. The ideal is to be men; but for them, to be men is to be oppressors."[39] The result of this conflict is that it has retarded the development of both groups. Migrants are so focused on making money through overtime as laborers that only a few of them have undertaken self development initiatives within the mine environment. Most of the migrant mine employees who were contacted in the study, despite being employed for over ten years, could only communicate in *Fanagalo,* which can be viewed as a tool used by the mining fraternity to keep migrants working in the underground. In order to be "promoted" to work on the surface, mine employees must communicate either in English or Afrikaans. Traditional authorities on the other hand, have for years focused on issues related to migrant employment while their real frustration is with the mining companies. Consequently, they have not been able to look beyond the basic mine laborer occupations in the mining sector for their people. Given the number of years that mining has been in their area, it is expected that they would focus more on self actualization in their jobs and consequently occupy more senior positions that have been reserved for the whites. The process of self actualization is being hampered by their competitive attitude towards the migrants.

In addition to this, the findings show that the issues of ethnocentrism and xenophobia are present and need to be discussed. Ethnocentrism is based on the belief of cultural "superiority"; the behavior of other groups being judged by the standards of "our own" culture.[40] Vander Zanden suggests that ethnocentrism is no stranger to nations, tribes, families, cliques, colleges, fraternities, businesses, churches, and political parties. It is about the feeling of solidarity, belonging to the "best people," and it can create social cohesion, (Vander Zanden, 1990). In moderation, ethnocentrism can thus be positive in terms of human socialization. It can be argued that ethnocentrism in the mining communities among the local communities and migrants were based on protectionism against the harsh apartheid regime as well as the migrant labor system. However a combination of poverty, differentiation integration processes and the continued circulatory and oscillatory nature of the migratory movements in the mining communities have resulted in extreme ethnocentrism. In turn this has culminated into xenophobia. What is interesting about xenophobia in the mining sector as well as other parts of South Africa is that it is mainly directed towards other black Africans by black South Africans. Kollapan suggests that not all foreigners are uniformly victimized; rather black foreigners, particularly those from Africa, comprise the majority of victims.[41] Morris[42] and Tshitereke[43] proposed three hypotheses to explain this phenomenon, namely "the scapegoating hypothesis," "the isolation hypothesis," and "the biocultural hypothesis." The scapegoating hypothesis suggests that in the South African mining context hostility towards foreigners is explained in relation to limited resources, such as housing, education, health care, and employment, coupled with high expectations during transition. Tshitereke suggests that people are more conscious of their deprivation than ever before, because expectations after apartheid have been heightened, (Tshitereke, 1999). The continued deprivation after apartheid has been blamed on the other black Africans because they are interpreted as threats to jobs, housing, education, and health care.[44] Morris argues that apartheid insulated South African citizens from nationalities beyond Southern Africa, (Morris, 1998). In this hypothesis, foreigners represent the unknown to South Africans. With the political transition, however, South Africa's borders have opened up and the country has become integrated into the international community. This has brought South Africans into direct contact with the unknown, with foreigners. According to the isolation hypothesis, the interface between previously isolated South Africans and unknown foreigners creates a space for hostility to develop: "When a group has no history of incorporating strangers it may find it difficult to be welcoming." Although this argument appears to contradict the statistics showing the high numbers of migrants in the mining communities over the last century, it must be interpreted with the differential exclusionary integration model forced upon the host communities and migrants. The same principles apply for the internal migrants who also experience similar hostility from the traditional authorities.

The "bio-cultural hypothesis," unlike the other two hypotheses, focuses on the physical and cultural attributes of foreign individuals. Unlike the other two hypotheses that treat foreigners as homogenous, the bio-cultural hypothesis focuses on physical and cultural differences exhibited by African foreigners in the country.[45] This hypothesis bears a lot of similarities to Freire's concept of power that suggests that in the early stages of liberation the oppressed tend to become the oppressors, (Freire, 1996). Black South Africans appear to be reflecting the oppression that they experienced during apartheid on black African foreigners. The analysis thus far has focused on the probable source of the conflict between the traditional authorities and migrants. What is important for this paper is to get a good understanding of the impact of this conflict on development projects in the area.

The study has also revealed disempowerment as the major cause of the poor relationship between the migrants and the traditional authorities.

Our analysis is that disempowerment of the two groups is the result of the Machiavellian "divide and rule" policy that the mining sector and successive government departments have imposed on the two groups. The mining companies and successive government departments over the years have disempowered these two groups on several fronts: First, the continued use of migrants at the expense of local labor, and at the same time providing them with poor living and working conditions. Secondly, the poor and inadequate service provisions provided in the communities by successive government departments.[46] Thirdly, the integration model (differential exclusion model) imposed on the two groups in response to the harsh labor migration and social policies of the mining companies and successive governments. The differential exclusive integration model does not promote positive integration. Castles and Miller suggest that communities that participate in the decision-making relating to migration into their areas are more accepting of migrants, (Castles and Miller, 1998). They argue that this approach facilitates the introduction of measures to prevent discrimination and exploitation of migrants and to provide social services to support successful settlement. These factors have significantly contributed to ameliorate the conflict between the two groups.

Positive relationships are conducive to successful development projects; however the process to achieve this may be complex. What is important to recognize at the outset is that although the study has focused on the impact of the conflict between migrants and traditional authorities, the way forward must involve all the stakeholders. It is therefore important to adopt a framework for analysis that includes the macro, meso, and micro levels. The microanalysis level refers to interpersonal relationships in the communities.[47] Analysis at the meso level relates to concerns with the local configuration of services, including the way in which policies are interpreted and implemented at the local levels.[48] Analysis at the macro level looks at the impact that policy guidance has on achievements of projects.[49] The success of projects will be influenced by the integration of the three levels of analysis. These analysis levels can help to identify the barriers inhibiting the development of projects.

Tembo argued that in any developmental process there is a need for empowering relationships between the donors, the recipients, and other stakeholders involved in the process.[50] Most international donors, such as the EC, in recognition of the need for this empowering relationship, now work within a framework whereby civil society organizations regarded as Non State Actors (NSA) are to participate "officially" in decision making process involved in development programming, implementation, and review. This is an important move from just viewing poverty eradication in

terms of donating money. However, there are issues of empowerment that
need to be considered when dealing with the subject of participation. As has
been revealed in this study, different groups within the stakeholder groups
participate and negotiate in development processes from their interests and
interpretations of what the development dialogue itself is about and the
various material and non-aspects within it, (Tembo, 2003). Tembo argued
that in some cases of negotiation and participation the power difference is
such that the poor and vulnerable groups either find other organizations
that represent their needs without really understanding the issues, take a
passive role, or they just do not take an interest. Therefore, inadequate participation methods can reinforce social exclusion and strengthen dominant
voices. In the end most negotiations and participation is usually based on
fund raising for projects that are unsuitable for the community members. It
has been the observation of this study that the mining company has focused
on setting up projects or donating money without achieving sustainable
development. The way forward in this study is therefore to utilize a framework of an empowerment-based transformation process that will ensure
genuine participation for those affected by the project.

The follow-up study found that despite the mining company employing a consultant company to promote community engagement, participation in community decision making and empowerment intervention, some
community members/groups felt further disempowered by the intervention strategy that the company adopted. One of the major complaints was
that the consultant company knew very little about the communities, but
despite this the consulting company initiated community interventions. The
result of this lack of knowledge was demonstrated by some of the observations and responses from the survey, which include: migrants were not
included in the empowerment process; traditional authorities took on the
responsibility of identifying the participants in the process, which resulted
in dissatisfaction of some community members who accused them of favoritism; one group in the communities threatened to take legal proceedings if
they continued to be excluded from the process; although the process was
supposed to have a "domino effect" in terms of communicating information in the communities, it appears that "hidden agendas" prevented people from passing information to the rest of the community. Better access
to the mine management for better job opportunities was one of the main
motivations for participation rather than empowerment purposes. In addition, job opportunities without competition from other community members were another objective for the "hidden agendas" by participants; the
participation of the usual suspects who continue to recruit their relatives
or friends further disempowered the vulnerable groups such as women,

youth, migrants, and the elderly. Their views, opinions and voices therefore continue to be ignored. It would appear that poor preparation in terms of social, economic, and cultural capital analysis in the communities may have exacerbated the existing inequalities and conflicts.

The analysis of this study reveals that sustainable resolution may not be possible without further research to elicit information on how people perceive, act on, and negotiate their interests. Stakeholders and social mapping are applied as participatory social research tools that document and feed back the values, interests, attitudes, and aspirations of a defined group of stakeholders, to encourage mutual understanding and enhance negotiation and deliberation over genuine conflicts of interest.[51] It is believed that analysis of information from the additional, more focused research may have potential to change the attitudes of all stakeholders.

In terms of integrating the micro, meso, and macro levels of analysis Tembo suggests that there needs to be a political economy of information, (Tembo, 2003). He argues that how information is shared, who shares it, to who, where, and under what circumstances, is critically important in the developing context. Analysis at the micro level in the mining communities gives an idea that information about projects is distributed through the traditional authorities. Observations have found that this communication structure has been selective, discriminative, and disempowering both to the local as well as to the migrant communities. The communities who are being represented must also have access to the right information at the right time in order to actively and intelligently participate and to influence decisions relating to the developmental projects and plans. This ensures that the weaker members in the communities such as migrants are not left out and their needs are also appreciated. At the meso level it is important that the company and local government departments are aware of the different community attitudes. In the same light it is also important for the different community groups to have access to the various local institutions as well as the company. Bellaart suggests that for a service to be accessible it must have the following features: it must be well known, open, friendly, nearby, trustworthy, recognizable, and competent, and must have a good image.[52] Therefore, access is about being able to get in and finding the appropriate service. One of the major criticisms of the South African public services is that the policies are very well written and appropriate for the needs of the population but interpretation and implementation at the local level is very poor. In terms of the macro level interventions the South African government has used its legislative powers to enhance development for the mining communities through the MPRDA.[53] Within the Act is a provision that states that mining companies must not discriminate against migrant workers. However, at the same time the Home Affairs Department has progressively reduced the number of work permits granted over the years, (Crush, 2003). In addition, media reports about government's views on migrants are poor, for example police and some government officials have been reported to place blame on migrants for the high level of crime, housing shortages and high house prices. This contradiction has unsettled a lot of migrants in these communities and perpetuates negativity towards migrants by the general public. The consequence of this is that migrants continue to use circulatory and oscillatory migration models into the area. The impact of this is that migrants are perceived by traditional authorities to show lack of commitment to the communities, therefore should not benefit from community development projects. The "Goodbye to Projects" found that political support for intervention aims and processes is important. Studies from Uganda (the PMA and the HIV/AIDS Program), showed that political support from the highest level was seen as being a significant factor in the reduction of HIV/AIDS transmission in Uganda.[54] What has come of this discussion is that it is not just about empowering people through participation but there is also a need for training at all levels to ensure full participation. If they are not well trained, institutional personnel may abuse their power as a way of hiding their ineffectiveness and lack of skills. Therefore, the situation will exacerbate the conflict within the communities and among the stakeholders as a way of scapegoating.

In addition to empowering in terms of participation and negotiation it is important to have an integrated social analysis framework. The aim of this analysis is to identify more specifically the opportunities, constraints, risks, and social inclusion.

Although the current study was not focused on the integrated social analysis framework, it is possible to identify some of these aspects within the communities. In terms of opportunities in the environment, the following were identified in the study: social diversity, economic opportunities brought on by the mine, stable institutions in the form of traditional authorities, and local government. The constraints identified by this study include poverty, poor access to information, lack of integration, the nature of poverty in the communities, economic and political instability in neighboring countries, isolation and the mixed nature of communities (neither rural nor urban), poor health provisions, and a poor or non-existent infra-structure.

In terms of the strengths and weaknesses of the two groups the study was able to identify some of the following: the traditional authorities must recognize their strengths in terms of being a structure that is well respected by communities, their knowledge of community needs, and their desire to be self determined. In terms of weaknesses the traditional authorities need to acknowledge that they have to balance the traditional values with the global values in their support of the communities, weak negotiating skills compared to international mining companies and the Government, and perceived xenophobic behavior. The migrants' strengths include: knowledge of the working world and being relatively skilled, their ability to integrate into new environments, a desire to work in partnership with traditional authorities and community members, and knowledge of organized trade unions. Migrants' weaknesses include: the persistent circulatory and oscillatory nature of their migration, the perceived careless use of money, the chronic identification of low level occupational positions in the mine by both communities as well as the mining companies. The sustainable livelihood approach suggests that successful interventions recognize that needs and problems can be tackled through working with existing strengths as one of its principles for project development, (Franks et al, 2004). All these strengths are weaknesses if they are used in isolation. At the same time, the weaknesses can translate into strengths if the two parties collaborate and are supportive of each other; there is a lot that they can gain from each other. What is positive about such an approach in relation to the migrants and the traditional authorities is that each group will be made aware of the contribution that they can make to the project as well as being in a position where they can identify what they can gain from the project. By working together to identify the strengths and the weaknesses the two groups (migrants and traditional authorities) are in a position to recognize the opportunities and constraints of their environment. At the same time, they may empower themselves by getting a better understanding of the source of their disempowerment and not allow the other stakeholders to manipulate or divide them.

CONCLUSION

What is coming out of this study is that both parties are the losers in the power struggle in the mining environment. Their relationship is based on the survival techniques they have adopted to hold on the small bit of dignity they have left. It is however difficult for them to perceive that they can achieve this without negatively impacting the other. Both groups appear to have internalized their role in the "divide and rule" strategy of the mining companies and successive governments. As a result, resolving the conflict between the two groups is complex.

In terms of finding the way forward, it is suggested that social frameworks be adopted, that take a holistic approach that includes all the stakeholders in the communities. At the end of the day it must be remembered that when all the mineral resources have been depleted, it is the traditional authorities, migrants, and the local communities who are left to "pick up the pieces."

NOTES

1. Broad-Based Socio-Economic Empowerment Charter for the Mining Industry, Pretoria: South African Government, 2002.
2. Mineral and Petroleum Resources Development Act (MPRDA), Act 28, South Africa: Government Gazette, Oct. 10, 2002; hereafter cited in text as MPRDA act 28.
3. Mineral and Petroleum Resources Development Act (MPRDA) Regulations: Amendment (Gazette 26942, Regulation Gazette 8087), 29 October 2004 (South Africa).
4. Ann Bowling, Research Methods in Health: Investigating Health and Health Services, 2nd ed. (Philadelphia: Open University Press, 2002).
5. Stephen Castles and Mark, J. Miller, The Age of Migration: International Population Movements in the Modern World, 2nd ed. (London: MacMillan Press, 1998).
6. Jonathan Crush, "Contract Migration to South Africa: Past, Present and Future," Briefing for the Green Paper Task Team on international migration, (Pretoria, South Africa, 1997), 3.
7. D.S. Massey, J. Arango, G. Hugo and J.E. Taylor, "An Evaluation of International Migration Theory: the North American Case," Population and Development Review 20 (1994).
8. Mark Schoofs, "All that Glitters: How HIV Caught Fire in SA: Part One: Sex and the Migrant Miner," The Body: An Electronic Journal, 1999. available at http://www.thebody.com last accessed on 28 August 2004.
9. W.R. Bohning, "Black Migration to South Africa—What are the Issues?," 1977. International Labor Organization, Geneva, Switzerland.
10. Jonathan Crush, "South Africa: new nation, new migration policy?" 2003. Migration Information Source Authoritative Data, Global Reach, Country Profile.
11. W. Gungwu, Global History and Migrations (New York: Perseus Books, 1997).
12. Francis Wilson, International Migration in Southern Africa (Cape Town: SALDRU, 1976).
13. "The Extension of the Pass Laws." Liberation, Johannesburg, March 1956. available at http://www.anc.org.za/ancdocs/history/people/sisulu/extensions.html last accessed on 1 February 2006.
14. Andreas van Wyk, Nuwe bier in ou kalbasse ["New Beer in Old Calabashes,"] Beeld, 11 March 2004.
15. Jason Meyers, "The Spontaneous Ideology of Tradition in Post-Apartheid South Africa," Politikon 26, no. 1 (1999): 33–54.
16. Justice Mohale, "Chiefs Ask for Land Rights," Sowetan, 5 June 2001.
17. Tallie Taljard, "Mine millions Go Missing," Citizen, 26 September 2003.

18. James M. Henslin, Sociology: A Down-to-Earth Approach, 4ᵗʰ ed. (London: Allyn and Bacon, 1999).
19. T. Coreno, "Fundamentalism as A Class Culture," 2002. available at http://www.findarticles.com/cf   0/m0SOR/363/92284224/p5/articlejhtml?term last accessed on 1 May 2002.
20. Anonymous interview conducted in January 2006
21. Anonymous interview conducted in January 2006
22. Anonymous interview conducted in January 2006
23. Anonymous interview conducted in September 2005
24. Anonymous interview conducted in September 2005
25. Anonymous interview conducted in January 2006
26. Anonymous interview conducted in January 2006
27. Anonymous interview conducted in August 2006
28. Anonymous interview conducted in August 2006
29. Anonymous interview conducted in August 2006
30. Anonymous interview conducted in August 2006
31. Anonymous interview conducted in August 2006
32. Anonymous interview conducted in September 2005
33. Anonymous interview conducted in September 2005
34. Anonymous interview conducted in August 2006
35. Anonymous interview conducted in August 2006
36. Anonymous interview conducted in August 2006
37. Tony Bilton, Kevin Bonnett, Pip Jones, Tony Lawson, David Skinner, Michelle Stanworth and Andrew Webster, Introductory Sociology, 4ᵗʰ ed. (New York: Palgrave Macmillan, 2002).
38. James Fulcher and John Scott, Sociology, 2ⁿᵈ ed. (New York: Oxford University Press, 2003).
39. Paulo Freire, Pedagogy of the Oppressed, (New York: Routledge, 1996).
40. James W. Vander Zanden, The Social Experience: An Introduction to Sociology, 2ⁿᵈ ed. (New York: McGraw-Hill, 1990).
41. J. Kollapan, "Xenophobia in South Africa: the Challenge to Forced Migration," Seminar, Graduate School, University of the Witwatersrand, Johannesburg, South Africa, 1999.
42. A. Morris, "Our Fellow Africans Make our Lives Hell: the Lives of Congolese and Nigerians Living in Johannesburg," Ethnic and Racial Studies 21 no. 6 (1998): 1116–36.
43. C. Tshitereke, "Xenophobia and Relative Deprivation," Crossings 3, no. 2 (1999): 4–5.
44. Charity, S. Chenga and J. Freek Cronjé, "Child and Family Welfare Issues in a Mining Community in South Africa," Paper presented to the 6ᵗʰ Pan African International Federation of Social Work, Regional Conference. Nairobi, Kenya, April 2005.
45. Bronwyn Harris, "Xenophobia: a New Pathology for a new South Africa?" in Psychopathology and Social Prejudice, ed. D. Hook and G. Eagle (Cape Town: University of Cape Town Press), 169–184.
46. Ralph Hamann, "Corporate Social Responsibility and Its Implications for Governance: The Case of Mining in South Africa," Paper submitted to

the oikos PhD Summer Academy, St Gallen, Swizerland, 28 July-1 August 2003.

47. L. Swartz, Culture and Mental Health: A Southern African View (Cape Town: Oxford University Press, 1998).

48. Charles Watters, "Good Practice in the Mental Health Care of Refugees: Perspectives on South Africa," in Migration and Health in Southern Africa, ed. Robin Cohen (Cape Town: Van Schaik, 2003), 224–231.

49. D. Pilgrim and A. Rodgers, A Sociology of Mental Health and Illness (Buckingham: Open University Press, 1993).

50. F. Tembo, Participation, Negotiation and Poverty: Encountering the Power of Images Designing Pro-Poor Development Programmes (Aldershot: Ashgate, 2003).

51. S.F. Jennings and S. Lockie, "Application of Stakeholder Analysis and Social Mapping for Coastal Zone Management in Australia," Cooperative Research Centre for Coastal Zone, Estuary & Waterway Management & Centre for Social Science Research, Central Queensland University, Rockhampton, Australia.

52. H. Bellaart, "Accessibility of Child and Youth Care for Migrants and Refugees," 17–19 January 2003. International Workshop Utrecht, Service Provision for Migrants and Refugees, University of Utrecht, The Netherlands.

53. Mineral and Petroleum Resources Development Act (MPRDA). Act 28 of 2002. Government Gazette, October, 10. South Africa.

54. Tom Franks, Anna Toner, I. Goldman, D. Howlett, F. Muhumuza, F. Kamuzora and T. Tamasane, "The Institutional Impacts of Adopting a Livelihoods Approach to Managing Development Interventions," Bradford, UK: Bradford Centre for International Development, 2004.

Part III
Migration and Survival Politics

Chapter Nine
Cultural and Ethnic Accommodation of New-Comers in South Africa

Gxowa-Dlayedwa Zodwa

BACKGROUND AND MOTIVATION

One may wonder how I came up with the idea of writing a chapter on cultural exchange between South Africans and non-South Africans living in South Africa. In my capacity as a lecturer of "Intercultural Communication," a module in the second year, I gave the students an assignment to work with 5 persons from other cultural backgrounds. The main objective was to find out how students interacted with each other. I thought the task would be easy for the students, only to discover that it was not. Most students found it difficult to interact, so much that others forfeited their marks. Students were tense and came complaining that it was difficult, but, as it was an assignment, and they needed marks, they had to do it.

The assignment was to be presented in groups, consisting of five students from different cultural backgrounds. For example, one group could have Chinese, Cameroonian, Congolese, South African and Tanzanian composition. They were 16 groups altogether. During the presentations, I could easily notice that South Africans, in particular, were not open enough with non-South African students. As a lecturer, I personally took it as a challenge to involve my students in cross-cultural communication, not only theoretically, but also in practice. Most non-South Africans expressed that they were ill-treated in this country by South Africans. They felt strong vibes of discrimination, and hated that exclusive attitude of being given diminished status like *Makwiri kwiri*. I needed to investigate what was happening in my country. Are we really in that state of hating other people and discriminating against them? What then was the need to fight apartheid? Is this not still apartheid in disguise? As a person involved in the transformation of my society through education, I was then moved to undertake this study in order to have a better insight of what is really happening in South Africa.

METHODOLOGY AND SITES OF RESEARCH

I decided to initiate further investigations by designing a questionnaire to interview people from various social classes, migrants as well as South Africans. The first idea was to ask people to complete the questionnaire we gave them. Some of the people responded, but they were not very descriptive. That is why I decided to go to the field in the company of my research assistants, who demonstrated much interest in this study. We questioned the people in the language of their choice. For instance, I questioned my people in my own language, Xhosa, so that they could express themselves better, opening up and exposing their innermost feelings about the migrants.

As my university is located in the Western Cape, my first targets were those in Cape Town. We designed two different questionnaires, one for South Africans and one for the migrants' groups who live in South Africa. The questions on the whole were open-ended, of which there were 37. The questionnaires were designed to understand the cultural and ethnical accommodation of migrants in South Africa and to find out how South Africans interact with those migrants' groups. All the people interviewed were adults. We visited places where we could find people who could feel free to express themselves. In addition, we targeted sites where we knew we could find people from various nationalities who interact with South Africans on a regular basis. In Cape Town, places such as Parow, Bellville, the center of the town, Salt River and Woodstock were visited. We were asking questions and using voice recorders so that we could easily transfer our findings onto the computer when needed. After transcribing the findings, we needed to type and keep the findings electronically.

The interviewees on the one hand had some expectations, while on the other hand they retained some valuable information in fear of being betrayed. That is why it was first necessary for us to explain the essence of the study. In spite of our explanations the Capetonians still did not open up fully; hence we had to move to the Eastern Cape. We went to Eastern Cape and to the rural areas to get more information from the indigenous people. In Eastern Cape, we got in touch with the rural people so that we could compare their reactions and responses to those of the Capetonians. We penetrated the villages and the towns. Some of the places we visited in Eastern Cape were Queenstown, Mthatha, East London and Lady Frere.

MIGRATORY SITUATION IN SOUTH AFRICA

We cannot talk about the migratory situation in South Africa without taking into account the history of the country. South Africa was once an international pariah and could not participate in exchange between countries. This situation was the result of the political system called Apartheid, which was based on the division amongst different groups of population that constituted South African society. This system gave advantages to certain groups, specifically whites, but other groups were excluded from the management of the country. Sanctions were taken against the political system and South Africa was not open to other countries. In fact, the system was promoting racism or more specifically, the feeling of superiority for the white race over other races. Since this political system went against human dignity, South Africa could not receive visitors from other countries and an embargo was imposed against it. The free circulation was thus infringed.

Since the end of the Apartheid era, the borders have been opened to other countries. People could come and visit the country since it is full of opportunities spiced by its geographical location as compared to all the other African countries. In short, she is considered as an "El Dorado" or a land of gold. Since many of the African people who want to go to other Western countries meet a lot of difficulties, they find it easier to access South Africa and benefit from the facilities and opportunities that the country has. Not only do Africans come to South Africa, but there are also people from other countries. Presently, the migratory influx is increasing. People from various backgrounds come in search of greener pastures. Migrants are classified in some groups e.g. asylum seekers or refugees, temporary residents, permanent residents, and tourists. Because of the geographical situation of the country, it is Africans who find it necessary to enter the country. The results of the study confirmed the revelations of what we had already discovered from the students of the University of the Western Cape; namely, that the South Africans are xenophobic; they are not open to immigrants.

If, I am permitted to use this common cliché 'from what you say we shall know," I will adamantly state that my people are fearful towards people coming from different countries. The reason for this attitude, I suppose, is because they themselves are harmful, proud, rude, brutal, lazy and xenophobic as one of my subjects stated in his response to the questionnaire. A person from another race or culture is therefore considered to be an enemy and thus, people would not collaborate with him. It is in this confusion and ignorance about other people, that the South Africans remain, psychologically if not intellectually, a needy race. My main concern is the fact that this attitude is mostly expressed towards other black African people, who constitute the majority group amongst the migrants. There are other groups, as well, such as Chinese, Pakistanis, Indians, Europeans, and Americans.

THE FINDINGS

I have to say first that we did not expect such a reaction from both sides when we went to interview people. We went first to interview people from other countries that we are calling "migrants" in this context. Cape Town is a big city and we really went to people from various nationalities who are involved in different activities. Migrants are from African countries such as the Democratic Republic of Congo, Congo-Brazzaville, Ethiopia, Somalia, Rwanda, Burundi, Tanzania, Nigeria, Senegal, Zimbabwe, Uganda, Angola, Benin and Ivory Coast, as well as from Europe and Asian countries such as China, Pakistan, and India. When interviewing people, we noticed that people were complaining about the behavior of South Africans towards those immigrant groups. The main complaint was that they feel that South Africans are not good with immigrants, especially when dealing with Africans. South Africans do not welcome other people on their land; they do not want to speak to them. This situation is creating tension between immigrants and South Africans. On the social level, particularly African immigrants are not integrated within the system; they feel they are even ignored. Most of the persons who come from African countries are refugees, but they find it unfair to be so discriminated against in South African society. Is it the fault of the government or the fault of the entire society? When we ask this question, we want to understand why the population is in tension with immigrant groups, especially Africans.

Immigrants are an important group in South Africa and they are contributing in some ways to the life in South Africa. There are however different assumptions held by each group, meaning immigrants and South Africans. My work as a cross-cultural lecturer was to see in which ways these tensions could be minimized so that people can come together to interact. Is it the list of assumptions that people make about other groups or the lack of knowledge, or the laziness to learn that make people not to understand each other, or the lack of will to get together with other groups, or different groups? Sometimes, people are not able to communicate with other people because of certain assumptions, or because of the stereotypes, or again generalizations that we make when considering other people. We wanted to understand if it was only the problem of South Africans or the problem of immigrants too because they also might not be willing to integrate in the South African society.

ANALYZING MIGRANTS' REACTIONS

When I went to interview immigrants, I had almost the same answers as with native South Africans. As mentioned earlier on, lots of them came to

South Africa in search of a better life—looking for jobs and to ameliorate their socio-economic living style. Most of the immigrants are qualified as economic immigrants. Many of the countries where they come from are in a situation of socio-economic and political crisis. Coming to South Africa is a way of surviving or of escaping the miserable situations that take place in their home countries. The other group from Asian countries such as Indians, Pakistanis, and Chinese come for business purposes. The rest of the immigrants who come from America and other Western countries, such as England, Netherlands, Germany, France etc., occupy high positions and are generally the owners of big companies. In short, they are therefore the real investors. From this classification, it is easy to understand how each immigrant interacts with the South African community. Because of this situation, we targeted those who were really interacting with the ordinary South Africans on almost a daily basis.

Most immigrants stated that they were not integrated in the South African community; they are usually under-employed and are robbed on daily basis because they were considered to be non-south Africans. For most of them, South African people are not friendly and do not really make it easy for immigrants to live freely in their country. As compared to other countries, South Africa is reflected to be the worst place to live in when you are a non-South African. The immigrants felt that they were not protected by the South African government. We also learned that most immigrants want to be integrated within South African society while waiting for things to get better in their home countries as they hope to return. To most of them South Africa is not helpful. When answering a question if they could encourage their friends or members of families to come also to South Africa, most of them said that they would not consider doing so simply because they do not want their families to suffer the same way they are suffering.

The major problem seemed to be language barrier as the immigrants also complained about South Africans not wanting to speak or learn other languages. One of the people we interviewed complained that South Africans become negative when they hear one talking in another language. Although English is the "lingua franca," they still do not even recognize when you speak English. The logical consequence is that these persons are not able to exteriorize their cultural features, such as clothes or music, as the immigrants expressed that they do not feel comfortable wearing their traditional clothes in South Africa because they will be identified and might even be attacked.

We asked the immigrants what efforts they were making to integrate within the South African community. They said that they are also trying to learn South African languages and adopt their habits as they want to be friends with South Africans. We were shocked to discover the complaints from the immigrants. Even the Asian group confirmed what the Africans said. One subject we interviewed said that he has been robbed too many times because he was a non-South African and thought to have a lot of money. For him, South Africans think immigrants have money and they must therefore be robbed. When asked why they think South Africans react so negatively towards non-South Africans, they said that there are assumptions that non South Africans come to take their jobs.

When the non-South Africans were asked why they ran away from their countries and came to South Africa, most of the people said that there was war in their countries, stemming from ethnical or tribal troubles. They came to find green pastures. There is poverty in their countries and they want a better living. Since South Africa represents a place where the conditions of living are better, business wise and economy-wise, people are tempted to migrate to South Africa. This is confirmed by Antonios K. Papantoniou when showing how globalization and migration are related, "Globalization has an ambivalent and somehow contradictory influence on the current migratory flows. On the one hand it creates situations and conditions which increase the pressure and intensify the desire to migrate: Growing economic inequalities, extreme poverty, breaking down of national economies, declining of traditional industry, environmental degradation, revival of tribal, ethnic, and religious fundamentalism, conflicts and wars, to name only a few of the direct or indirect results of globalization, contribute towards migration understood as a survival strategy."[1]

It is indeed only wars or tribal conflicts that make people run from their countries. Like other developed countries, South Africa receives a big flow of immigrants. There is evolution in communication and information that gives people ideas about the lifestyle of a country that might be far away. When people also know that the accessibility of another country can be facilitated by modern transportation, they are of course tempted to move from their own countries, maybe for economic reasons or to explore new horizons. Again, Papantoniou confirms this:

> The revolution in communication; the easiness and low cost of information flow and geographical movement of persons; the daily projection of prosperity and affluence pictures at a global scale; the cultivation through the mass media of the illusion of an increased familiarity with the North and accessibility of the Western way and quality of life to everyone living in the Western countries intensify the desire of participation—particularly among those who, for political or economic reasons, lived up to now isolated and deprived—and constitute a great

temptation and an urge towards taking *over the risk to migrate*. South Africa is now considered as a modern country compared to other Africans countries and there is access to information and people from other countries would like to participate also to those facilities since they consider themselves as citizens of this world and they want to benefit from the same opportunities. (Papantoniou, 2004)

These are some of the reasons that push people from other countries to come to South Africa, as is the case with other countries in Europe, Asia, or America. They encounter lots of problems, however, and are not easily accepted. When a country such as South Africa is coming out of a long period of isolation, it is not certain that there are enough skilled people on the national level. These immigrants are thus contributing to the economy of the country and they can even work at a cheaper salary. While migrants are not well integrated, they contribute strongly to the economy of South Africa. It would be devastating to imagine the South African economy without these migrants who are not only business minded, but they are also skilled in other domains. Most of the South Africans acknowledged that migrants are important to the national economy. They also represent a cheaper labor force because they have no papers. They cannot get proper jobs and they take even the most degrading jobs in order to survive. On the other hand, South Africans do not have skilled people in fields such as nursing and teaching and they turn to these migrants, even at a cheap salary. In fact, Papantoniou indicates that, "the functioning of a national economy increasingly depends on the fast availability of a (small) number of high-skilled migrants and a higher number of migrants belonging to the pool of low-paid workers (often undocumented workers constituting cheap and flexible but also vulnerable labor force). The capacity to manage and steer migration movements towards a country has thus become an important element of the global competitiveness for a global economy," (Papantoniou, 2004).

Immigrant groups are under the authority of South African government and since they are contributing in some ways to the active life of the country, they are supposed to be protected and given the opportunities to develop as human beings. South Africa as a country is a member of the United Nations and has also adopted the Universal Declaration of Human Rights. All immigrants in South Africa have certain rights. This means that South Africa must be prepared to receive people coming from other countries and accommodate them. The Universal Declaration of Human Rights stipulates in its article 14.1 that everyone has the right to seek and enjoy asylum in other countries free from persecution.[2] There are people who are coming and looking for refuge in South Africa and should be protected and given the opportunities to develop themselves. Not doing so is a violation of universal principles. On the other hand, culturally speaking, people are supposed to have the freedom to practice their cultural activities.

ANALYZING SOUTH AFRICAN REACTIONS

Since we could not conclude based on reactions from immigrants only, we decided to go to South Africans themselves to understand why the migrants did not feel comfortable and accommodated. We went to the same sites so that we could also have their points of view. The questions were reversed and we noticed that all the South Africans interviewed knew that immigrants were living in South Africa. On the question of knowing if they have interacted with them to ask why they came to South Africa, some said that they have interacted and they have asked. This group seems to know that many of the immigrants who come to South Africa left their countries because there were problems, and they wanted to find a better living. There was another group of people who said that they have not interacted with non-South Africans because of lack of time and interest. Those who said that they have interacted in some ways with the immigrants groups said that they found those immigrants friendly and they thought they were also human beings with whom they can be friends.

We wanted to know if they classify immigrants in terms of the countries they came from; meaning some were from Africa, Asia or from European countries. While some said they think all are immigrants, there felt there were people coming from different countries and this realization often influenced their appreciation of them. As a result, it was obvious that they liked those from Western countries better because they are believed to be investors who have come to create jobs. On the contribution of the non-South Africans to the economy of the country, South Africans said that they acknowledge that these persons do contribute in some ways to the economy of the country, because some of them are business-minded, and they can provide jobs. It does not matter which country they come from; they noticed that these immigrants are more focused and know what they came to do in this country. What about the assumption that these immigrants are in South Africa to steal the jobs of South Africans? In Cape Town, people seemed to believe this claim: immigrants want to have their jobs, while South Africans themselves are still struggling to find a place to work. However, we found that other South Africans thought positively and were sure that every person has the right to live. One of the subjects that we interviewed said that he considered every person as a human being.

I need to point out that in South Africa, we have different groups. We can refer to the division that was made in the Apartheid era not to support the system, but to show how people still remain segregated even today. I believe these realities still influence people. In Cape Town for example; there are four groups that are present, Blacks, Coloreds, Indians and Whites. One of the subjects we interviewed said that he was an African and that he would welcome every person as a human being and especially his fellow Africans. Interestingly, another South African subject expressed zeal to visit other countries and speak other languages. The same subject expressed remorse about the high unemployment rate in South Africa, which could be one of the reasons why South Africans have negative attitudes to non South Africans. Furthermore, the respondent is not against any non-South African partner. In fact, we learned that those who had the opportunity to interact with these immigrants were more open and very tolerant. This demonstrates that most open-minded South Africans are educated persons who have traveled to other countries and therefore, do not feel threatened by the presence of non-South Africans. This, in turn, motivates these South Africans to even do better. They seemed to appreciate the cultural features of those immigrant groups.

However, those who have never interacted with them appeared to be full of negative assumptions and hatred. When asked if they think that immigrants are involved in crime, some said that immigrants are involved in drug-trafficking and prostitution. And one could hear people say, "Those Nigerians are involved in those dirty things-criminal activities." It's true that some of the immigrants and especially Nigerians were involved in drugs, but now all non-South Africans are considered as Nigerians, and as such are also victimized. This again emphasizes the ignorance of South Africans who do not even know how to classify the people appropriately. When South Africans were asked if they have visited other countries, most of them said that they have never been outside and they did not know much about other places. Those who have traveled have only been to Southern African countries and Europe. South Africans also demonstrated that if they were given the opportunity to travel, the favorite countries are England and America. Some also chose Zimbabwe, simply because they heard many things about the Zimbabwean president, Robert Mugabe.

We also asked South Africans what they knew about other cultures. Most of them said that they have never traveled. They also felt that immigrants are not allowed to express their cultural values and are simply afraid of the South African population. Many South Africans suggested that the government should give time and opportunity to other cultures to show their colors. I am strongly in favor of this suggestion as it will allow South

Africans to discover some other realities and appreciate the diversity and learn many things. Since South Africans acknowledged that most of the immigrants are skilled and focused on anything they do, the government as suggested by other South African subjects should take care of those who contribute to the well being of the country. When at last, South African were asked to comment on what they think the government should do, people in Cape Town said that the government should enforce the laws on immigration and see who qualifies to have permanent residence or temporary residence status. The persons whom we interviewed in Eastern Cape were more open and suggested that the government should even provide shelter for those immigrants who are also contributing to the economy.

We were surprised that in the rural area people seemed to be more tolerant of immigrants than in the urban areas. For instance in their responses to this last question about what the government should do to accommodate the newcomers to South Africa, we noticed that the reactions were quite different. In Cape Town where people are surrounded with immigrants every day, they were not very tolerant. We wondered why urban South African responses were so much different to those from the rural areas. Was it because the rural areas are not over flooded with immigrants as in the urban areas? Or is it because they are still very "primitive," unlike those in the urban areas? These are some of the puzzles I wish to resolve as my project continues. In fact, the urban areas are places of competition and people do not accommodate other people easily when competition matters. Instead of considering each other as the colleagues or mates or as a friend, one is considered as a challenger and as someone who could steal opportunities such as jobs, partners, and so on. While in the rural areas there is a strong element of sincere solidarity, in the urban areas selfishness is the order of the day.

In Cape Town, for example, there are lots of immigrants and they all compete with South Africans. Sometimes, the immigrants are better-skilled, harder working and more business oriented as compared to South Africans. The result is that South Africans end up hating these immigrants because they take their places. In the rural areas, people are still helping each other and they have time for other human beings. What counts first is not the economic interest, but the human warmth. Even if they do not speak the same language, there was that genuine communication that is linked to the pure human nature of trying to accommodate another human being.

While we were in the rural areas, we had an experience that reminded us of the importance of human relationship. One day, while we attempted to leave a remote village, we got stuck in the mud because it had been raining for the past two days. Spontaneously, people from the village came to help us and they did all that they could to rescue us. This experience convinced us that in the rural areas, people are more accommodating. The word solidarity seems not to exist in the urban areas as it does in the rural areas. The problem is that people are not given an opportunity to get to know each other.

The ways that the media portray immigrants is another problem. South Africa is a modern country and people's behavior can sometimes be shaped by what the media says. Most of the South Africans who mentioned the involvement of immigrants in crime said they heard it on the news. The media never reports positive things on any group, and this influences the attitude of the local population. The attitude of the government is another problem. Immigrants are stigmatized in South Africa and the government has a great responsibility in this. When South Africans were asked to comment on crime in the country they mentioned that most brutal crimes like armed-robberies and killings are committed by South Africans themselves.

South Africa as a democratic country has voted a constitution and in its second chapter, the Bill of Rights, it stipulates in section 31 that everyone has the right to use their language and to participate in the cultural life of their choice, but no one exercising these rights may do so in a manner inconsistent with any provision of the Bill of Rights.[3] Persons belonging to a cultural, religious or linguistic community may not be denied the rights that other members of that community enjoy. On the other hand, culturally speaking, people are supposed to have the freedom to practice their cultural activities and to form, join and maintain cultural, religious and linguistic associations and other organs of civil society. We noticed that when asked about the freedom to practice their culture, people did not feel free to do so. Jandt (2004) quotes Kale on this point, who argues that "peace is the fundamental human value. The use of peace applies not only to relationships among countries but to the right of all people to live at peace with themselves and their surroundings."[4]

It is then important to give people from other cultures the chance to express themselves. In addition, the cultures of immigrants must be respected as we respect our own cultures. Every culture has its uniqueness and all cultures should be free to exteriorize their cultural values. The tendency to diminish other cultures must stop. Most of the migrant groups in South Africa responded that they were not free to practice their cultural activities because society makes them afraid to do so or the government does not give them the opportunity to practice. This is a violation of subsection 31 of chapter 2 of the South African Constitution. What does the government do to protect migrant people or other minorities who are also part of the South African society, whether they have been granted asylum, temporary residence, permanent residence, or not?

CONCLUSION

In this chapter, I have considered migration as a phenomenon that goes beyond the economic, but that also includes other aspects such as language contact, interethnic and intercultural contact. It is a global phenomenon. I have addressed it using South Africa as a case-study. South Africa was a country that was isolated due to its peculiar system of government before 1994. But, since the country opened to democracy; there is a big flow of immigrants. They come to the country as a consequence of globalization, looking for new horizons. However, there are still too many challenges blocking the way of these people who want to be accommodated. Most of the immigrants felt that they were discriminated against and we wanted to understand why. Is the problem at the level of the government or is it only the population that does not want to mingle with foreigners? It cannot be denied that immigrants are contributing to the economy of the country, but still they are discriminated against, and even though the law says that those people should be protected and given opportunities, there is still a huge gap between non South Africans and native South Africans.

As a lecturer and a South African, I learned a lot, but I also felt challenged by this issue and see that the country needs lots of changes. A country cannot live in an isolated way and pretend as if other persons are less important. We were told by both groups that there was a need for education, especially the geographical location of other African countries. In addition, South Africans need to know at least something about the cultures and history of other countries, especially African countries. Through education, people will have information and stop assuming that all other African immigrants are inferior. In fact, I wish to emphasize that there is a great need to know about the cultural values of other countries, giving opportunities to immigrant communities to show their cultural diversity. As a lecturer in the "intercultural field," I will promote this. South Africans need to discover the richness and the cultural diversity of other countries. The government at the level of the ministry of culture should think about the institution of cultural days so that those immigrant groups can also have the opportunity to display their cultures. In that way, every ethnic group will feel accommodated in South Africa. In support of Hanna, E (2005) I have the challenge not only to impart theoretical knowledge of multicultural and cross-cultural aspects of other countries; I also need to motivate them to put these into practice.[5]

On the political level, it is important that the government adopt open policies and practice them. When the policies are open, even media will follow suit. Immigrants and South Africans all said that they would like the government to intervene by employing practical measures to solve the problem of immigrants who want to feel accommodated. When the immigrants are victimized by prejudice at the government level, it's obvious that the population will follow. From interviews conducted in the Eastern Cape, South Africans indicated the need for the government to provide shelter for immigrants. From this we learned that the government could play an important role in making its people open up to the immigrants. This therefore suggests that the government has a great task at hand.

As a South African who has experienced how it feels like living out of one's own country and dealing with the younger generation, I think I am better placed to bring this change in order to make my people understand and to make my government change its people to understand the difficulty and hardship that exists when there is mismanagement of inter-cultural and multicultural identities. I am aware that this is indeed a long process but I intend to carry on and I wish to have the support of my country and the support of other countries so that South Africa can truly become part of the globalized world.

ACKNOWLEDGMENTS

I would like to thank the University of the Western Cape for granting me the funds that enabled me to undertake this study. It was a worthwhile academic project which has given me an opportunity to enlarge my knowledge and that of others. All the findings came from the answers I got from the people we went to interview in the Western Cape and in the Eastern Cape. I would like to thank them for consenting to answer my questions even if sometimes they needed to know what was this all about. Special thanks go to the people interviewed in East London who were very prompt to answer and to facilitate our work. Finally, I would like to thank the students from the University of the Western Cape who volunteered to interview people everywhere we went with them. This chapter is dedicated to all those who are involved in cross cultural communication as well as those who are prepared to change and associate with others, because we are all part of human culture.

NOTES

1. Antonios K. Papantoniou, *Globalization and Migration: Some reflections on the connection between two interrelated global phenomena*: A Dialogue

Between Europe and Africa, 2004. Available online at www.coe.int/t/e/
northsouth_centreprogramme/5_europeafrica_dialogue/c_HRand_Migra-
tion/globalisation: accessed on February, 04 2006.
2. Universal Declaration of Human Rights, Chapter 14.
3. *Constitution of the Republic of South Africa:* Chapter 2.
4. E. F. Jandt, *An Introduction to Cross Cultural Communication,* (Califor-
    nia: Sage Publications, Inc, 2004), 42.
5. P. Cowley, and B. E. Hanna, "Cross Cultural Skills-Crossing the Disciplinary
    Divide," 2005. Available online at http://www.sciencedirect.com/science.

REFERENCES

Constitution of the Republic of South Africa: Chapter 2, section 31.
Cowley, P. and Hanna, B. E. "Cross Cultural Skills-Crossing the Disciplinary
    Divide." 2005. Available online at http://www.sciencedirect.com/science.
Jandt, E. F. *An Introduction to Cross Cultural Communication.* California: Sage
    publications, Inc., 2004.
Papantoniou, Antonios K. *Globalization and Migration: Some reflections on the
    connection between two interrelated global phenomena:* A Dialogue Between
    Europe and Africa, 2004. Available online at www.coe.int/t/e/northsouth_
    centreprogramme/5_europeafrica_dialogue/c_HRand_Migration/globalisa-
    tion: accessed on February, 04 2006.
Universal Declaration of Human Rights, Chapter 14.

Chapter Ten

Pan-Africanism: The Impact of the Nkrumah Years, 1945–1966

Obinna Onwumere

INTRODUCTION

Kwame Nkrumah's emphatic outcry for African unity, political and economic independence in the late 1950s and early 1960s was most visible through the notion of Pan-Africanism. It is widely believed that Pan-Africanism revolutionized nationalism, and the amalgam of both necessitated the ebb of European empires in Africa.[1] While Pan-Africanism is considered to be a political ideology or movement that encourages all Africans and Africans in the Diaspora to unite in order to form a political union based on African ancestry, Nkrumah believed that Pan-Africanism was also the most viable option for Africa's total liberation and decolonization. Nkrumah's early Pan-African activities became fully manifest during his student days in London, including his effort in organizing the 1945 Pan-African Congress in Manchester. When Ghana attained independence in 1957, Nkrumah became Ghana's first President and he declared that Ghana's independence was pointless unless it connected with the entire liberation of Africa. Nkrumah used the notion of Pan-Africanism to guide his involvement in the Congo crisis, the liberation struggle of other African nations, and the historic formation of the Organization of African Unity in 1963.

By and large, Nkrumah remains a continental nationalist and a reputable African socio-political philosopher whose towering personality, ideas, and achievements pose an enormous challenge to modern biographers. Most recently, Nkrumah was voted in 2000, "The African of the century" by the BBC's African listeners and in 2004, the "Second Greatest African" that ever lived by New African magazine.[2] Nkrumah also had an enormous impact on other African leaders. For example, Kenneth Kaunda, Zambia's erstwhile President, revealed that Africa might not recover from the events of the 1966 coup in Ghana in the sense that Nkrumah was a great Pan-Africanist and visionary. In addition, Kaunda remarked that Nkrumah inspired many people of Africa towards independence and greatly supported the liberation of Southern Africa. Equally, Sam Nujoma, the founding President of Namibia, maintains that Nkrumah epitomized Pan-Africanism with an endless commitment to African liberation. Nujoma surmised: "Ghana's fight for freedom inspired and influenced us all, and the greatest contribution to our political awareness at that time came from the achievements of Ghana after its independence," (Ankomah, 19). Needless to say, Nkrumah set up Ghana as a model and guide for the entire continent of Africa, and he was aware that political independence without economic empowerment was futile. Falola elucidates that Nkrumahwas convinced that Africans would only progress with the total eradication of colonial rule, (Falola, 102). Therefore, a significant portion of Nkrumah's time was dedicated to developing theoretical and practical rudiments for African unity. Although Nkrumah's dream for Africa's total liberation was truncated by the 24 February 1966 coup, Nkrumah still occupies a lofty place in the annals of Africa's liberation struggle.

THE LONDON YEARS

Upon his arrival in London in 1945, Kwame Nkrumah's Pan-African ideals were quite discernible. He immediately enrolled in the West African Student Union (WASU), a pan-West African Organization and leading anti-imperialist organization founded in 1925 by a Nigerian lawyer, Ladipo Solanke and Bankole Bright of Sierra Leone.[3] By and large, the West African Student Union served as a social, political, and debating center for radicalism amid the African students in Britain. Nkrumah became actively involved in the affairs of WASU, which had a membership of approximately one hundred in mid-1945. In the October elections of 1945, Nkrumah was elected vice-president, and subsequently served as union member from 1946–1947.

    In London, Nkrumah met other pan-Africanists such as George Padmore, a Trinidad-born colonial agitator, C.L.R. James, I.T.A. Wallace Johnson, Ras Makonnen of British Guyana, and Jomo Kenayatta of Kenya, (Sherwood, 112). One of Nkrumah's most conspicuous Pan-African activities in London was to succor George Padmore in organizing the Pan-African Congress, which was billed for October 1945 in Manchester. Sherwood relates that Nkrumah became the Regional Secretary of the Pan-African Federation (PAF), a position that allowed Nkrumah to inform contacts of George Padmore about the proposed conference, (Sherwood, 117). The Fifth Pan-African Congress held in Manchester attracted roughly two hundred people in total, which comprised mainly Africans and people of

African descent, including W.E.B. DuBois, and Amy Ashwood Garvey, the widow of Marcus Garvey.

Interestingly, Nkrumah was appointed the chairman of the two sessions on Imperialism in North and West Africa. More encouragingly, however, this placed Nkrumah in a significant position in the sense that he had two resolutions emerging from the two sessions, (Sherwood, 122). By and large, the resolutions had political, economic, and social components in connection with the problems of North and West Africa. The role of chairman allowed Nkrumah to meet numerous political and trade union activists at the Manchester Congress. Amid the delegates were future African leaders such as Hastings Banda (Malawi), Jomo Kenyatta (Kenya), Obafemi Awolowo (Nigeria), Ibrahim Garba-Jahumpa (Gambia), Jaja Wachuku (Nigeria), and Ako Adjei (Ghana).[4] During the Manchester Pan-African Congress, Nkrumah enjoined that all Africans and people of African descent around the world should unite in order to address the ills and misdeeds of colonialism and imperialism. Thus, Nkrumah preached: "We believe in the rights of all people to govern themselves. We affirm the right of all colonial peoples to control their destiny. All colonies must be free from foreign imperialist control, whether political or economic. . . . The fifth Pan-African Congress calls on the workers and farmers of the colonies to Organize effectively. . . . The fifth Pan-African Congress calls on intellectuals and professional classes to awaken to their responsibilities. . . . Today there is only one road to effective action—the organization of the masses."[5]

Under DuBois's presidency, Nkrumah was appointed secretary of the working committee to effect sundry programs drawn up at the Congress, and to establish a headquarters. The *raison d'être* was that the office would maintain close contact with various political movements that would revamp the various colonies, (Sherwood, 123). The Manchester Pan-African Conference seminally advanced an international fraternity of black aspiration and solidarity. In hindsight, however, it is apposite to highlight that the Manchester conference emerged as Nkrumah's exposure to world stage politics, and he became the most accomplished of all of George Padmore's protégés.[6] Birmingham relates that Padmore's involvement in Nkrumah's early political career instilled the notion of an idealized commitment to African unity as a means of eradicating the existing colonial fragmentation in Africa, (Birmingham, 7). On the whole, the Manchester conference was a landmark in the annals of Pan-Africanism in the sense that it mustered leaders that led the struggle of Africa's independence in succeeding decades. It also enlightened Africans everywhere on how to break the colonial institutions for total liberation and political change. While the participants at the conference favored a socialist future for an independent Africa, they rejected the notion of violence as a means of attaining their objectives. Undoubtedly, the Manchester Pan-African Congress was meaningful in Nkrumah's life, because the conference's principles of anti-colonialism, anti-imperialism, and non-violence constituted the cornerstone of Nkrumah's political philosophy.[7]

While fully embracing the ideals of Pan-Africanism, Nkrumah was instrumental in the formation of the West African National Secretariat (WANS) shortly after the Pan-African Congress, (Sherwood, 127). Some notables in the group were Kojo Botsio, Wallace Johnson, Bankole Akpata, and Awoonor-Renner. The formation of WANS occurred in order to instill positive action in a radical sense for the achievement of African independence. Nkrumah became the linchpin of the organization as he assumed the role of secretary. This, of course, enabled him to travel to Paris in order to confer with the leaders of the French movement for African liberation like Leopold Senghor of Senegal and Felix Houphouet-Boigny of Ivory Coast.[8] Unfortunately, these leaders were not highly enthused with the notion of forming a Union of African Socialist Republics. Inasmuch as Nkrumah was deeply involved with WANS, he still worked closely with George Padmore. Jointly, however, they formed a discussion group christened "The Circle." Rooney maintains that the purpose of this discussion group was to effectively train activists with the aim of creating a Union of African Socialist Republics, (Rooney, 25). Equally, the group saw itself as the revolutionary vanguard in the struggle for West African unity and independence. It became clear that Nkrumah's commitment to Pan-Africanism remained resolute due to the fact that he attended many conferences as a guest speaker in Britain in order to disseminate the notion of Pan-Africanism. In addition, while with WANS, Nkrumah helped organize the publication of a monthly paper called *The New African*. In his autobiography, *Ghana: The Autobiography of Kwame Nkrumah*, he wrote: "As the volume of work increased I realized the necessity of a newspaper as an official organ of the Secretariat . . . And so I started to make plans for the monthly paper called *The New African*. . . . In March, 1946, the first issue appeared, sub-titled 'The Voice of the Awakened Action' and with the motto 'For Unity and Absolute Independence.'"[9]

Sherwood highlights that although Nkrumah struggled financially in London, he was able to publish a pamphlet called *Towards Colonial Freedom* in 1947, a publication that utterly denounces colonialism and imperialism, and explains what the colonies must do to attain colonial emancipation, (Sherwood, 168). Under the aegis of WANS, Nkrumah tirelessly embarked on preparing for the proposed All West African National

Congress, which was to be held in Lagos, Nigeria. However, a letter from his fellow compatriots Dr. J.B Danquah and Ako Adjei of the United Gold Coast Convention (UGCC) canvassed Nkrumah to return to the Gold Coast and to assume the role of general secretary. The UGCC was formed in 1947, but it lacked rudimentary organization and the ability to mobilize the masses, (Hadjor, 43). The objective of the UGCC was to attain self-government for the Gold Coast, but it lacked support of most Ghanaians in the sense that the movement was championed by a group of lawyers and businessmen who were not immensely popular among the people. Undeniably, Nkrumah's acceptance of the offer from the UGCC ultimately truncated his stay in London and doused the idea of the All West African National Congress. Nevertheless, Nkrumah's short stay in London not only engendered his political ideology and confidence, but it also bolstered the essence of Pan-Africanism in connection with colonialism and self-reliance.

AFRICAN LIBERATION AND UNIFICATION

After Ghana attained independence on March 6, 1957, Kwame Nkrumah immediately employed his Pan-African ideals as an instrument for Africa's total liberation, which had to be politically and economically sound. As a result, Nkrumah made two historic statements while delivering his independence address. Nkrumah acknowledged: "Today there is a new African in the world, and that new African is ready to fight his own battle and show that after all the black man is capable of managing his own affairs. We are going to demonstrate to the world, to other nations, that young as we are, we are prepared lay our own foundations." . . ."The independence of Ghana is meaningless unless it is linked up with the total liberation of Africa, (Ankomah, 12).

More encouragingly, Nkrumah invited Padmore to be his adviser in order to develop more Pan-African ideals. By employing Pan-Africanism, Nkrumah attempted to assist other African states in their independence struggles and to strengthen the independence of free states. In his book, *Africa Must Unite,* Nkrumah noted: "The first Conference of Independent African States met in Accra in April 1958. There were then only eight, namely, Egypt, Ghana,[10] Sudan, Libya, Tunisia, Liberia, Morocco, and Ethiopia. Our purpose was to exchange views on matters of common interest; to explore ways and means of consolidating and safeguarding our independence; to strengthen the economic and cultural ties between our countries; to decide on workable arrangements for helping fellow Africans still subject to colonial rule, and to examine the central world problem of how to secure peace."[11]

Unquestionably, when Nkrumah welcomed the delegates of the conference, it was historic in the sense that Pan-Africanism had moved into the continent. Nkrumah was delighted that free Africans were scrutinizing their own affairs, which was critical for Africa's liberation movement. Equally, in December 1958, Nkrumah hosted the All-African People's Conference in Accra. Representatives from 62 African nationalist organizations attended this mammoth occasion, (Nkrumah, 1963). Patrice Lumumba, the erstwhile Prime Minister of the Congo, gave plaudits for Nkrumah's effort to host the historic conference. In his speech at the conference, Lumumba asserted: "We thank the organizers of the Conference of the Assembly African Peoples for the friendly invitation they kindly extended to our movement. We would like to express our gratitude to His Excellency Prime Minister Kwame Nkrumah and to the people of Ghana for the fraternal welcome given us. We would also like to thank the representatives of the independent peoples present here for their continued defense of the Congo in international tribunals. I hope they will regard these words, delivered in the name of all our compatriots, as an expression of our sincere gratitude."[12]

In 1959, Nkrumah convened with trade union representatives all over Africa under the umbrella of an All-African Trade Union Federation. This is because the African labor movement was closely related with the struggle for political freedom, economic and social development. Further all-African cooperation was evident when the conference on Positive Action and Security in Africa opened in Accra in April 1960. This conference was held in consultation with other independent African states to examine the situation in Algeria and South Africa. Furthermore, the conference addressed the notion of the necessity to guard against balkanization and neo-colonialism.

One of Nkrumah's first attempts towards an African political union took place in November 1959 when Ghana and Guinea formed a kernel for the Union of African States. The political amalgam of Ghana and Guinea gained momentum after Guinea attained independence in 1958, thereby establishing a model for independence in French Africa.[13] Nkrumah's government organized aid to Guinea for various reasons immediately after the Guinean President Sekou Touré made a proclamation for the union of the two states. Nkrumah made further steps for a Union of African States by cajoling Liberia and Mali to join the Ghana-Guinea Union.

After a series of meetings Ghana, Guinea, and Mali formed a union called The Union of African States (U.A.S.) in 1961, which was to form the nucleus of the United States of Africa, (Nkrumah, 1963). The union was declared open to any African state in so far as they accepted its aims and objectives. The charter of the union rendered provisions for regular confer-ences between member states, and the executive organ of the union were the conferences. The conferences were held quarterly in Accra, Conakry, and Bamako, and were supervised by the Head of State of the host country. By and large, these conferences were geared towards exchanging views on African and world problems. After the second summit conference, a joint communiqué was signed in order to support the African nations' struggles for independence, especially in Algeria, Congo, and Angola.

In the 1960s, Nkrumah's cry for African unity became clearer because the imperialist mechanism was hampering the African liberation struggle. In 1961, there was a stark difference and polarization between what became known as the Casablanca and Monrovia bloc of states. The Casablanca group comprised of Ghana, Guinea, Mali, Egypt, and a few other states grounded in anti-imperialist ideals, while the Monrovia group consisted of twelve African states, which had French and English speaking, (Smertin, 1987, 87). These two groups took opposite sides in the issue of the Congo crisis and the Algerian fight for independence against French colonialism. The Casablanca group assembled in Morocco in 1961 in order to address the situation in the Congo, and it was agreed that the states should with-draw their troops only if the UN supported the central government.

By far, the best result of the Casablanca Conference was the publica-tion of the African Charter of Casablanca. This established a permanent African Consultative Assembly and three permanent functional commit-tees, and they were to meet at intervals to ensure a common defense of Africa. Although Nkrumah faced widespread obstacles in the creation of a Union of African States, Smertin maintains that Nkrumah's conviction that a union could be formed amid African states was based on the tenets of Pan-Africanism, (Smertin, 1987, 85). In this conception, the formation of a sole national government or community and the elimination of sundry colonial constructs would lead to the creation of a single African state. On the whole, Nkrumah's idea of Pan-Africanism was incongruous to those of other African leaders who claimed that African unity was premature.

THE CONGO CRISIS

Nkrumah used the events of the Congo crisis to elucidate the importance of African unity. In his book, *Challenge of the Congo*, Nkrumah wrote: "Although the struggle for national independence in the Congo has yet to be won, I see no alternative for the future of the Congo, except in the arms of a united Africa within the framework of a continental Union Govern-ment. Until this is achieved, the dangers facing the Congo will not only multiply but will be complicated by many factors which will involve the whole of Africa," (Smertin, 1987, 87).

Undoubtedly, Nkrumah's involvement in the Congo crisis, which started in 1960, demonstrated his tireless commitment to Pan-Africanism and African unity. His diplomatic efforts could not match the might of the Cold War forces, which dampened his attempt to solve the crisis by African nations under the United Nations. The melee in the Congo emerged partly because the May 1960 election produced three leaders: Tshombe from the wealthy copper-based province of Katanga; Kasavubu who hailed from Leopoldville; and Patrice Lumumba, the only leader in full support of a single Congo state, (Rooney, 206). Nkrumah mainly supported Lumumba in the sense that Lumumba favored Pan-African ideals. When a mutiny emerged, there was widespread violence and massacres. However, Tshombe declared that the Katanga province would secede from the Congo. Nkrumah saw the Katanga secession as an example of balkanization in Africa, by which new colonialism creates client states independent in name, but in actuality, they remain the pawns of the colonial power that has granted them independence.[14] At this juncture, Prime Minister Lumumba appealed to the UN to send special forces in order to squash the secession process. Lumumba held talks with Nkrumah in Accra for support, and in order to garner support for Lumumba, Nkrumah addressed the Ghana National Assembly. Nkrumah lamented: "This is the turning point in the history of Africa. If we allow the independence of the Congo to be compromised in any way by the imperialist and capitalist forces, we shall expose the sovereignty and independence of all Africa to grave risk. The struggle of the Congo is therefore our struggle. It is incumbent on us to take our stand by our brothers in the Congo in the full knowledge that only Africa can fight for its destiny," (Hadjor, 95).

As a result, Lumumba signed an agreement to join the Union of African States proposed by Nkrumah, and Ghana sent troops to assist in the Congo as part of the proposed UN force. It was widely believed that the Belgian forces were against Lumumba's legitimate government. When Colonel Joseph Mobutu staged a coup in September 1960, Lumumba was forced to transfer his government to Stanleyville. Still dedicated to the restoration of peace, Nkrumah desperately tried to broker a peace agreement between Lumumba and Kasavubu. It was his conviction that peace would preserve a united Congo free from imperialist penetration. Besides, Nkrumah made an overture on the Congo crisis when he addressed the UN General Assembly in September 1960. He stressed that independent African states should solve the Congo crisis, and proposed that the Non-Aligned Group should assist in solving the world's problems, (Rooney, 209). Inasmuch as Nkrumah's speech received plaudits, it failed to impact the entire Congo crisis.

Incidentally, after the arrest of Lumumba and the failure of the United Nations to handle the Congo crisis effectively, a conference was convened in Casablanca in January 1961. The centrality of the discussion was whether African states, particularly Ghana, Guinea, Mali, and Egypt should withdraw their troops from the Congo. They reasoned that the United Nations was not going to take serious action, and that the troops should no longer be available to the United Nations. Nevertheless, Nkrumah was in favor of allowing African troops to remain in the Congo, stressing that the withdrawal of the troops would be equivalent to betrayal of the Congo and the African revolutionary cause, (Nkrumah, 105). The agreement was that the troops should stay and the United Nations should augment its peacekeeping effort in order to restore the hopes of independence, integrity, and stabilization in the national economy. Eventually, the most significant result of the Casablanca Conference was the publication of the African Charter of Casablanca, which reinforced the need for African unity.

Regrettably, in February 1961, Lumumba was overthrown and murdered. One of the lessons derived from the Congo crisis is that Pan-Africanism was not inevitable and indeed was hindmost amid some African leaders. The Congo crisis revealed to Nkrumah that African puppet regimes served as the new link with the colonial powers; thus African unity remained elusive. Hadjor submits that the Congo crisis forced Nkrumah to rethink his approach towards the African revolution, (Hadjor, 95). Thompson maintains that Nkrumah designed his Congo policy to keep the Cold War out of Africa, (Thompson, 160). This is because the nascent independent nations were politically and economically equipped to fight the external forces.

OAU AND AFRICAN UNITY

For Ghana's Nkrumah, the achievement of national independence was only a necessary first step toward the ultimate objective of African unity. A failure to mention Nkrumah's instrumental role in formation of the OAU would be to render totally incomplete the annals of African history. It is important to note that the origins of the OAU could be traced back to the First Conference of Independent African States held in Accra in 1958. As previously mentioned, with the exception of South Africa, all independent states such as Ghana, Liberia, Ethiopia, and Sudan, as well as four North African states were present at the conference. One of the fundamental principles was the political unification of a United States of Africa. The first move to put this theory into practice was the union of Ghana, Guinea, and later Mali in 1959. Not surprisingly, Nkrumah was the brainchild of this union. The question of unity became complex, with many more states achieving independence in 1960. In essence, two major groups emerged in 1961: the Casablanca bloc and the Monrovia bloc. The Casablanca group brought seven of the more radical groups; the Monrovia group comprised a dozen former French colonies, the Brazzaville group and eight other states. The Monrovia group rejected the idea of a formal political union, concentrating instead on mutual recognition of equality and sovereignty, cooperation in economics, culture and scientific fields, and non-interference in each other's internal affairs.

The leaders of Nigeria, Guinea, and Ethiopia played a major role in bringing together the two political groups in Addis Ababa in May 1963. Nkrumah reiterated his call for a union for all African states, but it was not entirely welcome. Some leaders thought Nkrumah was ahead of his time. This notwithstanding, the representatives of thirty-one of the continent's states signed the Charter of African Unity, and a result, the Organization of African Unity was formed. Thompson notes that the leaders addressed their hopes and ruminations, (Thompson, 322). Abdel Nasser of Egypt recommended an African League, Ben Bella of Algeria did not embrace the notion of political unity. In fact, only Milton Obote of Uganda favored the total surrender of sovereignty within a union. Instead, many delegates undermined Nkrumah's vision, and therefore did not take him seriously. Nkrumah made it crystal clear that he wanted the OAU to adopt a Pan-African model for Africa's sustainability. In his historic speech at Addis Ababa on 24 May 1963, Nkrumah remarked: "I am pleased to be here in Addis Ababa on this most historic occasion I bring with me the hopes and fraternal greetings of the government and people of Ghana. Our objective is African union now. . . . We must unite now or perish. I am confident that by our concerted effort and determination, we shall lay here the foundations for a continental Union of African States. . . . Nothing will be of avail, except the united act of a united Africa," (Ankomah, 28).

Paradoxically, Nkrumah's resonance for African unity was a testament from a visionary rather than a self-seeking dictator. Hence, it was quite critical that Nkrumah signed the charter. It was clear that the Charter of African Unity was a pact with two schools of thoughts; the opinions of the revolutionary-democratic forces that approached the problem of African unity in a radical fashion; and the ideas of a large group of countries that took a simplistic approach. Nkrumah and other leaders ensured that the OAU was founded under the principles of anti-colonialism, anti-imperialism, and positive neutralism, (Smertin, 1987, 88). Thus, the founding of the OAU became a landmark in the chronicles of the African national liberation movement. Nkrumah's quest for the elusive Pan-African OAU was still unfulfilled. As imperialism kept permeating through the nascent independent nations through the nexus of the colonial masters and African puppet Heads of State in 1960s, Nkrumah posed an overture for joint armed forces for the OAU. While speaking at the OAU Summit in Cairo in 1964, he called on African leaders to endorse the notion of creating Union Government of Africa and a Joint African High Command. The leaders, of course, rejected Nkrumah's proposal. The last OAU meeting attended by Nkrumah was hosted in Accra in 1965. In Accra, he tried to coax the African leaders into adopting a new proposal for uniting the African countries, while retaining the sovereignty of each state. His proposal was rejected overtly and covertly, and Nkrumah was saddened because the OAU charter seemingly represented the embodiment of African unity. Nkrumah worked tirelessly for the unification of African states until the military coup on February 24, 1966.

CONCLUSION

Arguably, Kwame Nkrumah is best known as the architect of Pan-Africanism in Africa for the mere purpose of vehemently proposing a single Union of African States as a means to checkmate imperialism and balkanization in Africa. Although a majority of Africa's leaders in the 1960s did not adhere to Nkrumah's cry for African unity, his place in Africa's history is totally outstanding. Smertin notes that while Nkrumah became the first statesman in Tropical Africa to lead his nation to independence, he was also the first African leader to tackle the problems other African leaders faced later, (Smertin, 1987, 164). Additionally, Smertin purports that Nkrumah's name became a symbol of independence and national pride, and his considerations on national liberation have received international recognition, (Smertin, 1987, 164). A tribute from Kwame Toure, formerly known as Stokely Carmichael, acknowledged that the highest expression of "black power" is Pan-Africanism, and the highest expression of Pan-Africanism is in Nkrumahism, (Hadjor, 104). In delineating Nkrumah's achievements, Smertin wrote: "An entire era is linked with Kwame Nkrumah's name, an era not just in Ghanaian history but in the history of the whole African continent. This was an era of struggle for national liberation, the time when the independent African states took their first steps. Nkrumah was one of the most consistent fighters for Africa's liberation from colonialism," (Smertin, 1987, 164).

Unquestionably, Nkrumah's political ideology is still poignant for Africans today. For example, the Libyan leader Muammar Gaddafi gave adulations to Nkrumah's ideas and political philosophy in his speech during the 2005 African Union (AU) Summit in Sirte, Libya. Gaddafi remarked:

"Had we heeded his advice at that time, Africa would now be like the United States of America or at least close to it. But we did not heed his advice, and even worse we ridiculed those predictions. So we are still standing in the same place we were in 1963. . . . The call to achieve African unity gradually means the sacrificing of Africa on the altar of neo-colonialism. This is the speech Nkrumah made in 1963," (Ankomah, 32). As a devoted Pan-Africanist, Nkrumah, upon guiding Ghana to independence in 1957, invoked the Pan-African spirit of the Manchester Pan-African Conference to Africa. Nkrumah hosted several meetings in respect to achieving an independent Africa. These meetings turned out to be an impetus for the formation of the Organization of African Unity. Although the military coup of February 1966 is widely considered one of Africa's darkest moments, it did not erode Nkrumah's Pan-African ideals or political legacy. After the coup, Sekou Touré, the President of Guinea, made Nkrumah co-President upon his arrival in Conakry, a feat that is unprecedented in Africa. Emphatically, Kwame Nkrumah's political legacy has left an indelible mark on Africa's political history and it extraordinarily poses, to date, the most intelligible expression of Pan-Africanism.

NOTES

1. T. Falola, *Nationalism and African Intellectuals,* (New York: University of Rochester Press, 2001), 98.
2. B. Ankomah, "Never Again: Forty Years After the Coup that Derailed Africa's Progress," *New African* no.448 (Feb. 2006); 10.
3. M. Sherwood, *Kwame Nkrumah: The Years Abroad 1935–1947,* (Legon, Ghana: Freedom Publications, 1996), 112.
4. Hastings Banda led Malawi to independence, Jomo Kenayatta led Kenya to independence, Obafemi Awolowo became the first Premier of Western Nigeria, and Ako Adjei served in Nkrumah's cabinet.
5. K.B. Hadjor, *Nkrumah and Ghana: The Dilemma of Post-Colonial Power,* (New Jersey: Africa World Press, 2003), 27.
6. D. Birmingham, *Kwame Nkrumah: The Father of African Nationalism,* (Athens: Ohio University Press, 1998), 6.
7. Y. Smertin, *Kwame Nkrumah,* (New York: International Publishers, 1987), 29.
8. David Rooney, Kwame *Nkrumah: The Political Kingdom in the Third World,* (New York: St. Martin Press, 1988), 25.
9. K. Nkrumah, *Ghana: The Autobiography of Kwame Nkrumah,* (London: Thomas Nelson, 1957), 56.
10. Ghana was formerly known as the Gold Coast under British colonial rule.
11. K. Nkrumah, *Africa Must Unite,* (London: Panaf Books, 1963), 28.
12. J. Van Lierde, *Lumumba Speaks: The Speeches and Writings of Patrice Lumumba 1958–1961,* (Boston: Little and Brown, 1963), 55.

13. S.W. Thompson, *Ghana's Foreign Policy 1957–1966: Diplomacy, Ideology, and The New State,* (New Jersey: Princeton University Press, 1969), 67.
14. K. Nkrumah, *Challenge of the Congo,* (New York: International Publishers, 1967), 29.

REFERENCES

Ankomah, B. "Never Again: Forty Years After the Coup that Derailed Africa's Progress." *New African,* no.448, (Feb. 2006): 10–32.

Birmingham, D. *Kwame Nkrumah: The Father of African Nationalism.* Athens: Ohio University Press, 1998.

Hadjor, K.B. *Nkrumah and Ghana: The Dilemma of Post-Colonial Power.* New Jersey: Africa World Press, 2003.

Falola, T. *Nationalism and African Intellectuals.* New York: University of Rochester Press, 2001.

Nkrumah, K. *Ghana: The Autobiography of Kwame Nkrumah.* London: Thomas Nelson, 1957.

Nkrumah, K. *Africa Must Unite.* London: Panaf Books, 1963.

Nkrumah, K. *Challenge of the Congo.* New York: International Publishers, 1967.

Rooney, David. Kwame *Nkrumah: The Political Kingdom in the Third World.* New York: St. Martin Press, 1988.

Sherwood, M. *Kwame Nkrumah: The Years Abroad 1935–1947.* Legon, Ghana: Freedom Publications, 1996.

Smertin, Y. *Kwame Nkrumah.* New York: International Publishers, 1987.

Thompson, S.W. *Ghana's Foreign Policy 1957–1966: Diplomacy, Ideology, and The New State.* New Jersey: Princeton University Press, 1969.

Van Lierde, J. *Lumumba Speaks: The Speeches and Writings of Patrice Lumumba 1958–1961.* Boston: Little and Brown, 1963.

Chapter Eleven

African Political Instability and the Search for an Inclusive Society

Chika B. Onwuekwe

After decades of mismanagement and corruption, most African states have become hollowed out. They are no longer instruments capable of serving the public good. Indeed, far from being able to provide aid and protection to their citizens, African governments and the vampire-like politicians who run them are regarded by the populations they rule as yet another burden they have to bear in the struggle for survival.[1]

INTRODUCTION

For several years, African countries have been denied modest political leadership that fosters a progressive, just and inclusive society. Famine, corruption, insecurity, unemployment, civil wars, human rights abuses, rule of might rather than law, oppression of the minority group (race, gender and religion), and injustice have continued to plague the continent. As a result, most citizens who are tired of the incessant lack of opportunities for their self-actualization are constantly emigrating. The implication is that Africa keeps losing its best people to other continents, particularly Europe and North America. Unfortunately, the end of this mass exodus is not in sight as the endemic problems that support such migration are still in place.

Consequently, the desire to emigrate from Africa to other continents, particularly Europe and North America, in search of better life styles and opportunities, has become the rule rather than the exception. This chapter argues that political instability through forceful seizure of political power or election rigging, which often leads to denial of liberty and the security of the person, has contributed immensely to the current state of things. As a result, African intellectuals—both old and young—and industrialists perceive Europe and North America as safe havens for habitation, for development and for actualizing their short to long term life goals. It is on this basis that this chapter contends that the exodus of people from the African continent is mainly influenced by the desire of the migrant to realise her individuality, dreams and security of her person in a more welcoming and dialogue driven society. Additionally, it provides most migrants an opportunity to meet and fulfill some specific African oriented obligations to extended family and friends back in the continent. Lastly, the chapter questions whether Africans have a moral right to seek protection in other countries by abandoning their own.

THEORETICAL UNDERPINNING

Migration of any kind (internal or external) is mainly driven by the desire for better opportunities. The immediate reasons could be economic, political, institutional, social, religious, educational or a combination of all these factors. However, not every person in the society can take advantage of existing opportunities to migrate from one society to another. Often those who migrate are persons who are most knowledgeable about the opportunities elsewhere.[2] They are also those with the required survival instincts or economic power to survive the transition—between leaving home and fully settling in the new society—once they arrive at their chosen destination. As Simmons, *et al,* noted, "since migration is a response to regional differences in social and economic opportunity, the social and economic characteristics of migrants can vary across countries or regions as well as over time in any given setting," (Simmons et al, 83). The determinants of migration from one country (or continent) to another fairly resemble the determinants from rural to urban areas within a country. The major difference, which forms the focus of this chapter, is that political reasons play a huge factor in country-to-country migration. Politically stable countries of the West have continued to gain a steady supply of manpower through immigration programs that target certain categories of immigrants, mainly from Latin America, Africa and Asia. This policy is expected to boost the manpower population of western countries without compromising their core values, ideology and cohesiveness. Thus, as in rural to urban migration, the desire to "acquire education for one's own self and for one's children" (Simmons et al, 24), plays a strong role in narrowing down the countries to which people migrate.

Other factors include perception of the differences in the quality of life in one's country compared to the destination country, the presence of fellow Africans (friends and family mainly) in the targeted country, the possibility of quickly rebuilding, adapting and settling into the new society without pronounced differences or difficulties (such as language barriers,

and equal opportunity in employment). The rush and competition for qual-
ified immigrants in western countries makes it more attractive for unhappy
Africans to leave their continent. Recently, the new federal Conservative
Government in Canada requested the premiers of the country's provinces
to recognize foreign credentials of immigrants as a *sine qua non* to their
assimilation in their chosen communities.[3] Sharing this latest request from
Prime Minister Stephen Harper at a subsequent Provincial Liberal Party
Convention in his Ontario province, Premier Dalton McGuinty stated that
Canada is focused on attracting "top-notch immigrants." According to
him, Canada hopes to rise above the competition for quality immigrants by
addressing the following concerns: "A big question for any person choosing to leave their home country for another is: 'how long does it take me
when I'm over there to get up and running. How long does it take me to
have my credentials recognized and for me to be employed at my highest level of ability and training," (Livingston, 2006). Although made with
respect to rural-urban migration, the following findings by Simmons, *et al,*
are relevant for our purpose: "In Africa, migrants are predominantly young
adult males with somewhat higher educational attainments than their peers.
They are more likely to come from wealthier homes and from regions of
higher population density," (Simmons et al, 27). Unfortunately, since Africa
lacks functional and sustainable institutions that will support the political,
social and economic growth and social needs of its people, migration from
the continent in search of better livelihood is not likely to end soon. The
continent needs to rebuild its political institutions, for "unlike capital and
technology, (viable) institutions cannot be imported."[4] It is surprising that
the outside world knows of Africa's deficiencies, yet those in governmental positions appear ignorant of these problems. This is notwithstanding
their acknowledgment of various inadequacies during political campaigns
(where democracy exists) or when a military *coup d'état* occurs. However,
as soon as they assume power, these leaders deny the problems inherited
from the ousted regime, clamp down on dissidents, accuse the international
community of meddling in their local affairs, request Africans living abroad
to return home to rebuild with them, and occasionally pretend that all is
normal. Surrounded by cronies and political thugs, it becomes difficult
for those in power to listen, hear and dialogue with the opposition who
momentarily may represent the interests of the average African until they in
turn assume power. Osita Eze outlined the root cause of this problem when
he stated:

> In most of the African countries . . . election to political office is not
> often based on qualities the individual possesses. The determining factor

is often the amount of financial as well as other material resources available to the individual and his party. Votes are invariably bought and elections rigged, thus creating the prospect of a corrupt and selfish leadership, ascending to power and maintaining itself in office by corrupt means and other undemocratic processes. A leadership that is essentially imbued with an undemocratic spirit can hardly be expected to act as a citadel or guarantor of the democratic processes.[5]

Africa is indeed a continent where talent is not rewarded. It remains the poorest continent in the modern world. Robert Guest describes it as the only continent that, "despite all the technological advances that are filling stomachs and pockets everywhere else, has actually grown poorer over the last thirty years."[6] I am therefore inclined to agree with Meredith when he claims, "[I]n reality, fifty years after the beginning of the independence era, Africa's prospects are bleaker than ever before. Already the world's poorest region, it is falling further and further behind all other regions of the world," (Meredith, 681).

Civil wars and incessant unrests are some other reasons why Africans migrate to other countries. Guest reports that in 1999, one in every five Africans came from a country "racked by civil or cross border war," (Guest, 54). The victims of these senseless conflicts are civilians, mainly children and women. As a result, the country remains uninhabitable for the most part. Potential farmlands are loaded with landmines while farmers are disrupted from cultivating the land or harvesting their crops. This leads to increased hunger and *kwashiorkor* (a malnutrition disease) in Africa yet the leaders conduct themselves in provocative ostentation that mocks and minimizes the hardship faced by their citizens.

POLITICAL INSTABILITY

There is a common adage in most parts of Africa that 'east or west, home is the best.' This proverb refers to how Africans love their motherland despite occasional difficulties that may be traced to the transatlantic slave trade through the colonial period up to the present difficulties of unending internal conflicts. However, with increased exodus of Africa's people to foreign countries—old and young, skilled and unskilled, men and women—the above maxim is stripped of any meaning. It is no longer a secret that Africa is plagued with incessant but unnecessary political unrest. This has destroyed its political structure and creates an unbearable condition that is inimical to safety, healthy living and productivity. Wars and ethnic conflicts have not only left the continent in shambles, they have reduced its citizens to underlings and made them an instrument for mockery by the outside world. It is a situation that baffles some Africans and those sympathetic to their predicament. Unfortunately, the power hungry gun trotting individuals who find comfort in waging wars against their motherland from the bush; the disgruntled military personnel who rather than protect the country against external aggression wants a taste of political power for which they lack the skill; and the corrupt politicians who continue to create the atmosphere for unconstitutional interventions in governance have refused to cave in. The situation is fast crippling the continent as it experiences mass departure of its people to other continents in search of what Africa is unable to offer them. The migrants are disgusted by the carnage and tough conditions which the above developments have brought upon them. Looking beyond the shores rather than within the continent becomes an alternative, albeit a painful one at times, which Africans are forced to embark upon. In the end, the continent is the worse for it and if this trend continues, then the demise of Africa is nearer now than ever.

Admittedly, there are various reasons why Africans migrate to other continents in much larger numbers today than they did prior to when the first country in that continent secured independence more than fifty years ago. Previously, and shortly after independence, Africans travelled mainly to Europe—England and France—and occasionally United States for education, holidays, business and skills or professional training. At the end of their mission, they returned back to mother Africa. Most of the African people involved in the nationalist movements across Africa in the 1950s to early 1960s were educated in England, France or the United States. Upon return, these western educated Africans either joined the nationalist movement or took employment in civil service with a purpose to serve the motherland. To a large extent, most of these returnees were genuinely focused on making Africa great.[7] To their chagrin, governance was a difficult task to undertake. This was because most of them were either ill prepared for the position of leadership thrust upon them or underestimated their own people's expectations. Although made with respect to Kenya, Odhiambo's observation, "this was not, in reality, a very pleasant political community to inherit"[8] is also correct for other parts of Africa. In the process, most of these African leaders stumbled onto much wealth, became power drunk and being clueless on key projects to embark on to alleviate their people's well being, chose to loot the treasury and proceeds from natural resource deals.[9]

Subsequent to independence, and up to the present time, hooligans in military uniforms and disgruntled politicians have at different times organized forceful take over of the reins of governments they swore to protect, on the pretext that they wish to improve the poor conditions of the people. In the process, either a new political and economic agenda is started or in the event of some form of resistance, countless lives and properties are lost. For instance, the diamond rush in both Liberia and Sierra Leone was the mainstay of the fuelled insurgents led by Charles Taylor of Liberia against Monrovia and Foday Sankoh's rebel group in neighbouring Sierra Leone against the government in Freetown. Both Taylor and Sankoh recruited children (between ages 10 and 14) into their groups. They instructed their recruits to kill and destroy any opposition. The result was mayhem and a bloodbath in that part of Africa. Killings were indiscriminately carried out, with civilians being the biggest casualty. Their actions also rendered thousands jobless, wounded, hungry, malnourished, orphaned, homeless and displaced from ancestral connections. Irresponsible soldiers (both government and rebels) raped women and young girls with impunity. Women and young girls were also forced into prostitution as a means of earning some living. One wonders whether Taylor, Sankoh and many others like them would have ruled over emptiness if their carnage wiped out the entire population.[10]

The above represents some of the major political reasons why most Africans migrate to other countries in search of peace, stability and good governance. There are also some Africans who initially set out for further academic studies with a deep belief that they will return on completion of their programs. While overseas, they follow news and developments in Africa religiously. This indulgence is easier today because of the proliferation of the Internet than it was a few years ago. Often, news about Africa and tales of woes from folks and friends back home triggers another thought. They begin to reassess their decision to return to mother Africa after their studies and compare that with what opportunities are available if they decide to stay in their new home. Due to the poor political climate in Africa, over seventy percent of Africans that originally came over for studies in Europe and North America migrate officially at the end of their academic journey. Usually, they either stay back in the host country or move to another western country. Any of these is preferable than returning to the life of gloom, insecurity, uncertainty, devastation, and emptiness in Africa.

Interestingly, the above situation is not age specific. Currently, there are many African statesmen and women who now adorn academic institutions abroad as visiting scholars or professors. Most of these elders have distinguished themselves in their chosen fields but are forced to relocate abroad due to inefficient government policies or actions. In some cases, some of them were targets of government murder squads. These developments do not bode well for African youths. It is sad to grow up knowing that your future lies outside your mother's continent. Today, Africa is still boiling and troubled by leadership tussles despite the renewed hope of an African renaissance. Today it is a Sharia related issue in northern Nigeria that triggers off conflicts between Muslims and Christians leading to mayhem. Tomorrow, it will be an ethnic cleansing in one part of North Africa, such as Sudan that leaves millions of refugees in its wake, (Eze, 163). Africa is indeed a problematic continent and the conflicts plaguing it appear to justify its suspicious question-mark-like map depicting a convergence of people of different ethnic backgrounds arbitrarily put together for the convenience of imperialists during the infamous partition of Africa.

Most parts of Africa have been engulfed in wars at one time or another—Angola in 1990, Ethiopia and Eritrea border war in 1998, Nigeria fought a civil war between 1966 and 1970, Sudan in the 1980s, Côte d' Ivoire (now Ivory Coast) had its own civil war ignited by religious and ethnic divisions orchestrated by various military and political larders, Rwanda and Uganda were engaged in a fight over some land in the Congo, Liberia under Charles Taylor, and Sierra Leone. The Central African Republic was engulfed in tribal conflicts that threatened to tear that country apart. Following Sudan's independence, this country has spent over 30 years at war, often started by internal strife. The statistics are staggering and scary: "In 2000 there were more than ten major conflicts underway in Africa. One-fifth of all Africans lived in countries battered by war. Some 12 million were classified as refugees—40 per cent of the world's total. The cause of democracy and development, as *The Economist* said, seemed 'hopeless,'" (Meredith, 679).

The above political circumstances in Africa make me ask the following potent questions that interestingly run through the gamut of my analysis in this chapter. Is Africa a land of lost opportunities? Has the continent neglected, failed or refused to nurture, manage, reward and lead its growing human resources to the extent that it now loses them in droves daily to the West? Is Africa on the brink of extinction or on the dawn of another form of colonization triggered by the West's empathy to help its surviving but devastated people? Is Africa about to dissolve in the face of mounting debt, economic doldrums, social apathy, insecurity of life and property, political ineptitude, and endemic corruption at all levels of society and institution?

While this chapter hopes to touch on most of the above questions, its main purpose is not directly to answer them. Part of the reason for taking this approach is because the past and current political events and facts in (and about) Africa speak for themselves. It needs no further elucidation. I will only point to the above opening quote from Meredith as the foundational basis why the continent loses and will continue to lose its best and brightest people—both living and those yet unborn—to other continents, particularly Europe and North America, for political, economic and social security. African migrants departed their continent in search of better and different opportunities in the knowledge that if success smiles on them, they would contribute more to humanity than their continent would ever permit them.

GOVERNMENT WITCH-HUNTING

The basis for any political society is the preservation of life and property. Government institutions are able to perform this function by advancing the interests of their citizens within and outside their country. These interests are often summarized or described as the public good. It is not the same thing as the self-interests or biases of those in government. Achieving the public good in any society is usually a tough call as various conflicting interests seek attention at the same time. In modern times, democratic processes have assisted institutions to ease the tension associated with choice of policies to pursue and the order of priority accorded any conflicting projects. In fairer societies, guided by a constitution, government institutions make choices that will impact the generality of the population. This may be tantamount to what J.S. Mill described as the greatest good or the ultimate happiness of citizens.[11] Such inclusive programs or strategies, which do not diminish the minority's interests, can rightly be referred to as the public good. After all, an inclusive society is one that protects minority rights, safeguards the constitution and offers equal opportunity to all citizens no matter their tribe or color. Different from totalitarian governments, such a society encourages participation of all groups in decision-making processes and in the choice of who governs them. Its civic institutions are effective and constantly support the society to hold the people together.

A cankerworm prevalent in Africa is the government's desire to acquire its citizens' properties at will and without compensation. This occurs in democratic, autocratic, as well as pariah states in Africa. The forceful acquisition of citizens' properties may be achieved either through unjust laws, such as decrees, or by outright seizure with the help of law enforcement agents. For instance, on pretext of providing Zairians economic independence, Mobutu Sese Seko seized over 2,000 foreign-owned businesses without compensation. In a typical dictatorship style, the appropriated enterprises were given out to cronies with Mobutu retaining a large portion. Idi Amin of Uganda embarked on a similar venture during his totalitarian reign in that country. The self-acclaimed jihadist in Sudan, General al-Bashir, was known to confiscate citizens' property and assets at will without compensation. It was widely reported that he preyed on fellow Sudanese like a vulture and used torture to suppress insurrection of any kind. It is ironic that African leaders jet from one continent to another in search of foreign direct investment only to turn around and either national-ize or appropriate these businesses for themselves.[12]

Following the forceful take over of power in Sudan in 1989, General Omar al-Bashir embarked on a self-imposed jihad. Perceived enemies of government were killed, tortured or imprisoned without trial. His govern-ment terrified Sudanese of all walks of life, including fellow but dissenting Muslims. Meredith summed up the state of affairs in this North African state, thus:

> "One institution after another—the civil service, the army, the judi-ciary, the universities, trade unions, professional associations, para-statal organisations—was purged of dissent. Prominent Muslim sects . . . were silenced; much of their property and assets, including mosques and shrines, were taken over by the state. Christian activities were cur-tailed and suppressed. The press was rigidly controlled. Hundreds of politicians, journalists, doctors and trade unionists were detained with-out trial. Many were taken to 'ghost houses'—houses whose existence the government denied—where they were tortured. . . . detainees were subjected to burnings, beatings, electric shocks and rape to extract con-fessions from them," (Meredith, 589).

The late General Sani Abacha unleashed an unprecedented fear and terror in Nigeria that forced political critics, civil rights' groups and per-ceived opponents into exile. Amongst Nigerians that left the country included Wole Soyinka, the Nobel Prize winner for literature. Abacha and his security advisers (which metamorphosed into a killer squad) master-minded the disappearance or indiscriminate killings of numerous Nigeri-ans. Notable amongst their victims was Mrs Kudirat Abiola, wife of Chief M.K.O. Abiola who was acclaimed to have won the free and fair elections in June 1993,[13] ignominiously annulled by General Ibrahim Badamosi Babangida. Abacha's killer squad gunned down Mrs Abiola on a quiet morning in the outskirts of Lagos.

On another note, Abacha's corruption reached the greatest heights. Commenting on monies that Abacha had stashed abroad, Meredith said: "Abacha's greed exceeded that of all his predecessors. It was estimated that he stole more than $4 billion, taking money either directly from the treasury, or from government contracts, or through scams like the Petro-leum Trust Fund that he set up ostensibly to channel extra revenue from an increase in the domestic fuel price into infrastructure and other invest-ments," (Meredith, 581). Through his cronies, Abacha planted and lured his closest adversaries to coup plots. This provided him an immediate but untenable excuse to secretly purge Nigerian society of those perceived as enemies—both within and outside the military. It was on this pretext that both former Generals Olusegun Obasanjo (the current Nigerian president) and Shehu Musa Yar'Adua were arrested, tried and locked up for life.[14]

There is also the incessant inability of government institutions to provide basic services due to ineptitude fuelled by unprecedented corrup-tion. This undoubtedly is tantamount to government failure. Neverthe-less, African leaders clutch onto the helm of governance of their respective countries willing to die on that seat rather than attend to the social, politi-cal, economic and health needs of their people, to mention but the most vital. Africa remains a continent in desolation. Its problems are further confounded by politicians who perceive politics as "an arena for elite group on the look-out for money-making opportunities, not a vehicle for pursuing economic and social reform," (Meredith, 587). The World Bank's apt description of African political landscape in the 1990s is still correct in the 21st century. As the Bank then noted: "By 1990, half of Africa's states had military or quasi-military governments. In parallel with author-itarian military governments came a trend towards single-party rule under autocratic civilian leaders, largely pursuing interventionist economic poli-cies, in some cases under the banners of socialism or Marxism. Especially when combined with external shocks, the resulting economic decline and politicization of the bureaucracy eroded much of what remained of insti-tutional governance capacity and undermined many of the accomplish-ments of the 1960s."[15]

In Africa, government commits most of the atrocities and crimes against humanity either directly or through paid agents. However, some civilians who have grown powerful, rich and influential also indulge in vic-timizing opponents either in business related disputes or merely to settle personal conflicts. Like the government, they also utilize corrupt state insti-tutions such as the judiciary, the police and other law enforcement agencies to terrorize fellow civilians. As long as they remain faithful to the govern-ment, the actions of these wealthy individuals are beyond reproach.

UNEMPLOYMENT AND THE DENIAL OF BASIC RIGHTS

Both politicians and military juntas have failed to live up to promises of finding solutions to the persistent unemployment problems in Africa. Unemployment in Africa stems from various causes—civil wars, lack of education and required skills for some types of jobs, poor earnings to establish and successfully run private businesses, dependence on subsistence farming, inadequate government support for private sector enterprise, among others. Although noted for their self-belief and entrepreneurship, there are neither effective infrastructures nor financial assistance to support private initiatives, such as small-scale businesses. In both the public and the private sector, most employers expect their African employees to worship their bosses in order to guarantee job retention and promotion. Promotion is based not on how well a person has done in his job but on how well the employer likes the employee. This brings disaffection, as there is no merit in the system. To say the least, jobs are insecure, careers bleak and the future gloomy. Some Africans who find opportunities to escape this dejected society and its labour system vanish at the first instant.

Shortly after the Nigerian civil war, the Ibos that fought on the side of Biafra were not easily integrated into the Nigerian armed forces despite the declaration of General Yakubu Gowon's government that there was "no victor, no vanquished." In hindsight, it is likely that Gowon's declaration at the end of the war was to attract international support and aid to rebuild devastated Nigeria. Rebuilding human capital, especially soldiers of Ibo dissent who fought for Nigerian unity but on the other side of the fence was not on the government agenda. This was a great mistake, which sober Gowon, as a civilian currently living in Jos, Nigeria (his home state) now admits. That singular act of isolation in the face of hardship unleashed idle people and terror into the streets and communities of South-eastern Nigeria (the Ibo enclave). Gowon's decision turned some able-bodied men of Ibo origin who participated in the civil war into night marauders as a quick way to eke out a living. His outrageous policy also forced some erstwhile Biafran soldiers to scratch out a living in local areas by engaging in odd jobs. As a result, most of these erstwhile Biafran soldiers were exposed to illicit drugs both as smokers and petty traffickers. The worst hit by this unpopular agenda were those discharged army officers who out of frustration suffered mental imbalance. They became additional burdens to other members of their family who were already impoverished from the war, denied their properties located outside the Ibo region because of the policy of abandoned property initiated by the government, and therefore remained unsure of what tomorrow would bring.

Similarly, after Zimbabwe gained independence in 1980, Robert Mugabe promised to re-settle those who left school and joined his guerrilla war group—the ZANU—but were unable to get meaningful jobs when the rebellion ended. Mugabe's only assistance was the payment of stipends to this group of people for two years. Afterwards, he purposely ignored them and it was difficult for these people to eke out a meaningful living. The situation proved challenging for these individuals who have neither trade to ply nor proper education with which to seek "white collar" jobs. The approaches employed by Nigeria and Zimbabwe mirrors what other Africa states do after a major conflict. It is a winner takes all approach devoid of any form of inclusion. This brings disillusionment and sows the uncanny idea of how to seize power. It is also a catalyst and cogent reason to desert any country for a much better nation where people have more opportunity to succeed by doing honest jobs for honest reward.

Another problem of authoritarian and bad governments in Africa is the denial of fundamental human rights of citizens. One may argue that this is normal even in advanced countries where wars and conflicts may lead to declarations of emergency, the introduction of martial law in preference to the constitution, and the restriction of individual liberties, especially free movement, during such conflicts. Therefore, "emergency laws are inevitable in circumstances such as these."[16] During the Second World War, both Britain and France used extra-judicial measures to curtail incidences of violence in their countries. Notably, the British Regulation 18B empowered the Home Secretary in the United Kingdom to detain indefinitely any alien without trial as long as the war lasted. Following the terrorist attacks in United States on September 11, 2001, the US government passed the Patriot Act[17] which allows US security agencies to tap into or request corporations operating in the United States to supply personal information of their employees, contractors and so on. Information of this nature was hitherto unavailable to state authorities except through a formal court procedure, as it was contrary to existing privacy legislation. In contrast, emergency situations in Africa are constant, and often declared without proper review of the circumstances. The objective is usually to consolidate power while punishing opposition parties, individuals and their ethnic states or tribes. This portends great danger as citizens "whether by legislative or executive action or abuse of the judicial process, are made to live as if in a perpetual state of emergency," (Elias, 167).

In Africa, emergency laws are used to strengthen "naked force," (Elias, 167). It is used to legalize tyranny and oppression. Most times, the judiciary, if not well guarded, is used as a conduit for legitimizing illegality and downing the Rule of Law. Elias describes this as the "unparalleled example of the prostitution of the judiciary process in recent times," (Elias,169). An independent judiciary should see beyond a façade and know when either the legislative or executive wants to depend on it for atrocities perpetrated against their citizens. Trumped up charges should be seen for what they are and summarily dismissed. It surely requires guts to take such bold steps under a despot. Most oppressive governments in Africa perceive the judiciary as an extension of their institution. As such, they expect members of the judiciary to provide legal backing to illegal government actions no matter how oppressive or unjustified. They make scapegoats of a few unwilling members of the judiciary by removing them from their positions. Security of tenure of judges becomes an instrument of threat for subduing judges to compliance. It is a shameless blackmail, which leaves the common citizens at the mercy of tyrants, parading as leaders, and their supportive institutions—the judiciary and civil service.

In societies where the rule of might rather than the rule of law thrives, citizens live in constant fear. They have no means of expressing themselves because their freedom, liberty and dignity are suppressed. The press, which is the bastion of hope for the oppressed, is itself a victim under despotic regimes. Government press and media are used to feed lies and half-truths to citizens and the world in general. This development makes life unpalatable, brutish, and short. In the process, the security of most citizens—including their privacy—is jeopardized. Citizens are not sure of surviving the next day under the junta or despot. This is the bane of African continent in the 21st century and a genuine reason why its citizens seek shelter and solace in western countries.

THE CHALLENGE OF INFRASTRUCTURE

Africans are patient, understanding and always willing to support their leaders even in the face of adversity, ineptitude and dishonesty. At independence, African pride was rooted in the trust that their own persons—elites and educated Africans—would henceforth be in charge of government and also make economic decisions. They believed that this band of leaders would lead them to greatness. Being a continent blessed with abundant natural resources and a sustainable environment, it was left to the elites to drive development and orchestrate the distribution of the fruits of self-government. Unfortunately, this was not to be. Rather than bring prosperity and happiness, African mineral wealth became a burden and a source of corruption and endless wars. African leaders have at various times up to the present day shown themselves incapable of purposeful governance. They have continued to utilize the mineral wealth for themselves rather than the community of people over which they govern. It has become apparent that due to the huge deposits of natural resources in this continent, "people are prepared to fight for a share of power," (Guest, 14). For example, in Liberia and Sierra Leone, the fight for the large deposits of diamond in parts of the country led to a protracted insurgence masterminded by Charles Taylor

and Foday Sankoh, respectively. Similarly, the struggle for the control of
rich diamond, cobalt and tantalum deposits in Congo was one of the reasons for opposition to Mobutu's tyrannical government. Rebel and guerrilla fighters teamed up and used money from illegal sales of these resources
to fund their rebellion. When eventually Mobutu was overthrown and Lau-
rent Kabilla installed as the head of state of Congo, the citizens were hope-
ful that he would be better than Mobutu. Within a few months, Kabilla
showed his true person by proving the Congolese people wrong. Guest
summed up the situation in these words: "Kabilla was, if anything, more
cruel than Mobutu but lacked his predecessor's intelligence. He promised
elections but never held them. He jailed and tortured suspected opponents.
He tried to fine businessmen for breaking unpublished rules and to levy
taxes on as yet unrealized profits. He printed money with reckless abandon
. . . ," (Guest, 58).

Until 2002 when he died, Jonas Savimbi waged an almost four-decade
long war against the Angolan government during which he looted the country's natural resources. The Nigerian government has refused to negotiate
with the people in the delta area where the oil revenues are sourced. The
constant skirmishes and kidnapping of foreign workers in the (Nigeria) oil
rivers, which gained international attention under late Ken Saro Wiwa's
Movement for the Survival of Ogoni People (MOSOP) is still rampant.
The Nigerian federal government has resorted to constant intimidation and
occasional deployment of armed soldiers to the restive oil rivers to quell
disturbances. These are all short-term measures that scarcely provide a
lasting solution to the issues at stake. Granted that ownership of mineral
resources in Nigeria belongs to the federal government under the present
Nigerian laws, I am surprised that an amicable solution is not yet on the
table. As with other parts of Africa, this one-off protest by the delta people
of Nigeria may one day gain teeth and become a monster that tears the
country further apart. For the most part, both actions—attacks on workers
by indigenes and the government's nonchalant approach—are bad for business and the well being of Nigerians. With respect to Africa, Guest appears
correct in his assertion: "Governments that depend on natural resources
for most of their income are usually venal and despotic. Most oil-rich Gulf
states are, and African oligarchies, such as Nigeria, Gabon and Equatorial
Guinea, have a wretched record, too. But perhaps the country where oil has
proven most destructive is Angola," (Guest, 63). The deprivation that most
Africans are subjected to, coupled with the high-handedness of the political
leaders, may lead to justification for the frequent exodus of Africans from
their mother continent. Indeed, the circumstances may be explained by reference to John Locke's description of the state of war:

> . . . he who attempts to get another man into his absolute power, does
> thereby *put himself into a state of war* with him; it being to be under-
> stood as a declaration of a design upon his life: for I have reason to con-
> clude, that he who would get me into his power without my consent,
> would use me as he pleased when he had got me there, and destroy me
> too when he had a fancy to it; for no body can desire to *have me in
> his absolute power*, unless it be to compel me by force to that which is
> against the right of my freedom, i.e. make me a slave. To be free from
> such force is the only security of my preservation; and reason bids me
> look on him, as an enemy to my preservation, who would take away
> that *freedom* which is the fence to it; so that he who makes an *attempt
> to enslave me,* thereby puts himself into a state of war with me.[18]

In the entire equation, survival remains the first law of nature. With
the carnage and political tension that is seen constantly in Africa, people
have a right to defend themselves against oppressive regimes. African citizens have a right to fulfil their dreams within and outside their continent.
It is for individuals (either by themselves or through families) to determine
how best to actualize their individual dreams when political institutions
fail. The educational standard is fast declining while hospitals lack the
basic equipment (including beds) for teeming patients. Indeed, hospitals are
currently worse than consulting clinics, as the latter is usually staffed with
qualified physicians paid to examine and diagnose illnesses. It is a pathetic
situation and one that most honest Africans, within and outside the continent, are determined to remedy. The problem is that the entrenched establishments and those that benefit from the crumbs or largesse are ready to
maim, destroy and kill to maintain their proboscis on the endless flow of
corrupt wealth from government institutions. Ayittey captures the core
reason why government institutions continue to crumble in Africa: "Some
institutions decay and break down. Nobody cares because tenure of office
and promotions are based not on competence and merit but on personal
loyalty to the president, ethnicity, and sycophancy. Institutions such as the
civil service, the judiciary, parliament, and the police disintegrate and fail to
function since they have all been perverted."[19]

CONCLUSION

This chapter has shed light on the state of political affairs in Africa for
the past few years, and how that condition is a precursor to the flight of
its citizens to other parts of the world in search of success, security, economic stability and sane political sanctuary. It is a process which will not

end unless those entrusted with political governance in Africa understand and implement the basic agenda that will promote rather than diminish or rubbish the public good of its citizens. Unfortunately, except through refugee status brought about by senseless ethnic cleansing, conflicts or wars, only the rich and their families are able easily to migrate overseas for better opportunities. Most poor African families are struggling to feed themselves and their young, and have less money to embark on an unknown journey abroad despite the hardship. For the average families, their children may struggle to get out but it proves more difficult for them because of economic reasons. They lack the monetary resources to actualize this desire fully. Whichever way the migration occurs and for whatever level of family, Africa continues to lose its best people in numbers. This does not augur well for the continent. It needs these individuals to build a strong, independent and united Africa. At the moment, this is a pipe dream that is becoming fuzzier each day.

The desire for sit-tight governments, the ever changing pattern of election rigging and the selfish mentality that influences ethnic rather than national patriotism in Africa are the bane of political instability in the continent. A political society that divides rather than unites, excludes rather than includes or polarizes rather than coordinates its people is unsafe for human habitation. Such a society defeats the cause of self-preservation and provides no meaning to life. Lastly, such a society lacks free institutions that support freedom and equality of citizens duly protected by a superior constitution. Until Africa gets its leadership questions right and is able to provide a basic platform on which its citizens can realize their lofty goals, it cannot stop the emigration of its current and potential human capital. It is pathetic that the problem with Africa is its political leadership, which remains opportunistic and directionless.

NOTES

1. Martin Meredith, *The Fate of Africa: From the Hopes of Freedom to the Hearth of Despair: A History of Fifty Years of Independence*. (New York: Public Affairs, 2005), at 688.
2. Alan Simmons, Sergio Diaz-Briquets, and Aprodicio A. Laquian, *Social Change and Internal Migration: A Review of Research Findings from Africa, Asia and Latin America* (Ottawa: IDRC, 1977), 83.
3. Gillian Livingston, "Harper wants Immigrants' Credentials Recognized: McGuinty," Feb 25, 2006, Yahoo News Canada, available at http://news. yahoo.com/s/cpress/20060225/ca_pr_on_na/feds_ont_immigrants Last visited February 26, 2006.
4. Mwangi S. Kimenyi and John M. Mbaku, "Institutions and Economic Growth" in Mwangi S. Kimenyi, John M. Mbaku and Ngure Mwaniki,

eds., *Restarting and Sustaining Economic Growth and Development in Africa: The Case of Kenya,* (Aldershot, U.K.: Ashgate, 2003), 13. [Annotation provided].

5. Osita C. Eze *Human Rights in Africa: Some Selected Problems* (Lagos: The Nigerian Institute of International Affairs, 1984), 59.
6. Robert Guest, *The Shackled Continent: Power, Corruption, and African Lives,* (Washington: Smithsonian, 2004), 6.
7. They include Jomo Kenyatta of Kenya, Nnamdi Azikiwe and Obafemi Awolowo of Nigeria, Julius Nyerere of Tanzania, and Kwame Nkrumah of Ghana.
8. E.S. Atieno Odhiambo, "Democracy and the Ideology of Order in Kenya: 1958–1986 in Walter O. Oyugi, et al, eds., *Democratic Theory and Practice in Africa* (Portsmouth, NH: Heinemann, 1988), 111; 126.
9. See generally Patrick Chabal, *Power in Africa: An Essay in Political Interpretation* (New York: St. Martin's Press, 1994); Walter O. Oyugi, et al, 1988; Naomi Chazan, et al, *Politics and Society in Contemporary Africa,* 3rd ed. (Boulder: Lynne Rienner, 1999).
10. It should be noted that both Taylor and Sankoh were checkmated through the efforts of the Nigerian led Ecowas Monitoring Group (ECOMOG) military force.
11. J. S. Mill, *On Liberty and Utilitarianism* (New York & Toronto: Bantam Books, 1993)
12. On FDI in developing countries, see Chika B. Onwuekwe, "Reconciling the Scramble for Foreign Direct Investments and Environmental Prudence: A Developing Country's Nightmare (2006) 7 J.W.I.T 113.
13. This election was held on June 12, 1993. Nigerians, sick of years of corrupt military dictatorship seized the opportunity provided by the election to vote en-mass for Abiola who hailed from the South but had a reputable and likeable Northerner, Babagana Kingibe, as running mate. The election results so far released by Professor Humphrey Nwosu's electoral commission before Babangida's annulment saw Abiola in poll position to his rival Alhaji Bashir Tofa.
14. General Yar' Adua died in prison in what is believed to be a reaction from a deadly poison injected into his body by Abacha's paid physicians.
15. World Bank, *Can Africa Claim the 21st Century?* 2000, 53, cited in Guest, 47.
16. T. Olawale Elias, *Government and Politics in Africa* (London and Bombay: Asia, 1963), at 167–168.
17. President George W. Bush signed the USA Patriot Act (HR 3162) into law on October 26, 2001.
18. John Locke, *Second Treatise of Government,* C.B. Macpherson, ed. (Indianapolis: Hackett, 1980), 14.
19. George B.N. Ayittey, "Combating Corruption in Africa: Analysis and context" in Kempe Ronald Hope and Bornwell C. Chikulo, eds., *Corruption and Development in Africa: Lessons from Country Case-Studies,* (New York: St. Martin's Press, 2000); 104, 105.

Chapter Twelve

A Critical Analysis of the Social and Economic Impact of Asian Diaspora in Kenya

Francis Ogino, Felix Kiruthu, and Winston Jumba Akala

INTRODUCTION

For centuries, Eastern Africa had contact with people from other continents, particularly from Asia. The influx of Asian people into Kenya became more dramatic when British imperialists undertook to open up Kenya's interior by building the Kenya-Uganda railway between 1895 and 1901. Many Asians of Indian origin, hired as indentured laborers, were brought to Kenya to help with the building of the railway. The railway would open Kenya to a sophisticated web business and of social interaction. Later, at the height of colonialism, Asians, then settled in Kenya and less exploited by the colonialists, established and operated retail and wholesale businesses. Gradually, the Asian Diaspora in Kenya grew to dominate business and industry in post-independence Kenya. Today, Asians of Kenyan citizenship own great business empires across the entire East and Central African region, a phenomenon that has gradually elevated Kenya into a regional economic and social hub. This chapter therefore seeks to analyze critically the social and economic impact of the Asian Diaspora in Kenya. Specifically, the chapter utilizes the literature on globalization and ethnic identities to examine how the Asians in Diaspora in Kenya have managed to sustain their identities in Kenya while they remained major players in a complex regional economy. Further the study interrogates the post-independence education structures that promoted acceptance of diversity in an originally purely African environment, thereby enhancing the opportunity for diasporic Asian communities to flourish in Kenya.

BACKGROUND: IMMIGRATION OF ASIANS TO EAST AFRICA

The immigration of Asians to East Africa can be located within the forces of the early phase of globalization process. The *Periplus of the Erythrean*

Sea which is dated around the 1st century AD documents the various trading activities that took place between the East African coast and the orient; the Greeks; and Romans. In this trade the orient including Thai land and India acquired ivory, animal skins, ambergris and rhinoceros horns from East Africa. In return, these traders from the orient supplied to the communities of East Africa rugs/carpets, glassware and metal ware.[1]

The monsoon winds facilitated this trade by blowing the traders' ships to and from the East African coast. Although there is little evidence of the settlement of Asians in East Africa during this ancient phase of globalization, available evidence shows that by the 7th century AD, a number of foreigners had established settlements in the East African Coast. Among these were included the city state of Kilwa in modern day Tanzania. By the 15th century when the Portuguese sailor Vasco da Gama managed to sail to the East coast of Africa, there already existed a chain of prosperous coastal city-states in East Africa, which included Mombasa, Malindi, Lamu and Mogadishu. The fact that strong links with the orient existed was illustrated by the speed with which da Gama was directed to India from the Kenyan coast.

India was not the only part of the orient that transacted trade with the East African coast. It is reported that the Chinese Emperor was rewarded with gifts from East Africa around the 15th Century, including a giraffe. Archaeologists and linguists have already embarked on research along the East Coast in order to reconstruct these links with the orient. A recovery of a Chinese ship that is believed to have sunk along the coast of East Africa could unravel most of the details pertaining to these relations with the orient. The communities along the East coast provide tangible evidence of these ancient interactions between the land of Zenj (as the East Coast was known), and the orient.

Immigrants from the Indian subcontinent played a determining role in the development of commerce and industry in East Africa, particularly from the 19th century.[2] This was done in three main phases. The initial phase was characterized by the entry into the hinterland of coastal-based Indian merchants and financiers and the arrival of new immigrants from India in the 1840s, (Himbara, 1994). The Sultan of Zanzibar Seyyid Said contributed significantly to this immigration. He encouraged many Indian money lenders (Banyans) to come to the East African coast and provide money lending services to the Indian and Swahili merchants who dealt in the ivory and slave trades.[3] Some of the Asians were pursuing artisanal trades, including both Hindus and Muslims. Among the Muslims the Khoja, Bohra and Memon sects were the most active in artisan activity, while the lower castes among the Hindus worked as barbers, tailors and washer men.[4]

The intervention of the British East Africa Company (IBEAC) in 1888 and its establishment of stations along the existing trade routes accelerated the Asian advance into the interior. Nevertheless, it should be noted that the IBEAC utilized the existing infrastructure established by African and Swahili merchants who had already established trading centers such as Voi, Kibwezi and Machakos. The Asians therefore took advantage of this infrastructure to settle inland. Moreover, the IBEAC achieved its goals through the use of its private army, which consisted of Indian, Arab and Sudanese troops under British officers. At the time of penetration inland the armed forces of the company comprised 1120 such solders, divided between Mombasa, Machakos and Kismayu.[5] Asians, therefore, played a significant role during the early phase of Kenya's colonization. After the collapse of IBEAC in 1895, the British proclaimed formal colonial rule, and Asians continued providing useful services to the British.

Soon after declaring a protectorate status over British East Africa (Kenya) and Uganda, the British decided to construct a railway line from Mombasa to Lake Victoria named the Uganda Railway, for it linked the inland territory of Uganda to the outside world.[6] Thousands of Asians were contracted to provide labor for the railway construction. About 5000 subordinate Indian workers were recruited in addition to the more than 31,000 coolies. These Asian workers were supposed not only to help in the railway construction, but also in its running in a variety of capacities. Although the Asians as a whole were referred to as coolies, technically a coolie is an unskilled laborer. However, many of the indentured Asians worked as professionals such as surveyors, clerks, masons, carpenters and draughts men.[7]

In addition, a number of Asians came to East Africa on their own, mostly as traders, although some obtained employment on the railway as petty contractors.[8] Given the geographical spread of Indian skilled workers into small towns and centers during the colonial period, Nairobi, Nakuru and Mombasa were not the only urban spaces in Kenya where Africans interacted with Asians. Some of the Asians even opened shops at military posts and near the colonial administration *bomas* such as Fort Hall, Nyeri, Embu and Kisii.[9] A number of Asians even went beyond present day Kenya and established businesses in Kampala, Uganda, such as the famous merchant Alidina Visram, (Seidenbeng, 1985).

One of the outstanding Asian merchants who ventured into the interior of present day Kenya was Ali bhai Mulla Jeevanjee.[10] Jeevanjee started from humble beginnings as a cart driver who could neither read nor write. Through hard work and determination he became an astute businessman. By the time he came to Kenya in 1886 he had already set up a successful business empire in Adelaide, Australia, (Seidenberg, 1985). Jeevanjee played an important role particularly during the construction of the Uganda railway. His company was awarded contracts to supply masons, carpenters, locksmiths and carvers, most of whom were supplied from India, (Seidenberg, 1985). As a reward for his good services, Jeevanjee was allocated a lot of land by the British government. The Jeevanjee Garden in central Nairobi was part of the grant. Jeevanjee donated the gardens, which are named after him, to the government in 1906, (Patel 1997).

By the beginning of the 20th century, Jeevanjee's firm began to undertake the construction of several buildings in Nairobi, Kenya's capital city, as well as in other towns such as Mombasa and Kisumu. In 1905, he built the municipal market in Nairobi, which was described as the most up-to-date structure of its kind in East Africa, (Patel, 1997). By 1913, he had applied to be permitted to construct an iron building in River Road—Nairobi, containing 14 shops, 42 living rooms and 28 Kitchens and bathrooms.[11]

Indian masons and contractors erected schools, government offices and the most imposing business and residential dwellings in Kenya. These include the unique Kipande House in Nairobi, which was completed before the First World War by Gurdit Singh, (Seidenberg, 1985). Asians also erected the Shia Ismaili Mosque on today's Moi Avenue—Biashara street junctions in the 1920s. Asians also pioneered quarry operations in Kenya and in the process they apprenticed many Africans.[12]

After the construction of the railway, a number of Asians remained in the country although a majority went back to India. Those who remained carried their livelihood as artisans, traders or public servants. They also united their friends and relatives to come and settle in Kenya, (Zarwan, 1977). Therefore, globalization in Kenya has been characterized by the settlement not just of Europeans, but also of Asians. While the European missionaries spread their religion in the territory, the Asian impact was felt mainly in trade and artisan skills.

One of the main impacts of globalization in Kenya during the colonial era was the widespread use of money, and Asians were instrumental in this process. Asians introduced various Western commodities to Africans, including blankets, glassware, mirrors and cotton cloth. Africans were therefore encouraged to acquire Western currency in order to acquire these new commodities. It is important to note that the Indian rupee was the pioneer currency in Kenya during the colonial era. Similarly, the Indian penal code was used to administer law and order not only among the Indians but also among the Africans who resided in urban centers. This illustrates the dualism that existed during the colonial era. Both the Asian penal code and European laws were applied in the country.

It is interesting to note that during the early years of colonialism in Kenya, some Indians at home and in East Africa had hoped to include Kenya within an Indian Empire.[13] The fact that the British became hostile to the Indians soon after could explain the bitterness harbored by the Asians against British settlers. Asians viewed the British government as having betrayed their trust with regard to the colonization of Kenya. The Asians even formed a political association to promote their interests in the country, two decades before the first African political association, known as the Indian Association. The association was founded in 1900 and its chief motive was to fight for land in the white highlands. The British, however, refused to grant land to the Asians. British Governors including Charles Eliot and Percy Giroud categorically rejected the Asian demands for land in Kenya, (Cowen and Mc William, 1996).

This exclusion from land ownership in the white highlands became the basis of Asian political activism against the British in colonial Kenya up to the 1920s. Asian ambitions in Kenya received a rude shock in July 1923 when the Devonshire white paper declared that the interest of the Africans was paramount in Kenya. Thereafter, the focus of Kenyan Asian political activity was geared towards the struggle for the same political, social and economic rights which the Europeans had gained in the colony, (Gregory, 1971). A number of Asians even supported the African political associations against the British. M.A. Desai, for instance, assisted Harry Thuku's East African Association with transportation as well as published his articles in the East African Chronicles of Desai. Ironically, Asian traders also became the target of African bitterness against colonial exploitation, as they were deemed responsible for the overpricing of trade commodities as they dominated in the retail sector and acted as middlemen between African farmers and European export firms in colonial Kenya.

The Asians were also significant, particularly in the period following the First World War due to their participation in the trade union movement, (Stichter, 1982). Their significance in the movement was mainly enhanced by the fact that Asians dominated commerce, finance and insurance. Together with artisans employed in metal working, wood and furniture building and transport sector, clerks, draughtsmen and typists, Asians made up the majority of the wage–working population over the period, (Cowen and McWilliams, 1996). The Asians also participated in the establishment of several industries in the post World War II era. Commenting on this, the minister for commerce stated the following in 1957: "The Asian community is playing quite a considerable part in this development and Asians have in many instances shown themselves to be enterprising industrialists," (Himbara, 44). This unique position of Asians in colonial Kenya enabled them to interact with many Africans. There is no gainsaying the fact that many African artisans learned their trades from Asians on the job.

Moreover, many African trade unionists learned industrial militancy from pioneers such as Markham Singh, (Stichter, 1982; Cowen and McWilliams 1996). This support continued in the post-Second World War period, particularly during the Mau Mau revolt in the 1950s. Madally Manji is quoted as having opined how his elder brother Hassanaly assisted the Mau Mau guerillas in their war against the British, (Cowen and McWilliams, 1996). Since the Asian traders were not likely to be suspected by the colonial authorities of sympathizing with the Mau Mau, they effectively acted as couriers and financiers of the underground movement. As a consequence the colonial government punished a number of Asians. Makhan Singh was disallowed to enter Kenya from India during the period, while other leading Asian anti–colonialists, including Singh and Pio Gama Pinto, were jailed, (Cowen and McWilliam, 1996).

It is interesting to note that the dual nature of the Asians in Kenya was also clearly illustrated during this period. While some of the Asians supported the Mau Mau nationalists, another group began to support the colonial forces led by the Kenya Indian Congress. The protection rackets by Mau Mau activists targeting Asians and African traders also turned some of the Asians against the movement. The complexity of Asian attitudes towards Africans in Kenya can be explained in terms of the composition of the Asian community in the country. Asians were not homogeneous: whereas some were Muslim, others were Hindu and Sikh. Their religions faith therefore informed their varied altitudes.

THE SOCIO–ECONOMIC IMPACT OF ASIAN DIASPORA IN POST–COLONIAL KENYA

As political independence approached in the 1960s, the dual nature of the Asians in Kenya continued to be expressed. Asians continued to finance the emerging nationalist political parties such as the Kenya African National Union and the Kenya African Democratic Union, which were established in 1960. Most members of the Kenya Freedom Party, which was Asian dominated, disbanded the party in 1963 and joined KANU. Moreover, during the independence elections in 1963, Asian financial contributions played a big role in enabling KANU to win and to stabilize as a political party.

Unfortunately, during the first decade after independence, Asian prosperity provoked the envy of African leaders. With the onset of the Africanization program by the government, the small Asian traders were edged out of commerce and trade, especially in the smaller trading centers. Ironically, a number of factors still propelled the Asian traders to succeed in spite of the various challenges encountered. Himbara explains this success in terms of the Asian exclusion from non–commercial activities, which made them maintain a degree of internal solidarity, (Himbara, 1994). Most of the Asians organized themselves into close–knit communities based on religion. For instance, the Ismailia Muslim fraternity is associated with the Aga Khan institutions while the Hindus are associated with the Visa Oshwal. The main legislative measure used to facilitate the entry of Africans in commerce after independence was the trade-licensing Act of 1967, which was designed to limit the trading activities of non citizens, (Himbara, 59).

Consequently, Asians were excluded from trading in the rural areas, to make way for African traders. Following this development, a number of Asians left the country and opted to settle in the United Kingdom, India and Canada, while the others shifted from retail and wholesale trade to manufacturing. In spite of the above challenges, the Asian manufacturers benefited tremendously from the acceleration of economic growth among the African small holders whose fortunes were improving, (Cowen and McWilliam, 1996). The Asian industrialists and merchants soon reclaimed their former position of dominance in trade. Globalization has given the Kenyan Asians an upper hand in their commercial and industrial enterprises. Their strong links with their kinsmen in India and the United Kingdom has boosted their capital and commercial relations tremendously.

Since 1978 when president Moi took over as Kenya's president, Kenyan Asians began to benefit from political patronage as Moi sought to entrench his rule, (Cowen and McWilliams, 1996). This could explain why during the abortive coup of 1982, Asians and their enterprises and houses were the public target of widespread violence, which swept through urban centers including Nairobi, (Cowen and McWilliams, 1996). The fact that majority of the Asians have clung to faiths such as Hinduism, Jainism, Sikhism and specific Islamic sects in Kenya has further lent credence to the view that they are not ready to interact fully with other Kenyans. Indeed, a majority of the Asians in Kenya have avoided marrying Kenyans of African origin, a matter enhanced greatly by their socialization. Many young Asians prefer to marry fellow Asians either locally–based, or overseas. Commenting on the behavior of Asians, Marries and Somerset assert that they "were thrown back upon their distinctness as communities with their own religion and culture. Early sect closed in upon itself in mutual protection, reinforcing its family and cultural loyalties. This internal social cohesion promoted a style of family business, which could pioneer commercial opportunities without external support, and remained segregated from the society it served."[14]

Globalization has made it easier for Asians to maintain their relations with their kin overseas. This attitude has been strengthened by the hostile reactions expressed by a majority of the Africans in Kenya who view Asians as generally unsocial, proud and arrogant due to this seclusion. Moreover, the fact that Asians dominate the commercial manufacturing, insurance and whole sale trades in the country, has set them apart as the bourgeoisie that exploits the cheap labor of the African poor. As the giant Nakumatt super-market chain acquired the firestone franchise in Kenya in 2005, the Pan Paper Mills became associated with Asians. The identification of Asians with the forces of globalization, which have been seen as accentuating pov-erty and widening the gap between the rich and poor, has further alienated Africans from the Asians in Kenya.

Nevertheless, a number of Asians have demonstrated a deep commit-ment to the well–being of the country politically, economically and socially. The Kapila family, for instance has demonstrated a deep commitment to the welfare of the country through engagement in political participation alongside other Kenyans. Ishan Kapila a Kenyan advocate has represented many Kenyans in court, and identified with the common man including the urban poor. His role during the pro-democracy movement in Kenya that finally ushered in multipartyism in 2002, ranks with that of other leading lights such as Paul Muite and James Orengo in that crusade.

Although the social fabric of the Asian community in Kenya remained closely knit and more connected to the Indian subcontinent than to the African environment for many years, their contribution to African educa-tion cannot be overemphasized. Apart from establishing schools as busi-ness enterprises they rolled out scholarships through various funds. For instance, the Aga Khan Foundation provides education scholarships inde-pendently through the Aga Khan Education Services (AKS) and contributes immensely to Rotary International and the various Lion's Clubs in different cities in Kenya. All these funds are utilized in providing social amenities and educational opportunities for disadvantaged groups and for bright but poor children.

Practically all the major cities in Kenya such as Mombasa, Nairobi, Nakuru and Kisumu, among others, have witnessed immense presence of Aga Khan education and health institutions. These investments, perhaps the greatest Indian Diaspora initiative, spread throughout the East African region. The Asian schools have been at the center of perpetuating some forms of racism and separation through economic segregation. The fees charged are often beyond reach of many Africans and the schools pursue educational curricula that emphasizes "Asianness" and sports that have an Asian following such as swimming, hockey and cricket, rather than soccer and athletics, so that even if they are adhering to the local curriculum, they end up isolating Africans.

The hospitals also found in major cities, alongside the schools, are strengthened by Aga Khan's deliberate investment in the public print media. For instance, the latest initiative—the establishment of the Aga Khan University in Kenya—epitomizes the Asian involvement in tertiary education particularly in the fields of engineering and health sciences. Three years after the establishment of Aga Khan University in Nakuru, 100 miles northwest of Nairobi, and a health sciences campus within Nairobi, enrollment already exceeds 1,500 students, most of whom are of African descent. Apparently, this is a clear message that competitiveness in higher education is one of the challenges that arrived with the establishment of the university.

In the public print media, the Aga Khan initiative dominates the scene in Kenya and Uganda. Currently, the most popular newspapers in Kenya and Uganda are The Nation Newspapers and Uganda Monitor, all of which are owned by the Ismailia community under his highness the Aga Khan.[15] The readership of the Nation newspapers in Kenya exceeds 4 million while the Uganda Monitor attracts approximately 2 million readers. Through this print media the Aga Khan services in other areas of investment have been effectively marketed.

The Rahimtulah Trust is another of the Asian charity initiatives in Kenya. Through this trust, financial support has been extended to the less privileged to study. Other funds include Rattanzi, also heavily sponsored by the Asian business Community in Kenya and dedicated to funding less privileged but academically bright students to pursue their education. All of these have created an indirect social and educational inter-relationship between the African community and the Asian Diaspora in Kenya. On the other hand, it has helped to develop the requisite manpower required at the Asian-Diaspora-dominated industrial and business sector in Kenya.

Furthermore, the schools, hospitals and industrial establishments developed by the Asian Diaspora not only pay colossal taxes to the exchequer, but, also employ thousands of Kenyans enhancing their livelihood. Conversely, the often icy and sometimes exploitative characteristic of Asian businesses led to a very efficient and highly developed trade union movement in Kenya. Through many workers' trade unions, the greater section of Kenya's proletariat are unionized and adequately educated about their rights as employees.

However, in spite of awareness about the intricacies of the employer-employee relationship, the government of Kenya has been relatively slow in enacting sound laws to govern this relationship. As a result, exploitation of workers by the owners of the means of production (Asian Diaspora) is still rife in Kenya particularly for the non-unionizable temporary employees. For instance, while the laws of Kenya do not compel employers to employ permanently, they have no definite remedies for exploitation and injustice against temporary employees. As a result employers (predominantly Asian Diaspora) opt to keep employees in temporary status in order to limit their own liability in law, in case of any legal suits from such employees.

One of the most prominent Asian Diaspora industrialists that tried to address the problems associated with the work place and the immediate community is Manu Chandariah. A second generation Kenyan, Manu Chandariah rose from petty retail shop business in one of Nairobi's shabby streets to roll out a colossal metallurgy industry (Mabati industries) across Eastern and Central Africa, with the headquarters located in Nairobi. Other than re-organizing and addressing worker needs, Chandariah has addressed environmental issues such as pollution arising from industrial effluents. In Nairobi for instance the Manu Chandaria foundation beautified parks and re-carpeted roads as voluntary community service. In the area of education the foundation supports university research in engineering and environmental science on a competitive basis. This initiative has certainly contributed to the quality of education in Kenya and in the entire East African region. It is no wonder that several universities in Eastern Africa, including the Flagship University of Nairobi, have honored Manu Chandaria for his involvement in education and industrialization, among other things

The Asian Diaspora has participated in some of the scandals that rocked Kenya's economy leading to high inflation rates since the 1990s. Over 90 percent of cases at the anti-corruption court in Nairobi involve Asians. The largest corruption cases in Kenya (Goldenberg and Anglo-leasing) involve Asians at the top of the scandals, as master planners. It is no secret that Asian companies have been at the center of official corruption in Kenya. Thus, rather than fight the Asian Diaspora in business, key government corporations became victims of gullible executives within the government and in the various Asian-owned businesses. The most notorious of the scandals witnessed between 1989 and 1994 cost Kenya US$300 million and is popularly known as the Goldenberg scandal. In this scandal, millions of dollars were paid by the Kenyan government as export compensation to encourage export business in gold and diamonds. A national inquiry conducted between 2004 and 2006 revealed that although export promotion funds were paid by the Central Bank the gold and diamond exports were fictitious–a major setback to the economy.

Lastly, but by no means the least, some counter cultural practices such as homosexuality have been associated with Asians. In 1911, the first case of sodomy was tried in Mombasa and reported in the local newspapers such as Baraza and the Standard. The two men involved were Asians and although it was consensual, they were jailed for two years each and ordered to receive five strokes of the cane and pay a fine of 50 rupees each. Thereafter, Kenyans have increasingly continued to witness such cases in the courts involving mainly Asians and Arabs. In the past twenty years, about 90 percent of cases involving sodomy have been reported among Asians and Arabs, and whites (mainly tourists). The appearance of pimps in Kenya and the rise of brothels as places of sex is associated with Asian establishments. The gay clubs in some exclusive clubs in Westlands and Mombasa have the involvement of Asians.

CONCLUSION

It is not rare to see bi-racial people in Kenya. But they are likely to be a result of Western European and African families than Asian and African. It is amazing how the Asian Diaspora in Kenya managed for more than a century to remain socially connected to each other on one hand and to the Asian subcontinent on the other. Indeed, the Asian Diaspora in Kenya has effectively managed to maintain their ethnic identity. Yet business wise they freely, aggressively, and ingeniously operated and sometimes outmaneuvered the natives of East Africa. It is particularly noteworthy that even when government policies targeted and sought to limit their opportunities in the post-independence period, it triggered mutations in their business strategies in such ways that the inhibiting policies benefited them instead.

Thus the involvement of the Asian Diaspora in Kenya has been a mixed fortune. It will however be remembered that in terms of social and economic development they boast unrivalled contribution when compared to other Diasporic communities, not only in Kenya but in the entire East African Region.

NOTES

1. A. Sheriff, "The spatial Dichotomy of Swahili towns: The case of Zanzibar in the 19th Century," in *The Urban Experience in Eastern Africa C. 1750—2000*, (Nairobi: The British Institute of E.A. Publication, 2002).
2. D. Himbara, *Kenyan Capitalists, the State and Development*, (Nairobi: EAEP, 1994).
3. F. Cooper, *From Slaves to Squatters: Plantation Labour and Agriculture in Zanzibar and Coastal Kenya 1890–1925*, (New York: Yale University Press, 1980).
4. J.S. Mangat, *A History of Asians in East Africa 1886—1945*, (Oxford: The Clarendon Press, 1969); D.A. Seidenberg, *Mercantile Adventurers: The*

World of East African Asians 1750—1985, (New Delhi: New Age International Limited Publishers, 1985).

5. S. Stichter, *Migrant Labour in Kenya,* (Essex: Longman Group Ltd., 1982).

6. C. Elkins, *Britain's Gulag: The Brutal End of the Empire in Kenya,* (Washington: Pilmico, 2005).

7. R. G. Gregory, *India and East Africa,* (Oxford: Oxford University Press, 1971).

8. J.I. Zarwan, "Indian Businessmen in Kenya during the 20th Century: A Case Study," (PHD Dissertation, Yale University, 1977).

9. T. Zeleza, "The Establishment of Colonial Rule, 1905—1950," in W. Ochieng, (ed.) *A Modern History of Kenya,* (Nairobi: Evans Brothers, 1989).

10. Z. Patel, *Challenge to Colonialism: The Struggle of Alibhai Mulla Jivanjee for Equal Rights in Kenya,* (Nairobi: Nairobi Publishers Distribution Services, 1997).

11. Kenya National Archives. *Natives in Colonial: Nairobi Municipal Council. Nairobi, Kenya National Archives,* 1953; hereafter cited in text as (KNA/RN/4/53:178).

12. K. King, *Jua Kali Kenya,* (London, Heinemann, 1996); Stichter, 1982.

13. M. Cowen, and S. Mac William, Indigenous *Capital in Kenya,* (Helsinki: InterKont Books, 1996).

14. P. Marris, and A. Somerset, *African Businessmen,* (Nairobi: East African Publishing House, 1971), 75.

15. W. J. Akala, Modernization versus Culture Resilience in Education in East Africa, *Journal of Curriculum Studies,* 38 no.3 (2006); 365—372.

REFERENCES

Akala W. J. "Modernization versus Culture Resilience in Education in East Africa." *Journal of Curriculum Studies,* 38 no.3 (2006); 365—372.

Cooper, F. *From Slaves to Squatters: Plantation Labour and Agriculture in Zanzibar and Coastal Kenya, 1890–1925.* New York: Yale University Press, 1980.

Cowen, M. and S. Mac William. *Indigenous Capital in Kenya.* Helsinki: InterKont Books, 1996.

Elkins, C. *Britain's Gulag: The Brutal End of the Empire in Kenya.* Washington: Pilmico, 2005.

Gregory, R. G. *India and East Africa.* Oxford: Oxford University Press, 1971.

Himbara, D. *Kenyan Capitalists, the State and Development.* Nairobi: EAEP, 1994.

Kenya National Archives. *Natives in Colonial: Nairobi Municipal Council. Nairobi, Kenya National Archives,* 1953; (KNA/RN/4/53:178).

King, K. *Jua Kali Kenya,* London, Heinemann, 1996.

Mangat, J.S. *A History of Asians in East Africa, 1886—1945.* Oxford: The Clarendon Press, 1969.

Marris, P. and Somerset, A. *African Businessmen,* Nairobi: East African Publishing House, 1971.

Patel, Z. *Challenge to Colonialism: The Struggle of Alibhai Mulla Jivanjee for Equal Rights in Kenya*. Nairobi: Nairobi Publishers Distribution Services, 1997.

Seidenberg, D.A. *Mercantile Adventurers: The World of East African Asians 1750—1985*. New Delhi: New Age International Limited Publishers, 1985.

Sheriff, A. "The spatial Dichotomy of Swahili towns: The case of Zanzibar in the 19th Century." *The Urban Experience in Eastern Africa C. 1750—2000*. Nairobi: The British Institute of E.A. Publication, 2002.

Stichter, S. *Migrant Labour in Kenya*. Essex: Longman Group Ltd., 1982.

Zarwan, J.I. "Indian Businessmen in Kenya during the 20th Century: A Case Study." PHD Dissertation, Yale University, 1977.

Zeleza, T. "The Establishment of Colonial Rule, 1905—1950." Ochieng, W. (ed.) *A Modern History of Kenya*. Nairobi: Evans Brothers, 1989.

Conclusion
The Moral Ambiguity of Trans-Atlantic Migration

Toyin Falola and Niyi Afolabi

> African ancestors had in the past thousands of years moved into differ-
> ent global spaces. Contemporary African immigration to the West is not
> novel and neither is it an isolated phenomenon. African immigration to
> Great Britain has been well documented; as well as to France and other
> colonial metropolis. The African presence in Arabia, the Indian Ocean,
> and the former Soviet spaces are well documented, precluding the Afri-
> can diaspora to Europe, Caribbean, and the Americas due to the trans-
> atlantic slave trades since the 1500s.
>
> —Attah Anthony Agbali

The cost-benefit analysis of African migration has been blurred and complicated by the paradoxes highlighted in the preceding chapters. Unlike the
historical forced trans-Atlantic migration, voluntary trans-Atlantic migration raises a number of questions which remain either unanswerable or
silenced by the exigencies of survival and the possibilities of dreams fulfilled. Even in situations of dreams deferred, the migrant is placed in a subtle
but equally problematic quagmire—that of a permanent exile and the blues
of being stuck in that discomforting middle—wanting to go and having to
stay, wanting to stay and having to go. In essence, the migrant becomes an
entity permanently in transit both physically and psychologically. Despite
the catalogue of challenges and achievements, a conclusion is reachable: the
migrant would rather settle for a "moral ambiguity" in words and action
than contemplate a permanent solution because a "permanent solution" is
equally non-existent. Within this context, the most amoral and humiliating
form of migration is worth examining: human trafficking.

In a September 26, 2006 report, "Nigerian Women Trafficked to
Europe Mainly for Sex Trade," culled from *Nigeria Today Online,* the
International Organization for Migration (IOM) notes that "poverty, crime,
corruption, and violence are driving thousands of people to emigrate from

Nigeria, with young women particularly vulnerable to trafficking for sexual exploitation." As the most populous African nation with over 130 million citizens, the fact that the highest rate of such migrations from Africa comes from Nigeria is still not an excuse for the shameful practice. While there is an economic factor involved, the human cost is what makes the trend truly disturbing. Under the pretext that these innocent victims of migration are being "saved" from the dire economic conditions in their home countries, and with the reality that they will actually be working in the sex business, young women continue to be vulnerable especially when they are sole financial supporters of their families. Herein lies the moral ambiguity faced by African migrants: the economic conditions at their respective countries do not have easy solutions the same way that the voluntary migration at costs as high as $40,000 to $100,000 per victim, are not necessarily desirable but alluring. The situation is further complicated by the so called "binding contract/pact" which may or may not have religious and violent repercussions should the victim not honor such exploitative contracts. Although two countries in Europe are identified as the major destinations, namely Britain and Italy, others include Spain, Germany, Belgium, Austria, and France. Ultimately, the pain and pleasures of trans-Atlantic migration is in the eye of the beholder.

The future of trans-Atlantic migration for Africans may well be captured in the African proverb that "charity begins at home." The problem is that the African migrant is equally ambivalent about where "home" is. If Africa is considered home and the African migrant feels like a "sojourner" in his or her own home due to woeful economic conditions, then it is only reasonable for the migrant to locate and identify with a home where survival, freedom, and peace reign. On the other hand, if the African migrant considers the New World as home, the question then becomes what Africa represents for the African not only for him or her but for the immediate children, grandchildren and generations yet unborn. As much as we want to promote migration as a solution to immediate economic and political problems, we also want to encourage the amelioration of living conditions in Africa that will make the possibility of return not just a wishful thinking but a true and potential reality. As long as the disturbing conditions of living that threaten human and economic securities continue in Africa, trans-Atlantic migration will continue to be a viable option for Africans despite its moral ambiguity.

Appendix
Abbreviations & Linguistic Cluster

ABBREVIATIONS & ACRONYMS

AHEAD:	Association for Higher Education and Development
AIDS:	Acquired Immune Deficiency Syndrome
AKS:	Aga Khan Education Services
ANPP:	All Nigerian People's Party
APGA:	All Progressive Grand Alliance (Nigeria)
AU:	African Union
B.A.:	Bachelors of Arts
CAN:	Christian Association of Nigeria
CBCN:	Catholic Bishops' Conference of Nigeria
CDS:	Center for Democratic Studies
CMAG:	Commonwealth Ministerial Action Group
CUU:	Council for Unity and Understanding
DFW:	Dallas-Forth Worth (Texas, USA)
ECOWAS:	Economic Community of West Africa
ECOMOG:	Ecowas Monitoring Group
EU:	European Union
GNP:	Gross National Product
HIV:	Human Immunodeficiency Virus

IBEAC:	International British East African Company
IDRC:	International Development Research Centre
ING:	Interim National Government (Nigeria)
IOM:	International Organization for Migration
M.A.:	Masters of Arts
MESI:	Mobility Enhanced Stability Index
MIPH:	Mobility Induced Political Homogeneity
MNR:	Movement for National Reconciliation
MOSOP:	Movement for the Survival of Ogoni People
MPRDA:	Mineral and Petroleum Resources Development
NADECO:	National Democratic Coalition
NEPAD:	New Partnership for Africa's Development
NIDO:	Nigerians in the Diaspora Organization
NPRC:	National Political Reform Conference
NSF:	National Science Foundation
NUO:	National Unity Organization
OAU:	Organization of Africa Unity
PAC:	Pan African Congress
PAF:	Pan African Federation
PDP:	People's Democratic Party (Nigeria)
PhD:	Doctor of Philosophy
RCCG:	Redeemed Christian Church of God
SANSA:	South African Network of Skills Abroad
SDP:	Social Democratic Party
STD:	Sexually Transmitted Disease
UAS:	Union of African States
UGCC:	United Gold Coast Convention (Ghana)
U.K.:	United Kingdom

UN: United Nations

UNDP: United Nations Development Program

UNECA: United Nations Economic Commission for Africa

USD: United States Dollar

US / USA: United States of America

WANS: West African National Secretariat

WASU: West African Students Union

ZANU: Zimbabwe African National Union

LINGUISTIC CLUSTER

ZULU: An indigenous South African language.
Ex: *makwiri kwiri:* insulting and discriminatory term referring mostly to foreign laborers; an undesirable; a refugee.

Contributors

Niyi Afolabi, Ph.D., teaches African and African Diaspora Studies at the W.E.B. Du Bois Department of Afro-American Studies. He is the author of *The Golden Cage: Regeneration in Lusophone African Literature and Culture,* and editor of *Marvels of the African World: African Cultural Patrimony, New World Connections and Identities.* His current book projects focus on the Brazilian manifestation of Afro-Diasporan discourse and include bilingual volumes such as *The Afro-Brazilian Mind / A Mente Afro-Brasileira* and *Cadernos Negros/Black Notebooks.*

Anthony Agbali is a Ph.D. candidate in anthropology, and is concurrently pursuing a master's degree in sociology at Wayne State University, Detroit, Michigan. Presently, he is engaged as a Certified Hospital Chaplain at the renowned Barnes-Jewish Hospital, St. Louis, MO. An ordained Catholic priest, he studied philosophy, religious studies, and theology at the St. Augustine's Major Seminary, Jos, Nigeria, the University of Ibadan, Nigeria, and the Pontifical Urban University, Rome, Italy. His academic and personal interests are diverse. He enjoys music, poetry, spirituality and religion, prolific writing and reading, and horticulture. He is currently engaged in the ethnographic research for his dissertation on "African Immigrants' Experiences in Urban America: Construction of Social Identity, Religion, and Integration in St. Louis [Missouri]." His scholarly contributions have appeared in various volumes edited by Toyin Falola, including *Nigeria in the Twentieth Century; The Dark Web: Perspectives on Colonialism in Africa; Urbanization and African Culture* (co-edited with Steve Salm); and *Orisa: Yoruba Gods and Spiritual Identity in Africa and the Diaspora* (co-edited with Ann Genova).

Dr Winston Jumba Akala is a senior lecturer and Head, Department of Post-graduate Studies in Education at the Catholic University of Eastern Africa—

Nairobi, Kenya. He specializes in curriculum studies and civic education. His latest publication includes a chapter on *The role of the Catholic Church in curriculum development in Kenya,* in the International handbook of Catholic education (in Press Springer Science). Others include "The silent victims of HIV/AIDS in Kenya: The plight of uninfected children among nomadic pastoralists." In T. Falola and M. M. Heaton (Eds.). *Endangered bodies: Women, Children and health in Africa* (pp. 137–148). Trenton, NJ: Africa World Press—2006; and "Modernization versus Culture Resilience in Education in East Africa." *Journal of Curriculum Studies, 38* (3), p.368—372.

Charity Chenga is a Ph.D. candidate at the University of Kent, undertaking a comparative study of local black and migrant youths in their experience of the transition from school to work in a South African mining community. Her academic background includes an MA in Migration and Social Care Studies, a BSc in economics, and a diploma in mental health nursing. Her employment experience includes working at senior levels in banking, international trade, nursing, and research in the United Kingdom, South Africa, and Zimbabwe. Charity has been involved in three international research projects and two of her papers, "Health in the South African Mining Communities" and "Critical Factors Affecting Sustainable Development Projects in the Mining Communities," have been accepted for publication, one in a book and one in an accredited journal. Her interests and future plans include setting up collaborative research and developmental projects in both developed and developing countries.

Dennis Cordell is Professor of History and Associate Vice Provost at Southern Methodist University in Dallas, and Adjunct Professor of Demography at the Université de Montréal. His earliest research focused on the slave trade from Central Africa in the nineteenth and early twentieth centuries, leading to the publication of *Dar al-Kuti: The Last Years of the Trans-Saharan Slave Trade* (1985). Shortly thereafter, he joined with the late Joel Gregory and others to launch research on African historical demography. Early on, this endeavor resulted in the production of an essay collection jointly edited with Gregory, *African Population and Capitalism: Historical Perspectives* (1987), and numerous articles, including "African Historical Demography in the Years since Edinburgh" in *History in Africa* (2000). Since the 1990s, Cordell has focused more on the histories of African migration in the twentieth century; co-authoring a monograph on burkinabè migration with Victor Piché entitled *Hoe and Wage: A Social History of a West African Migration System, 1900–1975.* More recently he has studied the history of Malian migrants in France, publishing with Carolyn Sargent,

"Polygamy, disrupted reproduction and the state: Malian migrants in Paris, France," *Social Science and Medicine* (2003), and "Islam, identity and gender in daily life among Malians in Paris: the burdens are easier to bear" (2005). Along with three colleagues, he is completing research and fieldwork on the integration of immigrants in Dallas/Fort Worth, a National Science Foundation project which includes the Nigerian community. The paper he is presenting at this conference is one of the first products of that study on Nigerian immigration and immigrants. For more background, please see his website (http://faculty.smu.edu/dcordell).

Freek Cronjé is Senior Lecturer in the School of Social and Government Studies at North-West University in South Africa. He is also head of the subject group, Sociology within the school. His main field of specialization is sustainable development. and much of his research in this field has been done within the mining sector. Other issues within the development field that Dr. Cronjé has worked and published on include migration, health, and community development. His latest two publications are "The Interaction between HIV/AIDS and Poverty: A Psycho-Social Perspective" (*Social Work,* 2005) and "Critical Factors for Sustainable Social Projects" (co-authored by Charity Chenga, *Journal of the South African Institute of Mining and Metallurgy,* 2006).

Ntombizodwa (Zodwa) Dlayedwa is a linguistic lecturer in Design Features and Multilingualism at the University of the Western Cape in Bellville, South Africa. She taught language-literature at primary, secondary, and university/tertiary levels for sixteen years. Zodwa also trained many junior and senior primary school teachers before going to England, where she obtained a master's degree in Applied Linguistics and TESOL (University of Leicester) and a PhD in Language and Linguistics (University of Essex). While studying in England, Zodwa also had the opportunity to teach for nine years in primary schools as well as in special-need colleges in London and Ipswich before going back to South Africa. Zodwa is currently working on three papers: one focuses on morpho-syntax and the other two are concerned with an analysis of selected texts in Xhosa and their translated versions in English and Afrikaans. In analyzing these texts, Zodwa and her colleague use the framework and analytical approaches provided by Systemic Functional Linguistics (SFL). Zodwa's areas of specialty include formal linguistics, multicultural issues/communication, and storytelling.

Toyin Falola is a Distinguished Teaching Professor and the Frances Higginbothom Nalle Centennial Professor in History at the University of Texas at Austin. A Fellow of the Nigerian Academy of Letters, he is the author of numerous books, including *Violence in Nigeria: The Crisis of Religious Politics and Secular Ideologies* and *Nationalism and African Intellectuals,* both from the University of Rochester Press. He is the co-editor of the *Journal of African Economic History,* Series Editor of Rochester Studies in African History and the Diaspora, Series Editor of the Culture and Customs of Africa by Greenwood Press, and Series Editor of Classic Authors and Texts on Africa by Africa World Press. He has received various awards and honors, most recently the Jean Holloway Award for Teaching Excellence, The Texas Exes Teaching Award, the Chancellor's Council Outstanding Teaching Award, the Cecil B Currey Award for his book, *Economic Reforms and Modernization in Nigeria.* For his distinguished contribution to the study of Africa, his students and colleagues have presented him with a set of Festschrift edited by Adebayo Oyebade, *The Transformation of Nigeria: Essays in Honor of Toyin Falola* and *The Foundations of Nigeria: Essays in Honor of Toyin Falola.* His award-winning memoir, *A Mouth Sweeter Than Salt,* captures his childhood and received the Herskovits Finalist Award by the Association of African Studies and the E. Alagoa Award by the Oral History Association.

Dr Felix Kiruthu is a lecturer at the department of History, Archaeology and Political studies at Kenyatta University Nairobi, Kenya. He is specializes in economic history with a special focus on political economy and African history. His research mainly targets urban history, and has recently completed a study on the history of urban informal sector in Nairobi. Among his recent publications are: Voices of Freedom (2000) and the Evolving World History and Government book series (2005).

Isidore Lobnibe is a Ph.D. candidate in the Department of Anthropology, University of Illinois at Urbana Champaign specializing in socio-cultural Anthropology and West Africa. His research interests relate to themes including labor migration, social organization, the environment, historiography and the history of Anthropology. He is currently writing his doctoral dissertation based on field work he conducted in Southern Ghana among migrant farm laborers from Northern Ghana. His articles have appeared in the American Anthropologist and AFRICA.

Raphael Obotama is a Ph.D. student in the department of communication at Wayne State University, Detroit, Michigan. He is an ordained priest of the Catholic diocese of Ikot Ekpene, Nigeria. He has studied Philosophy and Theology and has earned degrees from the Pontifical Urban University,

Rome. His research interest relates to themes in African films with special emphasis on the Nigerian Video Films. He has published a work on Marian Theology, "Our Mother Who Art in Heaven." Other works in the pipeline are: *The Midnight Worshippers:* (Novel); *Crossed Lines,* (Screenplay), *The Green Card,* (Screenplay). His hobbies include writing, computer graphics, photography and video taping beautiful scenery.

The late Francis O. Ogino was until December 2006 a lecturer in the department of history at the College of Education of the University of Nairobi. Initially he lectured at the Catholic University of eastern Africa. Ogino has conducted extensive research on the history of the media in Kenya.

Godwin S. M. Okeke teaches Political Science at the University of Lagos. He holds a Bachelor and Masters Degrees in Political Science, and is also presently writing his Ph.D. thesis on "ECOWAS and Regional Security: A Study in Conflict Resolution in West Africa," at the University of Lagos— Nigeria. He has published articles in journals and chapters in books, including, "Interdependence and Integration: An Evaluation of the African Experience," "Guerrilla Warfare as a Political Strategy: A Case study of the RUF of Sierra Leone," "Political Violence, Democracy and Sustainable Development in Nigeria," "International Institutions and World Peace," among others. He has also attended several International Conferences and Workshops, including the 2001 ACUNS workshop on International Organisations, in Namibia; the Global Youth Exchange Programme on "Building World Peace through a Synergy of diversity," Japan 2003 and the Summer University Programme on "Ethnicity and Nationalism" at the Central European University, Budapest, Hungary, 2005, among others. He is a member of various professional bodies including the Academic Council on the United Nations System, ACUNS.

Chika B. Onwuekwe has earned the degrees of LLB (Awka), LLM (Lagos), and LLM and PhD (Saskatchewan). He is an attorney-at-law and a member of the Calgary, Canadian, International, and Nigerian Bar Associations. Dr. Onwuekwe is currently an Assistant Professor of Law and Society at the University of Calgary, Alberta, Canada. His research interests include the legal, economic, governance, and social issues of transformative technologies, emerging democracies, energy and natural resources law, and policy issues around patents. Dr. Onwuekwe continues to practice, teach, and publish in these and related areas. His latest works include "Reconciling the Scramble for Foreign Direct Investment and Environmental Prudence: A Developing Country's Nightmare" (*Journal of World Investment and Trade*,

2006). A book manuscript, "Access and Benefits Sharing of the Genomics Revolution," edited with Peter W. B. Phillips, is under review by Kluwer.

Obinna Onwumere is a Graduate student at School of Public Affairs, Baruch College, City University of New York. His research interests include Public Policy,Colonialism, Politics and Government in Africa, and Chieftaincy Institutions in Africa. He has also authored a book chapter.

Marie Rodet is a Ph.D. candidate in African studies at the University of Vienna (Austria). Her dissertation is entitled "Female Migration in French Soudan (1900–1945)" and is concerned with the invisibility of women migrants in the history of West Africa. In fall 2004, she published a paper in *Stichprobe,* an Austrian journal of African studies, on French colonial law, gender, power, and social change in French Soudan. In January 2006, she published a second paper, entitled "It Is the Glance That Shapes History or How to Use Colonial Archives Sources Which Are Witnesses Despite Themselves of African Women's History," in *Terrains et Travaux,* the journal of the Ecole Normale Supérieure. A third article is planed for spring 2006 and will be published in the *Journal of the French Colonial Archives* in Aix-en-Provence. It deals with female forced labor in French Sudan. From 2003 to 2005, Marie Rodet was part of a University of Vienna research project on African women's history. This project aimed to restore African women to French colonial history by analyzing the interaction between African women and colonial power. Since winter 2005 she has been part of an international research network entitled France Overseas, within which she works specifically on African women and the colonial legal system in French Sudan.

Index

For Product Safety Concerns and Information please contact our EU
representative GPSR@taylorandfrancis.com
Taylor & Francis Verlag GmbH, Kaufingerstraße 24, 80331 München, Germany

www.ingramcontent.com/pod-product-compliance
Lightning Source LLC
Chambersburg PA
CBHW070601270326
41926CB00013B/2384